RESTRUCTURING
PATRIARCHY

SUSAN K. BESSE

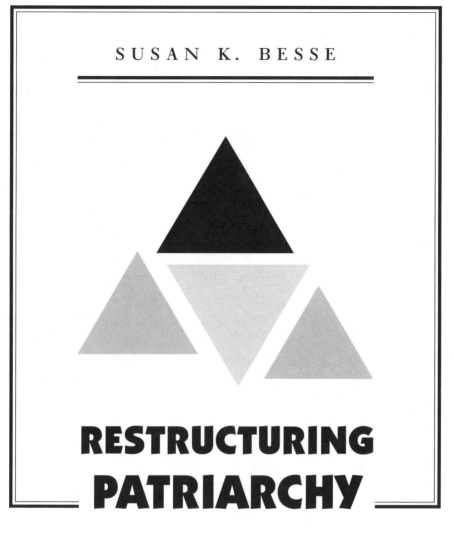

RESTRUCTURING PATRIARCHY

The Modernization of Gender
Inequality in Brazil, 1914–1940

The University of North Carolina Press ▼ Chapel Hill and London

▼ ▼ ▼

Library of Congress Cataloging-in-Publication Data

Besse, Susan K. (Susan Kent)

Restructuring patriarchy: the modernization of gender inequality

in Brazil, 1914–1940 / Susan K. Besse.

p.   cm.

Includes bibliographical references (p.   ) and index.

ISBN 0-8078-2252-3 (cloth: alk. paper)

ISBN 0-8078-4559-0 (pbk.: alk. paper)

1. Women—Brazil—History—20th century.   2. Sexism—Brazil.

3. Family—Brazil.   4. Brazil—Social conditions.   I. Title.

HQ1542.B47   1996

305.4'0981—dc20   95-23353

CIP

00   99   98   97   96   5   4   3   2   1

To my parents,
Richard and Janet Besse

CONTENTS

ILLUSTRATIONS

TABLES

ACKNOWLEDGMENTS

Over the long course of its gestation, this book has grown along with the fields of women's history and gender studies. Its conceptualization emerged only gradually, thanks to the work of the many scholars who have provided empirical groundwork and conceptual tools that were not available when I started research in the late 1970s. But to my family, friends, and colleagues who have supported and helped me along the way, I owe a more personal debt of thanks.

Emília Viotti da Costa first inspired me to study Latin American history when I met her as an undergraduate, and she has been an intellectual role model, brilliant critic of my work, and friend ever since. She enthusiastically supported my decision to study the history of women in Brazil (when few others did) and has contributed more generously to the development of this book with her time and keen insights than I can possibly repay. I also had the good fortune to be welcomed into the circle of women's historians at Yale University by Nancy Cott, who broadened my perspective, improved my work with her questions, and offered invaluable encouragement and support along the way.

I am enormously indebted to friends and colleagues, whose companionship, help, stimulation, and encouragement in many and varied ways helped keep me going: Sonia Alvarez, Ann Braude, Rosario Caicedo, Sueann Caulfield, Dana Frank, John French, Richard von Glahn, Terry Murphy, Chris Novak, Cookie Polan, Sharon Strom, and Mary Lee Townsend. Teresa Meade generously took the time to offer very detailed, perceptive, and helpful criticisms of the Introduction. Barbara Weinstein has followed the gradual evolution of my work over more than a decade, offering excellent advice as well as constant encouragement and support. The readers, Barbara Weinstein and Elizabeth Kuznesof, also provided valuable final suggestions and encouragement that prodded me on to sharpen the manuscript. Rosario Caicedo, Gerry Henze, and X Bonnie Woods offered their company and many hours of their very skilled help during the final stages of editing and proofreading. I also thank Bonnie for her photographic assistance. At The City College, I have enjoyed the intellectual support and comradeship of Beth Baron, Barbara Brooks, Carolyn Brown, Carla Cappetti, David Jaffee, Larry Kaplan, Gerardo Renique, Paul Sherwin, Robert Twombly, and Jim Watts.

My stay in Brazil would not have been the same without the warm friendship of Iumna Simon and her family, Horácio Costa, João Silvério Trevisan, Miriam Moreira Leite, and especially Jorge Schwartz and his mother Magdalena Schwartz. Jorge's boundless warmth, constant good advice, good humor, and generous hospitality left me forever in his debt. I regret that I did not thank Magdalena enough, before her untimely death, for her inspiration, the lunches she fed me while I was working at the Biblioteca Municipal, and the mothering she provided to a *gringa* away from home. Later, during a summer trip to Rio de Janeiro, Branca Moreira Alves generously welcomed me into her home and energized me with her friendship and her zest for life and learning. I also wish to thank scholars in Brazil who helped me along the way: Martha de Abreu Esteves, Mariza Corrêa, Michael Hall, Miriam Moreira Leite, and Margareth Rago.

For their patient help, I wish to thank the staffs of the Biblioteca Municipal de São Paulo, Arquivo do Estado de São Paulo, Arquivo da Cúria Metropolitana de São Paulo, Fundação Carlos Chagas, Instituto de Estudos Brasileiros, Arquivo do Hospital do Juquerí, Biblioteca Nacional do Rio de Janeiro, and Arquivo Nacional. I owe a special debt to Judge Pedro Luis Gagliardi, who not only allowed me to examine civil court cases of divorce from the Arquivo do Tribunal da Justiça in São Paulo but also generously put some of his assistants to work gathering information for me in civil court records that were closed to the public. Finally, I greatly appreciate his help in securing access to the Arquivo do Hospital do Juquerí. Bookseller Olynto de Moura took a lively interest in my project and succeeded in digging up dozens of old books that added immeasurably to the ease as well as the pleasure of my research.

I am grateful to the Doherty Foundation for financial support that allowed me to spend more than a year between 1978 and 1979 doing dissertation research in São Paulo. I also thank the PSC-CUNY Research Foundation, National Endowment for the Humanities, and Simon H. Rifkind Center for the Humanities at The City College, CUNY, for supporting revisions of the dissertation.

Through their example, my parents, Richard and Janet Besse, taught me to be adventurous and to set my sights high. And then, they gave me enormous independence, always supporting (even with trepidation) my many extended journeys abroad. I thank them for their trust in me, for their unfailing love and support, and for taking my choices in stride.

My grandmother, Blanche Mason Starkweather (1893–1991), whose greatest pride was having graduated Phi Beta Kappa from Vassar College in 1915 with a degree in economics, eagerly and lovingly supported my work all along the way, never doubting that I would succeed. Through her, I learned much about the history of women before I ever started to study it.

Sarah played a very special role in the final stages of this book. Without her, I would not have had nearly as much fun; nor would I understand the tremendous joys and inevitable frustrations of motherhood. She has also nudged me to rethink my priorities by asking the important questions—Why do you go to work, Mom? What do you do at work? Do you like work? Can we play hooky today?—and by loving me for reasons that have nothing at all to do with this book.

A Note on Brazilian Currency

▼ ▼ ▼

Until 1942, the standard monetary unit in Brazil was the *mil-réis*, or one thousand *réis*, written 1$000. One thousand *mil-réis* equaled one *conto*, written 1:000$000.

RESTRUCTURING
PATRIARCHY

INTRODUCTION

Quite suddenly beginning in the post–World War I period in Brazil, women appeared everywhere in print. Dressed in the most modern styles imported from abroad, they adorned the covers of the abundant new glossy magazines, and their snapshots were sprinkled throughout the inside pages. Advertisers used their bodies to sell products and exploited their anxieties to increase sales. A veritable outpouring of normative literature defined their new "duties" as wives, mothers, and housekeepers and offered detailed instructions on how to fulfill the escalating requirements. Novelists and social critics established their reputations commenting on the behavior of "modern" women and the much-feared blurring of gender distinctions. Educators, physicians, and psychiatrists built their careers defining and attempting to implement modern standards of female education and health. Jurists campaigned (in the popular press as well as in law journals and courts) to define and defend women's sexual honor as well as to "civilize" the passionate love that too frequently led to bloody crimes. The tabloid press flourished by offering lurid accounts of passionate crimes and voyeuristic details of scandalous private lives. Police journals spilled quantities of ink denouncing the styles and behavior of Brazil's "modern girls" and other "degenerate" women. Labor unions demanded protective legislation, and the Ministry of Labor undertook the task of defining and regulating appropriate female employment. Other government agencies worked to devise further means to guard against the "dissolution" and "perversion" of the institution of the family. Feminists succeeded in pressuring Parliament to pass female suffrage. The proliferating number of Catholic lay organizations demanded that the faithful adhere to the Church's conservative definitions of the "Christian family." Indeed, from the mid-1910s through the 1930s, there was hardly a prominent Brazilian professional, intellectual, or political authority who did not participate in the wide-ranging debates over the redefinition of gender roles.

Many considered the "woman question" and its correlate, the "crisis" of the family, to be of momentous importance.

On the one hand, women's appearance in print reflected changes in female roles and rising expectations that accelerated with the rapid expansion of the urban-industrial economy during the postwar period. Urban middle- and upper-class women quickly seized new opportunities within a society in flux to expand their social participation. And as they entered the public sphere as consumers, gained admission to schools and professions formerly closed to them, and formed feminist organizations to press for juridical and civil rights, their consciousness changed. They began to express—much more loudly and publicly than ever before—their dissatisfactions with the status quo.[1] They increasingly questioned traditional definitions of "female nature," protested male abuses of power inside and outside the family, and adopted "scandalous" modern fashions and habits as their own. While the press used their images to sell products, they used the press to vent their frustrations, to articulate their views and demands, and to communicate with one another.

On the other hand, the obsession with women's roles, behavior, and consciousness reflected deep and widespread anxieties among the rising urban elites over the rapidity and disorderliness of socioeconomic change. In a 1919 lecture, distinguished statesman Ruy Barbosa expressed the pervasive fear among the Brazilian intellectual and professional classes that the world in general (and Brazil in particular) was on the verge of "anarchy." The threat, he argued, was not "revolution" but "dissolution."[2] In the face of the disintegrative forces of massive European immigration and increasing rural-to-urban migration (following the abolition of slavery in 1888), explosive urban growth, sharp economic swings, intensified class conflict, and the introduction of dangerous new ideologies (of the political Left as well as feminism), the monopoly of power of Brazil's traditional rural oligarchy was crumbling and with it, the legitimacy of the republican government they controlled (the Old Republic, 1889–1930). Urban professionals, whether they placed themselves in the reformist camp or nostalgically looked backward to an idealized past, generally shared class resentments of the authoritarian and exclusionary politics of Brazil's traditional rural elite as well as class anxieties about the destabilizing impacts of the mobilization of the "popular masses." The political differences of these urban professionals, who were overwhelmingly male, also tended to dissolve in their suspicion of "modern women" and their opposition to real gender equality.

During the 1920s to 1930s, in a search for poles of order, rationality, "evolution," and "progress," Brazil's urban professional and intellectual community campaigned to "regenerate" the family and to elevate it (with women at its center) as the primary and essential social institution, capable of fostering economic modernization while preserving social order. Armed with prestigious educational degrees, the members of this community both challenged the "archaic" traditions of Brazil's oligarchical agrarian past and sought to establish their authority over (what they regarded as) the "unruly" and "uncivilized" Brazilian masses.

Increasingly secular in their thought, urban modernizers envisioned "progress" as occurring through the application of modern European scientific theories to Brazilian reality. By the 1920s through the 1930s, the enormous influence of eugenics—both a "science" and a social movement concerned with the improvement of the "race"—focused attention on reproduction as the key to overcoming the alleged "backwardness" and "degeneration" of the nation. Thus marriage, sexuality, maternity, and female education gained enormous significance in their eyes.[3] At the same time, more conservative urban intellectuals threw their energies into revitalizing Catholicism as a powerful reactionary force to stem the tide of modern scientific theories, democratic movements, and "immoral" modern fashions. And they succeeded in mobilizing hundreds of thousands of Catholics into lay movements. Militantly antifeminist, these organizations demanded strict adherence to the Church's traditional dogma and morality.[4] But if eugenicists' rationalistic and secular vision of "hygienic" reproduction, "puericulture," and "eugenic" education often clashed with Catholic activists' insistence on upholding the religious basis of family life and education, they concurred that women's primary and essential roles were wifehood and motherhood. And they shared the conviction that national regeneration (and Brazil's future as a world power) depended on the moral and physical health of individual families.

In 1930, after the worldwide depression knocked the bottom out of the international coffee market, Brazil's coffee oligarchy lost political power to a diverse coalition of rural oligarchs who had been marginalized during the Old Republic, urban middle sectors, intellectuals, nationalists, and young military officers. The coalition's populist leader, Getúlio Vargas—who came to power in a military coup and governed as provisional president (1930–34), constitutional president elected by Parliament (1934–37), and dictator (1937–45)—greatly strengthened the central government, fostered economic development, and instituted social and political reforms that mobilized the rising urban working classes into an effective base of personal political support.

Central to Vargas's program of modernization and political centralization was the gradual expansion of the notion of public interest to encompass realms that had previously been regarded as private (thus helping to usurp the power of the rural oligarchy while establishing government control over the rising urban masses). In justification of the state's increasing efforts to control intimate interpersonal relationships, professionals and political authorities echoed one another in reiterating that the family was the basis of the society and polity: that the state of the nation directly reflected the state of individual families. In 1940, a state functionary summed up what had become the canon of the age: "[T]he family is the foundation, the elemental and organic base of the State," and therefore "the perfection and civilization of the State depends fundamentally on the moral and legal conditions of each of the families which constitute it." He further proclaimed: "We consider the reconstitution of the family, in these times of dissolution of customs and infiltration of subversive theories, to be one of the most serious problems of public order, deserving the triple protection of the State." And he warned that if Brazilians did not help the state redeem the family while there was still time, they would be responsible for the "death of the fatherland" and the "extinction of our race."[5]

Among the favorite topics of concern for the new, increasingly interventionist state and for the urban professionals who elaborated its policies were the low rate of nuptiality within the urban working classes, the massive recruitment of women and children into the industrial workforce, and the extremely high rate of infant mortality. At the other end of the social scale, talk of "women's emancipation" within the small urban elite and rising middle classes alarmed men of both conservative and reformist persuasions, who agreed on the necessity of strengthening the model of the bourgeois family.[6] As women were exposed to the "pernicious" influences of the age—individualism, egoism, materialism—self-appointed guardians of public morality dreaded the breakdown of love, authority, and responsibility (or, one might infer, the breakdown of the sexual division of labor). Rapidly expanding urban freedoms for middle-class women—by-products of the booming consumer economy, growing educational and professional opportunities, new "female" jobs in the service sector, and the arrival of foreign cinematographic images of the sexy flapper and independent working girl—all threatened the power of the male head of household, which, if much diminished from the colonial period, was still considered (by virtually all men and probably by most women) to be fundamental to social order. Cartoons depicted the world turned upside down; and by ridiculing the masculinization of women and the feminization of men, they implicitly called for a return to normalcy and order.

To the emergent urban ruling classes, the stakes seemed very high. If the rebellion of the working class threatened property relations, the rebellion (or noncompliance) of urban women of all social classes seemed no less dangerous a threat to the relations of power within the family and therefore within society at large. In fact, the nature of these threats was similar. Maintaining social hierarchy (often defined as "morality") required maintaining binary oppositions between classes and between sexes.[7] Any attempt to dissolve either of these oppositions threatened the entire system of power. Thus as urban middle-class women invented a new discourse of individual rights for women and as they asserted themselves—sometimes powerfully—as agents of their own destinies, questions about sexual morality and gender relations became explicit political issues.

The formulation of public policy concerning gender relations was no more neutral than that concerning class relations. Especially after Vargas's rise to power in 1930, the Brazilian state played an increasingly active role in attempting to redefine the gender system: prescribing appropriate male and female educational curricula, employment opportunities, public roles, familial responsibilities, sexual behavior, and character traits. The importance of this ideological project lay in its centrality to the larger political project of promoting economic development while maintaining social stability, for this required reconciling employers' demands for female labor and women's demands for equality with the larger social need to harness women and the family more securely to the tasks of social reproduction.

Thus the struggle to redefine the gender system became an important part of the larger political conflicts of the era. Believing in the reformability of the human character, Brazil's modernizing professional classes struggled against the nation's conservative oligarchy and Church hierarchy to create new structures that would harmonize and rationalize social and political life. Vargas's seizure of dictatorial power in 1937 and his consolidation of a corporatist state structure in the Estado Novo (or "New State," 1937–45) represented the triumph of an authoritarian, co-optive model of economic modernization. This new state's corporatist project involved controlling the "anarchy" of the times by conciliating and arbitrating between conflicting interests. The state drew simultaneously on the expertise of populist social planners to devise paternalistic, co-optive responses to the "social question" and on the support of conservative groups linked to the Catholic Church and the army to uphold stable social hierarchies. The ideal envisioned was an "organic" society bound together (hierarchically) by ties of solidarity. With the proper place (rights and duties) of each group defined scientifically by "specialists," conflict would give way to peaceful collaboration toward a mutually desirable goal: capitalist development.[8]

In theory, at least, responsibility for controlling and disciplining the urban working class passed from individual factories to the state. The preferred techniques of social control also changed. Instead of relying solely on brutal force—

violent police repression—the state began to experiment with more "scientific" and "civilized" forms of control: proper socialization, moral suasion, institutional reform, and material benefits in exchange for political support and orderly social behavior. Most important, state-sponsored unionization effectively undermined autonomous labor organization (backed up by the continuing threat of force), while the passage of paternalistic labor legislation at least temporarily helped to co-opt protest. Through such means, the state sought to achieve the harmonious labor-capital relations necessary to guarantee capital accumulation.[9]

At the same time, the state increasingly usurped fathers' and husbands' traditional responsibility for disciplining women, invading what had been the most private and sacred of all relationships in Brazil: that of the family, and in particular, that of the husband and wife. State agencies, relying on the modern discourse of the rising class of liberal professionals they employed, attempted to impose new, more functional patterns of family relations. They maintained that it was no longer acceptable for husbands to behave like despots who wielded tyrannical power over their wives, nor for wives to be reduced to "slaves." Rather, modern, "hygienic" marriage should be constructed on a new "scientific" basis, in which reciprocity and mutual understanding gave rise to happy and stable—but still hierarchical—relations between the sexes.[10] Through the promotion of more subtle means of control (exercised through schools, medical facilities, social service agencies, the courts, and the legislature, as well as through renewed state support for initiatives of the Church), the state sought to legitimize marriage and the nuclear family as biologically natural and socially necessary institutions for all social classes and thereby to ensure the continued subordination of women's individual interests to collective interests.

In short, the professional classes and political authorities of the period concurred that rationalization of the emerging industrial-capitalist economy required simultaneous state intervention in the spheres of production and reproduction; the domestication of labor and the domestication of women (of all social classes) became complementary goals of the same corporatist project. Women—the guarantors of stable family life and the primary socializers of future generations—were key targets along with labor, since augmenting production depended (among other things) upon women's effectiveness in socializing a healthy, well-disciplined, and competent labor force. In the same way that the corporatist state attempted to depoliticize questions of labor-capital relations, transforming them into juridical and technical questions to be resolved by specialists, it attempted to depoliticize questions of sex and gender, transforming them into medical, juridical, and moral questions, best handled

by experts. By so doing, it not only sought to deny women (as it did labor) control over defining their problems and setting an agenda for action, but it also
provided a powerful "scientific" legitimation for this denial. This, in turn,
helped guarantee the differential access to resources that underlay the conception and consolidation of power in the authoritarian Estado Novo. The revised
gender system, itself a product of social and political conflict, became one of
the pillars on which the new polity was constructed and legitimated.[11]

This book studies changing gender ideologies, and as such, it is situated in
what is still relatively uncharted territory between women's history and political history.[12] It is not only about women but about the interaction of men and
women—in the family, school system, labor market, professions, polity, and
culture—in creating a new gender system compatible with Brazil's modern
era. The focus is necessarily on the urban middle and upper classes, especially
in Brazil's two major metropolises, Rio de Janeiro and São Paulo, since it was
this group that set social norms for the modernizing nation.[13] But the presence
of the poor majority is felt in the manner in which the Brazilian elite conceptu-
alized and articulated new norms; and attempts to implement these norms created new circumstances for those on the bottom of the social ladder (even if,
within Brazil's class-stratified society, the poor were unable to attain the middle-class ideals that were claimed universal and "natural").

Given the highly stratified nature of Brazilian society, the modernization of
the gender system affected women of different classes in different—and often
contradictory—ways. Changing economic necessities and social norms allowed women of the upper and middle classes new opportunities for higher education and paid employment that were not matched by equivalent opportunities for lower-class women. Well-educated women of elite families entered into
the professions; by the 1920s to 1930s, Brazil had a small but notable minority
of women physicians, lawyers, writers, and artists and even a few engineers and
scientists. A greater number of middle-class women took new "respectable"
white-collar jobs that were being created by the rapid expansion of the service
sector. Urban middle-class families, confronted with the declining value of
women's domestic labor, high rates of inflation, and the increasing need for
cash, began to regard women's wage work more favorably—as long as it did not
tarnish women's reputations (through association with working women of
lower social status), compromise their femininity (by placing them in direct
competition with men), or threaten the stability of the male-headed household
(by fostering women's individual ambitions or providing real opportunities for
economic independence).

In contrast, working-class women's employment, which had been accepted
as natural and necessary in the nineteenth century, began to be regarded as an

unnatural and unfortunate (if still necessary) evil, which endangered family stability and social and political order. Thus poor women, who had provided the labor power for the early textile mills in the late nineteenth century, faced growing hostility toward their labor force participation. While men of their class benefited from the industrial expansion of the early twentieth century, securing higher-skilled and better-paid jobs in the more modern industries, women remained segregated in the least-skilled and poorest-paid industries and jobs, thanks to the combination of social prejudices about women's "natural" abilities and proper roles, limited educational opportunities, the economic interests of employers (to keep a pool of low-paid workers), and protective legislation (which helped sustain sex segmentation in the workplace). In addition to "female" factory work, domestic service continued to provide the other major source of employment for poor urban women. While domestic servants freed middle-class women to pursue careers, they themselves remained trapped in the domestic sphere under the tutelage of their wealthier female employers. Not only did they suffer from a lack of legal protections, very low pay, and exploitative working conditions, but the nature of their work reinforced disempowering stereotypes of female nature.[14]

Within the family, it was middle- and upper-class women who could—more easily than working-class women—exploit new opportunities to gain power vis-à-vis their husbands. As the professional community endorsed the model of the companionate marriage, and as middle- and upper-class women took advantage of expanding social freedoms and new educational and professional opportunities, they gained clout in demanding greater equality, intimacy, and sexual fulfillment within marriage.

At the same time, the autonomy of working-class women (the majority of whom had remained unmarried and self-supporting during the nineteenth century) was being eroded by the increasing difficulty they faced in competing with men of their class in the labor market. The Brazilian Ministry of Labor, convinced that the rationalization of the bourgeois order required legal marriages and stable family organization within the urban working class, drafted protective legislation that restricted female employment to "appropriate"— and not coincidentally, less well remunerated—sectors and time shifts, thereby encouraging women's subordination to men through economic dependence. In addition, not only were working-class women the targets of campaigns (organized by state agencies as well as by the Church, medical community, and charity organizations) to impose modern "hygienic" standards of marriage and family life, but they also came under pressure from male-dominated labor unions, which agreed that women belonged at home. Union support for protective legislation—which ultimately helped protect men's space in the labor market—imposed stereotypes of female fragility on women who had worked brutal factory shifts, guaranteed women's unpaid domestic labor, and helped force the model of the bourgeois family onto the urban working class.

It was in the realm of politics that the emerging gender system contained the most acute conflicts of class. In response to the pressure of a small group of outspoken and well-connected professional women, the Brazilian Parliament passed female suffrage in 1932, and a few women went on to win local electoral campaigns. But suffrage was limited to literate women over the age of twenty-one, and, after the imposition of the authoritarian Estado Novo in 1937, no one voted for eight years. Working-class women (a large percentage of whom were still illiterate) were not only marginalized from political power through the denial of suffrage; in addition, as they were unable to compete with men for jobs in the modern industrial sector, their earlier importance as labor activists declined. Perhaps equally significant, a proliferation of new upper-class women's charity organizations buttressed state tutelage of working-class women. Striving to exert a "moralizing" influence over women of more humble backgrounds, these female charity workers often self-consciously allied themselves with the Church, industrialists, social service agencies, physicians, and educators to solve the "social problem."

By the late 1930s to early 1940s, public concern over changing gender roles, sexual morality, and family organization was on the wane. This can be explained in several ways. First, the gains achieved by women who worked inside and outside the organized feminist movement most likely eroded the constituency for feminist activism. And although more radical reforms remained on the agenda, the 1937 coup closed off channels of discussion and political mobilization, dashing hopes (and allaying fears) of further successes. Second, once the Estado Novo succeeded in demobilizing the urban working class (through its incorporation into state-organized unions) and pacifying workers with paternalistic labor legislation, the new urban ruling class no longer felt such anxiety over social "chaos." Nor, therefore, did they perceive such an urgent need to control women and to mold the family into a pillar of social stability and moral order. To the extent that this need persisted, it could now be safely handled by the growing state bureaucracy's new legions of technocrats. Third, the male urban modernizers, who had enhanced their own authority by attacking obsolete ("barbaric") patriarchal traditions, had achieved as much reform in the gender system as they desired. Having helped to break the power of the old order, and having ushered Brazil into the community of "modern," "progressive" nations, their interest lay in consolidating their gains. The modernized gender system that they had helped to elaborate during the 1920s to 1930s served them well in institutionalizing a more legitimate form of male domination.

Indeed, modernization of the gender system brought ambiguous progress. Women won all the "rights" of full citizenship; but given Brazil's authoritarian political traditions, few citizens could exercise any "rights" in practice, and women were warned not to allow the exercise of their "rights" to interfere with the performance of their most essential familial "duties." The ideal new woman was "liberated" from ignorance, but educators designed curricula to prepare her first and foremost to fulfill her "natural" role as rational household manager and intelligent socializer of the future generation. Although her enlightened mothering was increasingly valued, escalating requirements tied her to the domestic sphere while the emphasis on nurturing narrowly defined appropriate female character traits. Employers eagerly recruited her into the service sector of the booming urban-industrial economy, but the 1916 Civil Code defined her husband as the legal head of the household, who held power to authorize or forbid her to pursue a profession. Moreover, since she was channeled into routine, very poorly paid "female" jobs, her employment supplemented family income and promoted national development more than it allowed her individual autonomy or self-fulfillment. Male professionals cautiously endorsed the modernization of family and sexual life, but they did so in an attempt to contain conflict and postpone fundamental changes in the structure of family organization rather than to empower wives. The redrawing of social boundaries between the sexes, while ceding to feminist pressure to integrate women into formerly male spheres and seeking to improve the quality of male-female relations, ultimately left women's domesticity intact. In fact, the model of the family based on a specific division of labor that supported male domination and female subordination emerged perhaps even stronger for having been revamped and promoted within the urban working class. Despite the obvious contradictions in this model, it survived several decades until the massive entry of middle-class women into the paid workforce and access to contraceptive pills undermined the material compulsions on which it had rested.

This book begins by providing a historical context for the early-twentieth-century reconstruction of the gender system in Brazil. Chapter 1 focuses on the factors that threw the old gender system into disarray: the erosion of the material base of patriarchal power, the eclipse of home production by the rising industrial economy, the revolution in communications, the introduction of new symbolic representations of women, the rise of bourgeois values, and women's entrance into new social spaces. Chapters 2, 3, and 4 focus on the ideological and material reconstruction of the family that underlay the consolidation of the new authoritarian bourgeois order of the late 1930s. Modernization of the family brought measured accommodations to women's demands for greater intimacy and equality: while men were advised to become sensitive companions of their wives, women were urged to become active, competent collaborators. But at the same time, impassioned political campaigns strove to silence women's protests, suppress radical alternatives, and install mechanisms to harness women of all classes more securely to the process of reproduction. Chapters 5, 6, and 7 examine the reformulation of the gender system in the worlds of education, the labor market, and politics. Once old definitions of the proper place of men and women had become obviously dysfunctional, the resolution of heated public debates over sexual difference became crucial to the process of legitimating authority and protecting power. In short, understanding the revision of the gender system in early-twentieth-century Brazil is one key to understanding how modernization occurred without fundamentally upsetting the structure of inequality.

1

THE DEMISE OF PATRIARCHALISM

Until at least the mid-nineteenth century, Brazil was a rigidly hierarchical soci-ety bound together by ties of kinship and patronage.[1] Its export economy (with its successive booms of sugar, gold and diamonds, rubber, and coffee—and to a lesser extent, cotton and cacao) empowered the great *fazenderos*, rural patri-archs whose control of land, labor, markets, and capital ensured their political hegemony as well as near absolute authority over their extended households. Coexisting with (and within) the large extended patriarchal families were the smaller nuclear families of the less prosperous as well as the consensual unions and female-headed households of the poor and the slave population. For them, survival—given the absence of any effective central political authority, the precarious and limited economy, and the total lack of social services—gener-ally required allying with a powerful extended family (or *parentela*). In ex-change for protection, economic security, and favors, landed potentates com-manded loyalty, obedience, and service from dependent relatives, godchildren, needy friends, concubines, servants, tenants, free laborers, and slaves, as well as from their own wives and children.[2]

Children of the elite were reared to obey, even to the extent of accepting the right of the patriarch to choose their marriage partner. Romance was normally an irrelevant consideration; instead, elite families arranged marriages for their children (often with cousins or close relatives) with the aim of cementing polit-ical alliances and guarding property and status.[3]

Brazilian civil law (which until 1916 was an extension of the Philippine Code compiled in 1603 in Portugal) subordinated wives to their husbands, defining them as perpetual minors who were powerless to make final decisions about their children's upbringing or even to administer their own property.[4] Nineteenth-century travelers to Brazil painted a generally unflattering portrait of women of the elite. Frequently married off by their mid-teens to much older men, they were stereotyped as submissive, passive creatures whose cloistered domestic existence and superficial instruction (in playing the piano, singing, reciting poetry, dancing, and speaking a bit of French) made them exceedingly dull company. They quickly grew fat as a result of their indolent lives, deteriorated into stooped, wrinkled old matrons by the age of thirty (if they survived their many pregnancies), and were said to be characteristically bad tempered and abusive with their servants, especially with their husbands' mulatto mistresses.[5]

As historians have since pointed out, this stereotype is surely overdrawn, given that elite women directed large, complex households with dozens of slaves and servants engaged in the production of food, clothing, and other household necessities. Moreover, to them fell the responsibility for providing health care, socializing children, and organizing family celebrations and religious rituals. And in exceptional cases, rich widows, with the authority they acquired as legal head of the family, successfully managed *fazendas* or family businesses and wielded formidable political and social power.[6] Nevertheless, their example did not threaten the social norm of female seclusion, enforced (albeit with infractions) within the elite in order to guarantee the honor of the family and the racial purity of descendants.[7]

The vast majority of the population was separated from the elite not only by income and occupation but also by generally darker skin color, dress, and social customs. Legal marriage was a mark of status that the poor rarely achieved. For those without property to protect, consensual unions were the norm, illegitimacy rates were high, and female-headed households were very common. Female indolence and seclusion were impossible ideals. Beginning at very young ages, poor women labored in lowly manual occupations (as maids, cooks, wet nurses, laundresses, seamstresses, street vendors, or sometimes prostitutes) to eke out a marginal existence. And not only did their work take them into public spaces, but their income—however little—provided them a measure of autonomy.[8]

Brazil's political system reflected and reinforced its hierarchical social order. With the Napoleonic invasion of the Iberian peninsula, the Portuguese royal court fled to Brazil, installing itself in Rio de Janeiro in 1808. After Brazil declared independence from Portugal in 1822, a constitutional monarchy reigned until 1889, providing the powerful planter aristocracy (at least from 1840 until the 1870s) with a legitimate centralized state that served its interests. Elections were indirect, and the franchise included less than 4 percent of the population: adult males who met income qualifications. Given that many eligible voters did not vote and that others (through loyalty or intimidation or in exchange for payments) cast their votes for the slate favored by the extended family on which they were dependent, the electorate was easily manipulated and electoral fraud was common. At the local level, political bosses (*coronéis*)—generally the heads of tightly knit extended families—controlled the political parties and dominated municipal government, monopolizing local officeholding and distributing the spoils to their clients.[9]

After midcentury, and especially after 1870, socioeconomic transformations gradually eroded the material bases of patriarchalism. The speeding up of the industrial revolution in Europe brought railroads and steamships to Brazil, created high demand for Brazil's export crops, and offered unprecedented opportunities for profit, especially for landowners in the dynamic coffee-growing regions of western São Paulo. The rapid accumulation of capital allowed these coffee planters to accommodate to the ending of the slave trade by introducing modern technology to increase productivity and by gradually switching from slave labor to free immigrant labor. As southern European immigrants (whose passages were subsidized by the São Paulo and Brazilian governments) poured into the economically dynamic regions of the center-south, the internal market expanded. And as the cities of São Paulo and Rio de Janeiro mushroomed, wealthy coffee planters joined immigrant entrepreneurs in investing in infrastructure, banking, utilities, and the first consumer industries. Within these bustling, modernizing urban centers, the ascendant middle classes (of liberal professionals, bureaucrats, small entrepreneurs, shopkeepers, and clerical workers), along with artisans, industrial workers, and freed or runaway slaves, attacked traditional institutions and demanded reforms.[10]

In the face of rapid socioeconomic change, the formal institutions that had guaranteed social hierarchy collapsed. In May 1888, Parliament passed the Lei Aurea (Golden Law, which finally abolished slavery without indemnification) against only a few negative votes cast by representatives of indebted landowners in stagnant regions, and it was greeted with wild rejoicing in the nation's city streets. On 15 November 1889, a military coup overthrew the monarch, whose base of support had been reduced to the most traditional sectors of the rural oligarchy. The victors—the military, wealthy São Paulo coffee planters, and the urban middle classes—established a republican government (the Old Republic, which lasted from 1889 to 1930). But the franchise expanded only minimally to include all literate males over the age of twenty-one, and the lives of the majority of Brazilians did not change significantly. In practice, because the urban middle classes constituted a small percentage of the nation's population and had no base of support independent of the coffee export economy, they could be incorporated into the political system without undermining the power of the coffee elite, transforming the authoritarian character of the political system, or altering the neocolonial structure of the economy.[11]

While Brazil remained predominantly rural and dependent on the agro-export economy well into the twentieth century, its major cities grew at a much faster pace than the population as a whole, and they began to wield disproportionate political weight as well as cultural influence. Rio de Janeiro, after it became the seat of the Portuguese royal court in 1808, surpassed the northeastern cities of Salvador and Recife as Brazil's largest and most cosmopolitan center. It benefited from the opening of Brazilian ports to all nations and the consequent expansion of international trade. Especially after midcentury, increasingly rapid accumulation of capital allowed for improvements in urban services and public works, as well as the acquisition of more of the trappings of "civilization": the first national presses, new professional schools, a public library, theaters, coffeehouses, and elegant stores.[12]

Rio remained the nation's capital city after the formation of the Old Republic in 1889, and the liberal professionals who took over the city's administration imposed (forcibly, over the protests of the poor) policies designed to remake both the urban space and its population in the image of Europe and according to Brazil's new positivist motto, "order and progress." Between 1902 and 1910, in a dramatic reconstruction of the center city, slums were demolished (and their poor, largely nonwhite inhabitants relocated) to make way for wide boulevards, large public buildings with magnificent Beaux Arts facades, and embellished parks and squares (as well as for "respectable," generally white, families).[13] Expanding commercial and employment opportunities attracted foreign immigrants and rural migrants, almost doubling the city's population between 1872 and 1890 and more than doubling it again by 1920 (see table 1).

The city of São Paulo was even more quickly transformed from a muddy rural outpost to Brazil's leading commercial and industrial metropolis. Between 1888 and 1928, more than two million European immigrants entered São Paulo, approximately half of whom had been provided a free passage in exchange for going to work on the coffee plantations.[14] But many also migrated to the city, including those with sufficient capital to set themselves up as artisans, merchants, or entrepreneurs, as well as those who sought employment in the early textile, apparel, and food-processing industries. The population of São Paulo (city) more than doubled between 1872 and 1890, grew a spectacular 269 percent between 1890 and 1900, and grew again another 141 percent between 1900 and 1920 (see table 1). Immigrants provided cheap labor for the growing number of factories, which in turn supplied expanding local markets with manu-

Table 1. Population of Brazil and the Cities of Rio de Janeiro
and São Paulo, 1872–1940

	Brazil	Rio de Janeiro	São Paulo
1872	10,112,061	274,972	31,385
1890	14,333,915	522,651	64,934
1900	17,318,556	811,443[a]	239,820
1920	30,635,605	1,157,873	579,033
1940	41,236,315	1,764,141	1,326,261

Sources: Brazil, Diretoria Geral de Estatística, *Synopse do recenseamento realizado . . . 1920*, 39; Brazil, Comissão Censitária Nacional, *Recenseamento geral do Brasil . . . 1940*, série nacional, tomo 2, pp. 1, 140; série regional, pt. 17, tomo 2, p. 472.

[a] 1906 statistics. The 1900 census was set aside for Rio de Janeiro.

factured goods. The value of the state's industrial output more than doubled between 1905 and 1915. By 1920, São Paulo surpassed Rio de Janeiro as Brazil's leading industrial center and began to rival Rio as an intellectual and cultural center.[15]

Late-nineteenth-century urbanization dramatically increased opportunities for investment, employment, social mobility, and political mobilization— opportunities that in turn fostered transformations in consciousness and gradually loosened traditional patriarchal social relationships. Sons of planters who pursued urban careers escaped the tutelage of their fathers. Although their autonomy was compromised by their continuing dependence on patronage, their prestigious educational degrees, professional skills, and valuable political contacts gave them increasing leverage vis-à-vis their fathers. Moreover, liberal professionals and salaried bureaucrats no longer depended on receiving a substantial dowry from their wives' families, since they did not need the agricultural land and other means of production that had been essential for setting up a household in colonial Brazil. Thus, although such men might still be seduced by the luxuries, status, and advantageous family connections that a "good" marriage could bring, they gained much more freedom to follow the inclinations of the heart. Propertied families, which had traditionally arranged marriages for sons and daughters, responded by gradually eliminating dowries by the end of the nineteenth century, both reflecting and contributing to the erosion of the patriarch's power to control marriage choices. For elite women, marrying without a dowry meant total economic dependence on their husbands and a significant loss of leverage within the relationship. Nevertheless, they too gained greater freedom to choose (and responsibility to find) their own spouses. And propertyless women had a much greater chance of marrying legally.[16]

Legal reforms further reflected and contributed to the erosion of the power of the patriarch over sons and daughters. In 1831, the age of legal majority was lowered from twenty-five to twenty-one, thus allowing children to marry without parental permission earlier—a provision that children took advantage of only gradually, as they became more economically independent of parents. Early forced marriages were also restricted by the raising of the minimum age of marriage from twelve for girls and fourteen for boys to fourteen and sixteen in 1890 and sixteen and eighteen in 1916. And the 1890 civil marriage law forbade coerced marriages, specifying that windows had to remain open and doors unlocked when minors were married in private buildings.[17]

Accompanying the modernization of the economic infrastructure of the cities were notable changes in elite social customs. Garbage collection, underground sewers, street paving, gas lighting, and (especially) regular streetcar service allowed elite women to venture outside by the 1870s with a new degree of comfort, security, and ease. Their physical seclusion soon became an impossible and undesirable remnant of the past. Although always accompanied by relatives or servants, they were increasingly seen at public parks, beaches, tearooms, and elegant stores. And with the intensification of social life, they contributed to the enhancement of the family's status by displaying their stylish European wardrobes and social graces at the theater, balls, parties, and sports clubs.[18]

By the 1870s, urban intellectuals unanimously advocated improved public education as an essential means for ensuring Brazil's progress, although they defined proper female education as that which would make women good wives and competent mothers, capable of raising good citizens. Early feminists also justified female education as preparation for motherhood, but increasingly they demanded admission to institutions of higher learning and access to elite professions so that they too could contribute to the economic development of the nation, support themselves independently, and fulfill their own human potential. After institutions of higher learning were opened to women in 1879, only a very few women attended, given the high cost of obtaining the necessary secondary education and the strong social prejudices against such a novelty. Nevertheless, women's aspirations were rising and social realities were changing as urban middle-class families increasingly sought schooling for their daughters not only to prepare them for family roles but to ensure that they could earn an honorable living if and when it became necessary. Although the first women who took their places alongside men as physicians, attorneys, engineers, and scientists were more often denounced than applauded, their accomplishments gave them the credibility and the clout to demand female suffrage following the collapse of the monarchy in 1889. To the credit of early women's rights advocates, female suffrage was debated during the 1891 Constituent Congress (even if it was not yet taken seriously and was soundly defeated).[19]

By the mid-1910s, decades of erosion of patriarchal power had rendered traditional elite family organization and gender definitions obsolete. As extrafamilial institutions had taken over many of the functions of the extended patriarchal family, it was gradually replaced by the model of the urban, bourgeois nuclear family. And as the rapidly expanding market economy had progressively undermined women's productive roles in the household, middle- and upper-class women entered the public sphere in a variety of new roles. Although the lives of poor urban women did not change to the same degree, the "social question" and the "woman question" converged, reflecting the intensification of class conflict. Well-to-do women increasingly complained that their maids were becoming impossibly "uppity," while public authorities strove to curb the "immoral" behavior of "dishonest women," and conservatives strenuously denounced the employment of poor women outside the home as dangerous for family stability, social morality, and therefore political order.

This chapter describes the rapid and dramatic transformations in daily routines, styles, and social customs that marked Brazil's entrance into the modern industrial age. It focuses on the urban middle and upper classes, since they were the most affected and the most influential in redefining gender norms. The devaluation of women's domestic labor economically and socially, combined with expanding educational and professional opportunities, new types of recreation, and immediate access through modern communications to foreign images, styles, and values, changed the behavior, tastes, appearances, and expectations of Brazil's urban population—especially the female population—with a rapidity considered alarming by many of Brazil's most prominent intellectuals and professionals. Anxious over social and political "chaos" and economic instability, they often attributed momentous significance to what they regarded as an undermining of traditional gender roles and sexual morality.

During the late nineteenth century, elite urban households gradually lost their productive functions, becoming units of consumption. Whereas rural *fazendas* in Brazil had been relatively self-sufficient—relying on large staffs of servants and slaves to produce food, clothing, and other household necessities, care for the sick, educate the young, and provide entertainment—urban households increasingly depended on consumer goods and services provided by the market.

Rising industrial production from the late nineteenth to the early twentieth century increasingly replaced artisan and household production, providing textiles, shoes, hats, processed foods, candles, soaps, and other consumer goods for a growing market. By 1920, national industries had largely substituted imports in basic consumer goods.[20] Whereas the first department stores that opened in Rio de Janeiro in the 1870s sold nothing but expensive imports to an exclusive clientele, stores stocked with national products were catering to a mass market by the 1910s. Glittering tearooms and exclusive fashion shows continued to draw in wealthy shoppers, while middle-class shoppers were lured in by advertisements plastered on public busses, attractive window displays, sales, the introduction of purchase on credit, and the opening of a few five-and-ten-cent stores that sold nothing above a low fixed price. As the middle classes succumbed to the pressures of conspicuous consumption, new and ever larger department stores experienced a heyday.[21]

Until the beginning of the twentieth century, one of women's major tasks had been to supply their households with clothing, bed sheets, and table linens. Few stores sold ready-made clothing for children, and the selection of men's and women's clothing was very limited. Families with moderate wealth hired seamstresses, but even wealthy women were expected to do some sewing and embroidering. By the 1920s, those who could afford to pay retail prices purchased ready-made clothing as well as fashionable new accessories. Those with social ambitions but modest resources carefully copied store-bought models in the hope that others would not recognize their clothing as homemade. Those who subsisted on meager budgets treasured any item of store-bought clothing as among their most prized possessions.[22]

The popular women's magazine *Revista Feminina* provided readers with patterns for sewing clothing at home, but its pages were also filled with advertisements for ready-made clothing. In 1918, the fashion editor advised brides that it would be preferable if they sewed the intimate apparel for their trousseaux, carefully choosing the materials and tastefully decorating each piece with embroidery, lace, and ribbons. However, the editor quickly went on to concede: "Dear readers, if you don't have time, or if you lack patience, go to a reputable store . . . and buy your trousseau." She encouraged brides to shop at the "Mappin Stores," where they could find the finest assortment of embroidered and laced intimate apparel, as well as bed and table linens: "[A]ll you have to do is take a taxi, go down to 'Mappin,' ride the elevator to the second floor, and become enraptured with the beautiful and sumptuous displays."[23]

Shopping became an important social institution. Although no woman of a "good" family would have gone shopping unaccompanied at the beginning of the century, this became commonplace by the 1920s. Magazine covers featured women dressed in their best clothes ready to venture downtown alone. Saturday was the favored day for shopping, when the opportunity to display one's wealth was rivaled by the opportunity to see, to be seen, and to flirt.[24]

As the expansion of the market economy began to transform the structure of services, shopping also became a daily necessity. Even until the early twentieth century, elite women rarely needed to go out (or send their servants out) to provision their households. Routine purchases were made from door-to-door peddlers who provided the daily necessities: newspapers, milk, bread, ice, vegetables, fruit, firewood. Several times a week peddlers passed by selling eggs, chickens, turkeys, fish, and meat. Others sold sewing accessories and yard goods, brooms and baskets. Traveling handymen sharpened knives, fixed pots and pans, rewove straw seats, dyed old and soiled clothing, and so on.[25] Changes came rapidly with the inflation that accompanied World War I. When central market stall owners (from whom peddlers bought their wares) raised the prices of staples, the São Paulo government responded by establishing neighborhood street markets where small farmers could sell their produce directly to consumers without having to obtain a permit or pay taxes. Merchants also set up stalls in the new markets and provided shoppers with goods and services at reduced prices. The social effect was to encourage women to go out (or to accompany their servants out) to do their daily shopping.[26]

As industry undermined women's roles as producers, the professionalization of medicine undermined their roles as caregivers, turning them into the primary consumers of services provided by the growing medical community. From the mid-nineteenth century, doctors—who had discovered the poor health of women and children to be a serious social problem—launched strenuous attacks against folk medicine, midwives, and other "ignorant" noncertified practitioners. But, if we can believe early-twentieth-century doctors, their nineteenth-century predecessors did not succeed in bringing about the desired change. As late as 1918, Antonio Austregésilo Lima still found it necessary to insist: "[F]lee charlatans. . . . Always . . . believe in honest and friendly doctors; call on the sound reasoning you were taught in clinics or books."[27] And about the same time, educator Fernando de Azevedo and Dr. Francisco Vasconcellos lamented that young Brazilian women were weak. Indeed, according to Vasconcellos's calculations, even among elite women, 30 percent—a "legion" of young women—suffered from frailty. As a result, Azevedo claimed, they were destroying their health in maternity and producing sickly offspring.[28]

Nevertheless, professional medicine was firmly established by the early twentieth century, with doctors having secured strong influence within the government bureaucracy as well as within the middle- and upper-class population.[29] Gynecology and obstetrics had gained respectability as their (virtually all male) practitioners boasted new scientific knowledge and as the strict codes of decency and morality that had forbidden women from visiting male gynecologists gradually broke down.[30] Women whose mothers had given birth at home with the assistance of midwives now filled the growing number of maternity wards staffed by male obstetricians trained in performing cesarean sections.[31] Hospitals and specialized clinics offering new treatments and new services proliferated during the early twentieth century, both cause and consequence of the rapidly diminishing prejudices among the middle and upper classes against hospitalization.[32] Expensive clinics provided abortions—which were then (and remain) illegal—for the rich.[33] And plastic surgeons were in increasing demand, thanks to the popularity of eugenics (which stressed the importance of physical perfection) as well as to the modern cult of youth and beauty. Plastic surgeons not only corrected (real and supposed) defects of physiognomy but, more frequently, performed face-lifting operations for older women who sought to eliminate wrinkles.[34] Since the maintenance of health and beauty also required regular dental care, frequent visits to the dentist were advised as well.[35]

Psychiatrists versed in Freudian theories also prospered as elite women suffering from nervous disorders became accustomed to seeking professional help. According to Antonio Austregésilo Lima, nervous disability—neurasthenia—had reached epidemic proportions in modern society, and women were more susceptible to this new disease than were men.[36] In extreme cases, it became acceptable for men to intern female relatives whom they considered mentally imbalanced in one of the numerous psychiatric hospitals that had been founded since the last decade of the nineteenth century.[37]

The commercialization of leisure had similar impacts, transforming women from producers into consumers of entertainment and introducing new patterns of social interaction. Beginning in the second half of the nineteenth century, attractive alternatives existed to the traditional family gatherings at which women had played the piano, sung, and recited poetry; and women increasingly joined men of their class in public leisure activities. Theater and opera enjoyed great popularity from the 1870s in Rio de Janeiro, when the founding of the Teatro Lírico provided a space for the performances of traveling European companies, and from the 1880s in São Paulo, after the construction of the São Paulo–Rio de Janeiro railroad made it feasible to transport foreign companies to the city. By the end of the century, sports provided another form of public entertainment for a growing urban population. Horse racing clubs attracted elite couples eager to show off their chic outfits and socialize with their peers.

Among the less affluent, soccer matches—between rival neighborhood teams and later professional teams—drew increasingly large popular audiences. But young women (as well as men) not only watched sports from the sidelines. They began to participate in tennis matches and swimming races at the growing number of sports clubs. They spent leisure hours rowing or going on bicycle outings. And they played miniature golf and roller-skated at public rinks.[38]

However, it was film that first attracted mass audiences and caused the most stir. Cinemas proliferated after 1910, and by the 1920s, moviegoing had become among the most popular of pastimes for young and old, men and women, rich and the working poor. In São Paulo, the number of screenings of films quadrupled between 1915 and 1927 from 2,115 to 8,407, and the average seating capacity increased from 600 to 1,500.[39] Although the most luxurious cinemas required tuxedos for evening showings of Hollywood's best superproductions, modest neighborhood cinemas offered special showings for children and a ladies' night, when women paid half price. Many films were shown as serials in up to twenty installments, stopping at the moments of greatest suspense so as to attract audiences back week after week.[40]

Films not only provided a new leisure activity, but as they quickly captured the popular imagination, they introduced viewers to a new world of Hollywood stars and American styles and cultural values. Female moviegoers gained as role models sexy flappers and independent working girls who stepped out of traditional roles of resignation and modesty. Hollywood stars—especially female stars—became the heroes and symbols of modern life. In its opening editorial of 1922, the avant-garde magazine *Klaxon* declared the cinema and its image of the new woman to be indispensable components of the modern aesthetic: "Pearl White is preferable to Sarah Bernhardt. Sarah is tragedy, sentimental and technical romanticism. Pearl is reason, instruction, sport, speed, happiness, life. Sarah Bernhardt = 19th century. Pearl White = 20th century. Cinematography is the most representative art form of our epoch."[41] Popular magazines such as *A Cigarra*, *A Vida Moderna*, and *Eu Sei Tudo*, as well as new specialized movie magazines, regularly featured coquettish portraits of female movie stars accompanied by columns that fed the curiosity of moviegoers by revealing intimate details of the private lives of the faces on the screen.

The morality of the cinema became a highly contentious issue. An article in *Klaxon* asked: "How can a father teach his daughter about certain aspects of life?" And it answered:

The easiest way is to take her to the cinema, whose high morality, reduced to the most simple expression, gives the formula:

ALL BAD IS PUNISHED

THE GOOD ENDS UP WINNING

AND RECEIVES AS A REWARD MARRIAGE

OR IF MARRIED . . . A CHILD.[42]

But conservatives disagreed. In response to "innumerable letters . . . from female readers . . . demanding a campaign for the moralization of the cinema," the *Revista Feminina* published editorials urging women to boycott "immoral" and "licentious" films. The first of these editorials deplored the fact that the cinema, being an object of "universal public consumption, . . . sold the degenerate morality of its merchandise to whomever wanted to buy it." It argued that if legislation protected the physical health of the population by preventing the sale of spoiled food, legislation should regulate even more strictly "this dangerous vehicle of ideas" that could contaminate hearts with "the most malignant infection . . . if fraudulently nourished."[43] Editorials went on to protest that instead of educating the population in sound moral principles, the cinema exploited "scandal, futility, illegitimate love, . . . and crime"; it acted as a "fatal stimulus of abject appetite"; it encouraged "reprehensible desires" and "pernicious habits"; and it led to the "dissolution" of traditional Christian precepts and familial organization. The cinema, editorials claimed, taught the "pure" and "simple" hearts of children that "virtue is misery . . . and vice and wealth constitute triumph." And it "sows in the innocent hearts of loyal wives the poison of discontent, seducing their weak spirits with the false beauty of unrealistic heroes."[44]

Film was perhaps the most obvious of the modern revolutions in communications that challenged (at least to some degree) traditional gender stereotypes and roles along with the monopoly of information that the patriarchs had enjoyed. But it was not the only one. The phonograph enabled widespread distribution of the latest, commercially produced musical hits. And even more important, radios, which could be bought or built at moderate cost, brought the outside world into the home by the early 1920s. Housewives could now go about their daily chores accompanied by modern music and programs that exposed them to a wealth of new information and new (potentially "dangerous") ideas. Radio stations catered to the female audience by airing programs in which women who were strangers to one another communicated about common experiences, problems, and ideas—propelling discussion of "private" matters into the public realm. A few women took advantage of new opportunities to turn their skills as performers to commercial advantage (as did one female ensemble that was so modern and daring as to appear on the radio in 1928 playing popular music on guitars). But by making commercially produced music readily and continually accessible, the phonograph and the radio lessened the value of women's musical talents to their families and friends.[45]

Journalism also enjoyed a spectacular boom, thanks to increasing literacy and the growing market, and offered another new forum for debating and shaping gender relations. Whereas in 1890 only 19.1 percent of all Brazilian men and 10.4 percent of all Brazilian women were literate (amounting to only 2,120,559 people), by 1920 literacy had increased to 28.9 percent for men and 19.9 percent for women (7,493,357 people). The percentage of literates was much higher in the cities of São Paulo and Rio de Janeiro, where women were making the most rapid gains. By 1920, 54.5 percent of all women in the two cities and 65.8 percent of all men were literate (1,047,954 people).[46] In response to rising demand, the number of newspapers and periodicals multiplied quickly. The city of São Paulo, which had only fifteen newspapers and periodicals in 1901, boasted thirty-eight in 1910, fifty-six in 1920, and seventy-nine in 1927. Whereas no newspaper or periodical in the city had printed more than five thousand copies in 1901, more than half were printing over five thousand copies by the mid-1920s; and whereas 73 percent had fewer than four pages in 1901, 70 percent had four or more pages by 1927.[47]

The *Revista Feminina*, published between 1914 and 1927, became Brazil's first commercially successful women's magazine, and in so doing it established beyond question that a lucrative female market existed. The founder and editor, Virgilina de Souza Salles, was the daughter of a well-connected São Paulo family and the mother of the popular playwright Claudio de Souza. In addition, she was a brilliant and resourceful businesswoman. Beginning with a biweekly four-page leaflet entitled *A Lucta Moderna* (The Modern Struggle), she launched a major promotional campaign that entailed the national distribution of thirty thousand free copies of each of the first seven issues among sixty thousand potential subscribers.[48] By January 1915, the magazine changed its name to *Revista Feminina*, announced monthly publication, and enlisted 4,325 subscribers. It solicited advertisements to help offset costs and expanded to more than fifteen pages of text and illustrations. Prominent male writers and members of the Brazilian Academy of Letters began to contribute articles, as did most of the well-known female writers of the period.[49] By the end of 1916, the magazine was an elegant, glossy publication boasting over one hundred pages of text and two hundred illustrations, some printed in more than one color. The price of an annual subscription rose to 7$000 (seven *mil-réis*), and the number of subscriptions increased to 12,568.[50]

The magazine continued to grow at least until 1918, when it was printing between twenty thousand and twenty-five thousand copies of each issue.[51] Its success can be attributed in large part to an energetic campaign aimed at mobilizing readers to sell subscriptions to their friends. (Readers were told that by selling subscriptions they would help guarantee a better future for women and "perform an act of high patriotism."[52] As further encouragement, those who sold ten subscriptions received one free subscription.) The editors insisted that the magazine was "the first great work of our sex" in Brazil, and that it provided an indispensable "organ for intellectual communication."[53] Prominent men apparently agreed. According to the magazine's editors, endorsements poured in, including from Cardinal Arcoverde and from four bishops.[54] The daily newspaper *O Journal do Commercio* praised the *Revista Feminina* as the "best feminine publication that has appeared in South America" and stated that it deserved "enthusiastic public support."[55] The First Brazilian Congress of Journalists, held in 1918, paid homage to Virgilina de Souza Salles by placing her portrait in the Press Association's room of honor alongside those of other famous Brazilian journalists.[56] The *Revista Feminina* continued publication after the death of Virgilina de Souza Salles in 1918, but it gradually lost momentum and closed down in the late 1920s.

The *Revista Feminina* is interesting for its self-proclaimed mission of seeking women's "emancipation" within traditional Brazilian Catholic culture. Hence, on the one hand, in an attempt to provide readers with alternative role models, editors dedicated considerable space to publicizing and applauding women's social activism and professional achievements. And in an effort to broaden the spheres in which women felt competent to act, the editors published articles (written by women, if possible) on world history and politics, geography, scientific innovations, industrial development, artistic movements, customs of peoples of Africa and Asia, and feminist movements abroad.[57] The magazine provided a place for both well-known and lesser-known women writers to publish, thereby encouraging women to be producers and well as consumers of mass media. And it sought to build women's self-confidence by stressing that the issues and problems that concerned them were important social issues that warranted serious discussion and action. On the other hand, the "new female consciousness" that editors sought to promote did not include any questioning of Catholic social doctrine or of the division of labor within the family.[58]

Unavoidably, as a product and promoter of the growing consumer economy, the *Revista Feminina* (like virtually all successful popular magazines of the period) also fostered the development of another kind of "new female consciousness" by helping to initiate women into the mentality of the market. Regular columns on fashion and beauty—even if they occasionally attacked or mocked modern styles—ultimately heightened women's vulnerability to the dictates of the market. At the same time, advertisements—which assumed a more and

During the early 1920s, Brazilian companies eager to compete with foreign imports copied new advertising techniques pioneered in the United States in the late 1910s. Especially notable for their use of female sexuality to sell commodities were the prominent glossy advertisements for Lucy Toothpaste and the soft drink Guaraná Espumante that appeared regularly in the popular magazine A Cigarra.

more prominent position as the magazine expanded—not only extolled the wonders of modern products but exploited female sexuality to sell them. Using techniques of advertising pioneered in the United States and Europe, companies increasingly addressed the female consumer.[59] Advertisements sometimes exploited the image of the "new woman" in an attempt to sell women products commonly purchased by men.[60] But they also sought to create artificial needs, to breed insecurity that could be overcome through consumption, and to link consumption with sexual gratification.[61]

The *Revista Feminina* was by no means alone in eagerly and successfully wooing the large potential audience of female readers or in attempting to monitor and mold public opinion about proper gender roles. New glossy magazines of the post–World War I period competed with one another using a variety of innovative techniques, and as a result, the appearance and content of mass periodical literature was transformed. Catering to the delight that young women took in seeing their photographs in print, most of the successful popular magazines adorned every issue with dozens of unposed snapshots of smiling young women strolling in the streets or parks, attending sports events, sunning themselves in revealing maillots, attending parties or special events, and so on.[62] Formal portraits accompanied frequent articles about women in various professions and in the performing arts. And regular columns on fashion became mandatory, as did articles addressing such matters as love, marriage, female character, health and education, feminism, and domestic life.

Among other innovations, contests were highly popular among readers and successful in selling copies. Editors of *A Cigarra*, which in 1920 claimed to enjoy the largest circulation of any magazine in the state of São Paulo, ran continual contests in which they instructed readers to clip the coupon at the bottom of the page and to send in their votes for the most beautiful blond and brunet, for the young women best endowed with social graces and intellectual prowess, for the most eligible bachelor, for their favorite movie stars, and so on.[63] Following the announcement of the first "Miss World" contest to be held in Nice in 1922, *A Cigarra* joined with the Rio de Janeiro magazines *A Noite* and *A Revista da Semana* in organizing a national "plebiscite" to elect the "finest example of Brazilian beauty." Pictures of eligible candidates adorned the pages of the magazines for nine months, and readers sent in many tens of thousands of votes on clipped coupons.[64] *A Vida Moderna* took a slightly different tack, capitalizing on the debate over women's status by issuing inquiries to readers and "experts." In 1919, the magazine asked its female readers for their opinions on marriage and on the qualities of a good husband. In 1927, editor Apelecina do Carmo solicited responses from dozens of prominent male and female intellectuals to the questions: "How do you view female emancipation?" and "For women, does true happiness lie in taking advantage of the golden jail in which they live, or should they prefer the roughness of the struggle for existence?"[65]

A Cigarra also devoted fifteen to twenty-five pages of the sixty-five pages per issue to printing readers' contributions. This section, entitled "Collaboration of Readers," drew enthusiastic responses not only from young women of elite families but also from women of more modest means who were training to be seamstresses at the Female Vocational School or who worked as secretaries or telephone operators. It provided an open but anonymous forum for debate over modern customs and appropriate female behavior, and it served as a gossip and personal column. Complementing this section was another regular column called "Advice to Women," which was introduced in 1930. Editors explained that it was designed to help readers who suddenly found themselves confronted with an urgent and difficult problem.[66]

Bombarded with alluring advertisements of chic department stores and images of "Hollywood girls," young women discarded old fashions for daring new styles. Whereas nineteenth-century fashion had accentuated the differences between the sexes, reflecting their separate social roles and the rigid enforcement of a double standard of morality, postwar fashions suddenly blurred these distinctions. In the nineteenth century, men dressed starkly in dark colors, grew beards, and carried canes, emphasizing their seriousness and competence. Women wore highly elaborate and cumbersome dresses, emphasizing their submissiveness and dependency. Whereas men cut figures of aggressive public actors, women's appearance implied their status of passive and sheltered ornaments.[67]

By the 1920s, lighter, more practical dresses allowed women greater freedom of movement while also challenging the traditional female image of virtuous modesty and timidity. Hemlines crept steadily upward until they reached the knee by the mid-1920s, and the introduction of silk stockings and high heels called attention to newly revealed legs. Necklines plunged and sleeves disappeared. Fashionable wardrobes now included bright red, green, and purple dresses. Waistlines dropped, deemphasizing female curves. Rigid corsets were discarded in favor of lighter, less constricting bras and panties. Women cut their hair *à la garçonne* and adopted smaller hats with simple lines or wore no hats at all. Fans and parasols also disappeared as mandatory accessories. Powder no longer sufficed as makeup. Women plucked and lined their eyebrows and blackened their eyelashes. They applied rouge to their cheeks, painted their lips bright red, and changed the color of their nail polish to match different outfits. Even more scandalous, women went to the beach "almost naked" in new sleeveless maillots that extended only to midthigh, exposing bare arms and legs to public view. Paralleling trends in women's fashions, the rigidity of the lines of men's clothing softened, and sports clothes and light-colored jackets became more popular. Men shaved their beards and discarded canes.[68]

New poses accompanied new fashions in clothing. Discarding old canons of polite behavior, women began to sunbathe at the beach, use slang, and smoke in public.[69] Films and magazine covers popularized the image of the woman who smoked: modern, elegant, daring, voluptuous, seductive, and mysterious.[70] The media also canonized a new standard of beauty. Writers marveled that "the static woman became the active woman."[71] Corpulent matrons and frail, sickly maidens who swooned at the slightest provocation were declared obsolete. The new century valued energy, strength, thinness, agility: "In the age of the skyscraper, . . . female beauty is slender, long, perpendicular. . . . The elegance of women, like that of reinforced concrete skyscrapers, need not be heavy and round to be solid."[72] The Brazilian press reported that the great Hollywood stars were nearly all the same size: 5 feet 4 inches tall, 115 pounds, 33¾-inch bust, and 35½-inch hips.[73] Young women eager to emulate this ideal worried about their measurements and embarked on strict diets and programs of physical exercise.[74] Critic and cartoonist Belmonte protested that Joan Crawford "with her body of an infantry soldier and her legs of a soccer player is one of the models of the fair sex of my country." He ridiculed the mania of dieting that had so taken hold of young women, claiming that they were turning into "true 'stegomias' without shoulders, breasts, or hips—there being many who appear more like men dressed as women and others who don't appear to be anything at all, because they are virtual walking posts. The curved line, which used to be the highest expression of feminine beauty, is giving way to hallucinating angularities to such a degree that there are certain young women who end up admirable treatises of osteology."[75]

Changes in fashions triggered widespread unease about the apparent "masculinization" of women and "feminization" of men.[76] One male critic wrote that he was saddened to see a female friend smoking. He argued not only that it was in bad taste for women to imitate male habits but also that the smell of smoke took away from the sweetness of women's scent: "that mixture of powder and female flesh."[77] An editorial published by *A Vida Moderna* in 1925 lamented the passing of the days of long hair: "What do we see today? Men's heads on women's bodies. Bald heads that disappear in the nape of the neck, smooth, slicked down like the snout of a dog as it emerges from water. Oh! how horrifying . . . the hairdo 'à la garçonne.'"[78] The *Revista Feminina* published a satire on the confusion of the sexes entitled "The Mister or the Madam? Scenes of

*The Brazilian media canonized imported fashions of the 1920s even as it denounced
and mocked them. The caption on the cover of the 1 April 1921 issue of* A Cigarra
read: "With the [economic] crisis, everything rises astonishingly." (From A Cigarra
8:157 [1 April 1921])

The favorite subject matter for the covers of O Cruzeiro, *from 1929 (when the magazine began publishing) into the 1930s, was new female styles of dress and behavior.
(From* O Cruzeiro *3 : 9 [3 January 1931])*

Contemporary Life." It sketched a caricature of a modern couple both of whom wore pajamas, smoked, cut their hair *à la garçonne*, and kept slim figures. While she talked about sports with her friends, he discussed fashion with his friends. Upon the birth of their first child, the doctor found himself in a quandary about whether to entrust the infant to her or to him.[79] Cartoonist Belmonte also satirized the supposed trend toward unisexuality. In one cartoon a long-haired man commented to a short-haired woman: "Now it is men who are using preparations to make their hair grow." In a similar cartoon, a man justified his long hair by remarking: "I plan to introduce this new style to avoid confusions!" Another depicted a clown who, in the presence of two fashionable, short-haired women, remarked: "These two think they can confuse me. Now, am I not seeing that they are men dressed in skirts?" And, in a final cartoon, Santa Claus, looking through a window at a group of four unisex adults, asks: "You don't say! Are there no women in this house?"[80]

The new styles, which provided an outward sign of defiance for a new generation, were fiercely attacked for being immoral and for enslaving women to the dictates of the market.[81] Progressives and moderates were often offended by the artificiality and frivolousness of modern fashions as well as by the "almost obscene" exposure of women on the beaches to voluptuous stares.[82] Conservatives considered modern fashions to be antiaesthetic, anti-Christian, the "first step toward moral decadence," and a "very dangerous element" that could undermine the familial base of society and lead to a "tremendous cataclysm."[83] Editorials of the *Revista Feminina* echoed the opinion of many of the magazine's contributors. They urged women to reject the immoral fashions that were invading Brazil from abroad and to retain their individuality, autonomy, and traditional modesty. "Let's be *caipiras* [simple Brazilian backwoods women]," one editorial declared, not "international dolls."[84] Nevertheless, following the irresistible logic of the market, the magazine ran advertisements that kept readers up to date with the latest trends.

Urban lifestyles and modern technology transformed courting into a freer, more private affair. Although "honest" young women who wanted to marry "well" still had to take care to protect their reputations (which meant not only guarding their virginity but maintaining proper appearances as well), they were no longer segregated from young men by elaborate rituals or sheltered from potential suitors by constant chaperonage that precluded any direct or intimate contact. Young women whose mothers and grandmothers had rarely ventured outside (and then, always accompanied) met young men in public places; "footing" in public parks and downtown avenues provided chances for flirting, as did collecting money for charity on street corners and frequenting theaters, dance halls, tearooms, and sports events. At afternoon film showings, young men found the empty seats next to groups of unaccompanied young women especially attractive, and couples—shrouded by the dark and encouraged by seductive images—gave in to intimacies that appalled self-appointed defenders of public morality.[85] Comic strips noted the tendency. In one, a father remarked to his fashionable daughter: "I won't take you to the cinema. There isn't one that isn't showing corrupting or morally offensive films." She protested: "But Dad, I don't even look at the films."[86] Finally, as young women entered coeducational schools and offices, these too became places where the young might meet and flirt.

Revolutions in communications and transportation rendered the traditional furtive note obsolete. As telephone service expanded rapidly during the postwar period, rules of good taste that had previously forbidden young men and women from talking on the telephone relaxed, allowing for prolonged private conversations and for quick communications essential for arranging discreet meetings.[87] In addition, by the 1920s, automobiles became indispensable aids for courting among the urban elite. An automobile was not only a flashy outward sign of a young man's wealth and status, but it allowed a couple mobility and privacy formerly unimaginable.[88]

Jazz and the introduction of dances such as the tango, fox trot, Charleston, shimmy, and maxixe did away with the formal, ceremonious aspects of nineteenth-century dance. Gone were the waltzes and grand promenades of the prewar period, replaced by modern dances (of lower-class as well as foreign origin) that allowed for freer public expression of eroticism. Critics protested that "Freudian hallucination" had replaced romantic sentimentalism. Dance, they declared, was no longer an art form but a mere pretext for flirting—an opportunity to engage in conversation while "sinful[ly] entangling" bodies and "rhythmically agitating limbs."[89] Cartoons mocked the extravagances of the new dances by portraying them as animalistic or barbarian. One dancing couple was drawn with shadows in the form of apes; another couple was juxtaposed to barbarians semidressed in animal skins and carrying bones.[90]

Despite such objections, the children of the elite enrolled in the proliferating number of dance schools to learn (or practice) the complicated (and sensual) new steps. Jazz bands began to play at even the most conservative and exclusive *paulista* dance club, the Sociedade Harmonia, where young couples sipped whiskey and talked informally between tangos, fox trots, Charlestons, and maxixes.[91] Public bars and cafés also hired jazz bands to draw in customers for late-afternoon "tea-tangos." And new dance halls catering to a wide social

The uncomfortable rapidity with which customs were changing in urban Brazil provided satirists with rich and varied material. The most famous Brazilian cartoonist was
Belmonte, who published copious satires of modern fashions, including a series of cartoons entitled "Yesterday and Today." (From Benedicto Bastos Barreto [Belmonte,
pseud.], "Homtem e Hoje," O Cruzeiro 2:94 [23 August 1930], p. 13; 2:103
[25 October 1930], p. 5)

spectrum offered couples places to while away the night dancing. In 1923, the Casino Antártico sponsored a dance marathon in which the winning couple danced nonstop for 33 ½ hours.[92]

As the modernization and beautification of mushrooming urban centers displayed accumulated wealth and technological progress, the images of independent working girls and sexy flappers symbolized changing social relations. Alluring yet frightening, the "modern girl" was at once proudly displayed as a demonstration of national progress and denounced as a threat to national tradition. Her growing autonomy, assertiveness, and educational and professional accomplishments responded to the new freedoms, bourgeois ethic, and economic necessities of Brazil's expanding urban-industrial society. But her metamorphosis from the secluded, corpulent nineteenth-century matron demanded uncomfortable redefinitions of male-female relations, male roles, and family organization, as well as of "proper" female behavior. Critics feared that those who cultivated the new image of the independent, daring, sexually provocative women would undergo a revolution in consciousness that would profoundly threaten the family; it was also feared that women could not embrace the morality of the market without causing "materialism" to triumph over "human values" in the personal sphere.

Critics worried further that increasing exposure to foreign ideas and styles would subvert the national culture. One writer insisted that it was necessary to import "useful" technological innovations from Europe without also importing the "habits and customs that seriously threaten to stifle the good and pure aspects of our primitive soul, under whose domestic blessings we enjoy the integral happiness of our virtuous adolescence."[93] He lamented that the importation of foreign fashions was rapidly "destroying the primitive beauty of our soul with its artificiality," and he warned that if foreign ideas of female liberation were adopted in Brazil, women who were freed from the "delicious slavery" of domestic life would find only unhappiness.[94]

Rapid change generated so many conflicting messages that men and women frequently expressed anxiety over how to adjust their values to new realities and how to define proper behavior in light of new necessities and opportunities. Women who failed to acquire a lacquer of modernity suffered ridicule and social ostracism, while those who took to heart messages that communicated the possibility and desirability of women's social, economic, and sexual emancipation were either regarded as immoral or stereotyped as ugly, old battle-axes. Women were expected to cultivate an outward appearance of modern sophistication while carefully preserving the "eternal" female qualities of modesty and simplicity. They were to be both symbols of modernity and bastions of stability against the destabilizing effects of industrial capitalist development, shielding the family from "corrupting" influences. These contradictions were expressed in Oswald de Andrade's description of modernist painter Tarsila do Amaral, a somewhat romantic description that perhaps reflected more accurately what he wanted her to be than what she actually was: "*Caipirinha* [simple Brazilian backwoods woman] dressed by [the Parisian designer] Poiret."[95]

The following chapters trace in detail the debates over gender norms that raged during the 1910s through the 1930s. Out of struggles between men and women, housewives and career women, anarchists and reactionaries, liberal professionals and clergy, government bureaucrats and employers, there emerged new expectations and new patterns of behavior. As we shall see, Brazil's gender ideology was modernized to accommodate new necessities and opportunities while preserving the gender inequality thought necessary to guarantee the order and progress of Brazil's still hierarchical society.

MARRIAGE: A "DEFORMED AND DEMORALIZED INSTITUTION"

Controversy over the institution of marriage exploded into the realm of public discourse during the post–World War I period. Extremely rapid change during the late nineteenth and early twentieth centuries undermined the social and economic compulsions on which upper- and middle-class marriage had formerly been based and modified expectations of what constituted a suitable marital relationship.[1] As women of these classes began to acquire some social and economic power through access to education and paid employment, their rising anger over marriage relations found release in more public expression and their protests gained more clout. They grew bolder in demanding greater equality in marriage and in denouncing men's tyranny. For the first time, marriage was widely acknowledged to be an institution rife with conflict in which husbands and wives frequently assumed roles as adversaries. While women tended to blame tyrannical husbands for deforming and demoralizing marriage, male critics tended to blame a myriad of modern "evils," including feminism and female wage labor; unbridled egoism and individualism; the materialization of sentiments; the weakening sense of responsibility; and divorce, "free love," birth control, and abortion.[2] By the 1920s, there was widespread agreement among Brazil's intellectual and professional communities that marriage and the family were in "crisis"; many feared their rapid demise.

Threats to family stability may indeed have been real, but the exaggerated amounts of attention this issue received can only be understood within the larger context of the wrenching, disorderly process of change in early-twentieth-century Brazil. There is no reason to believe that earlier generations had enjoyed conjugal bliss. Prior to the mid-nineteenth century, prearranged marriages within the elite sought to enhance families' economic and political power; love, compatibility, harmony, and happiness had been at best secondary or irrelevant considerations. But these marriages of convenience (many of which were certainly far less than "perfect" by standards of the time, not to mention by twentieth-century standards) had never stirred up much public controversy. Their desirability generally went unquestioned as long as overwhelming social constraints guaranteed their stability.[3] What made marriages based on interest or convenience (rather than "true love") unacceptable to postwar society was their instability in the face of the expanding social and economic options available to women.[4] Women's anger over marital relations caused alarm not because it was new (there had always been female discontents) but because it appeared to be so widespread, so difficult to contain once old social and economic restraints had begun to crumble, and so dangerous at a time when "chaos" seemed to reign. Critics, terrified that society was coming apart at the seams, worried that marriages marred by unhappiness, conflict, or superficial commitments were dysfunctional in helping to preserve hierarchy and order in the society and polity at large.

The "crisis" of the family among the poor was discovered not by poor women but by bourgeois men who worried about the low rates of nuptiality among the poor and the instability of poor families. This they denounced as evidence of moral deprivation and vice, warranting serious social attention. In fact, the failure of the poor to marry legally and to bear legitimate children was nothing new. Marriage in Brazil had been until this time largely a middle- and upper-class institution. The poor, without property to protect or means to deal with the bureaucratic complications and expense of marriage, more often lived in consensual unions. Even when they accepted the dominant morality and valued legal marriage (as they frequently did), they could rarely achieve it. Instead, given the relative economic independence of poor women and the difficulty poor men had in playing the role of breadwinner, they fashioned their own moral standards for more flexible and symmetrical unions between men and women.[5] What made this behavior so threatening was its dysfunctionality in buttressing order and stability in Brazil's new urban-industrial society. In the context of intensified class conflict, political and ideological polarization, and tremblings of women's emancipation, male urban professionals and political authorities assigned ever greater importance to legal marriage. In their view, legally constituted and stable families among the urban working classes and poor were essential for maintaining social control and for ensuring proper socialization of new generations.

Contemporary literature implied that changes within the well-to-do classes had come very quickly. In 1901, José Veríssimo de Mattos declared that the controversies over marriage that were raging in Europe and the United States had been met with indifference in Brazil, since they seemed irrelevant to the actual conditions of life. According to him, women still resigned themselves happily and without question to their fate:

> Our woman, being still the same old-fashioned, kindhearted, and useful companion, modest and uninstructed, willingly submits herself to the inevitable difficulties and even to the troubles and disillusions that marriage perhaps brought her. Despite the obvious inequality of the Brazilian couple in the educated classes, this has no great consequences, being remedied by the sense of veneration that our woman must have inherited from the three formative races of our people, in which the woman occupied a secondary position. Even in the case of the husband's inferiority . . . this veneration mitigates the effects of inequality.[6]

By 1922, Augusto Cesar perceived the normal state of marital relations to be radically different: "Whoever lengthily observes the contemporary wife would certainly be aghast at the signs of perfidy, of obstinate and injudicious opposition which, at times, make the woman a true enemy, a tireless tormentor of her husband instead of his companion and partner in the serious business of life."[7] Obviously, both Veríssimo de Mattos and Cesar exaggerated their positions. Nevertheless, women's sense of injustice had heightened, they had gained a voice, and they had discovered that they could wield power in the public realm. Thus, suddenly women's noncompliance and rebelliousness became a socially significant issue, rather than a private matter that could be quietly handled behind the closed doors of individual family residences.

The Family under Siege

▼ ▼ ▼

The vast majority of women writers—of all political persuasions—held men (and male culture) responsible for the daily victimization of women and gradual destruction of the family. In impassioned protests, these urban middle-class women freely unveiled their contempt for men's bad behavior—their egoism, brutality, disloyalty, irresponsibility, and lack of consideration.[8] According to feminist Elisabeth Bastos, society was witnessing the destruction of marriage because "the great majority of men continue to be cave men, finding in marriage no more than the satisfaction of their physiological necessities," because they quickly cease to be loyal and dedicated husbands, and because they "lack a strong desire to protect a wife."[9] The more conservative novelist, chronicler, and columnist Chrysanthème (the pseudonym of Cecilia Bandeira de Melo Rebêlo de Vasconcelos), claiming that she had never erred in her evaluation of men, categorically asserted: "[E]very man, regardless of caste or race, looks down upon the female, all gracefulness and delicacy, that he does not begin to understand due to the inferior quality of the lenses through which he sees her."[10] Widely published columnist Iracema also attacked men for acting like "pashas" or "sultans" who forced women to resort to lying and dissimulation in order to defend themselves against their husbands' injustices, jealous pride, and anger. According to her analysis, women, whether innocent or guilty, were always the victims of the "matrimonial drama" in which their husbands esteemed them "but not 'as women,' rather as a neuter being, inferior though respectable, who is called 'a wife.'" She therefore took it upon herself to try to "clarify and reduce the deplorable error that still exists so deeply rooted among us" that a man could demand of his future wife the "renunciation of her personality" as a condition of marriage, forcing her to realize her love "through the rachitic door of submission" and reducing her to a "purely physiological being . . . without thought, without autonomy, [and] without will." Iracema protested, "What barbaric ideal of love is offered to a woman, requiring of her the total abdication of her personality! In the name of what rights or social rules, in the name of what moral is this inhuman sacrifice demanded of her?"[11]

Outspoken female critics, far from being isolated, articulated what seems to have been a pervasive sense of bitterness among urban middle- and upper-class women. Many anonymous letters to the editor cried out against men who betrayed or abandoned the women who loved them. One woman who found herself rejected by the man she had loved for seven years and for whom she had sacrificed her youth declared that she had decided to flee men "like the innocent dove flees the black martin." She warned that women's "greatest sin is to believe in the false words of a man," and she protested that it was the women who truly loved who were the first to fall victims to "black fatality." Men, she concluded, were false, faithless, ungrateful, cruel, and heartless in deceiving and abandoning innocent women—"Martyrs of Love": "The sole desire of men is to see us suffer, cry sad tears for their sake. They do not deserve to have a woman sacrifice herself for them. Men? They are devils that God forgot on the earth! They are the destroyers of homes! When a catastrophe occurs in a family, who is the sole culprit? The man! Who drags 'honor in the mud?' The man! For this reason they are and always will be the persons guilty for the disgraces of the innocent and saintly beings that are women!"[12] Another woman who signed her letter "Fairy of Good Advice" warned that women could not afford to have "fragile hearts." Instead of pardoning a man who betrayed her, she pledged: "I will place the man whom I love and who rejects me in the valley of oblivion and I will feel more than rancor for him: repugnance. And, as for other men, they don't merit anything but watchfulness." [13]

Female critics thus concluded that because of men's reprehensible behavior, women were finding wifehood to be among the most difficult and most disagreeable of occupations—a source of "cruel disillusion" and "bitter martyrdom." It became common for women to compare the institution of marriage to a jail, as did one reader who responded to a magazine questionnaire: "[Marriage is] like a prison as much for men as for women, with the difference that the man possesses the key and leaves when he wants, leaving his companion locked up, the tyrant!" [14] For the female characters in Chrysanthème's novels and chronicles, being good, humble, honest wives or lovers more often than not brought disillusionment, humiliation, and suffering. They recovered their peace of mind, their dignity, and their equilibrium only when they freed themselves of men. [15] Even archconservative Amélia de Rezende Martins declared that because of men's irresponsibility and lack of consideration: "Our daughters who marry, save blessed exceptions, are not happy; when they open their eyes to life, they open them equally to the most painful [and] most humiliating disillusions." [16]

Profoundly disillusioned herself, Chrysanthème warned that women had ceased to be the "timid and ingenuous cocoon[s], the innocent being[s]" who had once believed in the affection of men and who had been fondly attached to their domestic duties. Deceived, disillusioned, poisoned at heart, and with their eyes opened to men's "hypocrisy, . . . egoism, cruelty, and Machiavellianism," women had resolved to "take justice into their own hands": "The modern woman no longer wants to endure that which was suffered by her sisters, whose myopic sight did not completely discern the miseries and cowardice of their environment. . . . Today, latent but profound in female breasts, there are cultivated terrible hatred and ardent desires for revenge against men, who believe that they are loved when already the venom of revolt or of defense is rising against them." Referring to a number of famous cases in which abandoned or brutalized wives had killed their husbands, she warned that a "cataclysm is threatening our collectivity," as mothers, wives, and daughters were being transformed into "cruel criminals, into furies, thirsty for blood, avid for vengeance." [17]

Although she claimed to be terrified of this "dangerous unrest that exists in the conscience of modern women" and remained highly critical of feminism, Chrysanthème nevertheless concluded that until men reformed their behavior, women might be better off alone. She encouraged women to preserve their self-respect, their dignity, and their integrity by avoiding resignation and sub-missiveness, by trusting their own feelings and judgments, by standing up courageously to defend what they believed, and by energetically pursuing their goals and ambitions.[18] In some cases, she reluctantly acknowledged, this re-quired women to seek divorces, or to avoid marriage altogether: "Better celi-bacy, the noble individual existence, the honorable organization of a healthy and isolated life, than a bad marriage, a pernicious union."[19]

Other women were less ambivalent in advocating divorce as an essential means for women to liberate themselves from oppression and abuse or in rec-ommending celibacy. In 1912, schoolteacher and newspaper editor Andradina Oliveira published a book composed of letters by fictitious but typical women who found themselves condemned to the "pungent hospital of matrimonial miseries, in wait for the sole remedy"—divorce. She asked readers to listen carefully to each "agonizing scream of an imprisoned heart imploring that the metal chains binding her to her slavery be severed." And she insisted that her book was supremely moral, not only because it launched a "new blow . . . against the most noxious of all social conventions—indissoluble marriage, fount at the very least of shameful hypocrisies and cowardly captivity"—but also because it constituted a "cry of indignation against the unjust and crushing social situation of women." She hoped that her book might serve to mobilize women to demand divorce.[20] Elisabeth Bastos, like a growing number of pro-fessional women, supported divorce. But she also believed that until women succeeded in changing men's consciousness, it would often be better to seek paid employment as a means to live honestly and independently of men's "caprices": "[M]an does not merit confidence, and to marry is to bestow much confidence in him. . . . In certain and determined cases, it is better to struggle alone than badly accompanied."[21]

Women radicals had no more kindly things to say about men—"protectors and masters, knights errant, hypocritical moralists." But their attacks on the institution of marriage went deeper; they challenged the validity of its struc-ture and demanded its demise. Both Ercília Nogueira Cobra (apparently the black sheep of a middle-class family whose life remains obscure) and Maria Lacerda de Moura (schoolteacher, radical feminist, anarchist, and writer) vio-lently denounced the cult of virginity and the notion of "male honor."[22] They opposed marriage as a social ill, legalized prostitution, a perverse economic arrangement, and a highly developed immorality that reduced love from a sub-lime to a degraded act. In their opinion, the institution was a "fraud," a "lie," a mental enslavement of women, and a means for perpetuating women's servility and ignorance while exploiting their labor. In Cobra's allegorical (and perhaps partly autobiographical) novel *Virgindade inútil* (Useless Virginity), none of the difficulties faced by the heroine—poverty, the weight of social prejudices, discrimination, and prostitution—were portrayed to be as humiliating, suffocating, or oppressive as marriage. The triumph of the heroine consisted of the free development of her personality through unrestricted life experience, the maintenance of her independence, the discovery of true adult love, and the birth of a daughter outside marriage. Both authors protested against the morality by which women waited to be "picked like a flower" by men, used as ornaments or objects of pleasure until they shriveled up, and then discarded, deprived of roots for regeneration or resources for self-sustenance. As an alternative, they proclaimed free love to be the only responsible and moral type of intimate bond, and they advocated "conscientious maternity" outside marriage. Maria Lacerda de Moura's program for living life in its plenitude was a program of "integral liberty" that, by allowing for the maximum of self-knowledge and self-realization, would allow for the achievement of true adult love. In her own life, she followed the advice she gave to women: "Let us be deserters of the family, social deserters, free individualists—in order to think and dream and live in harmony with our conscience." Ercília Nogueira Cobra, in her even more brazen style, acted on the threat that prefaces her novel: "You can be sure, monopolizers of pleasure who call yourselves men when you should call yourselves monsters, the weak victim who you believe you can hold tight in your hand liberates herself just as you most constrain her. Your prisons are insufficient. . . . [Women's] bod[ies], martyrized by unsatisfied desires, will be free." [23]

Another middle-class rebel, São Paulo journalist and political activist Patrícia Galvão, who delighted in flaunting her disrespect for bourgeois sexual morality, took up the plight of poor women. In her novel *Parque industrial*, Galvão attempted to bring the exploitation of the female proletariat to public attention. With a frankness that was shocking at the time (and highly embarrassing to the Brazilian Communist Party, of which she was a member), she condemned the sexual abuse of female factory workers by villainous bosses and decried the tragedy of working-class women who were seduced by immoral bourgeois men with promises of marriage, only to be impregnated and abandoned to lives of prostitution. [24]

If poor women were obviously vulnerable to sexual abuse by men of higher social classes, evidence suggests that they were frequently dissatisfied in their intimate relationships with men of their own class as well. But it is not clear to what extent they were more dissatisfied than they had been previously. In any case, they continued (as before) to express their feelings in their choices and in their actions rather than in writing. Many valued their work, which gave them an independent source of income and thus a relative degree of autonomy. Freer than women of better means to leave husbands or lovers when subjected to bad treatment, they could demand a more equal relationship and, when unhappy, change partners. Although they were also subjected to male abuse, they were not prisoners to the extent that middle- and upper-class women felt themselves to be. Their outlet was to improvise in their daily lives more flexible and equal patterns of intimate relationships.[25] The threat they posed was thus the threat of "immoral" behavior rather than the threat of verbal protests and campaigns for institutional changes.

By the 1920s, women's aggressive protests and scandalous behavior had become a favorite topic of public discussion. The Rio de Janeiro police filled the pages of its weekly journal, *Vida Policial* (Police Life), with sensationalist crime reports blaming "fallen women," dishonest domestic servants, women-men, and "modern girls" for the ruin of the Brazilian family and hence for national degeneracy.[26] Chronicles, novels of social customs, and cartoons portrayed middle- and upper-class women openly attacking the values and rejecting the behavioral norms of patriarchal family organization. These "new women" contradicted or disobeyed their parents and husbands, advocated and sought divorces, had male lovers outside marriage or even maintained lesbian relationships, and asserted their right to hold paid employment and live independently.[27] Some conservative women held members of their own sex responsible for moral corruption, scandal, and family tragedies as a result of modern women's supposed renunciation of their "sacred role" as the "supreme priestess[es] of love, of good, and of virtue."[28] More interestingly, men began to write articles and letters to the editor complaining of the victimization of members of their sex by women who were fickle and capricious in their love, dominating men's hearts only to abuse and betray them later.[29]

Anxious, frustrated, and angry about losing control over women, male critics counterattacked. From their point of view, it was women who were destroying the family. They protested that women, corrupted by "Bolshevik liberties," had lost all sense of prudence, responsibility, and modesty: "What honest young man would accept a frivolous women for his fiancée, one whom he had already seen pretend to be engaged to everybody in the world while dancing the tango, the *remeleixo*, and the *maxixe*, or one of those sirens who parades down the Avenue exhibiting three-fourths of her body to the respectable public?"[30]

Female adultery became an obsessive concern for a number of male critics. José Gabriel de Lemos Britto expressed alarm over what he saw to be a spread of the plague of adultery from the upper classes to the middle classes: those that had formerly "appeared immune to this lamentable virus." He protested that "virgins" and "wives"—"the most valued thing that we possess in life"—were learning the "subtleties of the art of betraying a husband" from the cinema and theater. Women's adoption of "aggressive, gross, and provocative" behavior and styles, he warned, was undermining marriage and the family: "[S]ociety lacks knowledge except of a minimal part of that which occurs in the secrecy of alcoves and clandestine houses."[31] Judge Francisco José Viveiros de Castro concurred that with growing acceptance of the "erroneous [and] subversive idea of female emancipation," women had come to regard female modesty and timidity as "anachronistic" and "ridiculous." According to him, adultery had become a "custom, a style and a favorite sport" not only among elegant young men; modern women, savvy about the most unseemly matters, freed from religious restraints, and "avid only for luxury and excitement," were proving to be "easy prey, and often even spontaneously offered [themselves] to the conquest of men." As a consequence, he concluded, they had lost men's "respect, esteem, and consideration."[32] Augusto Cesar also warned that married women were adopting an eye-for-an-eye mentality. Rather than striving to curb their husbands' adultery by cultivating faithfulness, love, and harmony within marriage, he believed that they were imitating men's worst behavior: "Female morality [has] adopted with profound conviction the principle that the only means of cleansing oneself of the affront of an infidelity is to betray in return."[33]

Finally, both male and female critics considered that the much-decried "degeneration of modern customs" posed a further threat to the institution of marriage. They protested that both sexes had renounced the values of duty, responsibility, decorum, respectability, and abnegation. Modern marriage, they claimed, was no more than an irresponsible indulgence of impulse and superficial desire or a cynical surrender to economic interest; rarely was it based on real affection or mutual esteem. If men married for a "dowry or for a whim," women married for wealth or "to acquire their liberty: the terror of remaining single carried to the point of leading to all compromises and to all acceptances." Marriage was thus said to be based on a "tiny love . . . born between a shimmy and a tango" that was soon overcome by "caprice."[34] Chronicler Maria Eugenia Celso created a caricature of the young modern "Mademoiselle Futility" who justified her hasty marriage plans by scoffing at the idea that marriage was a serious matter: "—Serious? . . . those are old-fashioned ideas! . . . If you think too much, you won't marry . . . It's best not to think . . . Antonico is attractive, I'm pleasing to him, he doesn't displease me . . . We'll marry. Of what importance is the fiancé, my God? . . . The important thing is the marriage."[35]

If their marriages failed, couples could—to the dismay of many moralists—seek divorces abroad or *desquites* (legal separations that did not permit remarriage) in Brazil. According to lawyer Noe' Azevedo, *desquite* within the *paulista* elite had become "as fashionable and inoffensive as short hair": "To be *des-quitada* today [1927] in São Paulo is a characteristic sign of great elegance." He protested that the majority of *desquites* were the result of some "banality," citing as support a curious case in which he contended that a vain rich widow with social aspirations had coerced her reluctant daughter to separate from her loving husband.[36]

Critics further lamented the materialization of sentiments. Old-style love was said to have died in a "famous duel with greed": "[M]an sells himself to the fortune of woman, and vice-versa."[37] One cartoonist pictured "modern love" as the coupling of a thin, smiling man with a woman whose enormous money-bag torso bore a conspicuous dollar sign.[38] Letters to the editor and responses to questionnaires seemed to confirm critics' worst fears. One male reader wrote: "[A] wife only gives a kiss to her husband in exchange for a new dress. The woman no longer likes the home. She wants above all to enjoy herself. And, because of this, money has become the real incentive of love. Marriage is a practical accommodation in life. . . . Today's women! How different they are from what I dreamed!"[39] When the São Paulo illustrated magazine *A Vida Moderna* asked its female readers: "How do you view marriage?" several described it as a cold and calculated business deal:

As a way to go to Europe.

Like a factory in which our strikes are heeded by ever greater rises in salary: salary that is sufficient for all the expenses.

I don't even like to think about this. If I were a man, I wouldn't marry. The cost of hats, dresses and shoes alone. And the rent . . . ah! the rents of houses these days. And, beyond this, the theater [and] cars. How dreadful! So many expenses![40]

The last reader's ideal husband was he who, while taking into account all these expenses, still asked for her hand in marriage.

Other women complained that because modern life had materialized sentiments, true, disinterested, enduring love was difficult, if not impossible, to achieve. By the time a woman reached her late teens, sincerity and innocence had died, and the "pleasing" was quickly discarded in favor of the "useful." According to one reader, the pressure to maintain social status by dressing elegantly, frequenting society, and owning a luxurious house encouraged marriages doomed to a "tedious existence" and eventually, a "fatal collapse."[41]

In short, whether individual critics were most concerned with men's tyrannical treatment of women, women's aggressive protests and rebellious behavior, the threatening new discourse on "free love," or the "degeneration of modern customs," they agreed that marriage and the family were deformed and demoralized institutions. They bemoaned the rarity of "true love" in marriage and despaired over the small number of "perfect families."[42] According to one author's calculations: "Out of one hundred marriages, twenty-five fail completely, seventy end after a certain time in a monotonous 'modus vivendi,' and only five attain the ideal which they dreamed of when young."[43] An alarm was sounded: "[C]onjugal peace is the most serious problem that the majority of couples do not resolve."[44]

Strategies and Accommodations

▼ ▼ ▼

In fact, marriage among the middle and upper classes did not, of course, collapse. Men had little reason to reject marriage, since it provided status, emotional support, physical comforts, and sexual services without seriously constricting their social freedom. And for "respectable" women who experienced marriage as stifling, alternatives were neither very attractive nor viable. Concubinage and free love were regarded by the majority of the middle- and upper-class population to be little different from prostitution. And, if a woman wanted children, she could secure no effective legal guarantees that the father would support the children unless he married her.[45] Moreover, remaining single rarely gave those women who wished to escape domestic roles and family life the opportunity to do so. Economic dependence and social ostracism generally left them no option but to live with parents or siblings and help perform the drudgery of housework, uncompensated by the rewards or status that accompanied marriage. Even the few single professional women who succeeded in the uphill battle to eke out a decent living were subjected to constant surveillance and judgments on their personal lives.

A proponent of the establishment of an old-age home for unmarried women protested against society's "badly disguised contempt" for "these poor slaves of the family and of humanity who, with perfidious and cruel irony, are customarily given the deprecatory name of 'spinsters' [*solteironas*]." She went on to explain: "These prematurely aged women receive nothing at home but proofs of ingratitude; outside the home, they are granted nothing but humiliations. If they live with a married brother, they end up being considered as maids; for them, the work is little less than obligatory; the bread that they eat is almost alms."[46] Ercília Nogueira Cobra minced no words in describing the psychological plight of the unmarried woman:

The spinster suffers all martyrdoms, from the ridiculousness of a false social situation, permanent object of the mockery of other women who obtained a dowry to buy a husband, to the horrid attacks of hysteria, logical in a nervous system fractured by repression.

She lives unbefriended, in complete abandonment, without affection in life and she becomes silent.

She lives dead, and before knowing the solitude of the grave, where at least she will rest, little by little she dies in full life without ever giving expression to her strongest instinct, the sexual. She becomes a completely null being who lives frustrated, contemplating the pleasures of others. Everything is denied to her, and everyone makes fun of her "virtue."[47]

Given these circumstances, few women would have disagreed with the men who presumptuously affirmed: "marriage is the best female career" and "the supreme aspiration [of women] is to marry."[48] Even if women feared that their marriages might collapse, they could find some consolation in the fact that the situation of separated and widowed women was marginally better than that of single women. Their "virtue" was no longer so carefully guarded, and they sometimes received money or property through separation proceedings, through inheritance, or through the generosity of their children.

One woman who wrote for the *Revista Feminina* looked forward to the day when a woman could indulge in the luxury of asking herself: "Should I marry or not?" Yet in a world in which circumstances required that women still "entrust their past, their present, and their future to a man," she complained that they had little practical alternative but to "perfect their arms [of seduction]" so as to triumph in the "not always honest or dignified battle" to win a good husband.[49] If for a man achievement meant professional success, for a women achievement meant marrying well. In most cases, it secured her greater independence from her parents, adult status, and economic support.

Women's pessimism about marriage did not deter parents from actively collaborating in helping their daughters find suitable partners. (The marriage of a son was less problematic once he had demonstrated professional competence and the ability to earn a good living.) Marriage freed a woman's parents from the obligation of economic support, a consideration of growing importance owing to the burdens placed on family budgets by high rates of inflation and pressure to participate in ostentatious consumption. And for aspiring families outside the elite as well as for fallen aristocracy, the marriage of daughters could sometimes provide an easy means of upward social mobility and financial security for the whole family.

Although coerced marriages were technically illegal in both civil and ecclesiastical law, "coercion" was interpreted to mean very serious threats and ill treatment, not "simple reverential fear" of a parent who was exercising his or her "right or duty" to guide a child's actions and decisions.[50] In justification of the rejection of a petition filed in 1928 by Sophia for annulment of her seven-year marriage to lawyer Dagoberto, the ecclesiastical court maintained that she had married not under coercion but out of "obedience" to her father. The court's "defender of the marriage bond" explained:

> It is a principle of supreme prudence that children should listen to their parents' advice in all matters of importance.
>
> Marriage is a state of great transcendence, and therefore, in making the decision regarding this act, the rich sum of valuable observations of parents, their experience, already proven through many years, should be given preference over the influence of superficial and rash passions of sons and daughters, who, animated by youthful enthusiasms, lack prudence of their own. . . .
>
> To obey is to freely comply with the order of authority. Obedience is the sovereign law of human life, says the most excellent Jesuit orator. Under God, there is nothing more sacred than the authority of a parent. Nothing, therefore, is more just than for sons and daughters to obey their parents, to whom they owe their beings. Reason reveals this obedience that is owed to parents.
>
> Unreflective and inexperienced, sons and daughters need to be guided and instructed. And, how can they be directed if they do not obey? . . .
>
> It is for parents to command and for children to obey. In this lies the happiness of the family.[51]

The civil court also denied Sophia an annulment on the grounds that her father's coercion was not proved to have been sufficiently strong to invalidate the marriage.[52]

Given that divorce was not legal in Brazil (until 1977), Sophia may well have invented a story of paternal coercion in order to obtain an annulment of her intolerable marriage (rather than a *desquite*). Indeed, Rio de Janeiro's attorney general protested in 1942 that fraudulent marriage annulments were commonly granted in such cases during the 1930s.[53] Nevertheless, there is also evidence that in practice, parents still enjoyed (and sometimes exercised) considerable power to compel children (especially daughters) to marry partners chosen for them.[54] For example, Anna, a twenty-three-year-old woman with a handsome dowry of thirty *contos*, was forced in 1918 to marry and to stay married to a man who had ingratiated himself to her father.[55] Upon her father's death in 1924, her husband prevented her from seeking an annulment of their marriage for six months, until he had spent her dowry and abandoned her.[56] In 1923, the marriage of Clarice, a minor, and José, a medical doctor trained in Europe, was hastily arranged by their parents, who were intimate friends. Clarice's mother, indebted to José's father (her former teacher) for her career as a piano teacher, warned Clarice that were she to continue to resist the marriage, she would cause scandal to the family, ruin her mother's career, and suffer punishment and the withdrawal of economic support. At the same time, José feared that his father's poor health would become still more precarious were he to disobey his father's wishes. The marriage was performed in the bedroom of José's sick father, who died fifteen days later. After six months, Clarice's parents relaxed their surveillance, and she sought legal aid to annul the marriage.[57] In numerous other cases, widowed mothers, oppressed by economic difficulties and future insecurity, forced their daughters to marry men who appeared able and willing to provide their daughters—and even themselves—with wealth and social status.[58]

Few marriages, however, were actually arranged. Rather, parents resorted to indirect means to help their children secure advantageous marriages. More than ever, young women needed to acquire social graces and a basic education in order to compete in finding a husband. They also needed to frequent society in order to meet marriageable men. But as young women gained greater social freedom, elite parents grew increasingly concerned about whom their daughters might meet in public places. If most of these parents could no longer effectively compel their daughters to marry within the narrow boundaries of the old elite, they could try to influence their daughters' marriage choices by limiting the scope of social contact permitted. In 1916, a number of families of the "pure *paulista* nobility"—"legitimate descendants of the old *bandeirantes* [pioneers]"—joined together to form the Sociedade Harmonia: an exclusive "bloc of reaction" that they hoped would help them to "preserve themselves inaccessible to this invading wave of foreign elements that had no roots in [their] race." Organized and directed by several elite women, the Sociedade sponsored dances, concerts, and talks at which members of old *paulista* society would be able to maintain contact, preserve their identity, and protect their customs from the "contagion" of external influences.[59] An article written in 1920 claimed that membership in the Sociedade had become a goal for all those aspiring to enter elite society in São Paulo; it further implied that the desired exclusivity had been impossible to maintain, as more and more nouveaux riches were marrying into the "best families."[60] Marriages between children of nou-

At dances sponsored by the exclusive Sociedade Harmonia, the most "illustrious" families of the old paulista *aristocracy provided their children with opportunities to socialize with their peers and to seek suitable marriage partners. (From "Sociedade Harmonia,"*
RF 7:76 *[September 1920])*

veau riche immigrants and of the old landed *paulista* aristocracy were quite common by the 1920s. They were recognized to be socially and economically advantageous and were accepted as inevitable. Nevertheless, elite families jealously struggled to maintain control over which immigrant families should be admitted and which excluded.[61]

Besides going to great lengths to secure invitations for their daughters to the right social events, parents could—and did—invest in cultivating a daughter's social skills as well as in purchasing her an appropriately fashionable wardrobe.[62] But no longer were daughters expected to wait passively for their parents to arrange their marriages; nor were they to resign themselves to the idea that it was impossible to marry into a family of significantly higher status and greater wealth. The rise of the competitive social and economic order placed young women in stiff competition for the most promising bachelors. With the primary responsibility for finding good husbands placed on their shoulders, pressure increased for them to perfect the skills required to rise above their peers and achieve social mobility along with marriage. An article in the *Revista Feminina* commented that, unlike men, women regarded one another as competitors and rivals. It went on to say that women were the most careful observers and most severely critical judges of the details of dress and grooming of other women.[63] One woman complained that success in finding a good husband depended on a young woman's willingness to "surrender [herself] . . . unconditionally to the despotism of fashion."[64]

Finally, success also depended on a young woman's ability to learn to imitate the manners of upper-class society. One male writer commented that in order to please men of higher social status, "the bourgeois woman does everything, with an indefatigable tenacity, to identify herself with, or at least resemble in clothes, gestures, walk, speech, elegant touches, and even actions, the woman of high society."[65] An indispensable aid for young women with aspirations of upward mobility was *Boas maneiras*, the best-known Brazilian book of good manners. Written in the mid-1910s by Olga Meira, a founder and president of the São Paulo League of Catholic Women, the book provided nouveaux riches with guidelines on good taste and correct behavior.[66]

In short, among middle- and upper-class women, only the strong-minded, the deviant, and the unlucky remained unmarried. The alarm over the perceived rejection of marriage by the young seems to have been unwarranted. Although marriage coefficients for Brazil had traditionally been low, national censuses indicate that the percentage of the population aged fifteen and over that was married increased rapidly from 36.39 in 1872, to 44.68 in 1890, to 51.59 in 1940, while the percentage of those who were single decreased proportionately from 56.93 in 1872, to 48.46 in 1890, to 40.74 in 1940.[67] By 1939 to 1941, national marriage coefficients had reached a level considered respectable for "civilized populations": an estimated 8 to 9 per 1,000 inhabitants.[68] In the city of São Paulo, the marriage coefficient increased dramatically from 6.01 during the last five years of the nineteenth century to 8.58 between 1935 and 1939.[69] It was the statistics for the city of Rio de Janeiro that looked alarming. From 6.46 in the years 1920–21, the marriage coefficient fell to 5.79 for 1939–41. The high number of young, single rural migrants to the city as well as the postponing of marriage among the middle and upper classes could account to some extent for the very low marriage coefficient. But it is very likely that these statistics also contained significant gaps.[70]

The rising percentages of the married population are even more significant in light of the fact that couples—especially from urban middle- and upper-class families—were increasingly postponing their marriages. As more and more women enrolled in secondary and professional schools and were able to secure respectable paid employment for a few years between schooling and marriage, their age at marriage rose. In Brazil's two major cities, São Paulo and Rio de Janeiro, the median age at marriage for women shifted dramatically upward from under 21 at the beginning of the century to over 24 by the end of the 1930s.[71] The wealthier the area, the later the women tended to marry. For example, between 1939 and 1941, the median age of marriage for single women in Brazil as a whole was 21.5, and 47.51 percent still married under the age of 20; however, in the city of Rio de Janeiro, the median age of marriage for single women was 24.3, and only 25.28 percent married before they had reached 20.[72]

Statistics for São Paulo are especially interesting in revealing that the pattern of later marriage occurred first in the wealthiest neighborhoods of the city (Sé, Consolação, Santa Ephigenia, and Santa Cecilia). Between 1927 and 1937, the percentage of women in the city as a whole marrying under the age of 20 dropped from 30.8 to 25.1 percent, whereas the percentage of women marrying between the ages of 25 and 34 increased from 17 to 22.8 percent. The 1927 statistics for women who lived in the four wealthiest neighborhoods of São Paulo were nearly identical to the 1937 statistics for the city as a whole: 24.9 percent of women married under the age of 20, and 23 percent married between the ages of 25 and 34 (see table 2).

Since men too were postponing their marriages in order to complete professional training and establish financial security, the age differential between men and women engaged to be married remained. In Rio de Janeiro during the years 1939–41, the median age at marriage for single women was 24.3 and the median age for single men was 28.7, a difference of 4.4 years.[73] The 1929 statistics for the city of São Paulo show that 79.65 percent of engaged couples were less than 10 years apart in age. But the norm for women to marry older men remained very strong.[74]

Legal marital separation, although still very difficult to obtain, was a final option sought by some women suffering oppressive marriages. (Women were far more likely than men to file for separations, since marriage was more restrictive for them and since it was normally they who were abused or abandoned by husbands rather than vice versa.) The prodivorce arguments of both female and male professionals, along with growing social acceptance of the pressing need for and inherent justice of divorce, must certainly have facilitated women's struggles to escape undesirable marriages.[75] But it would be incorrect to imply that separation had become an easy or desirable option.

The grounds for obtaining a legal marital separation were still quite restrictive. The 1890 civil marriage law and the 1916 Civil Code specified that marriages could be annulled only in cases of coercion of one of the spouses or of "essential error of person." [76] The only other options were unofficial separation or *desquite*, which was allowed in cases of adultery, attempt to kill, ill treatment or serious injury, and voluntary abandonment of the home for two consecutive

Table 2. Age at Marriage of Women in São Paulo (City), 1901–1937

	16–20	21–25	26–30	31–35	36+
1901	55.4	29.3	6.9	3.7	4.7
1910	51.7	32.5	8.5	2.6	4.7
	Under 20	20–24	25–29	30–34	35+[a]
1915	36.1	48.7	7.1	3.5	4.6
1921	33.2	45.9	12.5	4.0	4.2
1927	30.8	47.4	12.9	4.1	4.7
1927 urban[b]	29.2	48.5	13.3	4.6	4.5
1927 suburban	35.7	43.6	11.3	3.5	5.9
1937	25.1	46.3	17.3	5.5	5.9

Sources: São Paulo (State), Repartição de Estatística e Arquivo, *Annuário estatístico de São Paulo* (1901) pt. 1, p. 417; (1910) vol. 1, pt. 2, p. 205; (1915) vol. 1, pt. 3, p. 84; (1921) vol. 1, pt. 3, p. 169; (1927) vol. 1, pt. 3, p. 138. Almeida Júnior, "Aspectos da nupcialidade paulista," 104.

[a] The age ranges used by the São Paulo Department of Statistics changed slightly between 1910 and 1915.

[b] The pattern of later marriage occurred in the wealthier urban neighborhoods much sooner than in the predominantly working-class suburban neighborhoods. Interestingly, the 1927 marriage statistics for women who lived in the four wealthiest neighborhoods of the city (Sé, Consolação, Santa Ephigenia, and Santa Cecilia) were nearly identical to the 1937 statistics for the city as a whole:

Under 20	20–24	25–29	30–34	35+
24.9	46.5	17.4	5.6	5.6

years. After two years of marriage, *desquite* was also permitted in cases in which there existed mutual consent of the spouses.[77] The rich who could afford the legal fees of securing a divorce from abroad (most frequently from Uruguay) could choose this option in order to remarry.[78] But Brazilian law did not recognize a divorce or second marriage from a foreign country.

Moreover, for women who qualified for an annulment or *desquite*, winning one could be an arduous (and expensive) task, and success did not necessarily resolve their troubles. Women frequently faced long, bitter struggles with husbands or family members before they could petition for a *desquite* or annulment, and even then, there was no guarantee that it would be granted. If a woman did secure a *desquite* and if she was the innocent partner, she was legally entitled to alimony, custody of her children, and child support.[79] However, such support could rarely be guaranteed, especially if she had been abandoned. A *desquitada* woman also faced enormous social prejudices and was condemned to either celibacy or concubinage. Whenever possible, therefore, women sought annulments rather than *desquites*, since the former permitted legal remarriage.

Especially interesting is the case of a successful professional woman of an old wealthy *paulista* family. In 1906, only three months after returning from a Catholic boarding school in Europe, Margarita was forced to marry a distant relative she barely knew. Despite Margarita's protests, her father remained intransigent in insisting on his right to choose her marriage partner. The wedding ceremony was an unhappy event attended only by her parents, godparents, and eight guests. After a few years, the marriage collapsed and Margarita's husband abandoned her. But when she sought legal counsel to annul her marriage, her father intervened. Fearing scandal and a blow to the family's reputation, he persuaded the lawyer whom she had approached not to represent her. Finally, in 1925, he gave up his active resistance, and Margarita was able to annul her marriage.[80] Although for wealthy women of prestigious families marital separation could be a liberation, for middle-class women it normally implied a substantial loss of economic security and social status. For the latter, separation was at best the lesser of two evils.

In fact, contrary to the common wisdom of the time, statistical evidence does not confirm that marital separation had become epidemic. Preliminary research in the São Paulo civil court archive uncovered an average of only fifty-five *desquites* and annulments granted per year in the city between 1922 and 1929.[81] And the 1940 census registered only 1,777 men and 3,027 women— 0.53 percent of the total population of the city fifteen years or older—under the category of "separated, *desquitados*, or divorced."[82] For Brazil as a whole, the 1940 census recorded only 0.28 percent of the population fifteen years or older as "separated, *desquitados*, or divorced."[83] These census statistics are of very doubtful accuracy because of the illegality of divorce and the underreporting of separated couples that had not legally formalized their situation. Nevertheless, it is likely that separated adults were conspicuous and threatening to polite society for reasons other than their numbers alone.

Although the great majority of middle- and upper-class women conformed to their prescribed familial roles, it was feared that this was a situation precariously based on tenuous restraints imposed by religious dogma and the still limited choice of viable social and economic alternatives, rather than on willing acquiescence. In the words of one anonymous (presumably female) writer:

Many wives hide in the silence of their abnegation a life of suffering and deception which, revealed, would yield bitter and terrible pages; they keep silent because resignation is not one of the lesser virtues of their sex; they keep silent through habit of submission; they keep silent because of familial and social considerations; they keep silent, finally, because during centuries and centuries of slavery, their hearts learned to obey without arguing, to suffer without protesting, [and] to cry without showing their tears![84]

For the first time, intellectuals, professionals, and public officials became fearful of the explosive possibilities were large numbers of women to unleash their unhappiness and their anger or to act on their desires for equality and independence. The increasing availability of formerly unimaginable educational and professional opportunities for middle-class women, along with the elaboration of a new critical discourse concerning the social and economic position of women, provided necessary preconditions for the development of a new female consciousness and for radically new patterns of behavior. Although marriage was not transformed overnight, postwar controversies over the institution opened up formerly ignored and taboo subjects to heated public debate, generated new sets of expectations, and provided support to women in their struggles to reshape their lives.

SHORING UP MARRIAGE

Between the mid-1910s and the early 1940s, an overwhelming consensus emerged among Brazil's most prominent intellectuals and professionals that the triumph of "civilization and progress" in the public sphere depended on "redeeming" the family. Judge Nelson Hungria articulated this consensus in typical language: "[The family] is the most indispensable of social institutions, for it is the germ of political association, the *célula-mater* of the State, [and] the basic element of human reproduction, of the formation of the inner character, [and] of the strength and health of the social body. . . . The destiny of the family is viscerally united to the destiny of society."[1]

While progressives campaigned to replace "archaic," "backward," and "dysfunctional" oligarchical traditions with modern "hygienic" standards, conservatives (especially those linked to the Church) insisted on the necessity of upholding the "traditional Brazilian family" in the face of rapid economic modernization. Nevertheless, they concurred that the "crisis" of the family was among the most serious and intolerable of social perils, and they subjected the institution to ever increasing scrutiny. Furthermore, they agreed that increasing state intervention was essential to preserve the institution of the family as a pillar of social and political order.

The struggle to modernize the family—and thereby to strengthen and legitimate the institution—became an integral part of the struggle of urban modernizing elites to transform the "anachronistic" oligarchical society that had survived into the early twentieth century into a modern, prosperous, orderly bourgeois nation. Much of their attention focused on reconsolidating middle- and upper-class families, since women of these classes were the most outspoken in attacking marriage and since these classes set societal norms. But their concern with shoring up working-class families was equally strong, since they believed that legally constituted and stable working-class families were essential for quelling working-class militancy, for guaranteeing continued male dominance (and by extension, the social hierarchy from which they benefited), and for ensuring sound physical and moral development of the children who would become future workers.

Feminists and antifeminists, reformist professionals and conservative clerics, industrialists and state bureaucrats articulated competing visions of proper family organization and sometimes worked at cross-purposes. But the sum of their efforts generated a complex combination of strategies—including reform, persuasion, the use of incentives, and repression—to shore up the institution of marriage and transform it into a pillar of the new bourgeois society. Broad societal debates on what constituted healthy conjugal relations had the effect of gradually modernizing norms and thereby helping to relegitimize the institution. Floods of normative literature sought to disseminate these modern norms and to achieve compliance through persuasion. The state not only introduced material incentives to encourage couples to marry and bear children but also employed more coercive techniques to enforce modern norms. These included passage of "protective" legislation limiting women's workforce participation, the use of old and new penal sanctions to discipline serious offenders, and the development of a corps of social workers charged with monitoring the behavior of poor families. The Church, with state support, developed a large network of lay organizations, which penetrated all aspects and classes of urban society for the explicit purpose of diffusing its conservative social doctrine. Psychiatrists defined the boundaries of "normality" and helped enforce these boundaries by establishing asylums where deviants were segregated from society. Finally, the industrial bourgeoisie attempted to control the domestic lives of their workers by constructing model villages where every aspect of workers' lives was carefully monitored and regulated.

In short, men's and women's intimate relationships became the object of increasing public scrutiny and control, a trend that paralleled and complemented growing attempts by the state to become involved in regulating all aspects of social life. As parents were losing control over the marriage choices of their children and as husbands were increasingly anxious about their ability to control their wives' behavior, urban professionals and public officials stepped in to fill the void. In justification of their assumed role, they maintained: "Marriage is an eminently social institution. It is of greater interest to the collectivity than to the individual himself."[2]

Reforming Marriage

▼ ▼ ▼

Efforts to reform marriage had a double thrust. First, in response to women's discontent, husband-wife relationships had to be modernized, acquiring at least a veneer of equality and reciprocity in order to redeem marriage as a legitimate, esteemed, and therefore stable institution. Second, reformers sought to make marriage more "hygienic," more rational, and therefore more functional in producing well-socialized and competent citizens whose behavior would further "civilization and progress." A consensus emerged among reformers on the need to promote companionate marriages, to "civilize" love, and to hygienicize sexual relations within marriage. More controversial was the opinion of a growing number of prominent male professionals that divorce was also necessary to moralize and civilize marriage.

Intimacy and love—rather than economic interest or social restraints—were seen to be the only possible and legitimate bases for ensuring the stability of modern marriages. Thus the vast separation of male and female cultures (which had formerly been accepted as natural and inevitable) now became a serious problem and obstacle to companionate marriage. Both men and women began to consider that the "abyss" that normally separated spouses was highly detrimental to personal well-being, conjugal harmony, and social stability. Marriages seemed doomed to failure in a culture in which couples were "so indifferent to one another, so disunited in thought, so divorced in sentiments, that they appear more as two alien beings, strangers united momentarily by mere chance."[3] Authors protested that because the two sexes shared no common ideas and no common language, they were incapable of communicating about issues of common interest or of achieving a harmonious coexistence. The result, it was feared, was incomprehension, silence, and tedium at best.[4] Worse, men's authoritarianism was a source of constant discord, while the curbing of women's liberty created exaggerated jealousies. In short, marriage soon brought "frequent fights, disregard and discord, rages, hatred and hypocrisies, laziness, growing disparities of opinion, and habitual disputes between the spouses."[5]

Reformers thus agreed that modern marriage had to be based on greater equality between spouses. No longer was it acceptable for a husband to act like a "taciturn, despotic, and omnipotent sovereign, more an owner than a spouse."[6] According to a number of Brazil's leading jurists, men's desire for absolute and exclusive property rights over their wives was evidence that they remained slaves to primitive animal instincts.[7] Such possessiveness, rather than being regarded as an expression of love, was now labeled "rape."[8] Public prosecutor Roberto Lyra insisted that the law ought to combat the "noxious," "absurd," "medieval" notion that a man's honor lies in his wife's uterus. "A woman is no longer a rib or an appendix, an object of luxury or a beast of burden," he claimed. "She has her own honor, like a man. She is responsible for her own acts."[9]

Nor was it considered healthy or advantageous for a wife to allow herself to be reduced to the position of a "slave." Modern society needed women who acted out of their own sense of initiative, conscientiousness, and duty, not those who were immobilized by tyrannical husbands.[10] According to Izabel de León, the ideal marriage was one based on intimacy and free association:

> The modern woman, free and conscientious, must build her home in a different manner than it has been built until now.
>
> It is absurd to want to apply old principles to the formation of a modern home, in the same way that it is absurd for the woman not to understand her social obligations in a new and elevated manner.
>
> The home based on principles of justice and perfect reciprocal understanding of rights and duties will be less subject to collapse.[11]

However, support for closer companionship and mutual understanding between spouses—companionate marriage—did not necessarily imply endorsement of the idea that women should be fully equal to or competitive with their husbands. If men's tyrannical exercise of their authority and women's servility were denounced as sources of conflict, the total elimination of hierarchy and authority was feared to be an equally dangerous source of conflict. The 1916 Civil Code made one formalistic concession to women's demands for greater autonomy and authority: the wife was legally described as a "companion, partner, and assistant in [attending to] familial responsibilities." But with its reaffirmation of the husband's position as legal head of household, a wife gained no effective power. She still had to depend on her husband to administer her property, to authorize her to pursue a profession, and to accept or relinquish an inheritance.[12] Jurist Eduardo Espinola explained that the necessity of establishing a single head of household barred absolute equality for married women: "[I]n the conjugal association, unity and direction are indispensable, making it necessary for one of the spouses to have the final word in cases in which there is a divergence of opinion regarding the best interests of the association; and, this power falls to the husband, whose capacity as head of the family is justified by considerations of traditional social order as well as by physical and psychological considerations."[13]

Thus the denunciation of female submissiveness was carried only as far as was thought necessary to quell conflict and to mobilize women's talents and energies without revolutionizing gender roles. Interestingly, the modern, progressive psychiatrist Antonio Austregésilo Lima revealed his true colors in the advice he gave to men: they should cease to *appear* authoritarian, trying to cede to their wives on small issues so that they might continue to prevail in larger matters.[14]

Continued legal inequality between husbands and wives was played down, however, by the stress on marriage as a partnership involving equally important and difficult—if different—tasks and responsibilities. Social need for hierarchy and women's aspirations for equality were reconciled through assigning wives their own sphere of authority and autonomy within which they could be relatively independent but from which they should not normally stray.[15] The notion that women should reign within the home as "queens" and "patronesses" enjoyed immense popularity. As "free," "equal," and "conscientious" beings, modern women were to embrace eagerly the role of "wise directors" of their homes: "Wide windows swing open in the spirit and mind of the woman toward the light and toward the beauty of liberty; all this dead sea of superstitions, prejudices, and puerile fears uproot themselves from her heart; the sun of conscience lights up in her mind in order to illuminate the path of her *duty*, and a gigantic step will be taken toward the ideal of perfection of the human species."[16] Women's "duty," of course, was to establish modern, hygienic families.

Reformers and conservatives alike emphasized that the sexual division of labor, rather than humiliating women, elevated them and, rather than being an obsolete form of social organization, was a modern economic necessity and "essential condition for human progress."[17] Stress was placed on the complementary nature of the sexes, and much effort was spent in justifying the appropriateness of the strict separation of tasks on the grounds that men and women were endowed with divergent physical and psychological qualities.[18] One author described the family as a small state in which the husband, as minister of finance, was charged with earning money, while the wife, as secretary of the interior, was charged with the political tasks of administration.[19] The wife's task was celebrated as both the most important of all social responsibilities and among the most difficult. Declarations such as the following abounded:

> [T]o the woman falls the most difficult, the most thorny, [and] the most meritorious role in forming societies and aggrandizing the fatherland.[20]
>
> The home embodies a ministry or a small country with a very complicated administrative apparatus, on which the normal functioning of the larger country depends.[21]

Reforming (and stabilizing) marriage also involved new efforts to "civilize" love—to replace "archaic" "illusions" about the nature of love with healthy modern ideas celebrating the domination of reason and responsibility over sentimentality and passion.[22] First, romantic love was pronounced dead and buried by modernizers who wished to "restore [love] to its biological and social function as the source of life, beauty, health, stability, harmony, and happiness."[23] According to Antonio Austregésilo Lima: "Men and women—but especially the female spirit—yield too much to the heart. They poison themselves with the false romanticism of love; they exalt excessively the nature of passions; they imagine the most false ideals; they construct symbols of love that are incompatible with human nature, and the result is soon evident: disharmony, discord, instability, disillusion; errors that cannot be amended; tearful misfortunes; shattered hearts, sickened spirits, fractured lives."[24] Afrânio Peixoto condemned nineteenth-century romanticism for exalting emotionality to such an extent that even bloody crimes of passion were glorified. Romanticism, he claimed, "begot this monster, perverse and murderous love, immoral and vile, which lives on, absorbing and gripping an entire society." He bid farewell to the perverse and obsessive love that had fallen "victim" to romanticism, and welcomed in a new modern love based on "self-control." "Reason," he insisted, "can and must check passions." By his definition: "Civilization does not signify merely material progress, but the inhibition of violent and egoistic impulses through customs of moderation [which are] indispensable to public order."[25] Roberto Lyra agreed: "[W]e must not allow [passion] free expression in this era in which the factors of disorder loom large and multiply." He even suggested that the state should intervene to prevent marriages based on "unpropitious, immoral, or infatuated love," since this was equally dangerous to civilization as were other motives for which the state denied marriage licenses. "Society needs healthy and well-balanced marriages," he declared, "in which reason is united with emotion in the interest of the children, the family, and the community. What is the desire of a retardatory romantic worth in face of the greatest human problems?"[26]

Couples were warned not to expect the initial sentimental love to endure.[27] Pleasure, they were told, was ephemeral; it was a great error to mistake passing ecstasies for the essence of true love.[28] As their marriages matured, couples were instructed to transform passion into "domestic love" and "conjugal friendship"—"love in its sweetest and purest expression."[29] This love—"hygienic love"—was praised as being "more spiritual, more durable, more useful to society, more profound, and more dignified."[30] As the base on which families were founded, its function was to inspire commitment to duty, respect for order, and resignation.[31] It was also said to preserve long-term personal happiness and health: "Dear reader, if you can pass your life without intense loves, you will live twice, because there is no greater poison . . . that threatens your days. . . . Happy are those who love only during youth, and who later let love weaken and be transmuted into serene friendship."[32]

Ideally, as conjugal love became "habitual" and "natural," it was supposed to develop into a "reunion of all affections" that would "survive very well in the most prosaic existence, in the midst of all the commonplace accidents of life."[33] In the interest of containing the threatening emotional instabilities of conjugal love, it was subsumed within the gender and generational hierarchies of family life and defined as an expression of friendship:

> For the wife, her husband's love takes the place of all other affections.
>
> In her husband's love, there is the love of a father, grave, tutelary, continuing to exercise protection and paternal vigilance over the wife.
>
> There is the love of a mother, forgiving her small defects and weaknesses, full of kindness and heedfulness.
>
> There is the love of a sibling, intimate, benevolent, full of trust and warmth.
>
> Finally, the husband is a dedicated friend on whom you can count in all circumstances, a friendly companion in daily life and in happiness.[34]

By equating the love of one's spouse with parental love, emphasis was placed on the absolute illegitimacy of any challenge to conjugal stability.

Optimistically, Antonio Austregésilo Lima predicted the dawn of a new era: "Happily, it appears that throughout the world, as men become more civilized, the impetuosity of love is diminishing. Romanticism slowly suffocates, becoming legendary, and humanity inaugurates the school of the possible, better adapted for loving."[35]

Despite the emphasis on the spirituality of conjugal love, there was a growing recognition among the medical community of the need to address problems of sexuality. Monogamous marriage was generally considered to be the institution best suited to furthering sexual hygiene and the healthy expression of sexual instincts.[36] In practice, however, doctors and psychotherapists acknowledged the big discrepancy between the ideal and the real, and they grew increasingly concerned that ignorance and errors in sexual practice could lead to unhappiness, disharmony, and the collapse of otherwise "perfect" marriages. Lima considered marriage to be the life transition experienced most intensely—and often traumatically—by women. He attributed women's feelings of extreme anxiety, neurosis, and frigidity both to their own fears and misconceptions about sexuality and to the traumas they frequently experienced during the first sexual contacts. He lamented that in many cases, adultery resulted from the inability of a husband or wife to satisfy the sexual needs of his or her spouse. He therefore claimed that a correct understanding of the principles of normal sexual intercourse was essential for healthy, stable marriages: "Man has no right to relegate this preoccupation of marriage [sexuality] to an inferior plane. . . . All the authors who treat the question of harmony and of happiness in marriage are in agreement that the sexual life shared by the two is the *sine qua non* for the success of the matrimonial union." [37]

Gradually and cautiously, the Brazilian medical community began to endorse the ideas of European psychoanalysts and sexologists. Lima insisted that the problems of the sexual lives of married couples were "infinitely complex," requiring the careful attention of specialists. [38] In addition to treating patients, he contributed to the growing literature of sexual manuals. In his *Conduta sexual*, he urged: "It is incumbent on the husband to study female sexuality and to know the degree of openness and shyness of his wife in order to captivate her. In the same way, the wife should seek to understand her husband so that, by making concessions and delicately refusing certain requests, she captivates him sexually to the greatest extent possible." [39] While emphasizing the importance of instructing women in basic principles of sexuality, Lima urged men to learn to be "artist[s] in matters of love." This meant being delicate and tender so as not to provoke in their wives pain, revulsion, or nervous crises; paying careful attention to foreplay; searching for ways to give their wives orgasms, or at least sexual pleasure; limiting their demands for sexual intercourse to two or three times a week; and abstaining altogether during menstruation, sickness, and "certain months of pregnancy." Couples were advised to avoid both frigidity and the "libidinous excesses" said to be typical of men's contacts with prostitutes. Lima also recommended that all couples interested in preserving conjugal happiness read the works of the famous sexologists Marie Carmichael Stopes, T. H. van de Velde, Paolo Mantegazza, and Augusto Forel. [40]

In fact, the well-educated public grew increasingly receptive to the idea of seeking expert advice on matters of sexual practice. Explicit sexual manuals were eagerly sought as respectable additions to the libraries of enlightened adults, and the active cultivation of pleasure in marital sexual relations began to be considered morally upright and socially useful. [41] Translations of foreign texts treating various aspects of sexuality suddenly became available during the late 1920s, and they sold well. In 1928, when the Companhia Editôra Nacional published a Portuguese edition of Augusto Forel's classic work *The Sexual Question*, the three thousand copies of the first edition sold out within two months. By 1929 the book was in its fourth edition. The same company published translations of the major works of Marie Carmichael Stopes in 1929, followed in 1933 by those of Havelock Ellis. By 1935 translations of five works by

J. R. Bourdon and three by T. H. van de Velde had been published. Also available in Portuguese editions were works by Sigmund Freud, Pierre Vachet, Paolo Mantegazza, Jean Marestan, Gregorio Marañon, Julio Barcos, Alexandra Kolontai, and Kenneth MacGowan.⁴²

In the prefaces to these translations, Brazilian editors and physicians denounced the hypocrisy, false modesty, and "superstitious prejudices" surrounding sexuality. They warned readers that they would find no scandal or obscenities and declared that there could be no immorality in that which was found in nature. They also stressed the importance of disseminating the "modern ethic based on Truth, founded in scientific knowledge."⁴³ In his preface to T. H. van de Velde's *Ideal Marriage* (an extremely explicit guide to human physiology and techniques of lovemaking), José de Albuquerque recommended that the book be included among the presents given to all brides.⁴⁴ Arnaldo de Moraes was more cautious in his introduction to *The Ideal Wife*. Whereas T. H. van de Velde had emphasized that his book's aim was to help women develop their sexual aptitudes to the maximum in order to assure more complete happiness in love, Moraes justified its translation as a useful source of scientific knowledge for gynecologists.⁴⁵

Another proposed means for reforming marriage (which was not implemented until 1977 because of Church opposition) was the legalization of divorce. Many of Brazil's most prominent male professionals came to agree with the women who were demanding divorce. But whereas female proponents were concerned with protecting women from oppression and abuse, male proponents were concerned with strengthening the institution of marriage. The latter argued that despite religious and legal constraints, incompatibility and adultery were breaking up marriages and sometimes leading to violent domestic crimes. Thus divorce, by legalizing and regulating the dissolution of inauspicious marriages, would help moralize and legitimate the institution. First, divorce would provide a necessary escape valve to reduce domestic violence and to compensate individuals suffering from disastrous marriages. Second, it would redeem marriage as an esteemed institution based on free will, not legal despotism. Third, it would promote health and social order by allowing separated adults to reestablish legal conjugal relations. Happy, stable, and legitimate second unions were considered preferable to first marriages torn apart by conflict and adultery or to illicit and legally unregulated bonds between separated adults. In essence, such prodivorce arguments were conservative. Advocates hoped that by allowing for the dissolution of socially dysfunctional marriages and encouraging the reentry of separated adults into new webs of family constraints and obligations (rather than into "free unions"), they could help buttress the institution of the family along with the hierarchical relations it embodied. They believed it was necessary to make marriage less rigid and less constricting in order to undermine criticisms, attacks, and outright rejection of the institution.[46]

Promoting Marriage and the Family
▼   ▼   ▼

These reform efforts, which were aimed at containing conflict within marriages and postponing fundamental changes in gender relations, were but one (albeit important) part of the larger project. Shoring up marriage also required new propaganda to promote the institution among the middle and upper classes as well as material incentives to encourage couples of more modest means to marry.

The realization that not all middle- and upper-class men and women absolutely had to form a family in order to survive reasonably well in modern society fed fears that large numbers might choose alternatives. If women were unhappy about the discrepancy between their ideals of marriage and reality, men, by admission of members of their own sex, were often terrified of assuming the responsibilities and duties of marriage.[47] In reaction, shrill propaganda insisted on the moral and medical necessity for all individuals to marry, and it also attempted to direct marriage choices in ways that would best preserve social hygiene and public order.

Marriage was declared to be the "perfect state" and also an obligation from which no one could shirk without committing a "grave fault, not only with regard to one's lineage, but also with regard to oneself, for [by not marrying] one deprives oneself of the most sublime treasure that the earth offers."[48] An alarmist article published in *A Cigarra* warned that unmarried men, lacking the emotional and physical comforts supplied by a wife, had a 50 percent greater chance of dying than married men of the same age. Although the article admitted that more married women in their childbearing years died than did single women, it concluded that the mortality rate was "frightful" among older unmarried women and widows who had few relatives to shower them with attention and affection. The author therefore advised all men and women to marry or remarry as rapidly as possible.[49]

On a more serious plane, Antonio Austregésilo Lima considered celibacy among healthy males to be "one of the most condemnable facts of society," since "[m]arriage constitutes one of the most secure conditions to guarantee the health of humanity and the greater longevity and stability of society." The same author also condemned female celibacy, but on different grounds.

> The female heart is sometimes a tuning fork, sometimes a sounding box, sometimes an instrument of harmonious and delicate chords from which harmony nearly always arises when it vibrates with man. At times, dissonance is born out of the consonance with other female hearts. . . .
>
> [Brazilian women] are too good to crave social independence. The programs of feminism will not soon concern our female patricians, for there is a golden chain that binds them to man—extreme affection. Feminine thoughts in Brazil (there are, to be sure, many and praiseworthy exceptions) are constituted by marriage.[50]

His insistence that the biological and physiological differences between the sexes should naturally lead to complementarity and to the willing dependence of women on men appears to grow out of his fear that female celibacy posed a dangerous threat to heterosexuality and male dominance. M. F. Pinto Pereira also stressed that women would not achieve happiness through economic independence but rather in the "unity of the two sexes." A strong proponent of the family as an "ardent sanctuary" in which Brazilian territory, history, and traditions were "immortalized," he attempted to combat the "dread" of the "magnificent institution" of marriage that he perceived to be commonplace among the young. He insisted not only that marriage was "the most noble female career" but also that it was a "civic duty" of all Brazilians and an "irrecusable necessity" for the healthy growth and evolution of the country.[51]

Having established the necessity of marriage, eugenicists and educators began to provide the young with advice on how to go about securing a good spouse—usurping what had been a parental role. They emphasized that the well-being of future offspring, of the family, and of society depended on healthy and well-balanced marriages. Most important, the young were advised that marriage should be a freely chosen association based on mutual love, not infatuation, passion, convenience, or material interest.[52] But this was not the only factor to be considered; marriage decisions were to be made on the basis of reason as well as sentiment. Women were told that the essential qualities for a good husband were honesty, sincerity, loyalty, uprightness, and dedication to hard work.[53] In order not to be deceived by appearances, every woman was urged to conduct long and patient studies so as to allow no aspect of her fiancé's character to remain unknown. Only then would she be capable of making a careful and rational decision as to whether sufficient compatibility of characters existed and whether his virtues outweighed his defects.[54] Another important practical consideration was whether he could support her.[55]

Relatively little literature was published instructing men on how to choose a wife. Physician and eugenicist Renato Kehl explained that it was easier to choose a wife than a husband, since it was women who had preserved the "ancestral qualities of nobility and humanity of the Lusitanian people." But he did suggest that men seek a wife who could play the triple role of lover, friend, and mother. Such a woman should be physically healthy and beautiful, intelligent, gracious, charming, pure, loving, and self-sacrificing. He went on to clarify that for a woman, to be well educated did not mean to be "emancipated" in the sense that she would question the sexual division of labor.[56]

Most of the literature describing the qualities of a good wife, however, was directed at young women rather than young men. It tried to convince them that men sought modest and dignified women for their wives: women who would willingly restrict their social lives, refrain from ostentatious or frivolous behavior, and work hard to become competent housewives.[57] It further insisted that women's greatest asset—that which would win them an honest man's love—was their "purity."[58] Lemos Britto believed in the absolute necessity of preserving traditional moral precepts:

> [The woman] knows that her social position derives from her reputation, and she puts herself on guard to defend that reputation. While a virgin, she sets out to obtain a husband and that relative independence that marriage gives. Now, she knows that without a scrupulous demonstration of virtues, she won't marry, and even if she doesn't intend to marry, without an unblemished reputation, a barrier will quickly be established between her and the society. . . . Everything advises the woman, for her own best interest, to be prudent.[59]

For marriages to attain the new eugenic ideal preached by a growing segment of the medical community, prospective spouses were also urged to consider factors of heredity. They were told that their interest in satisfying personal desires, while legitimate, should not overshadow their concern for the well-being of their offspring. Therefore, physicians encouraged all couples to undergo prenuptial physical examinations.[60]

Despite the growing consensus that happiness in marriage depended on greater physical, moral, material, and intellectual equality between spouses, it was still considered imprudent for a woman to marry a man she could outshine.[61] Editors of *A Cigarra* mocked the husband of Amelia Earhart, claiming that he must have been intolerably humiliated because no one could possibly think well of a man whose wife was so daring, independent, and successful.[62] Normative literature encouraged women to follow the dominant tendency to seek a husband who was her superior by virtue of age, strength, talent, and education.[63] An article in the *Revista Feminina* stated the case bluntly by applauding women's search for husbands to whom they would willingly subordinate themselves: "Some girls want to be selected by a man whose superior intelligence is for them a constant cause of admiration. I agree that they are delectably feminine, for they would like to find in a husband not a being that they can dominate or annihilate, but a protector so highly placed in their spirit that they would be grateful to let themselves be guided by him and have no will different from that of their well-loved."[64] Even Antonio Austregésilo Lima, who adamantly denounced the authoritarianism of husbands, who urged couples to understand that marriage depended on mutual concessions, and who encouraged women to further their education, did not in the end believe in the possibility or desirability of marriages based on full equality.[65] "Female enthusiasm for man is born in the notion of strength; the woman loves him who appears to her to be masterly; the notion of superiority can be physical or moral; however, it is indispensable that a woman submit herself in order to really love."[66]

If this propaganda expressed the views of and found its audience among the middle and upper classes, its irrelevance to the working classes and urban poor was obvious. Public officials recognized that promoting socially advantageous marriages and stable, healthy families required more than showering the young with advice and admonitions. According to the emerging corporatist doctrine, the state had the responsibility to "elevate, demonstrate esteem for, and improve the conditions of [the family], giving it all the support and all the guarantees necessary for its stability, security, and constant development."[67]

The state's desire to strengthen its tutelage of the family was reflected in the 1934 Constitution, which affirmed in principle that the federal, state, and municipal governments were required to dedicate 1 percent of their tax revenues to promoting the health and well-being of mothers and children.[68] The 1937 Constitution proclaimed more explicitly: "The family, constituted by indissoluble marriage, is under the special protection of the state." In order to implement these constitutional principles, the Estado Novo created the National Commission for the Protection of the Family in 1939. The commission was charged with elaborating appropriate laws, taking into account the following needs: to facilitate marriage (by eliminating all obstacles, making civil marriage free, recognizing religious marriage, and providing loans for newlyweds); to institute family loans to facilitate the purchase of a house; to protect maternity, infancy, and adolescence; to give family men preferential treatment in securing employment; to provide special benefits for large families; to aid poor families in supporting and educating their children; to define crimes against the family and specify sanctions and procedures for enforcement; and to create sources of income to aid the state in protecting families, including a special tax on single adults and childless couples.[69]

Two years later, Decree 3.200 removed the obstacles to marriage specified above and introduced material incentives for couples to marry and have children. According to this decree, newly married couples under the age of thirty who had obtained certificates of good health in prenuptial exams were eligible for special loans from public savings and loan institutions to buy and furnish homes. Payments on these loans could be partially forgiven upon the birth of each child, at the child's tenth birthday (provided that the child had been well cared for and educated), and in cases of sickness, unemployment, or death. This decree also committed the federal, state, and municipal governments to subsidizing institutions that provided impoverished families and their children with food, shelter, education, and other services.[70]

Given that the funds necessary to implement these policies were woefully insufficient, the significance of Decree 3.200 remained largely symbolic. A far more effective incentive for lower-class couples to marry legally was the gradual introduction of government social security benefits beginning in the 1930s, since only legally married wives could qualify for widows' benefits.[71]

Indoctrinating Wives

▼   ▼   ▼

Reams of normative literature demanded superhuman sacrifices of women once they became wives. This literature reached urban women not only through glossy magazines but also through the working-class press, youth groups, Church groups, schools, and medical clinics. As external constraints on middle- and upper-class women's social participation crumbled and as alarm over working-class women's freedom increased, this literature reflected the perceived need to reinforce internalized ideological constraints. It mystified women's subordination in the home by constantly emphasizing the dignity, importance, and grave responsibilities of the role of wife. The impact of normative literature on women is difficult to measure, but we can assume that its popularity derived from its usefulness to readers in clarifying and solidifying views that they were gradually embracing on their own. For readers anxious about changing female roles, this literature must have provided some degree of reassurance, as well as practical advice on how to cope.

Normative literature attempted first to reconcile housewives to their assigned role—to demonstrate that the sole path to true happiness and personal fulfillment lay in the assiduous cultivation of the role of virtuous wife. Second, it instructed them how to fulfill better their mission of preserving familial and social stability, creating a productive workforce, and furthering domestic and national prosperity. If much of the literature disseminated modern hygienic norms, the rest of it was more backward- than forward-looking, holding up a mythic golden past as a standard and reinforcing old stereotypes of female nature. Thus the messages were often blatantly contradictory, reflecting conflicting interests in the modern social and economic system. Women were relegated the difficult task of mediating between the past and present as well as between rational public standards of behavior, performance, and rewards and almost religious domestic standards of devotion and self-sacrifice.

Although women's desires for self-fulfillment, emancipation, and achievement were applauded, normative literature insisted that these should be realized within the "appropriate sphere": through attending to their families' domestic needs. The overpowering message was that marriage represented the "true and complete blooming of female life"; that "the true emancipation" of women consisted of "the perfect comprehension of their sacred duties"; and that the highest achievement to which a woman could aspire was the building of a happy marriage and a stable family.[72] Women were encouraged to use their newly acquired independence to transform and solidify marriage efficiently, not to escape the institution.[73] But should they not find marriage to be sufficiently fulfilling and liberating, they were warned that it remained a moral imperative. The widespread use of religious metaphors to describe family life and the appearance of normative literature in the form of "Ten Commandments for Wives" communicated to women that neglect of their familial duties was not only socially reprehensible but sinful.[74] One author insisted: "[T]he role that God entrusts to the young woman who marries before an altar encompasses such great responsibilities, in time and in space, that the truly religious woman must feel sinful, must feel that she is neglecting the duties imposed by Christian society when she is absent from her children or when she allows her thoughts to stray from matters of the home, without there being an absolute necessity—OF LIFE OR DEATH—for this."[75]

Women's familial duties included—first and foremost—continually pleasing their husbands. By making this task their "principal preoccupation," articles assured wives that they would themselves become more "perfect," be capable of accomplishing "miracles," and be guaranteed marital happiness.[76] Pleasing a husband was, however, an arduous task. Above all, it required a wife to devote all her attention to her husband, demonstrating that she lived only for him. She was told to exercise her superior female tolerance, gentleness, and delicacy so as never to exasperate her husband, provoke disagreeable sensations or bad humor, or cross him, even in situations in which she suffered.[77] She was given this advice for day-to-day life: "Treat your husband like a precious friend: like a highly respected guest, and never like a female friend to whom you recount the small difficulties of life."[78] In the words of one priest, a wife was to "make a true cult of respect, friendship, fidelity, and tolerance for her husband."[79]

Never was she to take any action that could be interpreted as being competitive with her spouse or that might threaten his feelings of superiority. Women who were so presumptuous as to imitate male behavior or seek to conquer and rule by force were warned that they would suffer "bitterness" and risk embarking on a "glissade" into the "abyss."[80] Rather than seeking to be men's rivals or engaging them in "ridiculous battles," wives were advised to use subtle feminine strategies for silently guiding and ultimately achieving domination over their husbands. Their power was said to lie in the exploitation of moral authority: "A virtuous woman always knows how to impose herself."[81] Or, in other words, "[Women] are forces because they are women, because they act in the social sphere as female elements and not as crows with masculine peacock feathers."[82]

Moreover, every wife was instructed to study her husband carefully in order to be able to decipher his thoughts and his moods and to foresee and satisfy his every desire even without his having to ask.[83] She was to respect his personality and inclinations, pretend not to notice his faults, avoid dominating or censuring him, and learn to become interested in and find pleasure in the things that he liked.[84] It was incumbent on wives to ensure a "perfect unity of desires, thoughts, and aims: a fusion so intimate, a harmony so tender, that it brings forth in the spouses the same ideas and the same feelings."[85] In practice, this much-praised unity and harmony might require the "eclipsing" of a wife's personality and opinions by those of her husband: "At thirty, a woman knows how to eclipse herself, placing herself like a fine decoration in the scenery of the life of a man, and how to diminish her pride so as to love better."[86] But a wise and honest wife was supposed to be glad to allow herself to be absorbed by her husband. By following these instructions, she could "shine like a queen of the home, under the title of Wife."[87]

Success in pleasing a husband also required that a wife understand the "irresistible urgency" of developing a serene, even disposition and of maintaining constant good humor; in this way she could become the "perfectly balanced, smiling friend of her husband"—the "kind, smiling messenger of peace."[88] In a world in which increasing value was being placed on individual self-fulfillment, one author claimed that women had a "right" to happiness.[89] More commonly, the cultivation of happiness was declared to be a duty and moral obligation of wives to be pursued to the benefit, rather than the detriment, of marital stability. Society stood to reap enormous benefits from the positive effects that perpetually smiling and cheerful wives could have on the stability and smooth functioning of domestic life.

Prescriptions for how to achieve happiness abounded. They consisted almost entirely of recommendations for attitudinal changes, rather than structural changes in women's lives or in social organization. Authors insisted that the achievement of domestic happiness was easily within the reach of everyone; it required only will power, optimism, and faith.[90] Women were advised that to achieve happiness, they had to "want it with all the energy of their soul," dedicate themselves fully to pursuing it, "build it like a bird constructs a nest," and "protect it from the small daily vexations of life."[91] Authors frequently emphasized that the path to happiness lay in the cultivation of altruism.[92] The popular playwright Claudio de Souza warned women not to step out of their domestic roles or to renounce their innate feminine charms. Rather than seeking the chimera of independence and liberation, he advised that they resign themselves to the idea that complete happiness could only be realized "in the tender subjection to their love, in the sweet slavery of their affection."[93] According to many other authors, it was apparently sufficient for a wife to be zealous in ensuring her husband's happiness for her to find happiness too.[94] Readers of one article were asked to consider the following "truths":

> Is it, by chance, so difficult for a woman to be affectionate and sweet, and so in control of her own feelings that conjugal happiness is never upset on account of her?
>
> Shouldn't it please her to attend to the easy task of giving her domestic life all the charm and affection, and the serenity and benevolence of constant good humor?
>
> In the end, doesn't she have everything to gain from the point of view of personal happiness and of her own reputation, as well as from the point of view of filling her work within the family with calmness, joy, and love?[95]

Another article declared: "It is not possible to imagine a marriage in which only one of the spouses is happy."[96] Happiness, being defined as the product of women's serenity, nobleness, inner strength, and willing acceptance of her familial roles, acquired the prestige of an important virtue. If any wife was unhappy, it was in her best interest not to show it; unhappiness became synonymous with incompetence, deviance, and moral degeneration.

Above and beyond these requirements, wives were told that ignorance of, or negligence in, performing household chores was "always censurable." No longer was it considered acceptable to leave the administration of the house in the hands of servants; even if a housewife did no manual labor herself, it became her personal obligation to supervise and instruct her servants diligently. If the house was not always spotlessly clean and tidy, if the children were not always neatly dressed, if the clothes were not always well washed and pressed, if an appetizing dinner was not always awaiting her husband upon his return in the evening, she would be failing in her "essential duties" and would inevitably displease her husband.[97] He might even become discouraged and "feel nostalgic for bachelorhood."[98] Articles stressed that a wife could "never sacrifice herself enough" in her day-to-day struggle to achieve the maximum possible degree of regularity, order, and discipline within her domain: "Nothing can affect a husband worse than a house in disarray, even if he himself is untidy."[99] No details were considered too petty to merit the closest attention; wives were advised that "these small nothings are what are most important in life."[100] The perfect housewife was she who, while never tiring of working twelve-hour days as a labor of love, was capable of saying (and believing): "I live like a princess. It is my husband who works and supports me."[101] In short, article after article attempted to convince wives that winning their husbands' esteem and establishing "profound conjugal friendship" depended to a large extent on their skills as housekeepers. How, such articles asked, could a poor husband be expected to admire or to feel attached to a wife who demonstrated no interest or skills in the art of household management? If he was so unlucky as to marry a woman who was ignorant in these matters, who could blame him for becoming impatient or annoyed![102]

However, this was still not enough. Articles warned wives: "[I]t is *indispensable* that you always present yourselves gracious and elegant to your husbands, because it is necessary that they always find you ever more captivating." To forget that the "best way to please a husband" was to maintain an attractive appearance was said to be a "disastrous result of ignorance," a "capital fault," and the "worst error a woman could commit."[103] Wives were advised to mobilize all their talents in conserving and adapting their "arms of seduction" so as to "create continually new sources of charm, to awaken lost illusions, and to perpetually rekindle the ashes of extinct desires." In this "most terrible and uncertain struggle" and "most difficult mission," it was stressed: "Female defense has the peculiarity of being exercisable only in the attack."[104] Coquettishness began to be widely praised as an important new quality for married women. One author claimed that intelligent women were those who could use coquetry "like a dagger with two cutting edges and wield it marvelously": that is, to catch, seduce, and dominate a man without his being aware of the game.[105] Chronicles announced that it was no longer acceptable for wives to turn into taciturn, unkempt matrons upon marriage:

> When he fell in love with you, weren't you, by chance, happy, smiling, buzzing as a bee, and brilliant as a ray of sun? . . .
>
> This should continue for all of life; . . . the woman, rather than diminishing, should seek to enhance the elements of seduction that won her her husband's love. . . .
>
> It is women who make the Brazilian husband taciturn, walking to the monotonous rhythm of creaking wheels, bent over under his burden.[106]

Warnings followed that the penalty for noncompliance was abandonment, loneliness, and misery: "During the period of engagement and the first phase of marriage, you accustomed your husband to the profusion of your kisses and affection. Why now do you change your behavior? If you change your behavior, you will be punished with lack of love, with indifference, with the love of a rival, with the disorganization of your home, and at last, with unhappiness."[107]

A wife's powers of seduction were, however, to be used only to seduce her husband. The "vanity" of wanting to please everyone was still judged to be a "grave defect."[108] Prudence was advised above all; nothing else mattered if her virtue and honor were compromised. It was a wife's "duty . . . not to permit that these qualities be put in question." Therefore: "[A] woman ought not only be honest, but moreover demonstrate that she is."[109] In practice, this precluded the possibility of a married woman having male friends. Since male-female friendships were seen to be based inevitably on sexual attraction, and since there was enormous fear that they were no more than a prelude to adultery, any private meeting or any exchange of affectionate looks was considered highly suspect.[110] A woman was seen to be "heroic" to the extent to which she repressed the extramarital expression of her natural instincts and sexual passions.[111] In her relationship with her husband, a wife was advised to cover up any "weaknesses of the body" if she had had them and to deny that her life had a past or a history. She was to assure her husband that before meeting him, she was "pure of body and pure of mind," and convince him that it was he who "awoke in her formerly frozen body the first tremblings."[112]

Through all these ways, women were held accountable for continually rekindling the fires of conjugal love. Most important, their own love was never to fail. In face of threatening anarchist notions of free love, articles declared outright that the essential characteristic of conjugal love was its permanence. The literature tried to convince women of the futility of the search for greener pastures. It stressed that only in the first, innocent love was there true sincerity; it was possible to love truly only once in one's life; perfect happiness did not exist; married life was the best way to obtain the maximum possible happiness; and, the only true and profound love was that which was eternal.[113] Wives were warned that whereas other faults could be overlooked, she who failed in her love would never be forgiven.[114] Even if her husband were to betray her and lie to her, she was to pardon him, say nothing, and accept that "for men, one woman alone is not enough." Through patience and careful cultivation of the "art of love," she was advised that she could reconquer him and bring him back to her, "more loving than before."[115]

Men graciously offered women help in learning how to cultivate the "art of love." *Arte de amar* (Art of Loving), a small book of verses written for women, won widespread acclaim from male intellectuals and enjoyed enormous success in bookstore sales. Reviews proclaimed it a "classic," an "extraordinary poem of tears, of thoughts, and of love," and a great work rarely equaled in Brazil. They advised that no woman should fail to keep a copy by her bedside if she was serious about learning to preserve and cultivate the great love for which she longed.[116] But the strategies recommended for winning and keeping a man's love made a mockery of the idea that true adult love could be based on honest communication between equal individuals. Love was reduced to an "art" that one could acquire like manners, or a game whose rules and tactics could be mastered by reading a few verses. Success depended on manipulation, deception, petty lies, avoidance of honest communication, and the lack of any expectation of reciprocity. The long list of essential female qualities emphasized innocence, shyness, purity, modesty, delicacy, absolute virtue, fidelity, submission, and resignation. Finally, the book warned women not to expect too much, encouraged them to hide their tears in times of disillusionment, and insisted that they resign themselves to whatever fate befell them. In the same way that women were held responsible for the blossoming of conjugal love, they were also blamed for its failure. To complain about a fate they had brought upon themselves was declared illegitimate.

On a more practical plane, wives' duties included bolstering their husbands' careers by providing the necessary material infrastructure, emotional support, and moral example. By turning her home into a "soft nest of innocent pleasure and captivating well-being," by carefully "removing the stones from the path, clearing the way, and shouldering the innumerable miseries of ordinary life," by alleviating his fatigue and worries with "the charms of her soft and loving voice, the caresses of her white hands, her smile, her shining eyes, and the refreshment of her red lips," she would enable her husband to "develop as far as possible his energies and his strength, leaving him to devote his heart and his body to his work."[117]

Women were instructed on the special importance of providing the material

infrastructure necessary for intellectual production. Articles declared that scientists and scholars needed modest, hardworking wives who shunned notoriety
and devoted themselves entirely to creating a distraction-free environment in
which their husbands could concentrate fully on intellectual pursuits. Rather
than seeking personal glory, a true woman would prefer to contribute to her
husband's glory.[118] According to various authors, a woman who emotionally
supported and inspired a male scholar played an "infinitely superior role" to
the woman who was herself a scholar.[119] In the words of one author: "Many
people suffer in the home on account of the woman, but the wife of a scholar is
capable of making a whole city suffer, a race, a people, and at times, all of humanity. How many important works were interrupted by the egoistic caprices
of a young wife! How many vocations unrealized because of female vanity!"[120]
Not only did he assume that vanity was the sole prerogative of men, but he dismissed women's personal ambitions and intellectual capabilities as insignificant.

Finally, wives were encouraged to embrace the bourgeois values of economy,
efficiency, and hard work within the home. Their zeal in practicing "scientific
housework" was proclaimed essential for domestic and national prosperity.[121]
According to Antonio Austregésilo Lima, one of the gravest faults of Brazilian
women was their aversion to matters of economy. Whether a family was rich or
poor, he declared, it was a wife's most urgent duty to learn to respect hard-
earned money and to protect the family from economic hardship. In the case of
a husband's death, a wife was to be capable of assuming the position of "true
small stateswoman of the family," demonstrating her expertise in managing
matters of finance, commerce, and inheritance, so as to protect herself and her
children from exploitation and ruin.[122]

The day-to-day responsibility for helping the family to conserve capital also
fell to women in a myriad of small ways. Rather than "tormenting their husbands with constant pecuniary demands," wives were counseled to practice
good domestic administration through careful accounting, moderate spending,
and skillful stretching of the available funds. Those who spent more than their
husbands earned were severely reprimanded; a wife was to make do with whatever her husband was able to provide.[123]

Readers of the *Revista Feminina* learned of numerous specific ways in which
they could contribute to the family economy. The magazine's editors, lamenting that many women continued to leave the task of purchasing food to maids,
attempted to convince readers that "this humble but dignified role of buyer and
inspector of food products is in no way incompatible with the finest education
[or] with the highest culture."[124] They urged Brazilian housewives to follow
the excellent advice of Julia Heath, president of the U.S. National Organization of Housewives, who instructed women that their new "mission" as house-

wives was to "know how to spend like [their husbands] know how to earn." Heath went on to claim that learning about the quality and value of products so as to become efficient consumers was not only a great "responsibility" but was also to be considered a "true profession." [125]

In 1917, editors of the *Revista Feminina* recommended that "in this moment of acute crisis," women could "easily" augment their husbands' salaries "through [their] own painless work." [126] Short of taking paid employment, they could cultivate kitchen gardens, preserve vegetables and fruits when they were in season, raise chickens, keep bees, and make delicacies (such as marrons glacés) at home in order to provide their families with delicious and nourishing food at a fraction of the normal cost. Articles providing instructions for knitting sweaters, sewing basic items of clothing, and remodeling out-of-style dresses stressed the considerable savings that such enterprises would bring. Emphasis was also placed on the value of handicrafts; patterns for embroidery, needlepoint, and crochet, as well as suggestions for how to refinish old furniture, sew pillows and rugs, and decorate lamp shades, filled many pages of every issue of the *Revista Feminina*. To further aid readers, editors of the magazine established crafts courses. [127] They also opened an exhibition of female handicrafts in 1917 at which women could earn "pin money" by selling the fruits of their labor. [128]

Finally, wives were encouraged to regard any instruction they had received in literature, painting, or music as a capital asset to be carefully conserved and transmitted. Rather than overburdening the family budget with the high and unnecessary costs of private lessons for their children, mothers could themselves provide adequate instruction. [129]

In short, contradictory messages on what constituted a good marriage as well as the sheer weight of the demands placed on women must have made wifehood a difficult part to play. A wife had to learn to walk a very fine line, trying to satisfy the new requirements of bourgeois society while at the same time carefully upholding traditional values. She was supposed to embody both the traditional female virtues of innocence, sweetness, submission, and resignation and the antagonistic bourgeois virtues of competence, self-reliance, efficiency, responsibility, and initiative. It also became important for her to be simultaneously an expert household manager and a glamorous social partner. As the glamorous social partner, she had somehow to be sexually attractive to her husband without being immodest or aggressive or attracting the attention of other men. As the expert household manager, she was told to develop her competence and her strength; however, this did not mean that she should be independent or self-sufficient, and never should she outshine her husband. On the one hand, she was encouraged to build her marriage on the basis of reciprocity and greater equality; but on the other hand, she was never supposed to question the necessity of the sexual division of labor, confront her husband in any way, or cease to take pleasure in serving him. Nor did reciprocity mean that husband and wife would share the responsibility for making a marriage succeed; this task was still assigned to the woman. Although closer companionship and mutual understanding in marriage were celebrated as modern ideals, in practice women were still expected to make all the necessary adjustments and concessions. It was emphasized that only in marriage could women find true self-realization; but it was precisely in marriage that their personal needs and ambitions were subordinated. Despite these contradictions, women who expressed their frustration or anger about the discrepancy between the ideal and reality or about the impossibility of satisfying antagonistic demands risked social ostracism. In the end, marriage was assigned more importance than the individual well-being of women. Happy resignation was mandatory.[130]

Policing Families

▼ ▼ ▼

How were modern hygienic norms enforced? And what were the sanctions for disobedience? To buttress the effects of normative literature, public officials, in collaboration with liberal professionals, the Church, and the industrial bourgeoisie, devised means for restricting women's options as well as for enforcing new, narrower boundaries on husbands' autonomy. State intervention in the "private" matters of the family—considered to be the "cell" of the state—was justified on the following grounds: "[State intervention] consists of the establishment of a just equilibrium between public powers and family authority, for the purpose of avoiding possible abuses and perversions within the family, the weakening or rupturing of moral and blood ties which should indissolubly bond parents and children and which are the connections capable of maintaining the family cohesive, indestructible and united, equal to its destiny."[131] Among the "abuses and perversions" that the state sought to control legally were excessive (and inappropriate) female employment, divorce, abandonment of the home, adultery, and crimes of passion.

In face of a broad consensus that female employment outside the home posed a serious threat to female virtue, family health and stability, and public morality, the state passed protective legislation restricting women's workforce participation. Although unable to eliminate the need for poor women to earn wages, the state could attempt to bar women from "inappropriate" employment and in so doing meet the demands of male-dominated unions both to protect "their" daughters and wives and to reduce competition from women for "male" jobs. In addition, protective legislation conveniently helped to reconcile the contradictions between the state's commitment to defend the family and its interests in maintaining a large pool of cheap laborers.[132] Reinforcing the discriminatory effects of protective legislation was the 1916 Civil Code, which specified not only that married women needed their husbands' consent to accept paid employment, but also that such employment should "always [be] for the benefit and improvement of the family."[133] Concerning the issue of divorce, the state sided with the Church, agreeing that continued prohibition of divorce was necessary in order to guard against dissolution of the institution of the family.[134]

Three other legal measures were aimed primarily at controlling men's behavior in the interest of ensuring "domestic solidarity." First, Decree 17.943-A (of 12 October 1927) and later the 1940 Penal Code (Articles 244–47) imposed penal sanctions for the material and moral abandonment of the family. Cândido de Morais Leme explained:

> Civil sanctions proved themselves ineffective and weak in face of the avalanche of profound egoism and vulgar materialism that were threatening to demolish the very foundation of the institution of the family. . . . The desertion of a spouse and children by a head of family were burdening society with the problems of prostitution and child abandonment, debasing the social standard and elevating the rate of delinquency, misery, vagrancy, and beggary. It was necessary that the legislator seek to thwart the increasing perversion of the familial sphere.[135]

The new, much harsher penal sanctions could be imposed if, "without just cause" (which included lack of means), a husband (or occasionally a wife) failed to provide support (food, shelter, clothing, medical care) for a dependent spouse; a parent failed to provide support for a minor child (under eighteen) or for an adult child who was sick or unable to work, failed to protect a minor child from harm (physical and moral), or failed to provide a school-aged child with primary education; an adult child failed to provide support for a sick or invalid parent or grandparent.[136]

Second, the 1940 Penal Code eliminated the distinction in the definitions of and penalties for male and female adultery. Previously, married women could be imprisoned for one to three years for committing any sexual act outside marriage, whereas only married men who kept a concubine were subject to such punishment. According to the new code, a sexual act outside marriage constituted adultery for both husbands and wives, but the penalty was reduced to fifteen days to six months. Jurists generally considered that the benefits of criminalizing male adultery and equalizing the treatment of husbands and wives before the law outweighed the risk of reducing the penalty for female adultery.[137] In the opinion of Judge Nelson Hungria, penal law should rightly constitute an ethical and tutelary force, attacking deeply rooted prejudices that threatened social discipline. And since "a necessary condition for the success and security of the family is the exclusive and reciprocal sexual possession of spouses," punishment of (male as well as female) adultery was necessary to protect the family and thereby ensure social order.[138]

Third, public prosecutors took up one of the causes célèbres of the period— the campaign to end the social and legal toleration of crimes of passion. (This term refers to homicides resulting from conflicts related to love or sexual relations. In practice, the crime was generally a male crime, involving the killing of women—or their suitors, or both—by husbands, fiancés, lovers, or fathers and brothers.)[139] Rio de Janeiro's most prominent public prosecutors, along with the powerful Judge Nelson Hungria and many of Brazil's preeminent lawyers, criminologists, social hygienists, and specialists in legal medicine, agreed with female critics that the "epidemic" of massacres of women by jealous men represented an "abominable revival of ancient barbaric practices" and an alarming "retrogression of civilization."[140] They worried, as did editors of the progressive newspaper *A Esquerda*, that Rio de Janeiro was living through a period of "authentic savagery": "[A] burst of insanity [has been] unleashed upon the family of Rio, shattering homes, destroying unformed youths, orphaning children, and throwing whole households into unexpected defenselessness and senseless ruin."[141]

On 25 February 1925, four public prosecutors—Roberto Lyra, Carlos Sussekind de Mendonça, Caetano Pinto de Miranda Montenegro, and Lourenço de Mattos Borges—founded the Conselho Brasileiro de Hygiene Social (Brazilian Council on Social Hygiene) to work toward the following goals: to expose the true (antisocial) motivations behind crimes of passion; to reeducate society, thereby destroying the social conventions and popular beliefs that protected these criminals; to repudiate legal doctrines that excused these criminals; and to rigorously impose harsh sentences as a necessary means of collective intimidation.[142] By the early 1930s, they were proclaiming impressive success in sending wife killers to jail, and in 1940 they took credit for winning a revision of the Penal Code so that emotion or passion no longer excluded criminal responsibility.[143]

The primary concern of the prosecutors, who billed their campaign as a great "work of social hygiene," a "campaign of moral and social prophylaxis," and a "true regenerating crusade," was clearly to protect the reputation (and therefore stability) of the family as an essential social institution.[144] Although their success in repressing crimes of passion was in actuality far less than they claimed, the importance of their campaign lay in its attempt to legitimate modern, hygienic standards of sex and family life and to establish the state's right and duty to impose these standards, usurping husbands' power over their wives.[145] They established in principle that to "civilize" and "elevate" Brazilian society, it was not enough for reason and rationality to triumph in the public sphere; men's jealous rages and use of violence against women in the private sphere had to be curbed as well.

On a more mundane and daily basis, psychiatrists relegated the task of "civilizing" husbands to women. Antonio Austregésilo Lima declared that if wives would only renounce laziness, passivity, and resignation in favor of the diligent cultivation of their minds, bodies, and spirits, they might succeed in reforming bad husbands who had the "airs or tendencies of a sultan."[146] Women themselves sometimes agreed that armed with a good education, intelligence, skill, tact, seductiveness, and patience, they could perform miracles:

> A bad man, quarrelsome and without religion, is the most intolerable companion, turns the home . . . into a true inferno, and makes his wife a poor victim, often incapable of reacting or defending herself.
>
> But since "where there's a will there's a way," the woman can transform him and organize her home as a place where she is the queen instead of the wretched slave. . . .
>
> The woman educated in the sound principles of morality and religion will not allow herself to be crushed by the ill treatment of her husband, nor will she abandon him.
>
> Using her strong determination, she will know how to convert him into a friendly and kind companion, and will be able to mold him to her will.[147]

Women were also enlisted to exert their influence over men's public behavior. According to the common wisdom, men's efficacy as workers required that their wives' moral example and the attraction of domestic comforts be sufficient to lure them away from the temptation to squander time, energy, and their families' financial resources on other women, liquor, and gambling.[148] The value of domestic peace and order in fostering ethical business practices, compliant behavior among workers, and political moderation was considered to be equally important. Women were warned that crime, rebellions, strikes, and political struggles were often born in small domestic problems. Everywhere, articles celebrated the power of women's moral domination over men and encouraged women to strive to cause moral virtue to prevail over political power and economic interest.[149]

As the Church campaigned to reestablish its influence within civil society during the 1920s and 1930s, it sought above all to maintain ideological control over the family and more forcefully than ever demanded adherence to its conservative social doctrine. Through a multiplication of Church journals and institutions, including the Centro Dom Vital, Confederação Católica, Ação Universitária Católica, Instituto de Estudos Superiores, Associação de Bibliotecas Católicas, Círculos Operários, Juventude Opérária Católica, Confederação Nacional de Operários Católicas, Liga Eleitoral Católica, and others, the Church formulated and communicated its doctrine to a wide urban audience. Its presence in civil society was also promoted by industrialists, who often welcomed the establishment of Church groups and the celebration of Mass in their factories and who secretly funded the Círculos Operários during the late 1930s and 1940s.[150] Even the state went as far as possible to strengthen the Church's social influence while maintaining the formal separation of Church and state. The 1934 Constitution not only upheld the prohibition of divorce as the Church had insisted but also recognized religious marriage (in addition to civil marriage, which had been the sole legally recognized form of marriage since 1890) and granted the Church access to public schools and to institutions of "collective interest," such as public hospitals and prisons. Through all these channels, the Church affirmed its doctrine on the proper organization of the "Christian family": the importance of female purity and chastity; the necessity of marriage; the inadmissibility of divorce; the sanctioning of sex within marriage only and for procreation only; the prohibition of birth control, abortion, promiscuity, and adultery; and the celebration of female abnegation, resignation, and submission to husbands' authority.[151]

The proliferation of private assistance organizations, followed by the rise of the social work profession, provided another means of social control, perhaps for middle- and upper-class female charity and social workers as well as for the poor women and children who were their clients. Philanthropy—the offering of alms as a temporary palliative—was no longer considered adequate. Rather, the modern "technique of charity" sought to defend the family, protect the collective economic well-being, and uphold public order by remedying and preventing misery. Even the term *charity* was gradually discarded in favor of *social assistance*, reflecting a new consensus that duty and the public interest, not magnanimity, were the real issues.[152]

Beginning in the 1920s, Catholic lay organizations, including the Associação das Senhoras Brasileiras and the Liga das Senhoras Católicas, mobilized women of "good" families to embark on a systematic tutelage of poor women and children. By the late 1930s, various schools of social work had been established (primarily in the cities of Rio de Janeiro and São Paulo) to train a new corps of professional social workers. The great majority of these schools were founded by Catholic organizations (but often subsidized by public funds), as were the two first and most influential ones: the Centro de Estudos e Ação Social de São Paulo (1932) and the Escola de Serviço Social de São Paulo (1936). Slightly more than three hundred students had graduated from these schools by the late 1930s. In accordance with their Catholic education, the first generation of social workers thought of themselves as social apostles (more than rational technocrats) who, imbued with a missionary zeal for spreading the social doctrine of the Church, devoted themselves to "stimulat[ing] a love for the home in young women workers and prepar[ing] them to fulfill the duties of their mission." Through Catholic organizations such as the Círculos Operários, Centros Familiares, and Associação Lar Proletário, these social workers focused on educating and assisting poor women in an attempt to prevent the disorganization and collapse of their families. To this end, they provided courses on domestic economy, child rearing, and family morality for housewives; day care, schooling, and moral education for poor children (with the hope that the lessons taught would reach parents); house visits to resolve family problems and observe standards of cleanliness; and services such as legal, medical, and financial aid, help in finding employment, and assistance in marrying legally.[153]

If the social work profession in Brazil originated as an extension of the Church's social action programs, government agencies gradually became the largest employers of social workers, assigning them to investigate and monitor the living conditions of the urban poor as well as to help promulgate bourgeois standards of hygiene and morality. The state of São Paulo pioneered in enlisting the social work profession in the task of transforming the problems of poverty and exploitation into problems of education, morality, and emergency assistance. In 1935, it undertook to promote and rationalize social assistance organizations through the newly created Departamento de Assistência Social de Estado, charged with coordinating, supervising, and funding public and private social assistance initiatives. At a national level, the passage of social and labor legislation during the 1930s and 1940s and the establishment of the Estado Novo in 1937 opened up new needs and new positions for social workers in the expanding government bureaucracy. Social workers were employed in increasing numbers to coordinate public and private social assistance programs, to administer the state's social security systems, to aid families in need (especially mothers and children), to mediate disputes between government bureaucracies and workers, and eventually (through the schools run by SENAI, Serviço Nacional de Aprendizagem Industrial, established in 1942) to help train workers in personal hygiene and proper social behavior as well as technical skills. Gradually the first generation of social workers educated by the Church was replaced by a new generation educated in modern secular theories of pedagogy, social hygiene, mental hygiene, eugenics, and so on. But their assigned mission remained essentially the same: to create a competent, compliant workforce by promoting "proper" family organization, health, and morality.[154]

Two other institutions—insane asylums and model workers' villages—also attempted to define and enforce boundaries of proper behavior for both men and women. During the late nineteenth century to the early twentieth century, psychiatrists joined the struggle to help resolve the "social question" by founding asylums designed to protect society from "degenerates." In addition to housing the mentally incapacitated, these asylums removed from society—and unburdened families of—individuals who were unable or unwilling to submit to the discipline required in their daily lives as workers, family members, and citizens. In the latter cases, men tended to be interned for transgressing the norms of work (and thus failing in their role as breadwinner). They included overworked factory workers suffering from delusions of persecution, drunks or vagabonds incapable of holding steady employment, and "bohemian" men of good families who squandered inherited wealth and lived off others. Or, they were "sexual perverts," usually homosexuals, who were embarrassing to their families and threatening to a society that held up marriage as essential for personal and social well-being. Women tended to be interned for transgressing the norms of family life and sexual propriety. They included prostitutes; rebellious (runaway, immodest, or sexually active) adolescents; stubbornly independent (and often caustic) professional women who refused marriage and remained distant from their families; women who cross-dressed or revealed tendencies toward lesbianism; hysterical, profoundly depressed, or delirious wives; dysfunctional housewives and mothers; and frustrated and angry spinsters.

Once these men and women were interned, the hospital routines attempted to domesticate them into accepting their appropriate roles. Men were assigned outdoor physical labor; women were confined to interior spaces and required to sew, embroider, and perform other domestic work. Any inappropriate or uncooperative behavior—defined according to gender stereotypes—was interpreted as confirmation of the necessity of their confinement. Those patients who adapted to the hospital environment, repented their previous antisocial behavior, and were able and willing to conform to social expectations were released "cured." But given the utter lack of treatment that most patients received during the early decades of the century as well as the very high percentage who remained interned until death, the only credible motivation for their confinement lay in "civilizing" society and "moralizing" the family rather than in "curing" the "ill."[155]

Brazil's industrial bourgeoisie also shouldered some of the responsibility for turning working-class families into bastions of stability, effective in curbing antisocial behavior. During the first decades of the twentieth century, industrialists reacted to workers' protests with a combination of repression and paternalistic acts of charity and social assistance. But the most comprehensive strategy for attracting and keeping a stable, compliant workforce was to build workers' villages adjacent to large factories. In the numerous villages constructed by prosperous industrialists, workers were provided with modest individual family houses designed according to modern hygienic standards, which required separate spaces for the kitchen, living room, bathroom, parents' bedroom, and children's bedroom, as well as a small yard. Residents shared communal laundry facilities, day care, schools, a church, recreational facilities and social clubs, stores, restaurants, and a medical clinic and pharmacy. In exchange, however, families not only paid considerable rent but also sacrificed their freedom and endured constant invasions of their privacy. The bourgeois morality of the responsible breadwinning husband and the loyal and dedicated wife and mother (who in this case, however, also worked) was imposed through innumerable rules regulating daily behavior. For example, residents of the workers' villages were frequently subjected to a nightly curfew, prohibitions on alcohol consumption and gambling, restrictions on social interaction inside and outside the village (covering everything from courtship to political activities), and requirements to attend church and to send their children to the Church-run village schools. Through the individual family housing design of the workers' villages and the highly programmed social interactions within these closed communities, employers attempted to integrate workers into the family and the home (the temples of morality, stability, and order), far removed from the street and public places (where vice and sin supposedly prevailed). Here, they hoped, the evils of promiscuity and prostitution, gambling, drinking, wife beating, child abuse and neglect, uncleanliness, and political conflict would be overcome—replaced by the useful and pleasant attention to matters of the home and family.[156]

Finally, the male-dominated labor movement also helped impose dominant stereotypes of female nature on women of the working class. Agreeing with the state that women belonged at home, labor unions campaigned for protective legislation, which in effect helped protect men's privileged space in the labor market and devalorized women's workforce participation, ensuring that the latter's financial contributions to the family remained secondary to those of the breadwinning male head of household.[157] To the extent that women participated in labor unions, they were generally (with a few notable exceptions) assigned supportive roles in line with their domestic functions.[158] And working-class men, who considered it appropriate that they should speak in the name of "their" women, reiterated upper-class men's protests against the exploitation of fragile working-class women who were wrenched from their true vocation as housewives and mothers to work in factories. Or, they reported (but distorted) the often successful political actions of "disorganized, weak and defenseless" women workers.[159]

By the 1940s, heated public controversy over marriage and the family waned. Although conservative upholders of tradition continued their efforts to keep progressive reformers in check, urban modernizers had decisively triumphed over the rural oligarchy. In that process of power realignment, a new, more "modern" set of gender norms had emerged, and the state worked in collaboration with competing social sectors—including liberal professionals, employers, and the Church—to apply these norms in practice through schools, legislation, police surveillance, courts, social service agencies, health clinics, and asylums. Although membership in the middle and upper classes generally required conformity to bourgeois sexual and family morality, efforts to impose these norms on the working classes must certainly have achieved more limited success. But with social and political conflict contained by the authoritarian Estado Novo, the need to transform the family into a pillar of stability and order lost much of its urgency. If the body politic was no longer perceived to be gravely sick, the health of the "cells" that composed it was no longer of immediate public concern. It was not until the decades following the 1960s, when middle-class women began to enter the workforce in massive numbers and thus experienced the restrictions and contradictions of their roles with new dissatisfaction, that questions of marriage and the family reemerged as urgent social issues.[160]

UPDATING CHILD REARING

On 2 May 1932, large numbers of women crowded into the courthouse in São Paulo to witness the twelve-hour trial of Antonia de Araujo.[1] Antonia, a thirty-five-year-old housewife and mother of five children, enjoyed a reputation within respectable middle-class society for being endowed with exceptionally high ethical standards. She had always zealously attended to her domestic duties, and despite her occasional mild oscillations between happiness and sadness, she rarely became irritable. Her dedication to her children was considered to have been exemplary, and her affection was said to have been accompanied by scrupulous attention to giving her children a strict moral upbringing. In addition, she was very well read in German and Portuguese and had familiarized herself with didactic literature so as to be able to give her children the best possible education.

It was therefore particularly shocking when she shot and killed her favorite son, João. The incident occurred on 24 April 1931 at five o'clock in the afternoon. A few hours earlier, João had returned home from the São Paulo Athletic Club with his father after having been turned in to the police for stealing a hat. When he locked himself in the bathroom and refused to give any explanation for his behavior on that day or for his history of petty thefts, Antonia went to her neighbor Clara to borrow money to buy a gun. She returned home to question João once again, but he continued to refuse to respond. Antonia then drove to a store, where she bought a revolver and ammunition. On her return, she found João sleeping. She kissed him; he awoke irritated, turned away, and covered his head with the sheet so as to avoid facing his mother. Antonia then fetched the gun and fired at her son. But, upon seeing the blood, she threw herself on top of him and hugged and kissed him frantically. And before she could carry out her plan to kill herself as well, her husband and oldest son appeared. Based on Antonia's statements, psychiatrists produced the following account of what had happened after she learned of João's theft:

> [S]he became transfigured, perplexed, shaky, saying not a word, and not even crying, which was odd, since she habitually cried for much less serious reasons. She told us that during this interim, ideas of ruin concerning her son passed through her mind, ideas that were not expressed at that moment. Among them we cite the following: her son would be expelled from the athletic club, defamed, and his name stained; he would not be able to enter the Navy as he wished because his certificate of conduct would stand in his way; she had no doubt about the incorrigibility of her son, since she had intimate reasons to believe this. Moreover, when her husband left to return to work, she told him "that this would be the last time that he would go to the Police to ask for his son, and that he should leave the case for her to handle." . . . While still under the shock of what had happened, and believing the future of her son to be irremediable, she concluded after hasty reflection that it would be preferable to see him dead than to see him continue in the path of crime, and because of this, she would kill him and subsequently put an end to her own life.[2]

Perplexed, male critics of the period pondered over why a woman of Antonia's stature, who seemed to embody fully society's ideals of perfect motherhood, would reason in such a way. The only explanation they could imagine was that she suffered from excessive sentimentality.[3] The psychiatrists who examined her offered no further clues. They reported that although she was repelled by the idea of killing and could never repeat such an act, she continued to believe that her dead son "enjoyed repose, removed from the sad path that he would have followed." Apart from this one lapse in her critical senses, they detected no psychological abnormalities. During her confinement in the state psychiatric prison, she conducted herself in a model fashion and demonstrated a high sense of morality.[4]

When examined as a case of social pathology, Antonia's actions reveal the psychological tensions created by the rising demands placed on mothers.[5] Until the last half of the nineteenth century, the lives of elite women had not been so circumscribed by responsibility for child rearing. With the patriarch at the center of the family, children existed at the margins. Although loved, they were nursed and nurtured by black slaves, subject to stern discipline and absolute patriarchal authority, and regarded as incomplete adults until adolescence, when they were ushered precociously into adulthood with the inheritance (and thus status) required to follow in their parents' footsteps. But urbanization and industrialization changed both the position of children within the family and the significance of childhood. The change occurred first within elite families, in which children gradually became the center of family attention, the guarantors of family well-being, and the most precious resource of the nation.[6] By the turn of the century, concern for child welfare broadened to include children of the working classes. As the smokestacks of new factories rose and white-collar jobs multiplied, the demand increased for a healthy, skilled, and well-disciplined modern labor force. As class conflict intensified and urban life brought a "degeneration of customs," the moral education of future generations assumed unprecedented importance.[7] In the eyes of Brazil's modernizing elite, children were no longer merely children; they were "human capital" necessary to "perpetuate and glorify our Fatherland."[8]

Thus parents (particularly mothers) were assigned new responsibility for the proper education and socialization of children.[9] Among the urban middle and upper classes—especially the professional classes—a child's disobedience or deviance was no longer explained and accepted as fate, as God's will, as the work of the devil, or sometimes as heredity. As they gradually secularized thought and promoted modern notions of pedagogy, urban professionals identified education as the primary determinant of a person's character (and, by extension, of his or her success).[10] In the words of Cândido de Morais Leme, a legal advocate for orphans for the state of São Paulo:

> It is proven, then, what high responsibility falls on the family in the moral formation of an individual, and how much dedication, sacrifice, and love ought to wrap the heart of parents so that they may fulfill this quasi divine mission. Quasi divine, we repeat, because God delivers into their hands ignorant and weak creatures, with a great many impulses and tendencies that must be guided and dominated. . . . It is incumbent on [parents] to polish, with skill, patience, and tenacity, the rough diamond that every person carries within his soul, in order to transform him into a valuable gem. The greater is the effort, the perseverance, and even the sacrifice of parents, the more dazzling and radiant will be the brilliance of the rough stone that they were entrusted. But, the greater is the negligence, the carelessness, and the criminal inertia on their part, the more coarse and insignificant this diamond will be. By the work displayed in this area are the capacity and the worth of parents measured.[11]

Antonia shared the assumption that it was possible—by using all the resources with which she as a well-educated, morally upright, and devoted mother was supposedly endowed—to direct her children in the path of honorable conduct, and she had dedicated her life to fulfilling this task. Once she became convinced of her impotence to control João's petty thievery, she suffered intolerable frustration and shame. So inseparable was her ego from her son's behavior that it became impossible for her to maintain her self-esteem and pride in the face of his wrongdoings. In contrast to a mother of a few generations earlier who would have regarded unacceptable behavior on the part of a son or daughter as a trial she had to endure, Antonia regarded João's crime as a direct reflection on her competence and character—as a testimony of her failure. The humiliation proved too great for her to bear.

This chapter argues that the enshrining of modern "scientific" motherhood as women's "natural" biological destiny and urgent social mission fundamentally shaped the emerging gender system. The overwhelming consensus that women's first responsibility was to give birth and to raise healthy, productive, and morally upright children constrained women's sexual behavior, defined their social relationship to their husbands, prescribed appropriate character traits and feelings, and limited the professional and social roles available to them (for both objective and subjective reasons). Even if the new ideal of motherhood was impossible to realize in practice, it provided the most powerful underpinning for the consolidation of the model of the bourgeois family and the continued sexual division of labor.

Mobilizing to Protect Children
▼ ▼ ▼

Few urban women could have remained untouched by the growing crusade to transform them into better mothers and to promote sound physical, moral, and intellectual development of their children. This crusade united strange bedfellows. The medical profession occupied center stage in defining the "rules" of modern "scientific" child rearing, in convincing mothers of all social classes of the urgency of absolute obedience to these "rules," and in promoting private and public initiatives to protect mothers and children. The state agreed that solving the "social question" and guaranteeing the wealth and progress of the nation required its active intervention to protect children and mothers. Public and private assistance organizations providing material aid, health care, vocational education, and moral instruction to poor and abandoned children multiplied during the early twentieth century. Labor unions campaigned energetically to curb the exploitation of women's and children's labor. Individual families, seeking to ensure the economic and social security of their children, dedicated increasing resources over longer periods of time to educating them.

And women themselves—both initiators and objects of the crusade—devoted ever increasing attention, time, and energy to child rearing.

Physicians, ever more convinced of the urgent need to "think socially," redirected their attention from the well-being of elite families toward families of more modest means and toward the formulation of public policy. At the end of the nineteenth century, Dr. Moncorvo Filho, pioneer in the field of infant hygiene, led the growing outcry against excessive infant mortality in Brazil, which he blamed on the ignorance and superstitions of mothers, on the precarious conditions in which the poor lived, and on factors of heredity. To help stem the "hecatomb of children," he founded the Instituto de Protecção e Assistencia á Infancia do Rio de Janeiro, which opened in 1899 with the endorsement of seven hundred politicians, journalists, physicians, engineers, lawyers, businessmen, and philanthropists. In addition to providing material assistance and medical care, the institute undertook to teach poor mothers elementary notions of child hygiene, to foster the establishment of new institutions dedicated to sheltering pregnant women and poor children, and to lobby for new legislation to protect mothers and children.[12]

By the 1910s to 1920s, the growing strength of the eugenics movement, both within the medical community and within society at large, elevated mother and child welfare to a new priority status. Proponents of eugenics proclaimed that cultivating this new "science of the moral and physical perfection of the human species" was the fundamental prerequisite for guaranteeing social harmony and political health.[13] At the same time, the continuing professionalization of medicine heightened the authority and power of doctors to intervene in all matters related to mothers and children, whether they were within the private sphere of the family or within the public sphere of politics. The founding of a host of new professional organizations during the 1910s and 1920s—including the Sociedade Eugenica de São Paulo, the Sociedade Brasileira de Pediatria, the Sociedade Scientifica Protectora da Infancia, and the Departamento da Criança no Brasil—further increased the political clout of doctors. Through sponsoring a new spurt of research, publications, and congresses, these organizations brought issues related to child welfare to the public attention and established doctors as the uncontested experts in the field. The First Brazilian Congress on the Protection of Infancy was held in 1922. Like other congresses on related issues of eugenics, hygiene, and public health, it focused on problems of social assistance, legislation, pedagogy, and sociology as much as it did on scientific or strictly medical matters.[14] By the late 1930s to 1940s, physicians and hygienists had secured decisive positions in the state apparatus, drafting legislation concerning the welfare of mothers and children, conducting sanitary inspections of schools and public institutions, defining normal-school curricula on hygiene and child development, and setting standards for the new corps of state-employed social workers to attempt to implement in practice.

Women, warned that they must no longer rely on "charlatans" (midwives and healers), increasingly deferred to male doctors, the new "experts" on child-birth and infant care. Poor women who began to use the newly opened clinics and public hospitals became prime targets for doctors' attempts to popularize modern "scientific" principles of health and hygiene. For example, at the Dispensario Moncorvo, Dr. Moncorvo herded them into classes on hygiene as early as 1901 and gave away thousands of free pamphlets containing the "rules" of proper child care. He also invented the concept of the "Concurso de Robustez," a baby beauty contest in which a jury of physicians awarded a monetary prize to the poor woman whose infant was the most perfect example of health and vigor.[15]

By the late 1910s to 1920s, the boom in the publishing industry offered unprecedented opportunities for doctors, educators, and hygienists to flood middle-class homes with articles on correct child rearing. The earliest magazine specifically dedicated to teaching women modern notions of child care, *A Mãe de Familia*, was published from 1879 to 1888, when, according to Dr. Moncorvo Filho, "few people perceived the utility of such information."[16] Three decades later, the growing popularity of new glossy women's magazines and of manuals on child care indicated the interest that women were in fact taking in the information. Reinforcing messages from these sources was melodramatic advertising by multinational pharmaceutical companies—both in the press and in public buses—lauding the miraculous results of modern drugs and the catastrophic consequences of nonuse.

From the late nineteenth century, pressure mounted for the state to assume responsibility for promoting the physical, moral, and intellectual development of all children. "[W]hat will we become," asked Federal Senator Lopes Trovão in 1896, "if the tolerance of the government continues, cold, indifferent, and apathetic in the face of the perverse environment which compromises our children's physical health and spiritual well-being?" He concluded with a strong case for greater state involvement: "We have a fatherland to build, a nation to establish, a people to mold . . . and in undertaking this task, what ingredient is more malleable and more easily influenced than children?"[17]

During the 1890s, the expansion of free public elementary education became a priority, and the state made its first attempts to regulate the employment of children in industry. Decree 1.313 of 1891 prohibited the employment of children under the age of twelve (except in the textile sector, where children eight years old could be hired), prohibited their nocturnal labor, and limited their

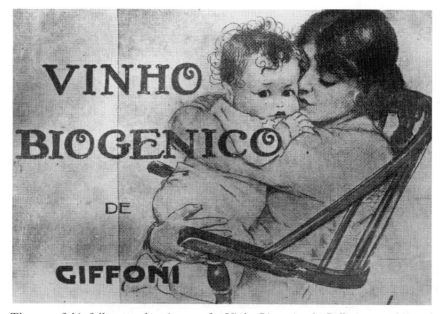

The text of this full-page advertisement for Vinho Biogenico de Giffoni warned "gentle readers and young loving mothers" that the beauty and strength of their infants depended on their own physical health and their ability to transmit this health through breast feeding. It went on to recommend that, to acquire the necessary strength, all new mothers take the fortificant Vinho Biogenico, the most "efficient" and "long-lasting" on the market. Readers were warned that failure to do so could result in sickness that would silence the happy laughter of their infants and introduce sadness and worry into their homes. Such admonitions abounded in the prolific advertising of the period. (From RF *12 : 139 [December 1925])*

workday to seven nonconsecutive hours. But these restrictions were observed mainly in the breach, as indicated by protests in the working-class press, the platforms of striking workers, and the succession of laws during the late 1910s and 1920s reiterating the same restrictions on child labor. The 1919 Código Sanitário raised the minimum age of employment for minors to fourteen, which was upheld by the 1927 Código de Menores. Restrictions on female labor and provisions for maternity leaves also began to be introduced in various sanitary codes during the 1920s, but it was not until 1932 that definitive laws regulating female and child labor were passed (Decrees 21.417-A and 22.042). According to Decree 21.417-A, mandatory maternity leaves for four weeks preceding and four weeks following childbirth were to be compensated with half pay, and the right to employment following the leave was guaranteed. Employers were required not only to give nursing mothers two half-hour breaks daily until their infant reached six months, but also to establish on-site day-care facilities in plants employing more than thirty women. Decree 22.042 again prohibited the employment of minors under the age of fourteen in industry and required as a condition of employment that employers obtain legal proof of age, authorization of the minor's legal guardian, a medical certificate of physical and mental health, and proof of literacy. In the case of absolute economic necessity of his or her family, an illiterate minor could be employed, but only if the employer provided primary education. The restrictions on child labor included prohibitions on nocturnal labor (with some exceptions for minors over sixteen years), the lifting of heavy objects, and employment in dangerous and unhealthy sectors.[18]

The 1934 Constitution extended in principle the state's responsibility for child welfare by mandating that the federal, state, and municipal governments protect mothers and children (including illegitimate children), assist families with numerous children, shelter children against exploitation and abandonment, curb infant mortality, and promote social hygiene, mental hygiene, and eugenic education.[19] Both the 1937 Constitution and the mandate of the National Commission for the Protection of the Family, created in 1939, reaffirmed the above principles. But it was not until 1941 that Decree 3.200 introduced incentives for bearing children and assistance for families with numerous children. According to this decree, preference was supposed to be given to applicants with the most children in hiring for civil servant jobs, and once hired, these employees were to receive a monthly bonus for each child. In addition, families with more than one child were granted reduced school tuitions and fees. To receive these benefits, however, families were required to present proof yearly that they had "provided their children not only physical and intellectual but also moral education, according to the parents' religious orientation, and appropriate for their social position, as their circumstances permitted." In contrast, single and widowed adults over the age of twenty-five who were childless were assessed an additional 15 percent income tax, and childless married adults were assessed an additional 10 percent.[20] In practice, these principles and laws remained largely ineffective and unimplemented. But if they failed to solve the "social question," they nevertheless reflected the new social consensus that child welfare was an urgent public concern and that the state had the right and responsibility to monitor how families raised their children.

The initiatives undertaken by public and private assistance organizations specifically to protect and educate mothers and children are far too numerous to list. They included the establishment of orphanages, day-care centers, reformatories, dispensaries and clinics, vocational schools, girl- and boy-scout troops, and lobbying organizations. Although their focus varied, their goals were mutually reinforcing: to provide shelter and a substitute family for abandoned children, to supply material assistance and medical treatment to children of needy families, to give poor children a solid vocational education, and, equally important, to provide religious, moral, and civic instruction aimed at turning children into responsible and productive citizens.[21] The urgency with which growing numbers of society women, health professionals, teachers, social workers, and others undertook the task of educating poor mothers and protecting poor children reflected not only a humanitarian concern for the welfare of these individuals but also the perceived need to prevent future generations from becoming pernicious elements in society. Stated negatively, the crusade sought to redeem the nation from "moral degeneration" and "political anarchy." Stated positively, it looked to provide the basis for future grandeur of the nation.

Among the central demands of labor unions were curbs on the exploitation of female and child labor. Using popular stereotypes, they warned that exposing fragile women to heavy physical labor, unsanitary environments, and morally compromising situations would prejudice their reproductive capacity. Similarly, subjecting highly impressionable and vulnerable children to the deplorable working conditions in factories would lead to their physical degeneracy and moral corruption. The interest of male-dominated unions in securing protective legislation dovetailed with the interests of those at the top of the social scale to tie working-class mothers more closely to their familial responsibilities. While respectable working-class men wanted their wives at home, policy makers sought to direct working-class women's energies toward building stable nuclear families and domesticating the "antisocial tendencies" of their husbands and children.[22]

In the rapidly growing urban environment, in which children no longer followed automatically in their parents' footsteps, families had little choice but to shoulder the arduous and lengthy task of carefully preparing their offspring to succeed in the increasingly competitive marketplace. A solid education became far more important in ensuring a child's future well-being than an inheritance. Only by assiduously instilling in their children the new bourgeois values and by providing them with adequate professional or vocational training could a family equip a child to become a good spouse and parent, a competent worker or professional, and a model citizen.

Finally, women themselves looked to child rearing for a sense of purpose and dignity in a society in which the value of their household labor had declined and in which their workforce participation was not only effectively restricted to the least prestigious sectors but was still generally frowned upon, at least as a long-term option. In fact, the deafening social consensus that child welfare was among the most critical issues facing the nation heightened women's power and prestige within the family and opened new opportunities for them to assume public roles related to the health and education of children. In the estimation of Brazil's feminist organization, the Federação Brasileira pelo Progresso Feminino (Brazilian Federation for the Advancement of Women), promoting and honoring the role of expert housewife and mother was an important means of increasing women's social power. The organization thus campaigned simultaneously for Mother's Day and for female suffrage, both of which were established in 1932.[23] As long as women had few (and very uncertain) channels for achieving acclaim and therefore few sources of self-esteem outside their success as mothers, it was logical for them to embrace this role uncritically, despite its often ambiguous rewards. Besides, in light of the overwhelming consensus that the fate of Brazilian "civilization" lay in the laps of mothers, and in the face of the bombardment of information on modern standards of child rearing, only the most deviant women could have afforded to ignore totally the mandate to devote increasing time and attention to their children.

Defining Modern "Scientific" Motherhood

▼ ▼ ▼

Although the emphasis of advice to women varied somewhat according to class, with lower-class mothers given more instruction in the rudimentary principles of health and hygiene and middle-class mothers given more instruction in the moral and professional training of children, the messages were remarkably consistent. First, motherhood was proclaimed both a natural, biological calling and a "quasi divine," God-given mission that fulfilled and ennobled women. Second, mothering was elevated to the status of a modern scientific profession: a worthy occupation for the most ambitious modern woman and a challenging undertaking for the best of female minds. Third, it was declared that mothers held the key to solving modern social problems through the correct moral orientation of their children. Fourth, women were charged with primary responsibility for inculcating the values and skills that would make their children successful and productive members of bourgeois society.

Everywhere, motherhood was celebrated as the crowning achievement and tangible demonstration of a woman's femaleness. Even more than in wifehood, it was considered appropriate that a woman's identity and vocation merge in motherhood. From self-proclaimed feminists, to physicians, to labor leaders, to representatives of the state, all concurred with the notion that "[a woman's] ultimate purpose in life will not be achieved as long as she does not fulfill her sweetest and most sublime mission, which is maternity."[24]

Science "proved" that maternity was a biological necessity for women: "Of all the callings that [a woman] could pursue, none is more urgent than is motherhood, because it is the most natural, constituting a sort of compulsory or forced vocation that biology granted to her, and that entails parallel and corresponding duties in the social biology."[25]

If this was insufficient justification for women to devote themselves to motherhood, the role was also held up as the surest path to self-fulfillment. Women who may have been disappointed by marriage were told: "Your life is not made for [conjugal] love that is never satisfied, but for a serious, sincere, and great [maternal] love."[26] Women who may have been tempted by worldly pleasures or professional achievement were advised that motherhood brought higher rewards: "Life loses the monotony of identical and repeated experiences and acquires different charms, always new and varied. No longer do you seek diversions with such eagerness. You now have something to engross your mind: the honest and legitimate preoccupations of the home."[27] Last and most important, women were promised that motherhood provided the ultimate stamp of moral goodness: "[M]otherhood is sacred; it purifies any sin, it adorns the most troubled face with serenity; it is absolution, redemption, the quintessence of any spiritual and corporal perfection."[28] In short, upon fulfilling this "quasi divine" mission, a woman could rest assured that "her function is . . . defined: she is queen, queen of the home."[29]

Motherhood, however, was not only declared to be women's "primordial mission."[30] It was also newly adorned with the aura of a modern scientific profession based on highly developed skills and specialized knowledge. No longer was it considered sufficient for women to be well intentioned, "full of heroism and love," and naturally endowed with a maternal instinct (female qualities that were taken for granted). Physicians and educators influenced by the eugenics movement insisted that women needed a rational, "scientific" understanding of childhood development and modern principles of hygiene if they were to fulfill their new patriotic duty and social function of "perfecting" the race.[31] Mothers were told that they had an urgent responsibility to stop the "day-to-day degeneration" and the "decline in health and beauty of the human race" by observing basic principles of good nutrition and hygiene. High infant mortality, physicians declared, was not to be regarded as "God's will": "[D]eath is not a fate but an accident due to the carelessness of parents."[32] Lamenting the low intellectual level of Brazilian women, they claimed that ignorance resulted in a "terrible hecatomb of children" who died "stupidly" and needlessly.[33]

Physicians thus set themselves up as women's closest collaborators. In a speech delivered to the First Brazilian Congress for the Protection of Infancy in 1922, Dr. Antonio E. Gouveia stressed the importance of the cooperation of professionals in educating women in modern scientific principles: "We must teach the Brazilian woman the new philosophy of civic duty: give her an elevated and useful education so that she can intelligently carry out the sacred mission with which the talented—protectors of the fatherland—are charged. How can the Brazilian woman be elevated to the position of Priestess of Eugenics if she, in general, . . . has not even heard of this social science that is primary among the sciences concerned with the future evolution of our race?"[34] A year later, Antonio Austregésilo Lima echoed the call for cooperation between mothers and professional health workers: "You are, dearest mothers, the social tree that ought to bear good fruits, and we physicians, hygienists, and adherents of eugenics ought to attend to the tilling of the soil and the conservation of the happy and noble plant, because social agriculture is the science of the future, and the fecund tree, which is the woman, ought to be the symbol of our force and our glory."[35] The "duty" of women who loved their children and sought the acclaim and glory of having produced healthy, successful offspring was to observe religiously and implement scrupulously the "rules" of hygiene and scientific child rearing set by physicians.[36]

Advice to women abounded, and minimum standards soared as children were portrayed as extremely fragile, vulnerable, and impressionable beings whose very survival could be jeopardized by the slightest error. The flood of new technical books on pregnancy, childbirth, and infant care subjected every minute aspect of children's lives to intense scrutiny.[37] Women's magazines such as the *Revista Feminina* regularly included articles giving detailed instructions on proper nutrition, hygiene, and clothing for children, as well as on diagnosis and treatment of common illnesses. It was thought that a good mother should be a good nurse.[38] Various authors even went so far as to outline strict schedules for how children should spend their day, specifying exactly when they should get up and go to bed, when and how often they should take baths, and when they should attend school, play, and eat.[39]

In addition, a new literature of sexual hygiene undertook the task of teaching mothers "correct" notions of sexuality. Among the topics addressed were menstruation, sexual intercourse, conception, prenatal care, and childbirth. Such literature informed women of scientific principles of heredity, warned of the potential dangers to offspring of alcoholism and venereal disease, and insisted that masturbation had disastrous effects on the physical and emotional health of children.[40] Furthermore, it advised mothers of their urgent duty to pass on this knowledge to their daughters, who presumably would themselves become mothers.

Alarm over rising social conflict and the supposed degeneration of customs in the modern urban environment led critics to urge women to be more vigilant in the moral education of their children. Time and time again, articles addressed to women stressed that the predominant responsibility for the well-being of the society, for the "future of the species," and for the "destiny of the fatherland" rested in the hands of mothers.[41] According to the common wisdom of the times: "Society is no more than the prolongation of the home; the nation accurately reflects the intimate life of families."[42] And the mainstay of the family—its "strength, . . . sentry, advance spy, and guardian angel"—was declared to be the mother.[43] If modern generations were dishonest, corrupt, frivolous, incompetent, and irresponsible, the blame was placed—often exclusively—on mothers who had not been sufficiently zealous and intelligent in providing their children with a solid education.[44]

Responsible mothers were thus charged with setting themselves up as a dike against conflict and disorder by waging a "silent battle" and "daily struggle" against their children's bad instincts and against the destructive influences of modern society.[45]

Women . . . should constitute the magnetic pole of inhibition against the chaotic life of Brazilians in the injudicious battles of our democracy.[46]

It is incumbent on women to curb excesses, condemn abuses, and correct the errors of modernity.[47]

Enormous faith was placed in the power of mothers. It was said that "[t]he influence of a mother over her child is absolute"; or, in other words, "[A child] will be that which we [mothers] want him to be. We will mold his spirit as a sculptor molds clay . . . , giving it the form we desire."[48] The source of this absolute power of influence was supposedly education: "Education in social life is much, almost everything. . . . To educate is to conquer impulses, errors of character, primitive and savage tendencies; it is to purify morality and the soul."[49] Vigilant mothers who succeeded in creating "perfect homes" were assured that their efforts were decisive in resolving social problems and guaranteeing national progress, for it was from these "perfect homes"—"sacred temples" and "friendly asylums" from the immoral, cruel, and corrupt world—that "perfect people" supposedly came and that civilization supposedly sprang.[50]

Beyond protecting their children's physical health and diligently overseeing their children's moral education, mothers were charged with inculcating bourgeois values and skills. By fostering the development of conscience, free will, responsibility, discipline, and initiative, they would be raising their children for the collective good rather than to satisfy their own egos.[51] Their children, in turn, rather than becoming "egoistic parasites of society," would become responsible patriots who cooperated in working toward the achievement of national economic prosperity and broad social goals.[52]

Old techniques of socialization were scorned. Brazilian women were widely admonished for their excessive sentimentality and for the overindulgence of their children.[53] Frequent pardoning of children's faults was said to weaken their health and debilitate their characters: "[I]t causes the virtuous plant of social good to die, and allows tufts of weeds to germinate, such as deceit, laziness, cowardice, character faults that later form the definitive personality of man."[54] In contrast, modern notions of pedagogy celebrated rationality, efficiency, utility, and realism. New emphasis was placed on the value of firm discipline for building character strength and courage, for instilling notions of justice and truth, and for teaching respect for authority.[55] Mothers were told that those who would triumph in modern society were citizens whose minds dominated their hearts and whose wills conquered their passions.[56] Children were therefore to be instructed in "healthy" principles of religious belief that built confidence in human reason and action, rather than those principles that encouraged submissiveness, fatalism, and lack of individual initiative.[57] Correct socialization further required that children gain a true appreciation of the importance and necessity of economy, as well as a clear understanding that fulfilling one's duty and working hard were the best guarantees of economic security and emotional well-being.[58]

Children were also to be given "realistic" expectations and hopes for life.[59] In the education of boys, it was considered most important for mothers to foster the qualities of energy, initiative, and independence over timidity, inertia, and resignation. Rather than constantly sheltering them from potential dangers, mothers were instructed to encourage their sons to enter into the "rough struggle of life" so that they might acquire the skills necessary to become professionally successful adults, competent to earn a good living.[60] It was also the task of mothers to build their sons' "manly courage" so that they would not hesitate to stand up and bear arms to defend their native soil.[61] If mothers could not themselves serve as role models for their sons, they could—by demonstrating "respect and admiration" for their husbands—encourage their sons to look up to their fathers as models of strength and power.[62] At the same time, however, mothers were warned that they should prevent their sons from becoming arrogant, despotic, and crude men who would be tyrannical husbands.[63] This feat was to be accomplished by always maintaining firm discipline and by refusing to allow their sons to see them as humiliated, weak, inferior, and submissive beings.[64]

Whereas a mother was to raise her sons to become responsible breadwinners, she was to prepare her daughters to carry out their "difficult, delicate, and transcendental mission of wife and mother, educator of [their] children."[65] Typical of statements of the period was the following: "To educate a woman is to solve the problem of education itself, because it is to form a mother with all the qualities necessary to fulfill the essential function which is her destiny."[66] Above all, girls needed to acquire the qualities of modesty, dignity, and virtue if they were to win respect and the social position and economic security that a good marriage brought. While encouraging sons' ambitions, mothers were to channel daughters' ambitions within narrow boundaries. For daughters to become useful and happy housewives, satisfied with the "delicious pleasure" of fulfilling their domestic duties, they needed to be brought up with "realistic" expectations. In the face of the growing emphasis on female education, some critics feared that girls were cultivating unrealistic hopes and an "exaggerated romanticism" that could give rise to "fantasies impossible to satisfy."[67] One article instructed mothers: "Restrain young women from devouring books, unless they be those that teach lessons of moderation, for excessive reading brings no benefit, but rather serves to give fodder to a curiosity that can turn dangerous."[68] The "danger" was that the inevitable disillusionment of a daughter's hopes and ambitions would bring pessimism, melancholy, and hypochondria, transforming the cheerful adolescent into a morbid adult described by one author as a "nightmare of the home."[69]

Authors encouraged mothers to talk to their daughters frequently and with the utmost seriousness about a woman's obligation to marry and raise children. Not a day or even an hour was to pass without teaching daughters their "multiple and complex" duties and helping them to develop the will power to conquer their own natures. By learning the "cult of doing one's duty" from an early age, girls would effortlessly "substitute duty for pleasure" and would willingly accept that their "noble and sacred" role required great personal sacrifice.[70] "Almost from the cradle," a daughter was to learn to be "docile, patient, and selfless," to defer to others, to care for the sick, to think always of her brothers before herself, to be undemanding and uncomplaining, and to regard her familial duties and obligations as "sacred." Under no circumstance was a responsible mother to allow her daughter to become a "haughty princess" or an idle, frivolous, or "vain ornament" of society. Instead, girls were to spend their time "usefully" engaged in mastering the "thousands of chores that a housewife should not ignore, such as cooking, cleaning, sewing, ironing, starching, etc."[71] Parenthetically, modern women were told that they should also provide their daughters with skills to earn an honest living. But this was regarded primarily as a means to protect them from having to enter into undesirable marriages or, alternatively, from falling into prostitution.[72]

The elevation of motherhood to a highly skilled profession of overwhelming social importance helped rationalize the assignment of even the most talented and highly educated women to the home. Middle- and upper-class women were urged to embrace the grave responsibility of raising their children themselves, rather than delegating the task to wet nurses, nannies, or maids—"ignorant women" whose influence would be "highly prejudicial" to the formation of their children's minds and characters.[73] The ideal image of the modern mother—a strong, intelligent, and indefatigable guardian of her children's physical, moral, and intellectual development—set new standards. For a mother to succeed as the primary educator and role model of her children, she needed above all "to have a consciousness of the grandeur of her mission, and consequently . . . to have an education, physical, moral, and intellectual development, authority, responsibility, and liberty, and full awareness and full enjoyment of her human rights."[74]

One author declared it to be undeniable that "maternity is noble to the degree to which it entails an understanding of its methods and its goals."[75] Thus *competent* mothering—not just mothering—was necessary for a woman to prove her social worth and moral virtue. In short, the normative literature of the period verified another author's claim: "The entire society expects something very great from the loving intelligence of mothers."[76]

Strategies and Accommodations

▼ ▼ ▼

Although social pressure and the unavailability of reliable contraception made it difficult for women to avoid motherhood, they could and did choose to bear fewer children than their mothers and grandmothers had borne. It was widely acknowledged that women in the urban middle and upper classes were practicing birth control. The authors who commented on this new "social infection" (or Malthusianism, as it was sometimes called) unanimously condemned rich and healthy couples who used contraception in order to limit their offspring to one or two or to avoid parenthood altogether. According to these authors, egoistic modern women increasingly shunned the task of raising large families because it was considered unfashionable (and even ridiculed in high society), it encroached on the time and money they could spend in the enjoyment of worldly pleasures, and it compromised their beauty, youth, and elegance.[77] Denunciations of abortion also grew stronger as physicians in expensive health clinics began to join midwives and healers in helping women defy legal prohibitions.[78] Dr. Fernando Magalhães (whose efforts in favor of motherhood included the establishment of an association called Pró-Madre in 1918) led an aggressive campaign for stricter penal legislation to curb this crime before Brazil took the "rapid path toward depopulation."[79] And spokesmen for the Catholic Church reiterated the religious doctrines that proclaimed all contraception as well as abortion to be a "grave sin."[80]

In practice, however, the new urban style of life and the high standards of child rearing made it impractical for women to continue to raise large families. If a mother was to attend to her children herself with little outside help, and if she was to provide all of them with the enormous amounts of attention and care that was thought necessary for their healthy physical, emotional, and intellectual development, she needed to limit their numbers. The increasing economic costs of raising and educating children also made it difficult for many middle-class families to provide adequately for large numbers of offspring. And finally, women could not both raise large families and also satisfy the new expectations that they remain attractive, available, and interesting to their husbands.

These changing social and economic circumstances provoked heated debate within the medical profession over birth control. Physicians, while continuing to propound the view that sexual intercourse not aimed at procreation damaged the physical and psychological health of both men and women, were forced to recognize the reality and modern necessity of birth control within marriage.[81] Gradually, the notion of "responsible maternity" gained acceptance. Progressive physicians no longer considered it to be in the best interest of society to demand of women maximum fecundity to the detriment of both their physical health and the economic well-being of their families.[82]

Declining fertility was especially marked in urban centers, where the economic and social pressures of modern society most strongly affected family life and where women enjoyed greater opportunities to participate in social and professional life. The 1940 census shows that in the city of Rio de Janeiro, the cohort of women born between 1881 and 1890, who would themselves have begun to bear children by the early 1900s, bore an average of 4.1 children each during their lifetime, whereas women who were thirty years older had borne an average of 4.9 children each. Fertility rates for younger urban generations dropped precipitously in relation to fertility rates for Brazil as a whole. In 1940, women under forty in the cities of Rio de Janeiro and São Paulo had given birth to about 40 percent fewer children than women of their age in the nation as a whole. Most interestingly, in the cohort of women who reached childbearing age just after São Paulo had surpassed Rio de Janeiro as Brazil's leading industrial center (women in their early to mid-thirties in 1940, who would have begun to bear children by the mid-1920s), fertility rates for São Paulo fell below those for Rio de Janeiro (see table 3).

Declining fertility reflected urban women's postponement of childbirth

Table 3. Cumulative Averages of Female Fertility by Age, 1940

Age/Birth Year	Average Number of Children Born Live per 100 Women		
	Rio de Janeiro (City)	São Paulo (City)	Brazil
15–19 (b. 1921–25)	9.1	6.0	12.2
20–24 (b. 1916–20)	67.2	56.3	103.0
25–29 (b. 1911–15)	146.8	136.6	245.3
30–34 (b. 1906–10)	221.0	219.7	385.1
35–39 (b. 1901–5)	286.3	305.2	508.8
40–44 (b. 1896–1900)	338.4	388.3	587.2
45–49 (b. 1891–95)	384.8	466.1	638.7
50–59 (b. 1881–90)	412.3	535.2	640.2
60–69 (b. 1871–80)	462.6	596.9	647.6
70–79 (b. 1861–70)	476.9	590.3	642.0[a]
80+ (b. 1860 or before)	490.6	596.2	623.9

Source: Mortara, "A fecundidade feminina," 55.

[a] Women over 70 years old in 1940 (born in 1870 or before) may in some cases have underreported the number of children they bore, which would explain why, in the statistics for Brazil as a whole, cumulative averages of fertility fall for these age groups, as compared to the average for women aged 60 to 69.

(which reflected their postponement of marriage) and their practice of birth control more than their rejection of motherhood per se. Whereas 46.3 percent of all Brazilian women between the ages of twenty and twenty-four in 1940 had given birth to a child, only 34.9 percent of women in this age group in the cities of Rio de Janeiro and São Paulo were mothers. In the thirty to thirty-nine age group, the gap narrowed: 72.3 percent of women in the two cities had given birth to a child, compared with 81.1 percent of women in the country as a whole (see table 4). But of the women aged thirty to thirty-nine who had given birth, those in the cities of Rio de Janeiro and São Paulo had had an average of only 3.6 children each, compared with the 5.5 average number of children borne by women in Brazil (see table 5).

Within urban centers, levels of fertility were significantly lower in wealthy neighborhoods than in poor neighborhoods. For example, 1940 fertility indices for Rio de Janeiro indicate that not only was the percentage of adults who were parents much lower in wealthy neighborhoods than in poor neighborhoods (44.9 percent, compared with 57.7 percent), but among those who were parents,

Table 4. Percentage of Fertile Women by Age, 1940

| Age/Birth Year | Percentage of Women Who Bore Live Children | | |
	Rio de Janeiro (City)	São Paulo (City)	Brazil
15−19 (b. 1921−25)	6.6	4.3	8.7
20−24 (b. 1916−20)	36.2	33.5	46.3
25−29 (b. 1911−15)	57.9	59.9	70.3
30−34 (b. 1906−10)	67.6	72.0	79.0
35−39 (b. 1901−5)	71.8	77.8	83.2
40−44 (b. 1896−1900)	73.5	80.7	83.9
45−49 (b. 1891−95)	75.0	83.3	85.1
50−59 (b. 1881−90)	75.7	85.4	84.2
60−69 (b. 1871−80)	77.1	88.3	84.1
70−79 (b. 1861−70)	77.1	89.1	83.6
80+ (b. 1860 or before)	75.1	87.9	81.9

Source: Mortara, "A fecundidade feminina," 57.

Table 5. Cumulative Averages of Female Prolificacy by Age, 1940

| Age/Birth Year | Average Number of Children Born Live per 100 Fertile Women | | |
	Rio de Janeiro (City)	São Paulo (City)	Brazil
15−19 (b. 1921−25)	138.5	137.4	140.6
20−24 (b. 1916−20)	185.5	167.8	222.7
25−29 (b. 1911−15)	253.5	227.9	349.1
30−34 (b. 1906−10)	326.9	305.1	487.3
35−39 (b. 1901−5)	398.6	392.3	611.5
40−44 (b. 1896−1900)	460.4	480.9	700.3
45−49 (b. 1891−95)	512.9	559.3	750.2
50−59 (b. 1881−90)	544.5	627.0	760.2
60−69 (b. 1871−80)	599.8	676.1	770.4
70−79 (b. 1861−70)	618.2	662.6	768.2
80+ (b. 1860 or before)	653.0	647.9	761.9

Source: Mortara, "A fecundidade feminina," 59.

Table 6. Indices of Fertility for Rio de Janeiro (City) in Wealthy versus Poor Administrative Districts, 1940

	District IV (Wealthy)	District VII (Poor)
Live births per 100:		
women aged 12+	142	237
men aged 20–79	138	231
Percentage of parents:		
women aged 12+	43.6	56.8
men aged 20–79	46.1	58.5
Live births per 100 parents:		
women aged 12+	325	418
men aged 20–79	299	395

Source: Mortara, "Brazilian Birth Rate," 494.

the levels of fertility of residents of wealthy neighborhoods were much lower than those of residents of poor neighborhoods (312 live births per 100 parents, compared with 406.5 live births per 100 parents; see table 6).

In light of the rising standards of what was required to transform infants into healthy, well-adjusted, and productive adults, the burdens of motherhood were not reduced by the fewer number of children that urban women bore. On the contrary, unrealistic expectations that mothers were capable of and responsible for producing "perfect" children greatly increased the pressure on women, as well as the frustration and guilt of those who did not succeed. One might expect that this pressure, along with the physical and professional restrictions that motherhood imposed on women's lives, would have provoked serious questioning and critical evaluation of the role. Clearly, not everyone found serenity, fulfillment, and true happiness in the sacrifices demanded of mothers. Worse, those who failed to mature into interesting, attractive, and competent adult women while attempting to fulfill the role of self-sacrificing mother were derogatively dismissed in Brazilian slang as "*cricri*" women—referring to extremely boring and tiresome persons, usually women who were obsessed with children (*crianças*) and housework (that performed by maids, or *criadas*).[83]

However, the taboos around questioning the sanctity and naturalness of motherhood remained so strong that even radical intellectuals remained silent or joined in exalting the role. Maria Lacerda de Moura—who suffered sterility, adopted two children (who remained strangely absent from her life and her thought), eventually repudiated marriage and the stultifying routine of house-wifery, and found a sense of purpose and a means of economic support in teaching and writing—went the furthest in attempting to redefine the role of motherhood in women's lives. She believed that motherhood should be volun-tary; she advocated the bearing and rearing of children outside the legal and re-ligious bonds of marriage; she denied that motherhood was a profession; and she insisted that motherhood should not interfere with the intellectual life of women.[84] Nevertheless, she continued to celebrate motherhood as women's mission and to accept the identification of femininity with motherly qualities.[85] She even condemned women who shunned physiological maternity unless they had chosen to apply their motherly instincts and qualities to solving pressing social problems. The latter endeavor—"spiritual maternity"—was, in her opinion, even more noble and dignified than the former.[86] Moreover, she pro-posed no alternative social structures to help women raise their children. Nowhere in her writings did she suggest that fathers should participate in child rearing or that this should be a social responsibility rather than the personal obligation of individual women. According to her view: "When all women know how to be mothers, humanity will be redeemed by maternal love."[87]

The mythology and romanticism surrounding motherhood flourished pre-cisely because any questioning of the sacredness of this role was extremely threatening to the vast majority of women who had no effective means to avoid motherhood altogether (except celibacy) and few attractive alternatives but to seek their identity and sense of purpose from motherhood. Even Maria La-cerda de Moura, who clearly came to loathe the daily routine of mothering in practice, fully embraced the role in theory. Demonstrating her "spiritual" motherliness became a central preoccupation in her life, presumably to prove to herself and others that she had not repudiated her femininity.[88]

If the celebration of women's motherly qualities and the emphasis on the so-cial significance of mothering served the interests of progressive women in the short run, it also undermined their long-term goals. The battles that feminists fought to secure greater professional opportunities and political power were furthered by the argument that society would be morally regenerated through the extension of women's motherly influence to the public sphere. But at the same time, this argument precluded any fundamental redefinition of women's social role. Motherhood forcefully and narrowly prescribed the boundaries of female character traits and appropriate social action in the minds of women themselves as well as for the society at large.

5

EDUCATING WITHOUT EMANCIPATING

In an age in which education was seen as all powerful—as the basis for prosperity, morality, health, social order, and international power—women's education (as well as men's) was accepted as an essential prerequisite for Brazil's national well-being.[1] Thus, from being a luxury enjoyed by a small elite during the nineteenth century, female education became, by the early twentieth century, a practical necessity both for urban women and for Brazil's rapidly urbanizing and industrializing society. As industry attempted to rationalize production, it demanded a workforce that was both better trained and morally and mentally disciplined through a modern "rational" and "scientific" education. And women themselves, who had predominated in the textile industry since its origins in the late nineteenth century, responded to the heightened demand for skilled employees in the expanding service sector. Not only did they enter in record numbers into traditional fields such as schoolteaching and nursing, but they took advantage of new opportunities offered by expanding commercial enterprises and government agencies, which were beginning to recognize the advantages of recruiting women workers. Employers not only lauded the efficiency of their female typists, receptionists, saleswomen, telephone operators, clerks, and so on, but they were also pleased to take advantage of the fact that women earned much lower salaries than did men with the same qualifications.

In short, virtually everyone—from the business and professional communities, to government officials, to feminists—agreed that female education was essential for fostering Brazil's "evolution" and "progress." But this consensus was based not only—or even principally—on the growing importance of women in the paid labor force. Brazil's intellectual community, profoundly influenced by the eugenic movement, considered that female education was essential for improving women's health and preparing them to meet the escalating requirements of expert mothering and efficient management of their homes. Only women with adequate intellectual, professional, physical, civic, moral, and domestic education were thought capable of fulfilling their "sublime mission" of protecting the health, nourishing the minds, and forming the characters of future citizens.

Within the urban middle classes, families began to regard female education (at least as far as secondary school) as essential for preparing daughters to cope with the new economic contingencies of life.[2] As the expansion of the urban economy gradually removed production from the home to the marketplace, families needed cash to purchase goods and services that female household members had traditionally provided. Growing pressure to consume strained family budgets, and high rates of inflation eroded families' monetary resources.[3] These new economic realities were reflected in the training of girls. In an age in which women (even of well-to-do families) could no longer rely on their relatives (or even husbands) for lifelong economic support, their education not only prepared them for marriage and motherhood but also provided them with basic skills necessary to earn a decent living in the event of economic need.

But if new social and economic conditions favored the expansion of female education, traditional cultural values weighed heavily in shaping the content of educational curricula. Leading eugenicist Renato Kehl insisted that for women, "to be educated does not mean . . . to be emancipated."[4] And in practice, schools that trained girls to function in the marketplace socialized them to accept women's domestic roles as "natural" and necessary. The social significance of women's education was thus limited by expectations—shared by both men and women—that women would continue to be the bastions of social order and the guardians of traditional social and gender relations. As long as women (including female educators) continued to regard their education as preparatory for marriage and motherhood, its function as a socializing force was more significant than its role as a liberating force.

Educational Access

▼ ▼ ▼

Pioneering Brazilian feminists raised the issue of female education during the second half of the nineteenth century. These feminists, most of whom were urban middle-class women (who through conviction or economic need, or both, pursued professional careers to support themselves and sometimes other family members), demanded the "intellectual emancipation" of women on numerous grounds. They considered equal educational opportunities to be not only a matter of justice but a practical necessity for fostering Brazil's "progress." On the cultivation of women's intelligence, they argued, depended the economic prosperity of the nation as well as the proper education of future generations. In short, how could Brazil hope to compete within the community of modern "civilized" nations without the enlightened collaboration of its female population?[5]

At the same time, new scientific and philosophical theories that rejected old beliefs about women's intellectual inferiority were gradually winning adherents among the rising urban professional classes. Positivists such as Raimundo Teixeira Mendes, while arguing that the proper place of women was in the home, believed that women were by nature morally superior to men—more altruistic, more devoted. Because of these qualities and because they possessed a more synthetic than analytical intelligence (being more emotional and sentimental than cerebral and rational), women needed a separate and different education than that given to men, but an education that was nevertheless "as complete as possible." Only then could women fulfill their mission as the "tutelary Angel[s]" of the country, prepared to join effectively the cause of regenerating society.[6]

The more progressive Tobias Barreto Menses, a jurist and proponent of German materialist philosophy, believed not only that women could and should be educated but that they should receive an education equal to that of men, since they possessed "the same natural aptitudes for higher studies" and had already proved their capacity in medicine and scientific research. In a speech delivered to the Pernambuco state legislature in 1879, he declared that the failure to admit women's equal capacity was an "unpardonable sin against the 'sacred spirit' of progress," and the failure to cultivate the intellectual development of women gave rise to "the great part, if not the greatest part, of our ills."[7] A decade later, physician Tito Lívio de Castro, in his medical school thesis, constructed an elaborate scientific argument designed to prove that women's retarded intellectual development was the result of social and cultural rather than physiological factors. He concluded that rigorous female education to raise women to men's level was the fundamental prerequisite for the evolution of the human species. To objections that this would threaten family stability, he replied: "If women's education, if their mental progress dissolves the family, [then] the first concern of a people striving to become civilized ought to be to extinguish the family—

to educate women. If the family is based on ignorance and slavery, it is incompatible with evolution. Either family or civilization."[8]

Nevertheless, nineteenth-century female education remained precarious and rudimentary. Although a federal law passed in 1827 provided for the establishment of free primary schools for girls, there were not enough qualified female teachers available to staff more than a few dozen girls' schools (even considering the watered-down curriculum outlined for girls' schools), and it was considered inappropriate for men to instruct girls.[9] As late as 1872, the census recorded only 18 women in the city of São Paulo and 313 in Rio de Janeiro working as primary and secondary school teachers.[10] Not until after 1879, when coeducation was legally mandated in public primary schools, and until the 1880s, when coeducational normal schools were definitively and widely established to train primary and secondary school teachers, did female primary education began to expand significantly.[11]

Apart from the normal schools, girls could obtain academic secondary education only in private schools (most of which were run by religious orders) or from private tutors, options that were frequently unappealing or unaffordable in addition to being inadequate.[12] Brazil's most prestigious secondary school, the Colégio Dom Pedro II in Rio de Janeiro (and the only one that granted a diploma automatically qualifying graduates to enter institutions of higher learning), did not become coeducational until 1922. Thus, despite the fact that the country's institutions of higher learning were opened to women in 1879, only a handful of women were able to obtain the academic preparation necessary to pass the entrance examinations.[13]

At the end of the nineteenth century, most women, even in Brazil's major urban centers, were illiterate (see table 7). And those who had learned to read and write were generally encouraged by parents, schools, and the Church to perfect their domestic and artistic skills rather than to develop their minds. In 1881, educator Félix Ferreira told a group of girls enrolled in the newly opened classes for women at the School of Manual Arts and Trades that they should not strive to become doctors, intellectuals, or freethinkers. Instead, he reminded them that they, as women, were "destined to provide happiness to a man" and should seek above all to acquire "the knowledge necessary to be able to run a household well."[14]

Nor were girls of wealthier families encouraged to pursue serious studies or to excel academically. Normal-school students learned needlecraft along with basic sciences, and those who went on to become teachers were expected to begin preparing girls for wifehood and motherhood during the earliest stages of primary school.[15] Daughters of wealthy families who were tutored privately

Table 7. Literacy Rates in Brazil, 1872–1940

	% of Literates among Total Male Population			% of Literates among Total Female Population		
	Brazil	São Paulo (City)	Rio de Janeiro (City)	Brazil	São Paulo (City)	Rio de Janeiro (City)
1872	19.8	32.1	41.2	11.5	17.1	29.3
1890	19.1	35.2	57.9	10.4	22.1	43.8
1920	28.9	64.3	66.5	19.9	52.1	55.8
1940	42.3	76.3	72.9	34.1	67.5	65.6

Sources: Brazil, Diretoria Geral de Estatística, *Recenseamento . . . 1872*, 21:1–2; Brazil, Diretoria Geral de Estatística, *Recenseamento . . . 1920*, vol. 4, pt. 4a, pp. xii–xiii, xvi, xxvi–xxxvii; Brazil, Comissão Censitária Nacional, *Recenseamento geral do Brasil . . . 1940*, série regional, pt. 16, pp. 4, 16; pt. 17, tomo 2, p. 472; and série nacional, tomo 2, p. 28.

generally received an even more superficial education, as described by pioneer feminist and schoolteacher Nisia Floresta:

> [The upper-class girl] is sent to learn to dance, not for the physical benefits that result from exercise, but for the pleasure of making her shine in public; to read and write Portuguese well is not a matter of great interest; [it is more important that she learn] to speak a bit of French and English, [even] without the slightest understanding of the literature of these languages; to sing and play the piano [even if it is] often without pleasure, style, or understanding; [to acquire] simple notions of design, geography, and history which she will abandon with her books upon leaving school; [to produce] a few pieces of tapestry, embroidery, and crochet that may be placed among the luxurious objects in her parents' parlors in order to bring forth frivolous praises of their creator.[16]

By the end of the nineteenth century, however, increasingly large numbers of urban middle-class women began to seek education as a means to guarantee their economic security as well as their social status. In response, the state of São Paulo took the lead in the early 1890s in reforming primary and normal-school education (to be followed later by other states). Two women assumed leadership roles under the direction of Antônio Caetano de Campos: Maria Guilhermina Loureiro de Andrade, who had studied in the United States, and the well-known North American educator Marcia Browne. Together, they helped introduce North American pedagogical techniques to Brazil. By 1894, the São Paulo Normal School was installed in a large modern building adjacent to a model school where students practiced teaching. The course of study was improved and extended from two to four years, and new normal schools began to open throughout the state.[17] The results were dramatic. Between 1893 and 1920, the number of female primary and secondary school teachers in São Paulo increased nearly sixteenfold (from 210 to 3,333); in Rio de Janeiro (between 1890 and 1920) their numbers increased nearly eightfold (from 790 to 5,979). At the same time, women came to dominate the profession heavily, making up 75.1 percent of all schoolteachers in São Paulo by 1920 and 81.2 percent in Rio de Janeiro.[18]

Still, women benefited from the expansion of educational facilities only gradually.[19] The school census conducted in São Paulo (state) in 1930 revealed that 46.5 percent of all primary school students were girls. However, although girls were entering secondary and vocational schools in far greater numbers than they had previously, they continued to be greatly outnumbered by boys, constituting only 38.5 percent of all secondary students. Moreover, girls were very heavily concentrated in teacher preparation courses and in commercial schools, where they were trained as stenographers and typists. The duality of Brazil's school system—in which primary, normal, and vocational education was disconnected from university and university-preparatory secondary education—functioned to preserve gender as well as class hierarchies. By the end of the 1920s, women still had made very little headway in entering institutions of higher learning except in the fields of pharmacy and dentistry, which were the least prestigious of the medical professions (see table 8).

Finally, after 1930, women began to make more rapid and significant gains in secondary and higher education. Reforms and expansion of secondary education, together with the founding of Brazil's first Faculty of Philosophy, Sciences, and Letters at the University of São Paulo in 1934, increased women's opportunities to obtain higher education. Yet even though Brazil's 1940 census recorded that 48.1 percent of the secondary school degree holders were women, these numbers hide the continuing inequality between girls' and boys' education. More than one-third (33.5 percent) of all Brazilian women who had received secondary school degrees had received their degrees in teaching, leaving university-preparatory education still heavily dominated by men. At the university level, only 9.0 percent of the degree holders were women. And although Brazil boasted increasing numbers of women trained as physicians, lawyers, and scientists, 59.2 percent of all women who had earned advanced

Table 8. School Enrollment in São Paulo (State), 1930

Type of Course	Enrollment	
	Men	Women
Preprimary and primary	244,483	210,780
Complementary	559	1,938
Secondary[a]	21,530	6,309
Vocational		
Ecclesiastic training	535	—
Pedagogy, teaching	691	7,010
Arts	178	1,584
Technical training[b]	11,827	6,912
Agronomy	138	—
Seamanship	83	—
Obstetrics	—	43
University		
Law	822	4
Medicine	284	11
Veterinary medicine	25	—
Polytechnic arts	447	7
Pharmacology, dentistry	1,516	536
Philosophy, literature	45	—

Source: São Paulo (State), Diretoria Geral do Ensino, Secção de Estatística e Arquivo, *Estatística escolar de 1930*, xvii.

[a] Includes students of ordinary secondary schools and commercial schools.

[b] Includes students enrolled in typing and stenography courses.

degrees had done so in the three fields of dentistry, pharmacy, and music (see table 9).

Educational Content
▼ ▼ ▼

The potentially radical effects of the expansion of female education were dulled by the content of the education that most girls actually received. As educators and government officials elaborated and instituted educational policies,

Table 9. Educational Degree Holders in Brazil, 1940

Type of Course or Diploma	Secondary		Advanced	
	Men	Women	Men	Women
General education	24,369	12,508	—	—
Teaching, cultural, or professional instruction				
Agriculture	771	91	3,652	47
Veterinary medicine	—	—	1,250	34
Domestic arts	240	1,730	—	—
Industrial or technical	2,072	234	—	—
Transportation services	2,226	46	649	49
Industrial chemistry	—	—	1,558	125
Polytechnic arts	—	—	13,912	96
Commerce	46,018	8,885	—	—
Economics	—	—	1,735	158
Law	—	—	20,145	482
Sanitary services and social assistance	1,419	3,728	42	89
Pharmacology	—	—	8,242	1,841
Dentistry	—	—	10,817	1,225
Medicine	—	—	18,042	543
Physical education	216	57	249	87
Pedagogy, teaching	4,874	57,871	1,665	305
Fine arts	480	137	581	187
Drama	35	29	—	—
Music	231	1,248	456	2,648
Ecclesiastic training	182	17	4,598	86
Military training	684	—	5,098	—
Administration	785	115	72	12
Supplementary instruction	147	87	—	—
Corrective instruction	46	4	—	—
Other (poorly defined or unspecified)	101,319	85,803	4,047	1,636
Total:	186,096	172,590	96,846	9,650

Source: Brazil, Comissão Censitária Nacional, *Recenseamento geral do Brazil . . . 1940*, série nacional, tomo 2, pp. 32–33.

it became clear that the purpose of "modern" female education was not only to provide instruction that would allow women to function as workers and citizens in the modern bourgeois society but, perhaps even more important, to prepare women for marriage and motherhood. M. F. Pinto Pereira explained:

> We understand that half of the task [of education] naturally falls upon the woman; . . . that her judicious instruction and proper education—being the guarantee of individual perfection and of the physical and moral strength of her children—accelerate the speed of national progress; that the problem of present day Brazil is to orient her rationally in the great work of our evolution; that without diverting her away from her normal function—her principal function—and without encouraging her to follow the extremes of feminism, we ought to educate her with great care so that she will be an intelligent and healthy mother of competent and enlightened men; that her principal education consists in the clear understanding of her principal mission [of motherhood].[20]

Educators justified this emphasis by claiming that women's intellectual capabilities—even if "equal"—were "different" from men's. Hence, according to Afrânio Peixoto, it was important to tailor education to the "respective aptitudes" of the sexes, thereby achieving "instead of absurd competition of the sexes, mutual assistance . . . in production and social benefits."

> Sciences developed in laboratories require mental syntheses for which you [women] are not inclined; but in addition to having a propensity for collaborating in indispensable and decisive experiments and observations, you can lend your cooperation in the task of teaching and applying [these principles]. . . . Women have little aptitude as prophets, philosophers, or great poets; [but] no one disseminates better the purity of the faith, the perfection of customs, [or] the charm of life [than do women] in their works of piety, in philanthropy, and in the comfortable beauty of their homes.[21]

These perceived differences in abilities and social destinies did not, however, preclude coeducation. In fact, rather than being regarded principally as an economic necessity (as it had been when introduced in public primary schools in 1879), coeducation came to be considered as a positive good. Peixoto claimed that coeducation was a "vital educational necessity" in order to ensure that boys and girls would develop harmonious relationships, full of "purity of thought and action." Educated together, they would come to understand and respect each other; and through practicing appropriate sports together, they would acquire "proper manners" instead of "precocious maliciousness." He argued further that coeducation would help bring about "cultural equality" (which did not, however, mean identity) between the sexes, thereby encouraging more and happier (and therefore more stable) marriages.[22] Although single-sex schools remained very common (especially among Catholic schools), leading educators and feminists agreed that coeducation was preferable, with the stipulation, however, that it should provide girls and boys with an education "in accordance with their natural aptitudes."[23]

Schools attempted to give girls a "practical" education aimed at training them first and foremost for domestic and family life and second for earning a living (in an appropriate occupation) if and when it became necessary. Maria Kiehl, researcher for the Ministry of Labor, argued that this kind of education was equally relevant for working-class girls as for middle- and upper-class girls, given that "the woman is naturally inclined toward marriage and motherhood" whether or not necessity forced her to accept paid employment.[24] The teaching of abstract intellectual principles was considered not only irrelevant to most women's lives but also threatening in its potential to "masculinize" women and divert them from their domestic roles.[25] Thus the inadequacies of the rudimentary instruction that most girls received in language, literature, history, mathematics, and sciences attracted less attention than the failings of the educational system to provide instruction in domestic science, child care, and suitable vocational skills accompanied by strict moral education.[26] Schoolteacher and feminist activist Branca de Canto e Mello agreed with São Paulo Council of Education member Aprígio Gonzaga that it was the task of public schools to prepare girls to fulfill the "mission that God gave them"—"to be mothers and housewives." In the opinion of both these educators: "Educating herself, the woman acquires the necessary character traits to arm her spirit and to continually improve herself; to elevate herself so as to understand her high social function [and] her responsibilities in the important problems of educating her children and running her household."[27]

Both in school and at home, women were encouraged to read; but some critics still believed that it was prejudicial for women to "devour" books, since this might lead them to aspire to unsuitable goals.[28] Increased attention was paid to providing women with books that taught morally sound lessons and presented models of admirable women. The *Revista Feminina* offered its readers two collections of books guaranteed to be "instructive, moral, and of high artistic value." Apart from a few children's books and several plays and books of poetry, the collections consisted of romantic novels.[29] In 1927, a survey of the reading habits of the eighty-six female students enrolled in the final year at the São Paulo Normal School found that the young women read little else but romantic novels. The author of the survey concluded that women read these books not only because they were attracted to stories of love and marriage but

Schoolgirls at the Colégio Nossa Senhora de Sion in São Paulo, posing for a picture in 1921. (From "Colégio Nossa Senhora de Sion," RF 8:81 [February 1921])

also because romantic novels were the cheapest and most readily available books on the market.[30]

The numerous schools run by religious orders for both rich and poor girls placed an especially heavy emphasis on moral and domestic education. At the elitist Colégio Nossa Senhora de Sion, girls of the "best" families were educated in the "healthiest principles of morality and religion, saving them from bad influences and preventing the perverse infection [of modern customs] from touching them." While learning sciences, languages, and domestic arts from the nuns, students were said to quickly "lose the roughness of their character, if they had any, and acquire a noble disposition and spiritual grace."[31] Catholic schools for poor girls attempted to instill the same discipline, sound moral principles, and respect for authority, but they placed much less emphasis on "intellectual" education. After very rudimentary elementary instruction, these girls learned manual skills and principles of hygiene thought necessary to prepare them to become good mothers and housewives.[32]

In the view of some moderates as well as conservatives, this kind of education was not only appropriate but crucial in the face of the "corrupting" influences of modern life. Archconservative author and reformer Amélia de Rezende Martins believed that "it is preferable [to have] complete ignorance and healthy morals, no science and much catechism, to all this semblance of instruction that serves only to cause unhappiness to a wave of Brazilian girls." In fact, the Church retained significant influence within the sphere of education, both through its own schools (which survived thanks to tradition and to the serious shortage of public schools) and through the institution of optional religious instruction in public schools by the Vargas government in 1931.[33]

Catholic school education, however, increasingly came under attack for its uselessness and hypocrisy by those who favored rational, scientific education. A chronicle of the period described the typical "chic" and "futile" upper-class woman: "She was educated, mainly, in a [Catholic] boarding school for rich girls, where she learned the rules of politeness, hypocrisy, lying, and dissimulation along with some pretenses of instruction. A little bit of practical French and theoretical English, music, imitative painting, flower [arrangement], rhetorical speech, classical dances and some other futilities. She left the prison of the school for the ample liberties of the salons."[34] Maria Lacerda de Moura denounced Catholic education for destroying students' energies, degrading their character, and combating any new idea in the search to hold on to tradition. Rather than educating them, it indoctrinated them, and rather than preparing them to make responsible moral choices in life, it drilled in useless "rules of conduct studied in the catechisms." If Catholic education meant "defeat" for women, it served as a "vaccination" for children.[35] The objections of Zélia Gattai were more immediate and practical. The daughter of Italian immigrants, her only option to continue schooling beyond the primary level was to enroll in a Catholic school that charged her family no tuition. But after a year, she grew tired of embroidering for the nuns (who, she remarked, received "many commissions"), and she dropped out.[36]

Even vocational education was conceived in such a way as to avoid conflicting with the primary goal of preparing women for marriage and motherhood. The São Paulo Female Vocational School, a tuition-free school established by the state legislature in 1911, provided working-class girls with a "rational preparation" for becoming "energetic, healthy, and useful" workers in the appropriate trades of design, dressmaking, needlework, flower confection, and hatmaking. Emphasis was clearly placed on the application of learned skills rather than on the development of initiative, originality, or creativity (which, in addition to reflecting social prejudices, was reinforced by the fact that the school was subsidized by the income earned by students in filling orders).[37] And although the state legislature created positions for four professors in Portuguese, arithmetic, geography, and history in 1917, the "educative importance" of the school, according to its director Aprígio Gonzaga, remained "first, to teach a secure occupation [to protect students] against moral deviance and crime; [and] second, to raise the intellectual level of the working class, developing their capacities of observation, reflection, and creation, [and] at the

Third-year students at the Female Vocational School of São Paulo taking a course on sewing in 1919. (From "A Escola Profissional Feminina de São Paulo," RF 6 : 66 [November 1919])

same time, rendering them capable of understanding their rights and social duties."[38]

To the extent that such vocational education included more than simple manual training, domestic and moral education increasingly ranked above "intellectual" education. During the early 1910s, Aprígio Gonzaga opposed obligatory domestic education in the Female Professional School on the grounds that it would undermine the school's mission of preparing women for paid employment. But he quickly relented under concerted attack from the educational establishment that he was antifamily, and he bowed to pressure to include home economics courses as part of the school's required curriculum.[39] In 1940, National Department of Labor employee Maria Rita Lira Schulz gave a public lecture praising Brazil's "first lady" for her initiative in establishing more vocational schools for girls: a "noble plan to elevate the proletarian woman to [fulfill] her sacred mission of creating a strong race." Schulz explained that the training of working-class girls in child care, domestic economy, nutrition, and "various arts" offered them a "valuable means of subsistence," for these skills were in demand in the marketplace as well as applicable in their own homes. She declared: "[I]t would be a great glory for our Country to succeed in orienting our girls in a more domestic direction, more towards the home, more in accord with the sublime mission of the mother of the family."[40]

As we have seen, very few women attended the university-preparatory secondary schools. Those who came from a higher social class than the students who generally attended schools of manual arts and trades attended commercial and technical schools to learn typing and stenography or normal schools to be trained as teachers. In these largely sex-segregated schools that did not offer the rigorous academic training necessary to pass university entrance examinations, women learned trades considered to be compatible with stereotypical notions of female nature and tendencies. Rather than fostering professional ambitions, such education directed women toward jobs that offered only meager economic rewards, little social status, and few opportunities for advancement. In addition, these schools continued to place heavy emphasis on domestic education. In a speech he delivered at the Escola de Comércio Alvares Penteado in 1931, pioneer reformer Fernando de Azevedo conceded that women had the capacity to enter any profession and the right to receive an "equal education"; but at the same time, he argued that it was necessary to remember the special, principal, and ever more important role that they played in the home. He went on to explain that domestic education for all girls figured prominently within his program for a "new" education for Brazil:

> Expanding the teaching of nutritional hygiene, child care and domestic economy in all primary, professional, and normal schools; instituting, obligatorily, domestic courses and classes for all [female] students in technical schools, and establishing [more] homemaking schools along with nurseries and day-care centers attached (Art. 395), the reform seeks not only to initiate the woman into domestic life and tasks, but also to equip her, through a more complete, scientific education, "for the struggle against infant mortality, through the better preparation of the woman for the mission which she should fulfill in the care and hygienic protection of children."[41]

In 1940, Decree-Law 2.072 made civic, moral, and physical education obligatory for all schoolchildren. It affirmed that "moral education" should seek to render boys and girls "capable of their mission as family men and women." And it went on to specify: "[Moral education] will bestow on women, in a special manner, a consciousness of the duties that tie them to the home, as well as a fondness for housework, especially the tasks involved in the rearing and education of children." Conspicuously absent from the text of the law was any explanation of how moral education should prepare boys to be good fathers and husbands.[42]

Clearly, academic and professional education for girls was still generally considered to be a safety net for those who needed it; those who achieved economic security and social status through marriage could apply the skills they had learned and the character traits they had acquired to housewifery and motherhood.

With the rising influence of the eugenics movement during the 1910s, leading educators and physicians began to call for the introduction of physical education for girls, which they regarded as even more important than for boys, given the greater physical and moral demands of motherhood. Its proponents celebrated women's physical education as the "cornerstone" of the "regeneration" of the Brazilian race (feared by eugenicists to be frail and sickly). Only strong and healthy women, they insisted, could "perfectly fulfill the mission of productive motherhood."[43] Orlando Rangel Sobrinho warned that inactivity led to organic decadence and threatened the very survival of the race. According to his calculations, infant mortality could be reduced by 70 percent with rational physical exercise. He therefore declared it to be a "basic patriotic duty to elevate the race by means of physical education, never forgetting the preponderant role of women."[44]

Physical education was also said to bring enormous moral benefits: persistence, discipline, self-control, courage, daring, initiative, a spirit of solidarity, self-confidence, and resolution.[45] Fernando de Azevedo believed that modern "scientific" programs of physical education would help destroy "epicurean morality," liberate women from the tyrannies of fashion, and restore moral purity to modern youth who were attracted to the dangerous pleasures and diversions of contemporary civilization.[46] Other proponents emphasized the importance of physical education for adolescent girls (as well as boys) in aiding sexual sublimation.[47]

Finally, physicians and educators celebrated female physical education as the means for achieving aesthetic "perfection."[48] The society that worshiped beauty and youth urged women to "awake from their lethargic somnambulism" and practice sports, or risk suffering from "fallen shoulders, enormous stomachs, twisted legs, double chins, and other defects that give the appearance of carelessness and disregard."[49] But if educators began to insist that women regard gymnastics as being "as serious a duty as eating, good grooming, working, and developing a character and personality," they continually stressed that women's participation should be ladylike.[50] Without exception, advocates of female physical education recommended against excessive exertion, which would inevitably result in the "rigidity" of the muscles, the "masculinization" of female forms, or the "fatal warping of true femininity."[51] The goal, far from transforming women into "Herculeses," was to emphasize and develop the natural differences between the sexes.[52] Therefore, women were encouraged to

Oarswoman on the cover of O Cruzeiro, *1931. Positive images of strong and radiant female athletes, in Brazil and abroad, appeared with increasing frequency in the popular press beginning in the late 1910s. (From* O Cruzeiro *3:45 [12 September 1931])*

take up "delicate" sports that would heighten their flexibility, agility, harmony, rhythm, and grace. Swimming, classical dance, Swedish gymnastics, fencing, tennis, and table tennis scored highest as the most appropriate forms of exercise. Rowing, bicycling, running, volleyball, and basketball were recommended only in moderation. Considered totally unsuitable were "violent" sports such as soccer, boxing, wrestling, weight lifting, long-distance running, and high jumping.[53]

Physicians and educators, having discovered that women's physical and mental health was closely tied to their sexuality, also began to advocate sexual education. In 1915, Dr. Francisco Vasconcellos described the severe trauma that the "fragile" young woman—"chaste and tender as a white lily"—faced upon finding herself "abruptly thrust into an unknown world" of which she was totally ignorant. Rather than welcoming menstruation, she was "profoundly tormented by surprise and mortally wounded by fear." And, the "great psychic shock" that she suffered left her with a "sad and bitter memory" of her transition to physical maturity. Vasconcellos went on to condemn parents who committed the "outrage" of allowing their daughters to remain in absolute ignorance of the sexual act even up to the point of signing a marriage contract. He blamed "sexual illiteracy" for the "shipwreck of generations of young women" who had strayed off the straight and narrow path of sexual purity: "Ignorance of the enormous evils that can result from the disturbance of menstruation or the practice of the solitary vice [masturbation] is what will lead her to sexual perversion, will destroy her organism, and will submerge her in the cruel quagmire of prostitution, her intelligence in the unfathomable abyss of sexual psychopathy." He went as far as to claim that sexual education would not only reduce the "army" of women suffering from neuroses by 50 percent but would also reduce the number of prostitutes by 60 percent.[54]

The number of physicians and educators who advocated sexual education rapidly increased during the 1920s. They argued that sexual education was essential to avoid moral perversion, sexual psychoses, physical degeneracy (through masturbation and venereal diseases), prostitution, and adultery and divorce, as well as to ensure healthy (eugenic) reproduction.[55] Eugenicist Renato Kehl was especially adamant that sexual education should aim to "civilize" the "savage" sexual instinct—in other words, to convince the young of the wisdom of abstinence, not sexual liberation. In his opinion, scientific instruction about reproduction was essential in order to "unveil the secrets and the mysteries of reproduction, to destroy dangerous naïveté, to put an end to erotic curiosity, [and] to recommend precautions against the dangers of [venereal diseases] and prostitution."[56] By the end of the decade, the need for sexual education was widely accepted among Brazil's professional community.

At the 1928 National Congress of Educators, delegates agreed that parents were incapable of providing adequate sexual education and endorsed (against only one negative vote) a statement supporting the adoption of programs of sexual education in schools for children of eleven years and older.[57] In a 1930 inquiry organized by the *Diario da Noite*, prestigious members of the medical community voiced unanimous support for sexual education, although their opinions differed about when it should be initiated and by whom it should be administered.[58]

In fact, sexual education was never instituted in the schools, thanks to both parental and Church opposition. Dr. Albuquerque speculated in 1933 that any school principal who attempted to initiate a course on sexual education would have immediately been forced to close down the school by fearful parents who imagined that their children would return home "impure and corrupted."[59] And Father Pascoal Lacroix (citing Pope Pius XI's 1929 denunciation of "naturalistic . . . sexual education devoid of all religion") insisted that sexual education should be administered privately and individually and only by parents and by the Church, since it was primarily a moral rather than a scientific problem, involving the training of the will more than the imparting of anatomical knowledge.[60] Even so, he contended that curiosity about sexuality is only awakened with adolescence, and therefore precocious instruction should be avoided:

> It is indispensable to keep and preserve children from knowledge of sexual life for as long as possible. Sexual ignorance is a natural necessity for their normal development. As long as no one tears off the veil of their innocence, nature veils from them sexual mysteries and conserves them, for many years, in a generous ignorance and enviable happiness. To tear this natural veil from them would be a cruelty and an impiety! It would be to destroy the child in the very child. It would be the equivalent of killing the child morally, taking from it what is most precious, that which gives it its value, charm, and happiness: purity, simplicity, and innocence.[61]

Once a child reached adolescence, Father Lacroix insisted that sexual education should demand chastity: "[T]he central problem of sexual education involves inhibiting mental concentration on this matter; guiding youth to diligently observe the very healthy and indispensable suggestions of modesty, and, principally, to consider sexual curiosity as their biggest enemy, from which, therefore, they should turn away. Therein lies the inestimable pedagogical importance of chastity."[62]

Despite this effective opposition, the goals of those who advocated sexual education paralleled the overarching goals of female education as they had been defined by leading educators of the period: to increase women's knowledge and skills and to improve their health without "liberating" them or, ultimately, upsetting the gender hierarchy.[63]

The expansion of educational opportunities for women allowed a small elite of women to achieve self-realization and economic independence through academic and professional achievement; and their conspicuousness (if not their large numbers) served to demonstrate the "progress" and modernity of the Brazilian nation. But the education that most women received was tailored to keep their aspirations in check—or, in the words of Professor Antonio de Sampaio Doria (psychologist and director of public education for the state of São Paulo), "to develop their capacity to adapt to the laws of life."[64] By directing women toward a narrow range of vocational courses at the secondary level, the educational system laid the groundwork for a sexual division of labor in the labor market that was crucial for preserving the gender hierarchy.

The goal of the educational system was not to foster female intellectual, economic, or social emancipation but to effectively mobilize women to promote physical health, national economic prosperity, and social and political stability. To this end, schools collaborated as much to keep "inappropriate" knowledge and experience unavailable to women as to make "appropriate" knowledge and experience available. In mediating between the old and the new, female education combined large doses of moral education and social discipline along with instruction in basic knowledge and skills. Women's assigned task was to "civilize," "elevate," and "redeem" the world, not transform it.

REDEFINING "WOMEN'S WORK"

By the 1910s, urban middle-class and even upper-class women were increasingly joining poor women in the wage labor force. This resulted from a combination of factors: (1) the gradual shift of household production to the marketplace and the consequent decline in the economic value of women's household labor; (2) the precarious economic situation of the expanding urban middle class, which was squeezed by high rates of inflation and by pressure to consume the products and services of the booming market economy; (3) the growing demand for female employees in the service sector; and (4) women's own embracing of the bourgeois value of work, which fostered their desire for greater economic self-sufficiency and professional achievement.

As the need for and the value of women's household production declined, leaving women "idle," and as idleness was increasingly scorned and forbidden by bourgeois morality, women's economic dependence on their relatives and husbands began to be commonly labeled "parasitism." Quite suddenly, both male and female intellectuals began to regard this "parasitism" as shameful, degrading, destabilizing of the family, inimical to "progress," and contrary to the laws of nature.[1] One female critic predicted:

[T]he day is not far away when women themselves will begin to be ashamed not to have an occupation in life: the sole means to win social respect and gain self-respect. The day is not far away—the signs of which are already apparent—in which women will be ashamed to be a parasite in life, a drain on the social beehive.

There is nothing more dignified than work. Future generations will despise women who live like a parasite off their families.[2]

Other women agreed that instead of being idle "dead weights" on their families, they should be intelligent and useful collaborators of men: "Tired of her secular parasitism, the modern woman puts her intelligence and her will power, unused until now, at the service of human progress."[3] Urban middle-class women increasingly understood that for bourgeois society, being useful collaborators meant holding paid employment: "Work is salvation, moral purity. We think . . . that all of us, men and women, ought to work. There is no more room in the world for the unproductive."[4]

Indeed, in the new urban-industrial economy, women's wage work provided much greater protection against inflation and economic depression than did household production. Even small salaries earned by unmarried daughters, widows, or—in the case of urgent need—wives could make the difference between precarious survival and some minimum comfort. In 1925, an article in a working-class newspaper claimed that petit bourgeois families were frequently facing the "hour of death" because their deficit at the end of the month was "ruinous." The article calculated that a typical small businessman who made 350$000 profit per month faced a deficit of 129$000 after paying for the basic expenses of rent, food, fuel, and electricity for a family of four. Even by moonlighting, he would be hard pressed to earn sufficient income to cover the costs of education for his children, medical care, entertainment, and consumer items (such as ready-made clothing, processed food products, household supplies, and electrical appliances) without the extra 250$000 that his wife or unmarried daughter could earn as a schoolteacher or in some other paying job.[5]

In addition, new patterns of female employment became necessary for national economic growth and modernization. Not only were women workers still needed in the industrial sector, but women with secondary education were eagerly sought to fill new respectable white-collar jobs in the rapidly expanding areas of banking, commerce, government administration, and social services. A survey commissioned by the Ministry of Labor found that male employers in commerce had become enthusiastic advocates of female employment. They were unanimous in praising the efficiency of their women workers, who, they claimed, unlike men, did not smoke, were more patient, tolerated routine, concentrated on their work for longer periods of time, and, being more modest, had lower ambitions that could be satisfied with lower wages.[6]

But if female employment was an inescapable necessity for women themselves, for their families, and for the booming urban-industrial economy, it posed serious problems for the society at large. The entrance of middle-class women into the workforce threatened the model of the bourgeois family, which demanded a sexual division of labor. And the continued presence of poor women in the workforce—especially in jobs that removed them physically

Caricature of the female professional going off to work, 1926. This sketch illustrated an article in A Cigarra *entitled "A Woman Can Do Whatever a Man Can Do." The text discussed, in a matter-of-fact, nonjudgmental manner, how mechanization had undermined the importance of women's domestic production, while the growth of the economy had created rising demand and new opportunities for female workers to prove their skills in varied occupations. It concluded with the statement, "As the world advances, likewise female independence increases." However, this sketch, in ridiculing the man who assumed female roles, obliquely but powerfully attacked the woman who opted to take advantage of those new opportunities to prove her abilities in formerly male spheres. (From "A mulher pode tanto como o homem,"* A Cigarra *14:273 [15–31 March 1926], pp. 44–45)*

from the domestic sphere—became more problematic. In an era of industrial growth, employers and the state worried about the physical health and "proper" socialization of children (future workers) whose mothers spent their days in factories. In an era of social conflict, women's absence from the home frustrated new efforts to foster the "proper" organization and stability of the working-class family. Conservatives deplored the need for women of all social classes to enter the workforce, predicting that it would corrupt them, destabilize their families, jeopardize their health and the health of their children, and undermine social stability and political order.[7] Law professor Augusto Olympio Viveiros de Castro considered the regulation of female employment to be "one of the gravest problems of the Social Question."[8]

Indeed, how could female employment be reconciled with the perceived need to tie women closely to their familial duties and to preserve the sexual division of labor within the family? How could women fulfill their mission as the bastions of family stability and morality if they were at offices and factories instead of at home? These contradictions were to a large extent irresolvable in the long term. But in the short term, efforts to attenuate the contradictions included defining women's paid employment very narrowly—as an extension of their familial roles—and restricting their entrance into "inappropriate" or dangerous jobs. Political, social, and cultural considerations required that female employment neither empower women to opt out of familial roles nor undermine the stereotypes linking femininity to delicacy, virtue, and altruism. It was crucial for the sake of family stability (and by extension, public order) and essential for employers seeking to keep labor costs down that female employment remain "complementary" to male employment.

Justifications for Female Employment

▼ ▼ ▼

Women's employment was justified on the grounds of both economic necessity and social utility. Single and widowed women who supported themselves and dependent family members as well as married women who supplemented their husbands' incomes would not only be ensuring their personal and familial well-being but would be augmenting the national wealth and fostering economic progress. In addition, it was argued that female employment could have a moralizing effect both on poor women (who spent at least a third of their day under the watchful supervision of employers) and on society at large (as working women infused their workplaces with female values). But the vast majority of social critics continued to regard women's employment as a necessary evil, required by the contingencies of modern life. And they insisted that it should neither change the definition of femininity, nor transform female consciousness, nor interfere with women's performance of their domestic duties. In short, if women were to work for wages, it should be temporary and incidental, not central to their lives and their thought.

Economic necessity was the most compelling justification for female employment. Not even the most conservative critics (who defined women's biological destiny as exclusive devotion to their homes and children) could deny the need for women to earn wages.[9] Reluctantly, they admitted that there was no alternative in Brazil, where the majority of the population ate inadequate diets, lived in squalid housing, and had little or no access to health care; infant mortality was disgracefully high; children as young as eight to ten years old were sent to work in factories so that their families would not starve; and urban households were frequently headed by women.[10] For single and widowed women of the middle classes whose relatives could not provide economic support, access to respectable paid employment was also considered especially important to protect them from starving, from falling into prostitution, or from having to accept an undesirable marriage offer.[11] The argument of economic need was so socially acceptable that a number of women used it to explain their workforce participation when this may not have been the decisive factor. For example, Maria José de Castro Rebello Mendes and Rosalina Coelho Lisboa, both daughters of prominent and wealthy politicians, explained publicly that they took jobs upon the death of their fathers in order to support their widowed mothers.[12]

A few progressive critics argued forcefully in favor of the employment of married women on the more positive grounds that it would enhance the economic stability and therefore the well-being of the family. J. M. Gomes Ribeiro declared: "In most homes today, the man's work does not provide enough [income] to cover household necessities. The woman must alleviate the almost intolerable burden that is imposed on the majority of family men by the abnormality of our times, by the increasing strain to earn a living. Only by so doing will the family be able to survive and prosper as the primordial institution of civilized nations."[13] Both he and Afrânio Peixoto maintained that men would be more eager to marry if their wives were wage earners who contributed cash to the family economy rather than merely consumers of their husbands' incomes.[14]

The obvious importance of female employment for the national economy was also a factor underlying justifications of female employment. With the rapid expansion of the service sector, employers invariably (and conveniently) discovered that women (who commanded much lower salaries than men) were "naturally" suited to fill new posts as teachers, nurses, social workers, sales-clerks, bank tellers, telephone operators, receptionists, and secretaries. Physicians, for example, appealed to the Department of Public Health to take advantage of women's natural qualities by training them to become visiting nurses. Employed by the state to inspect the living quarters of those who were sick and to teach the "rules" of hygiene so as to prevent the spread of contagious diseases, these nurses would be "multiplying" the work of more expensive (male) physicians (who would then presumably be freed to dedicate themselves to more lucrative tasks).[15] In the commercial sector, employers agreed that female workers were "more efficient, more reliable, and speedier" (as well as cheaper) in performing repetitive tasks that required no decision making, innovation, or responsibility (skills presumed difficult for women, given their natural "timidity").[16]

Arthur Henock dos Reis, a consultant for the railroad companies, also conveniently found that paid employment was in no way incompatible with femininity, and he concluded that the "rational and efficient use of the country's human element" demanded the use of female labor in appropriate jobs. He recommended that railroad companies follow the example of industry (which employed women to fabricate objects requiring a delicate touch) and the retail trades (which recognized women's intuitive ability to attract more customers) by employing women in jobs such as guards at railroad crossings and waiting rooms, ticket sellers, information booth staff, and telegraphists. In these "lesser important and less demanding jobs" that were "more suited to the female sex," the railroad companies could, he claimed, save considerable sums of money by hiring well-qualified women at less than two-thirds of the salary they would have to pay men. He noted that women (and their families) would benefit from the supplemental income these new jobs provided; the value of men's work would increase as they transferred to jobs that were "more appropriate for their sex"; the railroad companies would reap higher profits; industry, commerce, and the public would all benefit from access to railroad service at lower cost; and the national economy would take one more step toward achieving efficient and rational use of the labor force.[17] In all these ways, women's employment would foster the social good: "[O]nce again, women will be able to demonstrate how the latent patriotism of their hearts is always ready to cooperate with men, offering their labor power for the collective good without renouncing their [female qualities and roles]."[18]

As the demand for female employees grew, women began to be urged to opt for work—the source of health, wealth, honesty, dignity, personal satisfaction, and social well-being—over idleness, which was thought to breed degeneration, misery, and vice.[19] Energetic, hardworking women were held up as models of virtue over "frivolous" women who wasted their time and energy to no avail. In the eyes of one male critic, the glory of São Paulo lay in its well-educated and hardworking women, whom he described in glowing (but emphatically stereotypical) terms:

> [They are the] most resplendent sun of joy and happiness—the heroines of São Paulo, those who are the true pride of the Paulista home, divine women who dedicate themselves to the sacrifice of study and work—perfumed beauties who are always admired and never forgotten. . . . All of these admirable women who struggle and suffer are those who by the purity of their heart, by the nobility of their love, [and] by the brilliance of their virtue are the true flowers of Jericho, the beautiful and charming women who constitute the greatest, the most splendid glory of the pure home of the Paulista family.[20]

Ministry of Labor researcher Clodoveu Doliveira rationalized the exploitation of women factory workers by claiming that large industries "spontaneously" protected their female employees, providing them with "security and comfort, as well as relative freedom, [and] as a rule watching over the morality [of the environment], which . . . is generally satisfactory."[21] He lavished praise on the department store Casa Sloper and on the Rio de Janeiro Telephone Company. The former, "sensibly and liberally directed, . . . is a beehive of work, in a happy and smiling environment." The latter, he claimed, despite paying its female employees the lowest wages, was "worthy of mention as a social factor," since it provided a "true school of scientifically controlled work" and diligently "watch[ed] over the moral and material [circumstances] of its workers." In this "healthy environment," poor women were "surrounded by care and comfort." They were provided with a large, tastefully decorated, and hygienic restroom where they could spend their breaks, nutritious meals at cost in the company cafeteria, paid vacations, job security, and opportunities for promotion to office jobs or lower-level supervisory positions. In addition, should an employee miss work, one of the company's inspectors would be sent to her house to verify whether she was sick, to provide help if necessary, to inform her family in the event that she was neither at home nor at work, and to collect data on her living situation, including whether she lived with her family, and if not, why. With this information, the company could be sure that it employed only "honest girls."[22]

Supporters of female employment argued further that women workers would help redeem the corrupt world of business and government by infusing it with a high sense of morality.[23] The *Revista Feminina* applauded the victories of the first women who won posts in the upper ranks of public administration, and proclaimed:

> Now, the Brazilian woman can promise a new discipline and a new morality [flowing from] her religiousness, the power of her honesty, and the tenderness and integrity of her character that have resisted inundation by all the vices that pour through the cracks of the dam that used to isolate us from decadence . . . in the times in which we were still protected by the impermeable layer of our good traditions. It pleases heaven . . . that the entrance of the Brazilian woman . . . into the rest of the branches of the country's public administration may inaugurate a new age of morality, which all of us who live in this beloved land so desperately need.[24]

Leolinda Daltro, a candidate in the 1919 Rio de Janeiro municipal elections, justified her candidacy in similar terms: "As the woman that I am, with a superior sense of Altruism, I have preoccupied myself with the necessary alleviation of human suffering, investigating the practical means for diminishing misery and suffering, and for achieving a better distribution of justice." [25]

Thus the "duties" of modern women gradually came to include paid employment, not only during times when their households urgently needed the extra income, but also when familial responsibilities did not demand their full-time attention. Whereas during the nineteenth century women who worked for wages had suffered severe loss of social status, by the 1920s working women—especially professionals—enjoyed a certain prestige. "Working, [the woman] will cooperate in fostering the wealth and well-being of her community. [She will] not only comply with the demands of the biological law of work, but [will] also lend her help in the face of the present difficulties of life to social progress and the growth of the national wealth." [26]

But if women faced new pressure to demonstrate their worth through training for and dedication to some economically or socially "productive" task, enormous efforts were also spent in trying to reconcile female employment with women's household and familial roles and with stereotypical notions of female nature. In short, the new "biological law of work" was not to emancipate women from the old biological law of wifehood and motherhood.

First, a woman's employment and pursuit of career aspirations were laudable while she was single or while her family was in need, not as a long-term substitute for family obligations. The *Revista Feminina* explained:

> No one contests that it would be better if we women were responsible only for the duty of running the household. Nevertheless, the competition of

modern life has led us into the struggle, into the workforce, into hard labor because for many many homes, the man's income no longer suffices. Our incursion into public life is no more than an endeavor to ensure the satisfactory management of the home. It is clear that a woman who has a well-provided home will not go out on a mere whim to compete for a position as professor, saleswoman, typist, or whatever. If she comes out into the street, if she leaves her hive like a bee, it is because she senses that in her home signs of hardship are beginning to appear. It is not a movement of emancipation, nor a ridiculously extravagant movement of reaction that brings the woman onto the stage, that casts her poor delicate and hopeful heart against the sharp edges of the competition for work. No, it is a compassionate and benevolent movement; it is a very feminine, very womanly movement, full of piety and altruism, that tears her from her home, that throws her into [the labor market] searching . . . for the small allowance that her frail hands can earn, so that the children of her love do not shiver with cold or grow weak from hunger and thirst.[27]

The claim that female employment would neither emancipate women from their familial roles nor threaten their femininity was widely echoed. Ministry of Labor employee Maria Sophia Bulcão Vianna agreed, in a talk she gave to a group of girl scouts, that the need for married women to supplement their husbands' salaries was a very unfortunate necessity of modern life. But she insisted that in working for wages, the Brazilian woman—"naturally docile and attached to the home"—had not "abdicated" her former duties and obligations. She continued to be "a good wife, affectionate mother, and devoted sister" by sacrificing herself to help support her aged mother, younger siblings, or her own children.[28] Even feminists who passionately supported women's right to work felt the need to insist on the compatibility of work and motherhood. One reasoned: "[W]ork is a blessing, and as a blessing [it] will never impede [women] from also fulfilling their duties as mothers." While acknowledging that working women would gain independence, she claimed: "This independence will be conscientious and honest. It will not remove her from the home. Those who work conserve healthy thoughts and rarely go astray."[29]

Second, female employment was justifiable when it exploited female altruism and required the exercise of women's superior grace, sensitivity, compassion, and virtue, never when it demanded that they develop "male" character traits or compete with men. The overwhelming consensus was that women's honest pursuit of a living need not and must not require them to give up their peculiar feminine qualities: purity, sweetness, abnegation, maternal spirit, and so on.[30] But a 1942 study endorsed by the Ministry of Labor concluded that only a narrow range of jobs were compatible with female nature and did not risk rendering women less apt for motherhood physically or psychologically. These were teacher, social worker, nurse, doctor, dentist, pharmacist, laboratory technician, administrative assistant, secretary, saleswoman, interior decorator, hotel clerk, factory worker (in the areas of textiles, clothing, decorations, food processing, hatmaking, and finishing of various products), maid (cook, laundress, cleaning woman, or nursemaid), and small producer of agricultural products. These jobs, the study argued, did not demand more than a woman could easily do physically or intellectually. Equally important, they required "female" traits such as patience, cheerfulness, moral rectitude, delicacy, discretion, compassion, dedication to others (especially to the young, the old, the sick, the weak, and the suffering), knowledge of hygiene, artistic sensibility, manual dexterity, precision, attention to minute details, and (with the exception of women physicians) obedience to the directives of bosses.[31]

Professor J. P. Porto-Carreiro provided a more "scientific" justification for the strict separation of male and female jobs:

> The psyches of the man and the woman are mere reflections of their physical position in love: one seeks, grips, penetrates, possesses; the other attracts, opens up, surrenders, receives. Work, pure sublimation of natural impulses, will always be allocated by sex, in harmony with these dispositions.
>
> The foundry, the mine, large-scale commerce, the direction of industry, the initiation of action—these are properly masculine activities.
>
> Attending to the social good, research, education, providing material and psychic assistance—through preventive medicine, hygiene, and regeneration—these are properly feminine tasks.
>
> The two sexes will one day achieve the same status, but never [will they be] equal, for they are different so that they complement one another, not so that they compete.[32]

Indeed, sex segmentation in the labor market was widely regarded—not only by the state, by employers, and by educators but also by male workers—to be the essential means of reconciling economic needs with social interests. For example, the male president of the Association of Employees in Commerce (Associação dos Empregados no Commercio) argued that the most suitable manner to deal with competition between the sexes in the commercial sector was to differentiate strictly between "male" and "female" jobs and to train women in commercial schools only for those jobs defined as "female." Only in this way, he believed, could a "harmony of interests between the two sexes" be preserved.[33] In short, as long as women were set apart in appropriate "female" occupations, employers, male relatives, and male workers could hope that women's honesty and dignity would not be compromised, their peculiar female charms would not be tarnished, and they would remain complementary to and dependent on men rather than gaining independence. Obviously, in this case, they would threaten neither men's egos nor their salaries.

Since employment of married women was normally considered justifiable only as a last resort—as a means of survival for themselves and their families— it was still expected that well-supported married women would resign from their jobs and give up any career aspirations they may have had. Failure to do so was generally taken as a sign of bad taste, misplaced ambition, inappropriate egoism, and unsuitable competitiveness with their husbands.[34] For example, the *Revista Feminina*, which celebrated Maria José de Castro Rebello Mendes's success in winning a post as an official of the Brazilian Foreign Ministry in 1918, four years later pronounced her engagement to the consul to Bremen to be "one more victory of Brazilian feminism." The professional career of this "exemplary daughter" had, according to the magazine, protected domesticity and home life for those four years by providing income for herself and for her widowed mother. Upon her marriage, however, the magazine proclaimed her life to be "victorious"; it applauded her (presumed) respect for the home and her new undertaking of establishing her own family. Predicting that she would be a "model wife," the article valued excellence in performing domestic roles over professional achievement. The latter was praiseworthy only to the extent it served the best interests of the family.[35]

Women were constantly warned against seeking paid employment as a means to fulfill personal ambitions or to remain independent of men. Popular literature hammered home the message that no woman could secure a happy marriage while competing professionally with her husband, nor could she find true self-fulfillment until she gave up her career for motherhood. In a typical short story entitled "A Sad Secret," Amélia, an unmarried, ambitious, and highly successful professional woman, met an old friend who was a happily married housewife dedicated to raising her two children. When Amélia's friend described her children as the "delight of [her] life," Amélia burst out crying and declared: "Only now do I understand that I am not happy, that I cannot be happy. . . . I lack that which you have; I lack everything—I lack a child."[36]

Women who remained unconvinced by such stories were ridiculed, denounced for transgressing natural and divine law, warned that they were following the certain path to their own ruin and perdition, and accused of bringing doom upon the family and the nation.[37] Floriano de Lemos labeled independent professional women "women-men," "anomalies," and "errors of nature."[38] M. F. Pinto Pereira warned that if large numbers of women became economically independent, men would cease to provide support for them, fertility would decline, harmony between the sexes would be threatened, and the progress of the nation would be curtailed.[39] Oleno da Cunha Vieira made the point even more dramatically: "The totally independent woman—living her own life—by right of anarchist doctrines, is the masculinized woman, the negation of woman, wrapped up in the confusion of the business world, led astray from her destiny; she is not man's companion, but his enemy, in perpetual war with him. Imagine such a world. . . . What a horror! It would be the complete destruction of all moral values."[40]

Sex Segmentation in the Labor Force

▼ ▼ ▼

Social prejudices that demanded women enter jobs "compatible with their sex and abilities" severely limited women's options. Emphasizing women's proverbial patience, orderliness, attention to detail, submissiveness, lack of ambition, sensitivity, and maternal tenderness, educators, employers, and the state directed women toward occupations consisting of highly routinized work that required no innovation, responsibility, or authority; toward those in teaching, health care, and social work that involved dedication to others; toward suitable professional careers through which they could demonstrate their superior female morality and sense of social responsibility; or toward artistic careers that would provide outlets for their exquisite female sensibility.[41]

Backing up the weight of social pressure in limiting women's choices was the legal power of the 1916 Civil Code as well as protective legislation regulating female employment. Although the Civil Code granted married women the right to dispose freely of their wages, they were prohibited from accepting paid employment without the permission of their husbands.[42] As late as 1945, law professor Xavier Carvalho de Mendonça justified the husband's right to forbid his wife's employment: "Inasmuch as the exercise of a trade removes the woman from the home, exposing a bit of the privacy of the matrimonial bond [and] affecting the interests of the bond, one cannot but recognize the right of the head of the family to veto the wife's profession."[43]

Protective legislation passed in the 1930s—an important part of the Vargas government's effort to mobilize the political support of the urban working classes as well as to solve the "social question" in Brazil—went further toward restricting female employment. Previously, female employment had been regulated by federal, state, and local sanitary codes that were observed mainly in the breach. After 1930, the state took more energetic steps—for the supposed good of the family, future offspring, and the society at large—to forbid women to work at jobs that might endanger their physical health, jeopardize their maternity, or compromise their morality. According to Decree-Law 21.417-A passed in 1932, women could not be employed by industrial and commercial firms between ten o'clock at night and five in the morning (with some exceptions, including hospitals, clinics, asylums, telephone companies, radio stations, establishments in which female labor was "essential to avoid the interruption of normal functioning," and those in which only family members worked). Women were also prohibited from carrying weights considered excessive, from working underground or in construction projects, and from holding "dangerous and unhealthy" jobs (such as those in which they might be exposed to noxious fumes or dust or in which there was a high risk of accidents or poisoning). In an attempt to "protect" maternity, the law also specified that no female employee could be fired on account of pregnancy and that all employers were required to give pregnant women eight weeks of maternity leave (four weeks before and four weeks after the birth) with half pay and guaranteed employment after the leave. Upon returning to work, women who were nursing were to receive two half-hour breaks a day until their infants reached six months of age, and establishments that employed more than thirty adult women were to provide a nursery at the workplace for these infants.[44]

Whether intended or not, the law was more effective in discriminating against women in their search for equal employment opportunities than in protecting pregnant women and mothers.[45] Even within large firms, enforcement of maternity benefits lagged; outside large establishments, the legislation was meaningless for women who took in work at home, who labored as domestic servants, or who were employed in small shops—in other words, for the great majority of Brazil's working women.[46]

Brazilian censuses show that nonagricultural women workers were highly concentrated in a relatively small number of low-status and low-paying jobs; only a small elite were moving into professional, administrative, and social service jobs. Whether in menial jobs or professional occupations, women found it easier to secure employment producing products or rendering services that had traditionally been provided by women's household labor. Thus their workforce participation was defined as an extension of and complement to their domestic roles.[47]

Poor urban women had relatively few and unattractive choices. The persistence of the importance of domestic service as a source of employment for women is notable. In 1872, 51.3 percent of nonagricultural woman workers in Brazil were employed as domestic servants; the percentage dropped only to 33.7 percent in 1920, and increased slightly to 36.1 percent in 1940 (see table 10).

Table 10. Occupations in Brazil, 1872–1940

Occupations[a]	1872	
	Men	Women
Agriculture (including animal breeding)	2,279,273	964,325
Extractive industries (including mining, hunting, fishing, etc.)	22,074	—
Manufacturing[c]		
metallurgy, mechanical industries	19,461	—
ceramics (and nonmetal products of subsoil materials)	—	—
wood (and other products of vegetable matter)	39,492	—
leathers, furs (and other products of animal origin)	5,612	15
chemicals and pharmaceuticals	—	—
textiles	6,313	133,029
dyeing	422	127
clothing, shoes, hats	32,954	219
food and drink	—	—
construction	20,960	—
electricity and gas	—	—
products for sciences, letters, arts and other luxury items[d]	—	—
artisans[e]	14,496	4,870
seamstresses	—	506,450
other	—	—
Commerce		
banking, finance, exchange, insurance, brokerages, etc.[f]	93,577	8,556
merchandising		
Transportation and communications		
transportation[g]	21,703	—
communications	—	—
other	—	—
Armed forces, police, firefighters	27,716	—

1920		1940[b]	
Men	Women	Men	Women
5,705,404	606,919	8,183,313	1,270,199
138,261	946	345,202	45,358
106,800	14	150,506	3,044
20,011	2,952	68,963	9,203
69,215	1,202	177,538	18,164
6,764	1,525	24,681	1,343
6,081	1,067	23,701	8,526
30,821	57,548	101,218	189,080
—	—		
144,178	331,115	43,002	19,670
41,111	3,042	156,891	31,329
264,104	—	261,056	1,644
21,064	46	37,050	797
29,172	24,821	27,099	2,679
—	—	—	—
—	—	—	—
20,436	6,268	35,666	7,206
44,091	1,763	48,229	3,548
430,616	21,078	698,202	50,941
237,247	68	431,765	4,498
12,632	3,640	25,861	9,364
—	—	2,132	56
88,363	—	170,827	1,385

(*continued*)

Table 10. (*continued*)

Occupations[a]	1872 Men	1872 Women
Administration		
public administration (federal, state, municipal)	10,710	—
diplomatic corps	—	—
public school teaching and administration	—	—
justice department	—	—
private administration	—	—
Liberal professions		
clerics	2,332	286
jurists	6,958	—
medical practitioners	3,359	—
midwives	50	1,147
teachers and administrators[h]	1,307	2,218
artists	36,906	4,297
scientists[i]	—	—
writers, journalists	—	—
engineers, architects, agronomists,	—	—
economists, accountants, etc.	—	—
Services		
domestic service (remunerated)	196,784	848,831
other personal services[j]	—	—
entertainment and sports	—	—
social services	—	—
other services	—	—
unremunerated domestic service	—	—
Day laborers	274,217	135,455
Capitalists and proprietors[k]	23,140	8,723
Maldefined	(181,583 men & women)	
Profession unclaimed or without profession	1,984,053	2,188,061
Total	5,123,869	4,806,609

	1920		1940[b]	
	Men	Women	Men	Women
	94,487	3,225	203,890	21,624
	—	—	1,104	340
	—	—	14,984	60,882
	—	—	7,363	539
	37,303	2,864	2,163	301
	6,059	2,944	9,292	3,327
	18,597	32	9,086	220
	29,954	7,188	27,417	6,771
	—	—	—	—
	16,364	38,158	14,066	27,628
			3,317	678
	{ 42,719	6,096	279	78
			5,887	460
	—	—	4,040	149
	—	—	3,184	344
	70,335	293,544	87,755	549,117
	—	—	376,384	408,412
	—	—	20,985	4,089
	—	—	48,610	24,323
	—	—	15,642	1,329
	—	—	70,995	9,232,500
	—	—	—	—
	27,384	13,406	9,416	1,861
	369,911	46,657	90,618	10,985
	7,314,334	13,713,659	2,395,232	2,569,247
	15,443,818	15,191,787	14,434,611	14,603,238

(*continued*)

Table 10. (*continued*)

Sources: Adapted from Brazil, Diretoria Geral de Estatística, *Recenseamento . . . 1920*, vol. 4, pt. 5, tomo 1, pp. viii–ix, xii–xiii; Brazil, Comissão Censitária Nacional, *Recenseamento geral do Brasil . . . 1940*, série nacional, vol. 2, pp. 38–40.

ᵃThe categories listed are a combination of categories used in the three censuses. Where no statistics appear, the category was not used for that census.

ᵇIncludes population ten years old and older.

ᶜUnder manufacturing, the 1872 and 1920 censuses include factory production, artisanal production, and maintenance and repair services. The 1940 census separates manufacturing from maintenance and repair (which are placed under "services"), but the category of manufacturing still includes some artisanal production.

ᵈThe 1920 category includes publishers and printers only.

ᵉThis is an 1872 category, "manufactureiros e fabricantes."

ᶠIncludes other commerce that fits into neither category.

ᵍThe 1872 census had no category for transportation and communications. The statistics are for sailors.

ʰThe 1872 statistics are for "teachers and men of letters."

ⁱThe 1920 statistics are for "sciences, letters, and arts."

ʲIncludes restaurant and hotel services, personal hygiene, maintenance and repair of house as well as of domestic items, and fabrication, maintenance, and repair of personal items. This last category includes 386,057 women, most of whom were probably seamstresses.

ᵏThe 1920 census category is "persons who live off their revenues."

Besides performing housework and caring for the children of the middle and upper classes, poor urban women commonly earned their living as seamstresses who worked at home, in small dressmaking and repair shops, or, increasingly during the twentieth century, in factories. According to the 1872 census, 30.6 percent of nonagricultural women workers were seamstresses; their numbers and importance within the female workforce declined during the twentieth century, some being absorbed into the apparel industry, others continuing to provide personal services for individual clients. Brazil's textile industry was the one industry that, since its beginning in the mid-nineteenth century, employed more women than men; but women workers were also employed in the manufacturing of clothing, hats, shoes, and other nondurable consumer items such as food and drink, cigarettes, brooms and baskets, candles, soap, and matches, as well as various luxury items.[48] Gradually during the twentieth century some women moved into industries traditionally dominated by men—including ceramics, chemicals and pharmaceuticals, metallurgy, and wood and furniture making—but the growth of these industries (especially the more capital intensive and technologically advanced) did not benefit women to the same extent as men. Not only did the number of female employees in these industries remain relatively small, but they were usually segregated from male workers in less desirable jobs specially designated as "female," and they were paid even worse than were women in "female" industries.[49]

The most significant changes in the pattern of female employment during the early twentieth century came in the service sector. The development of new technologies and the expansion of government agencies, commercial enterprises, financial services, and communications provided a growing number of respectable white-collar jobs for educated middle-class and upwardly mobile working-class women. Public administration, which had been closed to women in the nineteenth century, offered significant new opportunities beginning in the 1910s. Between 1920 and 1940, the number of male employees in public administration slightly more than doubled; the number of female employees increased 671 percent (see table 10). Women also made notable gains in the commercial sector. Whereas they had traditionally worked as street and market vendors, they were now recruited to fill such jobs as salesclerk, typist, accountant, general office worker, and telephone operator.

Schoolteaching—which had provided one of the only sources of employment for educated women of "good" families during the nineteenth century—was also a rapidly expanding field that came to be almost totally dominated by women. By 1920, 75 percent of the schoolteachers in the city of São Paulo and 81 percent in the city of Rio de Janeiro were women.[50] Despite their low status and low pay, the widely shared conviction that "the most important function of the woman after maternity is that of educator" made schoolteaching a very respectable and sought-after profession for middle-class women.[51] In addition, with the construction of large hospitals, the demand for more and better-trained nurses increased, giving rise to modern nursing schools and a somewhat enhanced status for the profession.[52] Finally, social work—the "true creation of the epoch"—emerged as a new "female" profession that provided increasing numbers of jobs for educated women beginning in the late 1930s.[53]

Only a handful of successful female professionals escaped the boredom and exploitation that the vast majority of women in the workforce suffered. (And, of course, those who were married and had children owed their freedom to pursue careers to their maids.) Their significance, however, far outweighed their numbers, since their example challenged old stereotypes and provided models for radically new ways of being female. The opening of institutions of higher education to women in 1879 along with expanding opportunities in professional fields allowed a few women to become lawyers, physicians, dentists, pharmacists, engineers, scientists, and high-level administrators. The first female physicians and lawyers completed their training in the 1880s. However, very few actually practiced their professions, given the enormous obstacles they encountered. It was not until 1899 that a woman lawyer, Mirthes de Campos, was permitted to defend a client in court.[54] Three years later, when lawyer Maria Augusta Saraiva defended a client before a São Paulo court, a local newspaper commented that it "did not wish to see her example followed by our fiancées, sisters, or daughters."[55] Even by 1920, the situation had not changed much. Census figures for that year recorded only five practicing women lawyers in the city of São Paulo and nine in Rio de Janeiro.[56] Women physicians faced similar hostility, since few of their colleagues and few potential clients believed that the practice of medicine (apart from dentistry, perhaps) was appropriate for respectable women. Indeed, women's status in the medical profession declined in the early twentieth century; as male obstetricians displaced female midwives, women lost control of the one specialty they had previously dominated, and they were increasingly channeled into nursing, pharmaceutics, or, if they sought a medical degree, into dentistry.[57]

High-level government positions were finally opened to women in 1917, when Maria José de Castro Rebello Mendes became the first woman appointed as a ranking consular officer in the Brazilian Foreign Ministry.[58] Two years later, Bertha Lutz, a biologist who held a university degree from the Sorbonne, won the position of secretary of the National Museum in Rio de Janeiro.[59] After women won the vote in 1932 (and before the legislature was dissolved in 1937), a number of women were elected congressional representatives, mayors, and members of municipal councils.[60] And with the expansion of government administration under President Vargas, especially in the areas of labor and social welfare, women succeeded in winning many new administrative positions through competitive examination. Nevertheless, their positions remained tenuous. Perhaps in reaction to women's advances through competitive examinations, the Bank of the Nation, the War and Navy Departments, and the Foreign Service closed certain positions to women applicants during the late 1930s to early 1940s.[61]

If women faced formidable obstacles to becoming physicians, lawyers, engineers, scientists, high-level administrators, politicians, and businesswomen, it was somewhat easier for those inclined to become writers, poets, journalists, artists, and musicians to fulfill their professional aspirations. Not surprisingly, women in the arts and letters far outnumbered female professionals in other fields.[62] Not only could women writers and artists usually work at home on a flexible schedule, but their professional activities could be regarded as merely updating women's traditional role of reciting poetry, singing, and playing the piano at private social gatherings. In addition, these women seldom earned substantial or steady incomes. Rather than being considered threatening, they were praised by men for their sensitive and delicate characters—their true womanliness.

Because of their "exceptional qualities of observation," their "enormous sensitivity," their highly developed sense of "elegance," and their "female tenderness," women were thought to be naturally skilled at writing for other women and for children.[63] Thus, as the press sought to appeal to the growing literate female audience, opportunities multiplied for women to write regular columns in the most popular newspapers and magazines as well as to publish women's and children's books. Among the most successful women writers were Júlia Lopes de Almeida, Cecilia Bandeira de Melo Rebêlo de Vasconcelos, and Maria Eugenia Celso, all of whom published large numbers of articles and books about and for women. So expected had it become that women writers should address women readers that Claudio de Souza, son of the publisher of the *Revista Feminina*, Virgilina de Souza Salles, wrote the magazine's editorials during the 1910s to 1920s, as well as articles in many of the illustrated magazines of the age, using the female pseudonym Anna Rita Malheiros.[64] Even the conservative Brazilian Academy of Letters paid homage to women writers in 1921, when it awarded first prize in its poetry competition to a woman, Rosalina Coelho Lisboa.[65]

Numerous female artists also built brilliant careers. Brazil's foremost pianist during the 1920s was Guiomar Novais, who juggled marriage and motherhood with successful international tours. The foremost Brazilian painter during the 1920s was also a woman, Tarsila do Amaral, whose profoundly original use of brilliant colors, abstract forms, and intimately Brazilian themes won her an honored place within the Brazilian avant-garde.[66]

However, Brazil's successful professional women, if conspicuous, were exceptions. The vast majority of women were channeled into boring, routine, and unprestigious "female" jobs that rarely paid a living wage, making real economic independence an illusive goal. Having fewer job options than men, women had less bargaining power and therefore had to work for considerably less pay than men of the same educational level. According to the 1920 census, women employed in the industrial sector typically earned half to two-thirds of the salaries that men earned. The average daily wage of adult female factory workers in the textile, food, and apparel industries was 3$631, two-thirds of the average adult male wage of 5$449.[67] But given that women were concentrated in low-paying industries and occupations, the real wage gap between working men and working women was significantly greater. For example, men's daily salaries in the metalworking industry ranged from 7$000 to 8$000, and mechanics earned around 8$000 to 9$000.[68] But the many women who took in home work outside the factories or who worked in small confection or repair shops earned only a small fraction of what female textile workers earned.[69] Also subject to extreme exploitation were domestic servants, whose pay (in addition to room and board) was often a mere token sum.[70]

Telephone operators typically earned little more than did female factory workers, and even saleswomen started out at similar salaries.[71] Because these white-collar jobs were more "respectable," separating women of middle-class and upwardly mobile working-class backgrounds from women of poor working-class families, and because they offered somewhat better working conditions, employers found plentiful applicants willing to work for the miserable wages paid.[72] In 1933, Department of Labor official Clodoveu Doliveira admitted that a saleswoman could not even minimally support herself on the average salary paid; only in exceptional cases, after a woman had worked for more than six years, had demonstrated her loyalty to the firm, and had made it clear that she was not just working until she found a husband, could she hope to achieve real economic independence.[73] Even schoolteachers earned an insufficient wage to support themselves decently; unless they pooled resources and divided housing costs with other family members, they were condemned to poverty.[74]

Laws prohibiting wage discrimination on the basis of sex did little to close the gap between male and female salaries. Decree-Law 21.417-A of 1932, which proclaimed the principle of equal pay for "work of equal value" without distinction on the basis of sex, was watered down by the 1934 Constitution, which specified only that the "same work" must be compensated with equal pay.[75] In either case, women faced continuing wage discrimination. Not only did they perform different jobs than men performed (making the principle of equal pay for the same work largely irrelevant), but virtually by definition, a job normally performed by women was considered less valuable than a job normally performed by men (nullifying the principle of equal pay for comparable work). A 1935 survey of the living standards of 221 working-class families in São Paulo found that the median salary earned by women was only 62.5 percent of the median salary earned by men.[76] The 1938 statistics for average salaries of all adult male and female workers in Brazil as a whole showed that women earned only 47.6 percent of what men earned.[77]

If the economic advantages of sex segmentation in the workplace were obvious, the social advantages were no less important. In general, "female" jobs neither challenged stereotypes of female nature, nor placed women in competition with (or in positions of authority over) men, nor offered them opportunities for professional advancement or intellectual fulfillment, nor provided them adequate income and status to be comfortably self-sufficient. As a consequence, men preserved their privileged position in the labor market while female labor remained cheap for employers. The economy gained a large pool of easily exploitable labor without undermining a gender ideology that assumed the necessity of a binary opposition between maleness and femaleness for the preservation of political order and social hierarchy. And finally, the segregation of women in boring, unattractive, and ill-paid jobs helped keep them economically and emotionally dependent on their husbands and families, which in turn ensured that the majority would continue to orient their lives around fulfilling their domestic responsibilities.

Voluntary Work
▼ ▼ ▼

The prejudice and discrimination faced by the vast majority of women who entered the paid labor force did not affect middle- and upper-class women who engaged in voluntary work for charitable causes. Female charitable work in the United States during the nineteenth century had contained radical (as well as conservative) implications, providing women with new public roles, experience in organizing on their own behalf, and heightened social authority.[78] But in early-twentieth-century Brazil, where rapid urbanization and industrialization were accentuating the country's already highly polarized social structure and where ambitious middle-class women could choose to pursue new professional opportunities, the conservative implications of women's charitable work overwhelmed the potentially radical implications. Female charitable work, rather than undermining the gender hierarchy, reinforced it. Being unremunerated, this work posed little threat to women's primary roles as wife and mother or to their husbands' role as head of the family. And because participation in charitable causes was interpreted as proof of women's altruism and high moral virtue, it helped perpetuate stereotypes of female nature that narrowly defined appropriate public roles.

In addition, female charitable organizations, which were led almost entirely by upper-class women, unabashedly exploited women's moral authority for the interests of Brazil's upper classes. In contrast to U.S. middle-class moral reformers who sought to transcend class differences between themselves and their less-privileged "sisters" and who used the rhetoric of altruism to obscure their own class identities and interests, the upper-class female leaders of Brazil's charitable organizations worked self-consciously as members of their class and often employed rhetoric that emphasized their class identity and goals: to attenuate class conflict and to legitimate the social order.[79]

Female charitable work was welcomed by male professionals and intellectuals—from the most conservative to the more progressive—as an important means of fostering social peace and "moralizing customs." Antonio Carneiro Leão suggested that "distinguished" women should support such organizations as the YWCA (which he believed provided working-class girls with healthy recreation, practical instruction, and sound moral lessons), or the Girl Guides (which he envisioned could become a moral and intellectual training ground for future generations of female civic leaders), or the International Women's Federation (whose goal was to develop new educational curricula and provide health care and instruction to poor women and children). He emphasized the "highly moralizing" influence that upper-class women who offered "their lessons, their company, and their time" could exert over women and girls of more humble backgrounds.[80] Similarly, M. F. Pinto Pereira believed that upper-class women should establish day-care centers where the children of working women could be "morally educated and instructed in life." In addition, he encouraged them to develop assistance programs to save impoverished and abandoned women from falling to "vice," as well as to redeem those already corrupted by prostitution and alcoholism.[81] Antonio Austregésilo Lima also joined the chorus of men who praised women's charitable organizations, and he encouraged women to continue to expand the scope of their activities to provide greater numbers of "abandoned children, prostitutes, unfortunate women, orphans, and cripples" with both "daily bread" and spiritual guidance. In addition, he advised them to work to eliminate begging, which he believed seriously undermined the bourgeois ethic of hard work.[82]

Women's charitable organizations proliferated and flourished beginning in the late 1910s. Middle- and upper-class women eagerly joined the growing ranks of volunteers, for participation gave them both a means of entering the mainstream of public life and an outlet for their talents and energies. Moreover, in a society that was assigning increasing importance to educating women to be "useful" citizens, volunteer work in charitable causes provided an acceptable means for well-educated and well-supported married women to make a public contribution to society.

In 1923, Maria Jacobina de Sá Rabello warned an audience of the São Paulo elite that many women were suffering from idleness and boredom and were turning to narcotics and frivolous diversions. As an alternative, Sá Rabello urged women to seek happiness through "dedication" first to their families and second to women's "mission," which she defined as charitable work. In her view, this was an especially suitable task for women, since their nature led them to devote themselves to others: "[T]he most beautiful works of charity arise from female initiative."[83] Maria Sophia Bulcão Vianna agreed that dedication to charitable work was a most noble and appropriate activity for well-to-do women: "Women ought always to be the arm that supports, the voice that consoles, and the conscience that guides humanity, which oftentimes vacillates due to the contingencies of modern life."[84]

According to government statistics, the number of charitable organizations in the city of São Paulo increased from ten in 1901, to fifty in 1910, to well over one hundred during the decade of the 1920s.[85] The membership in most of these organizations was entirely female and often consisted of hundreds of women.[86] Among the most active of these organizations were the League of Catholic Women (Liga das Senhoras Católicas), Brazilian Red Cross (Cruz Vermelha Brasileira), Pro-Mother (Pró-Madre), Pro-Infancy Crusade (Cruzada Pró-Infancia), Women's Civic Alliance (Alliança Cívica Feminina), Women's Alliance (Alliança Feminina), and the Society for the Assistance of Lepers and the Defense against Leprosy (Sociedade de Assistência aos Lázaros e Defesa Contra a Lepra). For the most part, they organized, administered, and raised money for social assistance programs designed to provide moral and practical instruction along with material aid and health care to needy single women, poor and abandoned children, poor mothers, and the working class.[87]

For women of the social elite, affiliation with charitable causes provided a means to gain respect and social prominence through their own efforts rather than through mere identification with their husbands. Setting an example for women of her class was the wife of President Getúlio Vargas, who founded and patronized the Brazilian Association of Social Assistance (Associação Brasileira de Assistência Social), dedicated to promoting social assistance work in many different areas.[88] In some cases, elite women made a career of voluntary social assistance work. For example, Countess Amália Ferreira Matarazzo, the wife of perhaps the wealthiest Brazilian industrialist of his time, not only founded the Instituto Santa Amália, which trained girls in domestic science, manual skills, nutrition, and hygiene, but she was also a cofounder and president of both the League of Catholic Women and the Brazilian Red Cross, as well as a member of dozens of other organizations.[89]

For archconservative Amélia de Rezende Martins, charitable work was more explicitly a means of political activism. In the late 1920s, she initiated an enormously ambitious plan to organize a national network of social assistance organizations. In her opinion, the "grave crisis of morality" in Brazil urgently demanded an organized response. And, sensing a "wave of energy arising" within the female population, she threw herself into mobilizing women to save Brazil from "moral bankruptcy."[90]

According to Martins, upper-class women—who possessed innate moral superiority (over men of their class as well as over lower-class women) and whose competence was increasing "daily"—were naturally suited to this task. But she insisted that her work would not be "feminist": "We need men, with their clear vision and practical spirit. We will work sustained by men who are our natural support." And exploiting her class connections, she appealed to potential male donors in government, industry, and commerce for financial sustenance.[91]

Like many other female charitable organizations run by upper-class women, Martins's organization openly declared its reactionary political objective: to solve the "social problem." First, Martins advocated bolstering the influence and moral authority of the upper class over the lower classes:

> The group of the upper class that sets a good example for society is nearly being suffocated by the wave of ostentatiousness that threatens to demolish everything. We must enlarge this group until we form a legion that can demand the respect of the nation and the world.
>
> In my opinion, this is the most serious aspect of the social problem, since it is from above that the example comes. It is from above that comes the protection for all other social classes, and this sector of society, the upper class, ought to be a pure fountainhead rather than a corrupted spring.[92]

Second, Martins considered it essential to solidify the family by reestablishing the authority of parents over children and by teaching children lessons of morality, patriotism, and respect for authority. She believed that the nation could be redeemed if the youth of all social classes were shielded from the corrupting influence of modern liberties.[93] Third, she explained that social assistance programs designed to alleviate the misery and hunger of the poor would quell the anger of the working class, preempt strikes, and eliminate the danger of social revolution.[94] Although Martins's organization was relatively short lived and failed to establish branches outside Rio de Janeiro, its appeal for public funding set a precedent for women's charitable organizations in Brazil, which began to receive substantial public support by the 1930s.

Less ambitious but more successful was the Association of the Daughters of the Divine Heart (Associação das Filhas do Divino Coração), founded in 1920 in Petrópolis (Rio de Janeiro). Its stated objectives were to promote the moral and religious education of the proletariat and to study means by which to harmonize capital and labor. The organization received liberal financial contributions from industrialists, which it used to build workers' recreation centers next to factories. There, upper-class women attempted to teach workers the evils of anarchism and socialism and to instill conservative Christian values. The organization proudly took credit for having averted numerous strikes during its first year of operation.[95]

For most women, participation in charitable organizations did not involve a large-scale commitment. Hundreds of young single women volunteered to sell flowers in city centers on Saturday afternoons. In addition to raising money for charities, this activity gave them a legitimate reason to be downtown, an opportunity to flirt with young men, and a chance to have their photographs published in *A Cigarra* or other glossy magazines.[96] The Red Cross also mobilized hundreds of women to knit and sew clothing for soldiers during wartime and for hospital patients and orphans during peacetime. Thus, the traditional institution of the sewing circle began to be used not only as a means for women to socialize but also as a means for them to demonstrate their patriotism and civic responsibility. Finally, it became fashionable for women to organize fund-raising teas, dances, and festivals that drew the social elite together. Notices of such events, accompanied by the names of the organizers, routinely appeared in the social columns of the major daily newspapers next to announcements of engagements, births, and special events at exclusive clubs.[97]

Regardless of the motivations that led individual women to participate in charitable causes and despite the skills that the leaders acquired, female charitable organizations functioned as a mechanism of social control both of the benefactors and of the recipients. Charitable work provided a safe alternative to paid employment for well-to-do married women who wanted to participate in the public realm. Those who were most involved developed organizational, fund-raising, public-speaking, and other professional skills; but they were invariably praised for their altruism, dedication, and moral virtue, while their professional capabilities went unacknowledged. Moreover, because charitable organizations were directed by upper-class women and liberally funded by government and industry, they served the interests of the upper class in their attempts to assuage the suffering—and in the process, quell the furor and "moralize" the behavior—of the exploited. To these organizations fell the task of maintaining the appearance of noblesse oblige in the booming urban industrial society.

Women's Attitudes toward Employment

▼ ▼ ▼

To the dismay of many conservatives, expanding employment and professional opportunities for middle- and upper-class women did indeed bring notable changes in the consciousness and behavior of at least a prominent and conspicuous (if small) group of women. Feminists agreed that women's employment was essential for the well-being of families and for social progress. But they were adamant that women should pursue careers for their own good as well. Neither Mariana Coelho—feminist activist and poet from the state of Paraná—

nor many other professional women felt the need to deny that their careers gave them more than money: independence, pleasure, self-fulfillment, and a sense of personal worth and accomplishment. Coelho's "profound conviction that true female emancipation is in work" led her to conclude that "the woman who knows only how to be a housewife . . . is fatally condemned to be a slave": "Unable to emancipate herself [through paid employment] from the modest role of housewife, all power is concentrated in the egoistic hand of her husband, for she lacks the basis even to recognize that in her position of slave, the noble dignity that ought to glorify her perished."[98] She further lamented: "The female sex . . . has lived for centuries and centuries absolutely asphyxiated under masculine predominance and conforming tradition, during which [time] our precious abilities [and our] work have been suffocated with impunity."[99]

As early as 1921, another enthusiastic young woman writing from the rural state of Goiás also declared work to be the all-absorbing ideal of "modern" women. Even while conceding that women of her generation were destined to be "martyrs," forced to fight the inevitable battles of the period of transition, she still proclaimed:

> I have no fear of erring if I say that the ideal of modern young women is summed up in one word, in this magical word that is the *sesame* of life, for it unveils for all to see fabulous treasures, captivating perspectives, extraordinary worlds—and what is even more, pleasures, joys, in short happiness!
>
> And this word endowed with a magical power also sums up the masculine ideal. . . . I need not say that . . . the word [is] "work."[100]

The tiny minority of women who pursued paid employment as exhilarating and personally satisfying attracted much social attention. These women—who tended to be single, widowed, or separated—presented a new positive model of the unattached female: she was accomplished, proud, and independent in contrast to the frustrated, ridiculed, superfluous, and dependent "spinster." Among the most conspicuous of the new breed of professional women was Bertha Lutz, feminist leader during the 1920s and 1930s and founder of the Federação Brasileira pelo Progresso Feminino, secretary of the National Museum, official Brazilian delegate to numerous international conferences on women's status, skilled public speaker and author of many articles and books on women's status, congresswoman from Rio de Janeiro (1936–37), and president (and the only female member) of the Special Commission on the Status of Women established by the Brazilian Congress in 1937. Highly educated, articulate, and diplomatic, she won respect and praise not only from her female followers but also from many male professionals and politicians. Judging from her poised, discreet, and optimistic public posture, her professional and political accomplishments must have provided her with the satisfaction necessary to overcome whatever isolation, frustration, or anger she may have felt as a single professional woman struggling against social conventions.[101]

Yet women who built much more modest careers sometimes derived great personal satisfaction from their work as well. For example, Lola Delgado, the daughter of a respectable carpenter, chose to work as a saleswoman rather than marry. Over the strong objections of her father, she took her first job selling cosmetics in 1924 and continued working as a saleswoman until 1950. By that time, she had saved enough money to open a small store of her own. With the profit she made from her store, she bought a small house. Finally, Delgado ended her career as an official in the police department. At the age of sixty-six, this remarkable woman expressed no regrets about remaining unmarried; instead, she declared herself "fully realized."[102]

More typically, however, pioneering middle- and upper-class women who opted to pursue careers rather than to marry found that success was often bought at such a high price that it could be a dubious victory. The constant struggle against all odds and against social conventions brought many women as much anguish as it did satisfaction. Expressionist painter Anita Malfatti's fascination with very modern things—more shocking when coming from a woman than from a man—isolated her from her family (who disapproved of her "modernity") and from the Brazilian artistic community (which found her early work incomprehensible and "disagreeable" until years later). Her daring 1917 exhibition, which scandalized the public and critics alike, was so viciously attacked that her self-confidence as a very young woman was irreparably damaged. Lacking the firm support of friends, family, and even Brazil's artistic avant-garde, Malfatti was crushed by overwhelming hostility toward her work and by economic necessity, which forced her to paint on commission. As Malfatti came under pressure to conform her style to the taste of her patrons, her work lost its early audacity and vigor.[103] In a letter she wrote in 1921, she admitted her frustration and discouragement: "Holding on to this ambition [to pursue a career as an artist] certainly comes much more out of torment than out of pleasure. And yet I would die if I abandoned my life."[104]

For Maria Lacerda de Moura, the price paid for striving to achieve her goal of self-realization was also extreme isolation. Initially, as a young middle-class woman growing up in a provincial town in the 1890s, she did what was expected of her: she attended normal school, married at seventeen, and for ten years "led the life that every recently married woman leads:—embroidering, sewing, painting decorations for the house, playing the piano, ironing, chatting purposelessly, sleeping well and eating better, reading novels, and enjoying relatively good health."[105] But by her late twenties, she began dedicating herself to serious study and eventually abandoned her family in favor of writing, teaching, and political activism. Once liberated from the "antifeminist notion that the woman was born exclusively to be mother, to be housewife, and to play with and entertain men," she viciously attacked marriage and the routine of domestic life:

> Female work . . . by tiring the eyes, demanding energy, [and] emptying the imagination, results in mental fatigue. It contributes to the nervousness and irritability peculiar to women. The small details of life are what sap our energy, our intelligence, and our judgment. . . . Female irritability is the product of mental atrophy and of misdirected and misapplied activity. Female lives slip away and are extinguished amid sewing, embroidery, cleaning, and automatic care for "uncared for" children; [it is a] life without ideals, without any notion of what a future society could be, without a vision of beauty, without concern for action aimed at securing improved well-being. Always routine.[106]

Economically independent, she lashed out in word and in deed against constraining social conventions and injustice. Proudly identifying herself with "the discontented, the disinherited, and the righteous," she searched for "isms" that would satisfy her intellectually and for means to bring about her vision of a better future in which all forms of exploitation would end: bourgeois capitalism would be toppled, religious dogma condemned, corruption and vice overcome, human misery abolished, charity rendered obsolete, women liberated from their subservience and economic and mental slavery, unwanted pregnancy avoided, wanted children born out of wedlock to emancipated women, militarism outlawed, and peace achieved.[107] But after years of struggle, she found no lasting community of support and no political party or "ism" with which she could identify. Disillusioned with the power of education and embittered by the obstacles she had encountered in fighting for change, she retreated into mysticism and lived out the final years of her life in solitude on an island.[108] Generalizing from her experience, Maria Lacerda concluded: "All women who have achieved self-realization have been either single, widowed, divorced, or badly regarded by their entire family [and by society]."[109] "Thus the affliction and the tragedy with which the superior woman fights, alone, heroic, swimming against the current, committing suicide every day in the absorbing work [of earning a living] so as not to slip into the innumerable snares, the trap in every corner aimed at taming her in order to prostitute her in the immense hall of the social brothel. The tragedy of precursors!"[110]

Less prominent single career women—even those whose work conformed better to female stereotypes—also suffered from a sense of isolation, disrespect, and social irrelevance. "Brites," the daughter of a politically progressive engineer, received a good normal-school education and encouragement to be self-supporting. By the time she finished school in 1921, her father had died, and she began teaching—the profession that was to sustain her for the rest of her life. Reflecting back on her life, Brites declared that she had always loved to teach. "While I was a teacher," she said, "I lived." Thanks to her career, we can believe her disclaimer: "I am not a frustrated old maid." Yet she seemed to envy her sisters, who had all married well and had children. And she certainly resented the low pay and low social status she had received as a teacher.[111] But even more angered by society's continuing scorn for the single woman, she concluded the story of her life by protesting: "The single woman has no social prominence. . . . I was 'NN' [nothing and nobody] in life: the actor in the play who serves the coffee, passes the tray, closes the door. The actor who says nothing: who enters silent and leaves mute."[112]

A few single professional women suffered much worse fates. Eunice and Maria—both bright unmarried schoolteachers—were punished with internment in the Juqueri insane asylum for behavior (intelligence, ambitiousness, nonconformity, independence) that might have been tolerated, or even praised, had they been men. Eunice was taken to the asylum at age thirty (in 1910) by her family and diagnosed as suffering from manic depression. The psychiatrists noted:

> Our patient is the youngest daughter and was therefore accustomed to excessive pampering and loving. Very intelligent, she studied at the Normal School, where she stood out, always receiving the highest praise, which turned her prideful. Actually she deserved it, for three years after her graduation, she was appointed director of the elementary school in Santos. There, she distinguished herself, working very hard. . . . For a trivial reason, she became displeased and asked to be transferred to Araras; she found the environment very limiting for her talent and she abandoned the school. She worked too much: she possessed an intellectual hyperexcitation; she wrote school books that became models; she founded night schools; she bought books and books to read; during this time she became completely independent; she would not allow any intervention or even advice from her parents or older brothers; she relied exclusively on herself.[113]

After five months of hospitalization, Eunice was discharged "cured," having succumbed to pressure to give up her valued independence and move back into her parents' house.

Unlike Eunice, Maria refused to conform. Maria received a "superior" education, was endowed with the highest intelligence, and, except for her biting tongue, was known to be a person of excellent conduct and upright character. Her family reported that she had begun to show signs of nervousness and irritability from the age of about thirty (in 1907). During her forties, she was hospitalized three times for several months each time, until at age fifty she was interned for the rest of her life, until she died at age eighty-one. Because of her agitation, she was initially diagnosed as manic depressive. However, after ten years of hospitalization, the doctors concluded that she could no longer be diagnosed as such; instead, they declared: "It is evident that she is afflicted with a psychopathic schizoid personality." During her long years of internment, she conserved her intelligence and remained lucid and capable of work. But she was said to be egocentric, disinterested in the outside world, indifferent to her family, bad tempered, and solitary ("neurotic" characteristics typically assigned to independent women). The doctors noted that she never recognized that she was "sick." On the contrary, they quoted her as saying: "Since childhood I've had a ferocious tongue, evil and shocking. Everyone tells me this. . . . I have always been this way and it is not a sickness."[114]

The more common pattern for middle-class women (and for upwardly mobile working-class women) was to sacrifice (or perhaps more often, happily abandon) their career in favor of marriage and motherhood. Very few women could have realistically aspired to be a physician, lawyer, high-level administrator, successful businesswoman, or self-supporting artist or writer. For the majority, a career meant living with boredom, frustration, subordination, and pay discrimination. Many women therefore welcomed marriage as an escape as well as a more secure means to social status and economic security. Célia, for example, delighted in the prospect of quitting her clerical job at a bank and dedicating herself (in the time that remained after fulfilling domestic responsibilities) to what she really loved—playing and teaching the piano.[115]

If those women who might have achieved professional success regretted having to choose between the opportunity to pursue their careers freely and the social and economic benefits that accompanied marriage, their feelings were generally hidden beneath flowery rhetoric about the joys of married life. Even Anna Amelia de Queiroz Mendonça, an accomplished poet and leading member of the Federação Brasileira pelo Progresso Feminino, declared: "The woman should work, study, conquer all the pinnacles of thought and activity. But each time that a great love lights up the heart of a true woman, she will not feel humiliated in relinquishing certain rights that her ego has striven for, in order that she may conquer her terrestrial happiness in the secluded charm of her home."[116] The story of Aracy Pereira Lopes, a successful medical student, was typical. She withdrew from the São Paulo Medical School during her fifth and final year when, in the words of one of her best friends (who was herself a successful writer), "an angel from heaven turned the rudder of her destiny." "[W]ith her same smile, Aracy closed the book she was studying, arose from her chair in the school and, without looking back, left everything to be the goddess of a home full of affection, tenderness, and love. She was to be wife and mother [of five]: the angelic companion of a public man, a famous doctor, a cultured, kind, and refined gentleman." [117]

Lavinia, a born rebel who was brought up by her father to believe that marriage was not a career for women, was perhaps more honest in expressing the ambivalence that many intelligent and ambitious women must have felt. Although she had taken great pleasure in working as a schoolteacher while she was single, she later subordinated her personal aspirations to helping her husband Raphael build his career. Reflecting back on her life, she remarked: "[M]arried I was no longer myself. I was [La]vinia-Raphael. My life was his life." [118]

It is important to emphasize that only a tiny number of privileged women could have contemplated pursuing a career for the purpose of achieving life-long self-fulfillment. Clearly, the vast majority of working women regarded their employment more instrumentally. Sometimes they saw it as a means to secure a good marriage, thereby liberating themselves from the need to work for wages as a long-term means of survival. In an age in which movies fostered the fantasy of the secretary marrying her boss, women could hope that they might find their prospective husbands on the job: men they would otherwise not have met. "Paquita," an orphan who worked her way up from seamstress, to typist, to proprietor of a small candy store, to student of a commercial school, and finally to secretary in a large industrial firm, regarded her achievements as the source of her security and happiness. But her "confidence in [her] future" was based not only on the professional skills she had acquired; more important, she credited professional success for her success in finding a fiancé who met her expectations and through whom she could fulfill her social ambitions. [119] Even if the fantasy of marrying the boss remained a fantasy, women sometimes regarded their earnings as protection against having to accept the first marriage offer. Free from immediate economic need, they could, in the words of one female writer, use their profession as a "dowry with which to obtain a more advantageous marriage." [120]

For the great majority of women in the workforce, however, employment was an urgent necessity to ensure the economic well-being of themselves and their families. It was their guarantee of survival—protection from starvation should their parents be unable to provide, should they be widowed or abandoned, or should their husband be unemployed or inadequately paid to support a family. If they bothered to contemplate the advantages or disadvantages of working for wages, their "choices" were not made freely. Most of these women (who generally worked under arduous, unhealthy, dangerous, abusive, or stifling conditions) would surely have given up their jobs had they been able to afford to do so. (And indeed, many moved in and out of the workforce as their families' material circumstances changed.) A 1942 survey of 261 female workers found that the vast majority (not only of factory workers but also of middle-class white-collar workers) worked only out of economic necessity, quickly became bored with the routine and the lack of stimulation, were discouraged by bad working conditions, low pay, and lack of opportunities for advancement, and would very happily have stopped working if possible.[121]

Yet this does not negate the fact that women—even in menial jobs—took pride in doing their jobs well, in being "useful" to society, and in providing for themselves and their families. "Risoleta," who began working as a maid at the age of eight, valued work and took great pride in being an excellent cook, even while she deeply resented the pitiful wages she earned, the sixteen-hour days, her lack of rights to paid vacation, days off, and social security, and the disrespect and disregard shown to her by employers. Nevertheless, it was the income she made working as a maid—supplemented by taking in laundry and boarders after she was widowed during her second pregnancy—that allowed her to raise her two daughters as well as five other abandoned children. Beginning in her late forties, she gradually went blind from the many hours she had spent at the hot, smoky wood stove, and she had to stop working. But if her life was, in her own words, a "struggle without respite," she was very proud to have supported and educated her children, including her two daughters, who both graduated from secondary school with degrees in accounting.[122]

In practice, the inclusion of middle- and upper-class women in the labor force probably benefited Brazil's economy more than it benefited women themselves. Only a small number of women gained real satisfaction and independence from their wage work, whereas the booming economy gained a large efficient pool of easily exploitable labor that could be channeled into routine, low-status jobs. Moreover, the entrance of an elite of women into new, more prestigious careers only very gradually modified stereotypes of female "nature." The potentially radical impact of female employment was undermined by the segregation of the vast majority of women workers in "female" jobs that provided them with very little pay, demanded only minimal skills, and allowed for no exercise of authority—in short, jobs that kept them powerless.

If a few pioneering women clearly valued their careers above family life and consequently arranged the latter around the former (or rejected marriage and motherhood altogether), the great majority of women continued to place family interests and needs first. Their ambivalence about women's domestic identity was matched by their ambivalence about rejecting it. And thus even as women won the "right" to work, they more often accepted it as a "duty" to be performed to the advantage of their families, not themselves. As long as women themselves regarded their work as secondary to wifehood and motherhood and as complementary to their husbands' work, female employment brought about neither rapid nor radical changes in gender relations. The potential threat of female employment to male power, family stability, and social order was thus contained, at least in the short run.

THE POLITICS OF FEMINISM(S)
AND ANTIFEMINISM(S)

What it meant to be a "feminist" was an issue of great contention in the late 1910s to 1930s in Brazil. Self-defined feminists ranged from "Catholic feminists" who preached that "without God, Fatherland, Honor, and Family, there is no feminism possible," to single professional women who looked abroad to Europe and the United States for models and who regarded paid employment as the most essential prerequisite for female emancipation.[1] In addition, a number of women who were labeled by others as "anarchist and libertarian feminists" rejected the label of "feminism" altogether, denouncing it as "bourgeois." Even within the organized feminist movement, the Federação Brasileira pelo Progresso Feminino (FBPF), very divergent views coexisted. As the organization increased in size during the 1920s and early 1930s, it brought together under one umbrella a diverse group of women's suffrage, professional, civic, and charitable organizations from all the states of Brazil. And its membership was divided between those fighting to secure social and political rights for women and those concerned primarily with elevating and celebrating women's domestic roles.[2]

In 1932, the FBPF won two political victories: women's suffrage and the establishment of Mother's Day.[3] The federation's president, Alice Pinheiro Coimbra, accepted the combination as natural and correct. "The cult of familial sentiments," she declared, "fits perfectly well within our program." She explained that from the time of its founding in 1922, the FBPF had aimed to make women more competent housewives as well as more competent actors in public life.[4] This dual focus was at once the federation's strength and its weakness. The breadth of the FBPF's program encouraged collaboration among career women and housewives, suffragists and charity workers. But by accommodating the concerns of very diverse groups, the FBPF avoided confronting the conflicts between women's public and private roles, as well as the contradictions between definitions of women as innately different from men (usually "superior," but still unequal) and potentially the same (thus equal). And so, although the FBPF played an important part in winning key political victories for women, it never succeeded in bringing about the far-reaching social and cultural changes its leaders envisioned.

Between 1918 and 1937, Brazil's feminist movements played a key role in shaping the ways in which their country's gender order was redefined.[5] Well educated, accomplished, and in numerous cases politically well connected, feminists commanded attention from Brazil's professional and political communities to their demands for social, economic, and political equality. And they won significant victories: greater access for women to education and employment opportunities, female suffrage, and other legal and institutional reforms.

However, they quickly ran up against the narrow limits set by Brazil's socioeconomic structure and traditional cultural norms. Committed to a reformist program of integrating women more fully into bourgeois capitalist society, they could not bridge the wide gap between social classes. If female suffrage challenged patriarchal power as institutionalized in the state and marked women's formal entrance into political life, the vote was meaningless for the majority of Brazilian women who remained unenfranchised (because of the continued literacy requirement) and largely useless as a tool for improving the conditions of the vast majority of Brazilian women's lives (owing to the elitist and authoritarian nature of Brazilian politics). Because relatively few Brazilian women had gained the educational and professional opportunities that so profoundly affected the lives and consciousness of the urban middle- and upper-class feminist elite that dominated the FBPF, the latter's feminism remained alien to the vast majority of Brazilian women. And so the feminist movement lacked the grassroots support that would have been necessary to bring about rapid and radical cultural changes, enforce implementation of institutional and legal reforms, and effectively confront the strong antifeminist reaction that built during the 1930s and 1940s. After 1937, this reaction, fueled by the installation of a dictatorship, crushed the still young feminist movement.

Organized Feminism
▼ ▼ ▼

The undisputed leader of the organized feminist movement was Bertha Lutz, whose family background, education, and life choices set her apart from mainstream Brazilian society. Lutz was born in 1894 in São Paulo to Adolpho Lutz, a Swiss-born specialist in tropical medicine, and Amy Fowler, an English-born nurse and founder of a school for neglected boys. Lutz earned degrees in biology from the University of Paris and law from the University of Rio de Janeiro. In 1919, she won the post of secretary of the National Museum, thereby becoming the second woman to hold a high civil service post in Brazil. From there, she went on to build a highly successful career as an administrator, politician, and scientist. Neither marriage nor motherhood ever figured in her life.[6]

While a student in Paris, Lutz was influenced by European feminist movements, and upon returning to Brazil, she undertook the task of organizing Brazilian women to campaign for their social, political, economic, and intellectual emancipation. She began cautiously in December 1918 by publishing an appeal to women in a popular Rio de Janeiro magazine. She called on women to join together to form "an association [not] of suffragettes who break windows in the streets, but a society of Brazilians who understand that the woman should not live parasitically off [the prerogatives] of her sex, taking advantage of the animal instincts of man, but ought to be useful, educate herself and her children, and become capable of fulfilling the political duties that the future cannot but share with her."[7]

The organization that emerged from her appeal, the League for the Intellectual Emancipation of Women (Liga para a Emancipação Intellectual Feminina), campaigned for women's rights through issuing proclamations, circulating petitions, and writing articles for the press. Bertha Lutz set the agenda for the campaign: education, employment, and suffrage. First, she appealed to the Ministry of Education to provide rigorous secondary education for women so that they would be adequately prepared to pass university entrance examinations and compete with men in securing paid employment. Her appeal was answered in 1922, when women were for the first time admitted to the prestigious Rio de Janeiro school Colégio Dom Pedro II.[8] Second, she voiced her conviction that the emancipation of women lay in wage work:

> [W]ork is the most powerful instrument in the hands of a woman, with which, guided by a new ideal, she will seek not only to improve her social position, but also to become more independent and useful. Personally, I believe that both present social circumstances and future trends require, for

the interest of humanity and the woman, that she seek economic emancipation and intellectual expansion in work. For this reason, I consider that in Brazil the true "leaders" of feminism, correctly understood, are the innumerable young women who work in industry, in commerce, in teaching, and in other spheres of human activity.[9]

Third, she argued for the justice and necessity of female suffrage, stressing that it would both dignify and empower women. Lutz believed that once women were enfranchised, they would be able to ensure their future material and moral well-being.[10]

Lutz's position as a government employee provided opportunities for her to establish formal contacts with women's organizations throughout Europe and the Americas. These contacts greatly enhanced her personal prestige and the authority with which she spoke. In 1919, she was chosen as Brazil's official delegate to the International Labor Organization's conference on the conditions of working women.[11] In April 1922, she represented Brazilian women at the first Pan American Conference of Women, held in Baltimore. There, she joined with other Latin American delegates to form the Pan American Association for the Advancement of Women. The League for Female Intellectual Emancipation was designated the Brazilian branch of this organization; Lutz was elected one of its vice presidents.[12]

Impressed by the organization and tactics of the women's movement in the United States, Lutz solicited the help of Carrie Chapman Catt in drawing up a constitution for a new national feminist organization in Brazil that would supersede the Rio de Janeiro–based league.[13] On 19 August 1922, Lutz founded the FBPF. It was designed as an umbrella organization that would bring together women from all states in Brazil who were working to achieve women's rights or involved in social action and charitable organizations.[14] The FBPF's goals echoed those of the Pan American Association: to promote female education and raise the level of instruction available to women; to win civil and political rights for women; to protect mothers and children; to obtain legislative guarantees for female labor; to promote female organizations and open up new opportunities for women to engage in social and political action; and to strengthen friendly links with other American nations in order to guarantee the preservation of peace.[15] Its directorate included professional women, the prominent novelist Júlia Lopes de Almeida and her daughter Margarida, the wives of several leading politicians, and Bertha Lutz.[16]

The FBPF quickly gained national prominence upon staging a five-day international convention in December 1922. It was attended by female delegates from various states in Brazil, by representatives of women's social service, charity, and professional organizations, and by numerous congressmen and government officials. The presence of Carrie Chapman Catt and Elisabeth Babcock from the United States, Ana de Castro Osório from Portugal, and Rosa Manus from Holland lent further prestige to the gathering. A luncheon held for Bertha Lutz by Edward Morgan, United States ambassador to Brazil, brought together the leaders of the Brazilian feminist movement with Brazil's vice president, minister of foreign relations, director of public education, and various congressmen.[17]

Commissions were established to set priorities for action. The commission on female employment heard testimony from representatives of the Teachers' League, the Rio de Janeiro Union of Employees in Commerce, and the Bureau of Employees of the Young Women's Christian Association on the problems faced by working women: poor transportation, excessive hours, low pay, sexual harassment, bad hygiene in workplaces, and the lack of legal guarantees. At the same time, these representatives protested the limited opportunities for women to enter the labor force.[18] Upon the commission's recommendation, the convention resolved: "[C]onsidering the urgency of ensuring legal protection for female labor, which has been subject to inhuman exploitation, reducing women to an inferior position in the competition for industrial and agricultural salaries, as well as in other activities of modern life, it has become necessary to call to the attention of political leaders the need to incorporate protective measures for women into our social legislation."[19] The FBPF endorsed the 1919 recommendations of the International Labor Organization for legal regulation and protection of female employment.[20]

The commission on the improvement and extension of female education resolved that the FBPF should support coeducation at all ages, obligatory primary education, the extension of domestic, civic, and vocational education for women, and the admission of women to all secondary and university courses.[21]

Following addresses given by Senator Justo Chermont and Carrie Chapman Catt, the commission on political and civil rights established the Brazilian Female Suffrage Alliance (Aliança Brasileira pelo Sufrágio Feminino). Justo Chermont's wife assumed the presidency; two of the three vice presidents chosen were also wives of leading politicians; and Bertha Lutz filled the position of secretary-general.[22]

Immediately after the convention, Carrie Chapman Catt's visit to the state capitals of Bahia, Pernambuco, and São Paulo provided momentum and publicity for local branches of the FBPF. In São Paulo, Catt's visit coincided with the founding of the São Paulo Women's Suffrage Alliance (Aliança Paulista pelo Sufrágio Feminino). At a public forum attended by prominent members of the *paulista* elite, Catt shared the stage with the São Paulo alliance's president, lawyer Walkyria Moreira da Silva, and its secretary-general, writer Diva Nolf Nazario.[23]

Throughout the 1920s, members of the FBPF campaigned to promote women's rights. They obtained publicity through interviews, public forums, petitions, and manifestos.[24] They used the press to respond to the arguments of antifeminists. They supported politicians who favored women's rights and attacked others who did not.[25] They secured a formal statement from the Brazilian Association of Lawyers that the Constitution did not specifically forbid female suffrage, and many attempted to register to vote, thereby bringing the issue to public attention.[26] They pressed for reforms in the Civil Code that would eliminate the relative incapacity of married women. They lobbied for labor legislation to protect the interests of women workers, and they used their skills and influence to improve female education. They maintained contacts with the international women's movement through copious correspondence and frequent travel abroad. Bertha Lutz attended the 1923 and 1929 conventions of the International Woman Suffrage Alliance in Rome and Berlin, as well as the 1925 Pan American Conference of Women in Washington, D.C. Margarida Lopes de Almeida traveled to Paris as Brazil's official delegate to the 1926 International Woman Suffrage Alliance convention.[27] Finally, the members of the FBPF mobilized greater numbers of women to participate in their campaigns by establishing new women's organizations: the Association of University Women (União Universitária Feminina), the Association of Women Civil Service Workers (União de Funcionárias Públicas), the League of Independent Women Voters (Liga Eleitoral Independente), and the Professional Women's Association (União Profissional Feminina).[28] Their activities and successes were recorded in books published by Diva Nolf Nazario, secretary of the São Paulo Women's Suffrage Alliance, and Mariana Coelho, member of the Pernambuco branch of the FBPF.[29]

The October 1930 revolution brought about a political opening that was quickly seized by the FBPF. Although the leading members of the new government were not advocates of feminism, their commitment to electoral and labor reform and social welfare presented the organized feminist movement with new opportunities. In June 1931, the FBPF held its second international convention in Rio de Janeiro. This time, the convention ran for eleven days and was attended by representatives from every state in Brazil, from twenty-eight women's civic, social service, professional, and suffrage organizations, and from eighteen foreign organizations. Following formal presentations and debates, the convention formulated official policy recommendations for constitutional and legislative changes as well as for social policies that would further women's rights.

Among the most important of the resolutions passed was that which declared women's economic emancipation to be a central problem of the feminist movement. To hasten women's economic emancipation, the convention recommended that modern public education be oriented toward preparing women to exercise a profession. And to facilitate the entrance of women into paid employment, the convention called for the establishment of a bureau of women and children, the creation of a corps of inspectors to ensure rigorous enforcement of hygienic standards in workplaces, and the effective implementation of minimum salary, equal pay for equal work, prohibitions on sex discrimination in civil service hiring, and paid maternity leaves. In addition, the convention emphasized the need to rationalize public assistance programs, and it argued that this required fostering the social work profession and relying on the expertise and human relations skills of women. Yet at the same time, because large numbers of Brazilian women remained outside the paid labor force, the convention resolved that the FBPF should stress the importance of domestic economy for the national economy and strive to win acknowledgment that the economic activities of housewives were as valuable as other productive activities.[30]

Following the 1931 convention, women's participation in formulating public policy increased rapidly. It was to a great extent thanks to the unrelenting pressure of the FBPF that Brazilian women won the vote through a decree issued on 24 February 1932.[31] In May of that year, Lutz was appointed to the government commission charged with preparing a draft of the new constitution. She produced a document entitled *Thirteen Principles* that drew on the technical advice of the female lawyers who were members of the FBPF and on policy proposals that had been hammered out during the federation's conventions.[32] At the FBPF's national convention in 1933, Lutz's *Thirteen Principles* won official endorsement.[33] Although no FBPF candidate was elected to the Constituent Assembly, the federation successfully lobbied for acceptance of its proposals. Included among the changes introduced in the 1934 Constitution were the right of Brazilian women to retain their citizenship and pass it on to their children despite marriage to a foreigner; female suffrage and equality before the law without distinction on the basis of sex; the establishment of the following guiding principles for labor legislation: equal pay for equal work, minimum salary, the eight-hour day, annual paid holidays, maternity leaves, and insurance to protect workers against sickness, accidents, disability, and retirement; the right of women to occupy all public positions without distinctions based on civil status and the right to take three-month maternity leaves with full pay; the requirement of preferential participation of qualified women in the direction and administration of social assistance programs concerning maternity, child welfare, female labor, and the organization of the home; and the requirement that all levels of government assure the support of mothers and the protection of children through legal guarantees, the establishment of specialized services, and the allocation of 1 percent of tax revenues to this end.[34]

Following the achievement of female suffrage and the drafting of the 1934 Constitution, the FBPF directorate outlined an extremely ambitious set of new objectives. Bertha Lutz, in two articles published in the FBPF *Bulletin*, proclaimed that female suffrage was not an end in itself but an instrument to be used to improve women's status. She warned women that their newly won rights were precarious and that the real battle still lay ahead: women had not yet entered the "Promised Land"; they had only arrived on the margins of the corrupt political system—the "outskirts of a camp of gold seekers." Women's task, therefore, was to unite in defending their sex, use their democratic rights, elect idealistic and uncorruptible feminists to public office, change the country's laws in favor of women and children, and infuse the political system with "profoundly social, pacific, and humanitarian values."[35] Lutz recognized that in an international climate in which feminism was facing mounting opposition, the achievement of these goals would be difficult. Yet she continued to set her sights ever higher. It was her conviction that feminism should be understood as more than a peaceful reform movement that arose naturally at the historical moment when household production was transferred to the marketplace; it was also a movement that sought a "permanent revolution" in customs, habits, and laws.[36]

The FBPF's commitment to this "permanent revolution" was expressed in its 1935 "New Plan of Action." Among the stated goals was to create a new type of woman—conscious of her dignity and emancipated through education, wage work, and participation in political life—who would infuse Brazilian culture with female values.[37] On a more concrete level, the conventions held in 1934 and 1936 hammered out an elaborate program aimed at consolidating and extending the gains that had been achieved. Members of the FBPF turned their energies toward securing juridical implementation of constitutional rights and guarantees, educating and encouraging women to assume new social, economic, and political roles, and building a broader base of public support for feminism.[38]

The conventions placed primary emphasis on equal employment opportunities. Bertha Lutz argued adamantly that economic emancipation was the precondition for all other forms of emancipation for women.[39] And the FBPF's strongest statement in favor of equality was contained in its 1936 demand that the government institute a "Statute on Women" that would guarantee to all women, regardless of civil status, the freedom to engage in any profession or economic activity of their choice, as well as protection against all restrictions based on sex, including discrimination in hiring and firing due to marriage or pregnancy.[40] In order to further ensure equal treatment, the organization demanded a prohibition on the segregation of women in low-status and low-paying female occupations, a practice that resulted in the undermining of the principle of equal pay for equal work.[41] It also opposed "false protectionism," such as restrictions on female labor after ten o'clock in the evening, which in effect deprived women of equal opportunities to earn a living.[42] In an attempt to resolve the tension between protectionism and equal treatment that arose over the issue of maternity, the FBPF demanded that maternity be declared a source of rights (not privileges).[43] Bertha Lutz expressed concern that laws requiring employers to contribute toward maternity benefits might in practice increase discrimination against women in hiring as well as encourage more frequent firing of married and pregnant women.[44] Nevertheless, the FBPF supported the extension of the right to take paid maternity leave to employees of private as well as public enterprises.[45]

In the area of legislative reform, the conventions also devoted energy to securing changes in the Civil Code that would establish the absolute equality of married women with their husbands and changes in the Penal Code that would establish equal treatment of men and women involved in adultery and prostitution.[46] However, on the extremely controversial issue of divorce (which was opposed by the Catholic Church and probably by many of the FBPF's members who were practicing Catholics), the FBPF backed away from taking a position, calling instead for a national plebiscite.[47]

Despite the FBPF's commitment to the principle of equality, it favored preferential access for women to certain jobs. Plans were coordinated to push for an enormous expansion of federal, state, and municipal social service agencies whose programs would not only benefit women directly (as the recipients of aid) but would also open up new jobs for female administrators, social workers, and inspectors of workplaces.[48] The FBPF insisted on the strict observation of Article 121.3 of the 1934 Constitution, which specified that the direction and administration of social welfare programs should by preference be entrusted to qualified women. The federation emphasized that this was appropriate and necessary not only because women had greater experience and expertise in this area but also because women's "patience, dedication, attention to detail, objectivity, thrift, and high moral sense" made them better suited to performing social service work than men.[49] Bertha Lutz interpreted this "female vocation" in social service as an extension of women's maternal vocation and looked forward to the day when it might assume "colossal proportions."[50] She believed that the creation of a large corps of social workers was desirable both because it would help destitute women and children and because it would encourage treatment of delinquency and criminality through rehabilitation rather than repression.[51] The FBPF proposed the creation of a female police force that would be responsible for handling women and children, both as criminals and as victims. Furthermore, the federation argued that inmates in women's and children's prisons should be treated exclusively by female jailers, physicians, and psychiatrists.[52]

To guard against misinterpretation and misapplication of constitutional and legal provisions, the FBPF lobbied for the establishment of a national "technical council" of nine women charged with promoting social welfare and popular culture, consulting in the elaboration of such programs, supervising their administration, and reporting annually on their progress.[53] In addition, the FBPF demanded not only the participation of women in all other legislative, advisory, administrative, and technical bodies of the government concerned with finances and labor but also the appointment of women to a certain percentage of leadership positions in these bodies.[54] In the case of the all-male National Labor Council, direct pressure was exerted in the attempt to force the minister of labor to appoint female members. The FBPF collected the signatures of seven hundred working women on a petition demanding proportional representation for women on the council.[55]

The FBPF recognized that successful consolidation of gains required a large-scale mobilization of women throughout Brazil. Therefore, various commissions of the FBPF together with the League of Independent Women Voters made attempts to raise the political consciousness of women, to involve them in discussions of social and political policies, and to encourage them to vote. Tactics included setting up voting registration stations for women and disseminating information about women's new rights and civic duties through literature, lecture tours, and traveling caravans. In 1934, the immediate concern was sponsoring female candidates for public office and endorsing male candidates who supported feminist objectives. Long-term plans included building an active network of local branches of the league throughout Brazil and establishing new female organizations of schoolteachers, mothers, and workers through which feminist ideas could be spread.[56]

In addition, the FBPF campaigned for the establishment of a government women's bureau that would have provided increased legitimacy for the feminist movement, as well as significant financial backing. According to a proposal made during the FBPF's 1936 convention and refined by Bertha Lutz, the bureau was to be run by women through national, state, and municipal branches. Its preliminary tasks would be research into the actual conditions of women, organization of a system of maternal insurance, preparation of didactic material to be used for radio broadcasts, and training of professional social workers.

It was envisioned that the bureau would eventually direct and oversee all services related to female employment, maternal insurance, female education and vocational training, and social welfare.[57]

Bertha Lutz's inauguration as a federal congresswoman in June 1936 and her assumption of the chair of the Special Congressional Commission on the Statute on Women raised the hopes of feminists that the FBPF's demands and proposals would receive serious consideration by Congress.[58] Their hopes were short lived, however.

The November 1937 coup abruptly cut off the channels through which the FBPF had worked. The authoritarian Estado Novo dissolved Congress, suspended the vote, disbanded political parties, imposed press censorship, and rewrote the Constitution. The political skills that feminists had acquired and their tactics of lobbying and petitioning were useless under the dictatorship, as were arguments based on liberal democratic principles. Many of the constitutional guarantees won in 1934 were lost before they had been implemented; the 1937 Constitution neither specifically prohibited discrimination on the basis of sex, nor guaranteed equal pay for equal work, nor required women's participation in public programs that affected women, nor declared the protection of maternity to be an obligation of the government. Bertha Lutz's fears that women's access to paid employment might easily be restricted were fulfilled. After 1937, the consular service dismissed female officials, and several other government agencies ceased to consider women's applications to certain positions.[59] The FBPF discontinued publication of its *Bulletin*, plans for the organization of a large-scale feminist movement collapsed, and the hope that significant changes could be brought about in women's status and consciousness evaporated.

Any evaluation of the FBPF must recognize that it developed within the confines of severe objective and subjective constraints. Although feminism was most appealing to urban middle-class and upper-middle-class women whose lives had been deeply affected by the changes brought about by rapid urbanization and industrialization, even among this group organizing was extremely difficult. Until larger numbers of women chose (or were forced) to look beyond the family and domestic roles for self-fulfillment, social status, and economic security, their continued material and psychological dependence on men severely limited the possibilities for a revolution in female consciousness. Even among women who agreed with feminist critiques and goals, organizing was hindered by the absence of a tradition and experience in working together for social and political goals, as well as by women's vulnerability to ridicule and humiliation (especially to attacks of being "unfeminine," "un-Christian," or "immoral"). Outside urban centers, tradition hung even heavier. Women of small towns and rural areas had little or no access to higher education and respectable paid employment. Moreover, even their freedom to venture unaccompanied beyond the confines of their homes was often still restricted.

Another factor that limited the possibilities for organization was the wide gap between social classes in Brazil and the intensity of class conflict during this period. On the one hand, the vast majority of middle-class feminists were unwilling—and perhaps unable—to cross class lines. Not only did they share middle-class fears, prejudices, and patronizing attitudes about the working class, but they also depended on low-paid domestic servants to run their households while they pursued professions and engaged in political activities. Although the FBPF programs always included demands for improved working conditions for working-class women as well as protections for pregnant women and children, linkages to poor women were tenuous at best. The professional women who made up the FBPF directorate spoke in the name of working-class women rather than mobilizing the later to speak for themselves, and they declined to support confrontational tactics, including women's strikes. Even the large numbers of schoolteachers and civil service employees who filled the rank and file of the FBPF, along with nurses, typists, salesclerks, seamstresses, typesetters, bookbinders, and others, rarely participated on an equal footing with the smaller number of professional women who made up the federation's directorate and who made the key decisions. Factory workers and maids did not figure among the FBPF membership. Such women participated only in very rare instances, such as in 1924 when hundreds of factory workers signed an FBPF petition to include women on the National Labor Council, or in 1933, when waitresses convinced the FBPF to oppose legislation that prohibited female employment between ten at night and five in the morning.[60]

On the other hand, working-class women had little reason to join the feminist movement. If achievement of political and civil rights and equal access to higher education and professional employment were crucial to middle- and upper-middle-class women, these were largely irrelevant to the majority of Brazilian women who were still illiterate. Moreover, working-class women lacked the skills required to participate in the FBPF's tactics of political campaigning and petitioning; and they would certainly have been quite out of place at the gala luncheons held by the federation at the most exclusive social clubs.

Beyond this, the effective limitation of organized feminism to "respectable" middle- and upper-middle-class womenfolk served the purpose of maintaining the image of moral unimpeachability and ladylikeness that was undoubtedly important in winning the favor of liberal male politicians. And the high academic, artistic, and professional achievements of most of the FBPF's active members made it impossible for opponents to contend that these women were incapable of responsibly exercising political rights. Had the FBPF mixed in class politics, feminists would have compromised their carefully cultivated image as highly skilled, peaceful, and reasonable reformers. If feminism was already threatening in itself, feminism linked to the class struggle in this highly conflictive and class-bound society would have been intolerable.

The FBPF's tactics were carefully adapted to the limitations of the context in which the organization operated. Skillful diplomacy was required to win respectable middle-class allies, male and female. Special care was taken to avoid direct criticisms of those aspects of ordinary middle-class women's lives that had traditionally provided the only sources of identity, meaning, and purpose and to which most of these women were firmly committed. Never did the FBPF explicitly attack the family and domesticity as a source of female oppression (although some of its members did so as individuals); instead, the organization sought to encourage women to regard their skills in household economy as valuable assets that could and should be used in paid employment and political participation. Bertha Lutz, in a speech delivered to the Chamber of Deputies on the occasion of her entrance, argued: "The home is the base of society, and the woman will always be integrated into the home. But the home no longer fits within the space of four walls. The home is also the school, the factory, the office. The home is principally the parliament where the laws that regulate the family and human society are made." [61] Such statements implicitly rejected the role of wife and mother as an adequate source of self-fulfillment, social status, and economic security without, however, directly attacking the family or women who were content with their domestic identity. In what was probably a fairly conscious attempt to preempt hostile attacks, FBPF members also frequently emphasized their femininity. They used stereotypes about the "natural" differences between the sexes as the most effective justifications for the entrance of women into new areas of social and political participation. Finally, because of the importance that religion played in most women's lives, the FBPF also exercised great care to avoid confrontation with the Catholic Church.

Federation activists chose to fight on the fronts where they felt most self-confident and saw the clearest opportunities for success. The competence of FBPF members in organizing, public speaking, and learning the rules of the political system earned feminists the respect and support of influential men. And the cultivation of links with international feminist organizations enhanced their legitimacy and prestige in the eyes of liberal congressmen, many of whom, eager to demonstrate their modernity and true liberalism, were easily persuaded to support the early feminist reforms. For a number of women, a leadership position in the FBPF served as a training ground for later entrance into municipal, state, or national politics.

The commitment of FBPF members to reformist politics was founded in the belief that liberal democracy was a relatively favorable system for women and in the expectation that initial political gains could be used to pry open the system further for the benefit of all women.[62] They demanded not political revolution but what were nevertheless radical steps for the time: the application of the liberal ideal of equality to women and family relations and the incorporation of women's concerns, opinions, and values into the public sphere. They believed that the emancipation and empowering of women through effective political participation and through paid employment that ensured economic independence from men could eventually bring about radical transformations in women's consciousness and in Brazilian society and culture.

Ultimately, the most ambitious goals of the FBPF's leaders were frustrated, however. Political repression and formidable obstacles to women's economic independence were compounded by unanticipated difficulties in uprooting the attitudes that sustained patriarchal power. The feminist movement itself did (and perhaps could do) little to effect significant changes in women's consciousness. The time may not have been ripe for attacking stereotypes about female moral superiority and "natural" abilities, but the cost of using such stereotypes was to leave intact the mystique of "female nature." Even among FBPF members who were experienced political activists and who enjoyed economic independence, not all developed what could be considered a genuinely new feminist consciousness. One São Paulo delegate to several FBPF conventions was physician Carlota Pereira de Queiroz. In 1931, as the only woman delegate to the Constituent Assembly, and later as a congresswoman, she staunchly opposed the FBPF's proposal for the establishment of a government women's bureau. She maintained that such a bureau would foster a "struggle between the sexes" rather than a "natural collaboration—true and harmonious with our traditions."[63]

The FBPF brought professional organizations and unions of working women together with typically conservative charitable organizations. Professional women such as Mariana Coelho, Carmen Portinho, and Bertha Lutz passionately believed that women's inferior status was the direct result of the sexual division of labor and that employment was the precondition for women's emancipation—the only guarantee of economic security, independence from men, and ultimate happiness.[64] All three of these women clearly rejected the Church's position on women, although only Coelho openly accused the Catholic Church of humiliating and fostering social contempt for women.[65] And all three remained single, although Coelho alone publicly rejected all platitudes about the glory of married life and motherhood.[66] The caution of Portinho and Lutz suggests that the goals and tactics of many FBPF-affiliated organizations reflected more closely the assumptions and ideals of the Catholic Church than the secular feminist program of Bertha Lutz. For example, Luiza Roberti Soares, speaking as secretary of the Brazilian Women's Civic Alliance, proclaimed: "I am a fervent defender of the great ideal of women's rights, of [women's] emancipation from the absurd prejudices that have kept them in an inferior position." Yet her overriding concern was to teach women to be model wives and mothers. No longer, she declared, could women be "objects of luxury." They were to work for "social equality" but not through "revolutions or [boisterous] meetings." In her view, the "first step of feminism" involved educating women in "correct principles of hygiene and morality." Only then could they be "sincere cooperators at home and in real life, and above all . . . vigilant educators of the spirit and character of their sons—future men."[67]

The program of the 1931 convention encompassed these disparate viewpoints. Although an "Exhibition of the Home" demonstrated women's skills in home economics and applied arts and displayed modern appliances for simplifying and beautifying the home, the convention as a whole declared women's economic emancipation to be the central issue deserving attention.[68] Such oppositions existed despite the official unity of the FBPF's affiliated organizations behind statements of purpose and programs of action. Federation president Alice Pinheiro Coimbra's 1932 declaration of the solidarity of Brazilian women was belied in practice.[69] As a federation, the FBPF brought together women who held primary commitments to very different causes. Although the opinions of Bertha Lutz and her close followers prevailed in the formulation of the FBPF's program, members interpreted these programs in vastly different ways, using whatever elements furthered their particular purposes and ignoring others. The radical impulses that underlay the FBPF's programs were easily sapped at the point of implementation by women who lacked Lutz's convictions. To a large extent, Lutz remained a spiritual exile in Brazil, alienated not only from the masses of Brazilian women but also from many—perhaps most—of those who made up her organization.[70]

Other Feminisms
▼ ▼ ▼

Much more threatening in the popular imagination were women labeled "anarchist and libertarian feminists." Impatient with the organized feminist movement's timidity in attacking women's subordination within the family, its silence on the issues of divorce and sexual freedom, and its failure to address seriously issues of central concern to the female proletariat, these women denounced feminism as "bourgeois" and rejected the label altogether. The two most conspicuous and outspoken feminists (if we can use this label that they rejected) on the Left were Maria Lacerda de Moura and Patrícia Galvão (known as Pagu).

Maria Lacerda de Moura—born in a small town in the state of Minas Gerais in 1887, educated at the normal school, and married at seventeen—began rejecting her domestic identity at the age of twenty-seven, when she embarked on an intellectual pilgrimage that was to lead her to a radical, but isolated, feminist position. In 1919, she joined Bertha Lutz in founding the League for Female Intellectual Emancipation. But her move to the city of São Paulo in the early 1920s, and her exposure to the living conditions of the urban proletariat as well as to leftist political ideologies fostered a profound change in her consciousness. She began participating in educational projects organized by the group of anarchists who ran the Biblioteca Social A Inovadora (a library, bookstore, and educational center) and became the editor of its short-lived journal, *Renascença*, in 1923.[71] In the second issue of the journal, a statement of principles included the following: "Our Director [Maria Lacerda de Moura] is in fact an advocate of the rational emancipation of women, although her latest works have gone beyond this. Female emancipation is one link in the chain that will liberate all humanity. This arises from the following point of view: the woman is the slave of modern slaves."[72]

A year later, in her book *A mulher é uma degenerada?* (The Woman Is a Degenerate?), Maria Lacerda explicitly and publicly attacked the feminist movement she had helped organize: "What good is the equality of legal and political rights for a half-dozen privileged women, themselves a part of the privileged class, if the majority of women continue to stagnate in the misery of their millennial slavery?"[73] As an alternative program, she demanded not only the end of bourgeois capitalism in order to liberate women from misery but also profound cultural transformations in order to liberate women from mental slavery: "Against [the power of official education and religion to restrict women's consciousness] it is necessary [to use] a very sharp stiletto that wounds without pity and leaves inside the subtle thorn of doubt . . . and the necessity to seek asylum on firmer ground."[74]

The problems of family organization and love became increasingly central to Maria Lacerda's thought by the late 1920s. Finding support in the writings of Russian feminist Alexandra Kolontai and free-love advocates Ellen Key and Han Ryner, she vehemently denounced marriage and urged women to become economically independent so they could seek love and sexual fulfillment out-side the boundaries of social conventions and legal bonds.[75] She also practiced what she preached.[76] In the face of an escalation of attacks on her views, Maria Lacerda lashed out at her opponents, accusing them of narrow-mindedness and bad faith.[77] At the same time, she became increasingly alienated not only from mainstream society but from the causes and parties she had previously endorsed. In 1932, in her book entitled *Amai e . . . não vos multipliqueis* (Love and . . . Do Not Procreate), she declared:

> [The woman], eternally tutored, doubly enslaved, in the name of re-claiming her rights, in the name of female emancipation, in the name of so many banners, so many idols—fatherland, home, society, religion, moral-ity, good manners, civil and political rights, communism, fascism, every other ism, revolutions, and barricades—continues to be the slave, an in-strument skillfully manipulated by men for their sectarian, power-hungry, economic, religious, political, or social causes. . . .
>
> Within all [parties], with the most varied platforms, I know those who are interested only in their own freedom and the victory of their own party, without the slightest concern for women, and without the least understand-ing of women's rights and needs. They are libertarians and their legal fam-ily is very bourgeois. . . .
>
> Every [reformer], absolutely every one seeks to stifle the true inner ne-cessities of women.[78]

Embittered and discouraged, Maria Lacerda ceased publishing after 1934 and embarked on a private, tortured search for love and self-fulfillment. She moved to an island to find solitude and self-sufficiency, retreated into mysti-cism, and lived out the advice she had given to women: "Let us be deserters of the family, social deserters, free individualists—in order to think and dream and live in harmony with our conscience."[79]

Patrícia Galvão (Pagu)—the irreverent, liberated, and politicized child of the next generation—had nothing but scorn for the political agenda and moralism of bourgeois feminism. As a teenager in the late 1920s, she delighted in shock-ing middle-class *paulista* society by flaunting her disdain for the canons of po-lite behavior. Using her sexuality as well as her extravagant and rebellious manner to win her way into the *paulista* avant-garde, she quickly occupied the spotlight. More than anyone else, Pagu embodied the *antropofagist* creed: "[to] constantly and directly consume the taboo" or "[to transform the] taboo into totem."[80] Her admirers proclaimed her the "ultimate product of São Paulo": "Pagu abolished the grammar of life"; "she would be capable of devouring var-ious venomous bishops."[81]

*Sketch of "Pagu" (Patrícia Galvão) by Emiliano Di Cavalcanti, 1929.
(From* Para Todos, *27 July 1929, p. 21)*

In mockery of the bourgeois institution of marriage, Pagu collaborated with avant-garde novelist Oswald de Andrade (who was then married to her friend and mentor Tarsila do Amaral) in arranging her farcical marriage to painter Waldemar Belisario de Amaral (who had been raised by Tarsila's family). As the newlyweds were driving to the coast for a honeymoon, Oswald took Walde-mar's place. The marriage was officially annulled several months later. By that time, Oswald and Pagu had already consummated their "romance of the anar-chist epoch" by "marrying" in front of his family's tomb in the city cemetery— in Oswald's words, "the ultimate defiance." And Pagu was pregnant with a son, Rudá, born in September 1930.[82] But wifehood and motherhood occupied little of Pagu's time and energy. She hired a nurse to care for Rudá, rejected house-keeping for political activism, and separated from Oswald within a few years. Later in life she summed up her attitude toward marriage: "Women in all civi-lized times have only known one goal—marriage. Her place in the sun, shel-tered by the virile and protecting shadow of a man who takes upon himself all the initiative. All [women's] longings and needs are cut off at this point, with the consequent suffering implicit in the contract."[83]

In 1931, Pagu joined the Brazilian Communist Party, followed its orders to "become a member of the proletariat," and took up the cause of socialist revo-lution. She immersed herself in the lives of the female proletariat, working at the worst of jobs and experiencing firsthand the arrogance of bosses and the humiliation and rage of women workers.[84] During this period, she wrote a col-umn entitled "A mulher do povo" (The Woman of the People), in which she commented on the behavior and values of São Paulo's female population. She viciously attacked the hypocritical, sterile bourgeois (and Catholic) morality that prevented women from using their minds and bodies freely, thus fostering triviality and neurotic perversions rather than healthy sensuality. Pagu's con-demnation of the bourgeois feminist movement was also ardent. She mocked the notion that Brazil's feminists were in any sense a "vanguard" or had any-thing "revolutionary" to propose. Not only did she attack the FBPF's suffrage campaign as elitist and naive, but she also scorned the campaigns by Maria Lacerda de Moura and other anarchist women for sexual liberation and "con-scientious maternity." Instead of living like "parasites," dependent on the ex-ploitation of their maids for their freedom, she proposed that feminists first fight to overcome poverty and class exploitation.[85]

Eventually, however, Pagu looked back at her experience as a party activist with profound bitterness, for the party could not accommodate her individual-ism or her radicalism as a woman.[86] In 1933, when she published her "proletar-ian novel" *Parque industrial* denouncing the sexual exploitation of the female proletariat, the puritanical Brazilian Communist Party was so offended by the novel's sexual explicitness that she was forced to publish under a pseudonym. Ultimately, Pagu's unorthodox revolutionary vision did not fit within the party's project; it threatened the party's public image and its grassroots support as well as its internal discipline, which—among other things—required no "amorous adventure[s] or sexual scandal[s]."[87]

Too far ahead of their time and separated even from each other, Maria Lacerda de Moura and Patrícia Galvão were gradually but systematically marginalized. Their revolutionary vision as women fit neither into the projects of leftist political parties of the 1920s and 1930s nor into the programs of Brazil's organized feminists. Although they—and other lesser-known women like them—clearly posed the greatest threat, they remained isolated individuals on the fringe who never formed a movement that could attract significant support or pose a serious challenge to the status quo.[88]

At the other end of the political spectrum—to the right of the FBPF—was "Catholic feminism," zealously espoused by the *Revista Feminina* and endorsed by prominent male conservatives and (presumably) by the magazine's tens of thousands of middle-class female subscribers. From the magazine's inception in 1914 until it ceased publication in 1927 (following its founder's death), the editors proclaimed their enthusiastic support for and commitment to feminism. And they sought to make their magazine into a forum of debate over women's issues as well as a vehicle of communication among women's groups. But their feminism was quite different in its tone and goals from that of the FBPF (which refused to collaborate with the magazine).

Editors of the *Revista Feminina* constantly emphasized the conservative nature and origins of "real" feminism in an attempt to change what they considered to be a common misconception of feminism: "the derangement of old maids who did not find a husband, and who aspire to disorganize life and the home with an inversion of social values."[89] They repeatedly claimed that feminism, properly understood, was the fruit not of revolutionary desires but of profoundly conservative instincts. Its goal was not destruction or subversion but the preservation and reconstruction of Christian morality.

> Not this revolutionary feminism that preaches the destruction of the family, that disavows the idea of God, that ignores the sentiment of honor and proclaims a liberty that necessarily will be transformed into slavery. [But] pure and Christian feminism, supported in our traditions, claiming for women the rights that are theirs, equalizing them with men, demanding the equal-

ity [that is] indispensable, always seeking the collective happiness and the progress of the nation, trying to instruct women so that they will know and be able to fulfill their duties with the highest judgment and intelligence.[90]

They took it upon themselves to preach the "great truth" that "without God, Fatherland, Honor, and Family, there is no feminism possible."[91] The editors explained that feminism as they defined it was a natural reaction of women against the destructive invasion of home life by the "corrupting" influences of modern society and against men's inability to continue to provide adequate economic support for their families. The necessity of self-protection, they claimed, was the primary motivation for women's entry into the political sphere and into paid employment.[92]

Nevertheless, the *Revista Feminina* endorsed "progress" and proclaimed feminism to be a necessary and inevitable part of human evolution. In the century that espoused the doctrines of equality, liberalism, and individual rights, the editors argued, feminism represented women's just desire for liberation from the "ignominious captivity" that had restricted their physical movements, left their intellectual capabilities undeveloped, curtailed their initiative, and wasted their energies.[93] They argued that as society was undergoing extraordinary technological development, it did not need obedient slaves but women who, as free individuals, would use their awakening consciousness and rehabilitated spirit for the benefit of all society: "[O]ne of the greatest discoveries of the century was, undeniably, that of the wealth of energy, will, intelligence, and finally 'power' accumulated in that half of the human species that has been enslaved throughout the centuries by the tyranny of unjust and inhumane prejudices."[94]

The editors applauded the dawn of a "new phase" for women, in which they would achieve a "natural emancipation" without revolution or noisy battles.[95] Feminism, they predicted, would "penetrate into our life silently by way of infiltration," and women would be transformed into a "useful and productive [social] force after twenty centuries of inaction."[96] The emancipation envisioned by the *Revista Feminina* was to be an "emancipation from ignorance, from misery, from dishonor, and from vice," not absolute equality with men or the liberation of women from the "eternal chain of laws that the Creator established."[97] The editors denounced the meaning assigned to emancipation by "anarchistic and libertarian feminism"; this, they believed, "threatened to strip women of their natural charms" and "would result in the unbalancing of the harmony between the sexes established by God." In their view, women's "emancipation" and "conquest of autonomy" meant the establishment of their "right to collaborate in the great work of reforming the world," and it implied their duty to assume new social responsibilities.[98]

Primary among the social responsibilities assigned to modern "emancipated" women was the preservation and moralization of the family. The editors of the *Revista Feminina* assured men that there was no need to oppose the emergence of a "new female psychology," because women would continue to be the same loving wives and mothers they had been previously.[99] According to their view, any "elevated and humane" form of feminism had to acknowledge that the home was "the cornerstone of all well-organized human societies" and the realm in which women could and should exercise most fully their talents as socializers and educators.[100] Therefore, as an integral part of its feminist program, the *Revista Feminina* urged women not to imitate "Ibsenian dolls" or seek the "ruinous pleasures of vain worldly-mindedness" found at frivolous salons, tea tangos, theaters that exalted adultery, and beauty parlors.[101] Instead, for the benefit of their homes and children, women were advised to spend their free time "perfecting [their] spirits" through studying, reading the *Revista Feminina*, and reflecting on serious issues.[102] The editors also urged readers to react against the "moral epidemic" of divorce—that "tremendous wave of perversion of customs that threatens to destroy the moral unity of modern societies."[103] In their view, divorce would not only decrease women's rights, their dignity, and their happiness, but it would also destroy the realm in which women enjoyed uncontested reign.[104]

The *Revista Feminina* agreed with the FBPF that women should demand the right and accept the responsibility of political participation. But the rhetoric used by the magazine, as well as its conception of what "participation" implied, buttressed tradition as much or more than it promoted change in gender relations. No longer, the editors argued, was it possible for women to sit at home and watch men lead the country further and further down the path of "moral misery," until "little by little, we see all that was noble of what we inherited from our ancestors sink under a wave of degradation, corruption, embezzlement, robbery, and plunder."[105] To do this, the editors claimed, would be an act of "almost cruel indifference": "In no hour of the century have we, women, been so gravely summoned by the cries of human desperation. And we must enter into this cruel carnage [of politics] as examples of consolation, peace, [and] love, carrying crossed on white nurses' smocks the merciful rosary of the sister of charity. We must prepare the medicinal water for the body and for the soul."[106] Extending the metaphor further, the editorial called on women to become the "hazy, vaporous shadow, the nearly immaterial crepe" that could quietly slip into the "lugubrious corridors of the hospitals late at night as a beatific vision that consoles, soothes, cures, [and] restores."[107]

Never did the editors doubt that women had the potential to regenerate politics, for they believed in women's innate and profoundly moral character. If men had led society astray, it was women who could "lead society back to a more sane understanding of its duties and its morality." Women's advantage in this undertaking was precisely their distance from the contamination of opportunism and personal ambition. As a "new and virgin force" in politics, women could redeem the corrupt political system with their new energy and ideas, their honesty, and their respect for religion, family, and national tradition.[108] But the only way in which women should carry out this patriotic duty, according to the *Revista Feminina*, was by exercising the right to vote, which, because it required very little investment of time, would not interfere with women's domestic responsibilities.[109]

Finally, the editors of the *Revista Feminina* asserted that women's right to hold paid employment was a fundamental aspect of the feminism they supported. But they argued that women's entry into the workforce could be justified only as a necessary evil brought about by the contingencies of modern life. And they insisted that it should neither change the definition of femininity, nor transform female consciousness, nor revolutionize gender relations. The magazine applauded only those women who, in the spirit of self-abnegation, dedication, and sacrifice, entered the workforce with the goal of helping their husbands or parents maintain the economic well-being and stability of the family. Women who appeared to have taken jobs as an act of social insubordination were severely criticized.[110]

The *Revista Feminina*'s breed of feminism was palatable even to conservative high officials of the Catholic Church, who praised the magazine. The magazine demanded new rights for women only insofar as these were deemed necessary or expedient for the preservation of religious morality, tradition, and family life; the moralization and revitalization of politics; and the promotion of individual and collective prosperity. Behind its sometimes progressive rhetoric, the *Revista Feminina* constructed a feminism whose goal was not the achievement of equality between the sexes or any real intellectual and economic emancipation for women. Never, in fact, was the question of what was beneficial for women as autonomous individuals considered. The overriding concern of the magazine's editors was to find ways to accommodate extremely rapid socioeconomic changes within Brazilian culture without fundamentally changing gender relations or provoking competition and conflict between the sexes. Even the layout of the magazine communicated to women that their identity was to be circumscribed by the role of wife and mother. The texts of articles about female education, employment, and political participation were frequently interrupted by photographs of the young children of the magazine's readers.

The *Revista Feminina*'s use of stereotypes about female nature was not a tactic aimed at achieving progressive reforms in the short run. Rather, it grew out of and reinforced the belief that the sexual division of labor was both natural and inevitable. As a corollary of this belief, there is a striking absence of any critique by the magazine's editors of the imbalance of power between men and women. It was only men's *abuse* of power that they protested; men's possession of superior power was accepted as legitimate. The utopia envisioned by editors was one in which women would remain dedicated and loyal housewives and loving mothers without, however, becoming slaves to their husbands. They would both preserve their female charms and learn to be highly responsible household managers who took initiative within their appointed realm to help improve the material well-being of the country. Moreover, they would carefully guard their "purity" so as to be qualified to fulfill their responsibility for bringing about a moral regeneration of society through the correct socialization of future generations. Men, in turn, would provide economic support for the family, treat their wives with deserving respect, and avoid all abuses of power.

The conservatism of the *Revista Feminina*'s feminism (or, one might say, its antifeminist feminism) perhaps better reflected the consciousness of Brazil's urban middle-class women than did the more activist, professional, and secular feminism of the FBPF leadership. Women who considered themselves feminists but remained unaffiliated with feminist organizations were frequently inhibited by their fear of rejecting traditional norms and torn inwardly by ambivalences. Among those attracted to modern ideas concerning female equality, many found it extremely difficult to put these ideas into practice in a country in which social and economic structures severely limited women's options. As one angry widow explained, it required enormous courage for women to stand up to defend their rights in the face of men's hostility: "To do this . . . one needs great heroism, a high spirit of sacrifice, and the resolution to confront even ridicule. Yes, because we women live so enslaved by narrow-minded prejudices [and] by a thousand obstacles that are the legacy of old generations, that the few most courageous women who risk taking a step outside the circle drawn by old and odious routine will be pointed at as abnormal beings deserving ridicule and mockery."[111] Her writings, like those of many other self-proclaimed feminists of the period, were full of contradictions that dulled the impact of her social criticism and anger. Few feminists hesitated to denounce the inconsistencies of liberalism or to demand formal legal equality, the right to a good education, and access to jobs that would allow women to support themselves decently. More controversial, however, was the issue of how women's political equality, education, and employment would or should affect gender relations. On this point, Brazilian feminists generally backed down from carrying feminism to its logical conclusion. Bound by strong taboos against provoking conflict or acting "selfishly," they adopted conciliatory positions that undermined demands for equality between the sexes. The unwillingness or inability of many feminists to reject the idea of a male-dominated "natural order," to redefine femininity, to attack aspects of Catholic dogma that subordinated women, and to demand a reorganization of family life stood as formidable obstacles to female emancipation.

It was common for feminists to endorse the idea of a "natural" God-given order that required the sexual division of labor. One woman, while stressing the need to fight for political equality and to "combat the prejudices that restrict women's full enjoyment of their rights," urged women to understand that it would be "nonsense" to think that men and women were equally endowed with the same aptitudes. And, although she declared that women both needed and had the right to hold paid employment, she continued to believe: "Predispositions exist. It seems to me that women's delicate hands, their sensitive hearts, [and] their loving souls are much more suited for child care [and] housework than are the rugged arms of men. It is a matter of dividing work. In this manner, aptitudes are perfected through practice and even become hereditary."[112] Like many feminists, she failed to confront the fact that her understanding of biological and moral imperatives inevitably perpetuated men's power and women's subordination. While declaring their commitment to securing equal rights, independence, and autonomy for women, many feminists thought it was unnatural—and therefore reprehensible—for any woman to want to escape wifehood and motherhood, to compete with men, or to usurp men's roles. In the words of another feminist: "A woman can be independent, enlightened, active, [and] a prominent builder of civilization and remain modestly in her home."[113]

Women wanted emancipation, but they clung to stereotypes of femininity that affirmed the value of weakness and submissive behavior. Emília de Sousa Costa, a Portuguese feminist who was well known and frequently quoted by Brazilians, prefaced a lecture in which she denounced the cruel subjection of women in marriage and the hypocrisy of female education as follows: "No one would say upon seeing me to be this tiny inoffensive person in a very feminine dress whose gestures and expression betray an almost infantile timidity, that you have before you . . . an authentic feminist!"[114] She was not alone in insisting that female emancipation could and should be accomplished without "masculinization" or the loss of female charms. A female editor of the São Paulo magazine *A Vida Moderna* claimed that feminism would stimulate women's "natural qualities": "virtue" and the "charms and sweetness of the most exquisite femininity."[115] Educator Else Machado declared that no discreet woman could reject the accepted norms of female behavior: "honesty, tenderness, patience, energy, trustfulness, tolerance, resigned suffering, and love." Nor did she believe that women should question the definition of femininity as "weakness, the necessity of protection [and] a person to confide in, respect, [and] serve, and the strength with which women suffer, protect, defend, and support." She criticized professional women who, by adopting a "manly posture," failed to please their male colleagues with their charms. And she attacked women who sought intimate friendships with men for transgressing the boundaries of morally acceptable behavior.[116]

Even physician Alzira Reis, who desperately wanted to achieve liberty, dignity, and autonomy for herself and for all women, had difficulty redefining femininity. Her impassioned call for women to rise up, to assert themselves, and to pay more attention to their own needs and less attention to men's needs was followed by an apology for the "heat of [her] words." She quickly retreated even further from her aggressive stance, advising women that their struggle for emancipation must not be carried so far as to provoke conflict between the sexes. "Altruism is in our hearts. Even while proclaiming our autonomy, we must voluntarily, conscientiously, and actively subordinate ourselves to our duties, as the integral part that we are of the social being, of the Fatherland. Everyone must fulfill her duty to the maximum of her ability."[117]

So strongly was femininity identified with Christian piety that few feminists dared to attack openly the Catholic Church's ideology about women. Indeed, the current of feminism espoused by the *Revista Feminina*—which considered Christianity to be the source of female dignity and the basis on which feminism had to be built—was extremely popular among Brazilian women. But while participation in Church-inspired charity or social reform activities provided some women with opportunities to escape purely domestic roles, adherence to Catholic dogma crippled women's attempts to overcome their subordination. As Brazil's more radical feminists pointed out, the belief in the necessity of hierarchy within the family kept women submissive; the value placed on self-abnegation and resignation precluded women's self-realization; the requirement that women remain absolutely pure and virtuous limited possibilities for women's social participation; and the unacceptability of divorce prevented women from escaping tyrannical husbands. Within traditional Catholic dogma, power and equality were absolutely denied to women.

Finally, feminists were frequently torn by enormously contradictory feelings about family life. Because so many regarded marriage and the family as the source of both women's identity and their oppression, they often vacillated between angry attacks on men's egoism and celebrations of family life. Especially interesting is an article entitled "Pro-feminism" in which the author, Joanita de

Souza, struggled to reconcile her desire for independence with her belief in the sacredness of the home. She called on women to rise up, to emancipate themselves from the fears that had kept them weak, to educate themselves, to act independently, to distrust men's generosity, and to tirelessly combat men's egoism—women's "most terrible enemy." "[A]s long as you subject your virtue to the narrow limits of a jail, as long as you are conquered by slavery, as long as liberty is not a fact, instead of strong [individuals] you will be slaves, instead of noble [human beings] you will be hypocrites." She denounced marriage as a "degrading prison" in which women were not only humiliated and exploited by irresponsible and demanding husbands but were defeated and rendered impotent to protect their dignity and their rights. At the same time, however, she declared the home to be women's "throne" and insisted that well-adjusted and responsible women did not want to abandon the home in search of other sources of satisfaction. After having identified marriage with slavery and feminism with women's emancipation, Souza curiously claimed: "Feminism without home is absurd, degradation, but never feminism. Do you think that we are going to change the natural laws? The Law is permanent; outside of it there is no salvation." Souza proposed no structural reforms in family life that might have made the institution supportive rather than oppressive to women's personal development. Nor did she offer her readers any practical advice on how they could change their husbands' behavior. Finally, she backed down from her impassioned demands for equal rights by qualifying the type of "liberty" that she believed was appropriate for women to seek: "Liberty within the limits of virtue, within the path of duty, abnegation, altruism . . . liberty in the exact sense of the word, not utopia [and] not transgression which is the most degrading slavery!"[118]

The vast majority of Brazilian feminists (both inside and outside the FBPF) who preached a serene, noncombative feminism won the approval of many prominent men, but they generally failed to convince these men to alter their worldviews to any significant extent. In the absence of a radical and large-scale feminist movement that had the potential to transform women's consciousness, men could afford to endorse feminism generously. The movement posed little immediate threat to the established routine of daily household life or to the polarized definitions of masculinity and femininity, and it presented only a theoretical challenge to the patriarchal power structure. Many liberal politicians eagerly supported female suffrage as a symbol of their modernity and proof of the consistency of their liberalism.[119] In addition, men welcomed feminism as a means for channeling middle-class women's talents and energies into socially useful and economically productive tasks. More often than not, male support was based not on the hope that feminism would bring about greater individual well-being and happiness for women but rather on the expectation that it would prove useful for promoting public morality, social order, and economic prosperity.[120] Thus, not all men who declared their support for feminism were true advocates of women's emancipation. In fact, they often advanced very narrow definitions of feminism that in effect denied women the possibility of using political power and economic gains to contest male authority. The modernization of men's discourse was not necessarily accompanied by real changes in their attitudes toward women.

The responses of seventeen male intellectuals to *A Vida Moderna*'s 1927 questionnaire about feminism revealed the wide range of opinion that existed. There were at least a few men who were willing to declare unreserved support for women's intellectual, economic, social, and political emancipation. Being less bound by the tyranny of social pressures than were women and free of the internal feelings of anxiety and guilt that plagued women who sought nontraditional channels for self-realization, a few men eagerly espoused radical positions on the subject of family organization and appropriate female roles.[121]

More commonly, well-educated men, including those who responded to the questionnaire, tended to be reluctant to denounce feminism outright, but very few could tolerate the idea of real equality between the sexes.[122] Couto de Magalhães announced that he had repudiated his former antifeminism and was "with sincerity . . . ready to take up the cudgels in behalf of female emancipation: ample, complete, unrestricted emancipation." "Women can and should compete with men in the struggle for existence," he declared. "They have completely equal rights." But in the next sentence he stated that women naturally could not engage in professions that compromised their "grace" or their "modesty"; nor should they be elected to public office.[123] Oleno da Cunha Vieira declared that only those with "fossilized minds" could deny women the right to determine their own lives. Nevertheless, he violently attacked women who remained independent of men on the grounds that they negated their femininity, transgressed human and divine laws, and fostered anarchy: "[A] woman's happiness is, above all, in being the Senhora of her home. . . . A woman should not break this chain [of domestic life] which is, after all, her charm, her triumph, and her life."[124] Afonso Celso found no contradiction in proclaiming himself a monarchist, a devotee of the cult of the Virgin Mary, and a longtime supporter of feminism.[125] Both Aureliano Leite and Stiunirio Gama clearly stated their preference that women stay at home. But they skirted the question of women's emancipation by arguing that women were already emancipated: they were sovereigns of their own homes and could conquer men simply with their smiles.[126] Of the men who answered the questionnaire, only Moacyr Chagas denounced feminism outright.[127] Laurindo de Brito declared that although he had great "sympathy" and "enthusiasm" for feminism, he believed that female emancipation was still an impossible and inappropriate goal for Brazilian women.[128]

Of the men who declared their support for feminism, among the most interesting was Antonio Austregésilo Lima, a psychiatrist, professor at the Rio de Janeiro Medical School, member of the Brazilian Academy of Letters, and prolific writer. Upon publication of his book *Perfil da mulher brasileira* in 1923, he was hailed as a true friend of women's emancipation. He subtitled the book "A Sketch of Feminism in Brazil" and cast his "vote of sympathy" for the "complacent feminism" that he claimed was "peacefully spreading" throughout Brazil by force of the "inevitability of social evolution."[129] However, Lima's primary concern was clearly not the liberation of women per se. He declared that the aim of his book was to strengthen the Brazilian family, and he believed that the proper goal of feminism was the mobilization of women's energies and the rational use of their aptitudes for the collective good of society.[130] In his view, the task of the feminist movement was not to elaborate a radical critique of women's oppression or to develop tactics to overcome that oppression; rather, its task was to prepare women to fulfill the roles assigned to them by modern society.[131] He called upon women to become a dynamic element in society, an influential moral force, and the catalysts of national progress by responsibly carrying out their mission of educating new generations to value truth, justice, hard work, social cooperation, patriotism, and the fulfillment of their duties.[132] He proclaimed that the services performed by women in the home were of "incalculable" social value, since the home and the school were the two "temples of the spirit, in which the mother's milk of yesterday is transformed into the spiritual bread of today."[133] In addition, he welcomed the entrance of women into a wide range of professions, but only on the condition that there would be no scandals, struggles between the sexes, or radical changes in traditional customs or in family organization.[134]

Lima's book was not a description of Brazilian feminism. It was a prescription. It attempted to demonstrate that extraordinary women had always acted and must always act out of altruism and a sense of social responsibility, not out of a desire for personal achievement or glory. And it denied the value of female emancipation and self-realization except to the extent that this was necessary to ensure the evolution of the race and the prosperity of the nation. In essence, Lima stripped the term *feminism* of its meaning by using it indiscriminately to refer to any endeavor undertaken by women that, in his opinion, fostered orderly national development.

Antifeminisms

▼ ▼ ▼

While critics such as Antonio Austregésilo Lima applauded feminism but an-nulled its message, others mounted direct attacks on the movement. Among antifeminist strategies, ridicule and trivialization of feminism were perhaps the most efficient. In this, the popular press played an important role. It restricted the public's understanding and acceptance of feminism by repeatedly associat-ing the movement with issues that were of only marginal significance to the problem of women's emancipation. Any reading of the popular press of the pe-riod verifies Maria Lacerda de Moura's observation: "In whatever newspaper, we see at every step the expression—'victories of feminism'—referring, at times, to a simple question of styles. To occupy a prominent position in any government office, to travel alone, to study in schools of higher education, to publish a book of poetry, to be a 'goddess' or 'directress,' to get divorced three times in the columns of *Para Todos*, to swim across the English Channel, to be a champion in any sport—all this constitutes 'victories of feminism.'"[135] In popularizing the idea of feminism, the press trivialized its seriousness and distorted its meaning. The message conveyed was that being feminist meant being modern and fashionable; no fundamental transformation of conscious-ness was necessary. In addition, ridicule was widely used to intimidate women and thereby to keep feminism within acceptable boundaries. Women who were so rash as to usurp what were considered to be men's roles were repeatedly hu-miliated and mocked as sexually aberrant—ugly old battle-axes void of female charms.[136]

But antifeminism ran deeper than this. Throughout the post–World War I period, avid antifeminists—who were generally political conservatives—opposed liberal democracy as well as feminism and all other challenges to tradi-tional hierarchical social relationships. These they regarded as dangerous tides of social disorganization and frightening assaults on the "natural" God-given "order." The anger and fear that feminism inspired in many men was occasion-ally expressed in outbursts such as the following: "In short, [feminists] want, consciously or unconsciously, to turn the world upside down, to render it more and more uninhabitable, to anarchize it, [and] to set it in opposition to today's paradise that may be found on a country estate where female grace prevails, [and] where the daughters of Eve are, by virtue of their tenderness and affec-tion, mistresses of the home and queens."[137] Underlying male antifeminism was the conviction that women were innately inferior to men and that their powerlessness was an integral part of their charm. The author cited above ex-pressed his wish that women would remain "the same beings made of sensitiv-

"Suffragists" on the cover of Fon Fon, *16 May 1914.*

ity and delicacy, fear and hysteria, tears and fantasy, vows and volubility, voluptuousness and dreams, futility and exhibitionism that they have been un- til now."[138] Another male author expressed his dread of women's growing in- dependence, proclaiming that it was necessary for women to remain in the home, dedicate their lives to pleasing men, and willingly submit themselves to the whims of their husbands. In his view: "Women were born to be adored in our homes like irresponsible angels, founts of happiness and smiles."[139]

Antifeminists not only appealed to the public's emotions; they also attempted to construct scientific and moral justifications for antifeminism. They frequently argued that the denial of political and social equality to women did not imply women's inferiority. On the contrary, they claimed, women enjoyed a position of superiority that stemmed from their moral purity and that required isolation from the corruption of politics and the greed and ambition of the work world. Any descent from their pedestal of honor would result in the immediate "destruction of the immense social power" that the "privileged sex" supposedly enjoyed.[140] Another—more disingenuous—version of this argument was advanced by Tristão da Cunha, who claimed that Brazil had always been a matriarchy: "[T]he woman has always governed the man, and through the man, the country. The organization of the State has been, in the end, a projection of the domestic [realm]. The mother, the wife, the daughter, the sister have invariably been the definitive regulators of male activity. . . . [Women] have been the invisible and decisive powers, like that of fairies." He protested that feminists, by falling victim to "egalitarian nonsense," were seeking to debase women and to rob them of their "secret and effective sovereignty."[141]

Antifeminists also argued that women's entrance into the public sphere represented a fatal violation of true female nature and would inevitably destroy the natural harmony between the sexes. They insisted that normal women could not possibly be as happy enmeshed in the confusion of politics as they were as "queens" and "angels of the home," for, according to the "natural order of things," it was only in the role of wife and mother that women could truly fulfill themselves. In the words of one author: "The air of liberty and of politics will kill women as though they were delicate tropical flowers that only live and flourish under the crystal of their greenhouses. Therefore, let's leave [women] there so that they may live among hymns and benefit the world with blessings. The moral world turns around two forces: the masculine, which is the reason of humanity, and the feminine, which is the heart of humanity."[142] Other authors stated in shrill language that any emancipation of women from "the noble destiny that was predetermined for them by the Omnipotent" would lead to their certain "ruin and perdition."[143] "[T]he insurrection of women against the condition that nature bestowed upon them could transform humanity into an enormous bonfire in which everything humane was consumed, leaving mankind to start anew. But to revolt against laws of nature is to revolt against invincible forces [and] to rebel against an intangible power; rebellion under these circumstances is an insane rebellion."[144] Granting political equality to women would not only "[frustrate] the plan established by Divine Providence" according to which the husband enjoyed "natural rights" over his wife but would also provoke bitter battles between the sexes.[145]

Another argument used by antifeminists was that feminism, by questioning the validity of the rigid sexual division of labor, threatened to undermine the modern family—the glorious product of a long process of evolution and the base of all Christian civilization. Far from humiliating women, they argued, the sexual division of labor was the essential condition of women's dignity and of human progress; any flight of women from their "sublime mission" and "primordial function" of housewife and mother would provoke moral degeneration and social collapse.[146]

Finally, a number of antifeminists argued that women were either temperamentally unsuited to participating in public life or incapable of assuming this responsibility until they were better educated and better informed.[147]

What most threatened Brazil's feminist movement was the revitalization of Catholicism as a reactionary intellectual force during the 1920s to 1930s. Under the leadership of Sebastião Cardinal Leme (who sought to overcome the apathy within the Catholic community and transform the Church into a powerful social and political force), hundreds of thousands of Catholics were mobilized into lay movements. Among these were the Brazilian League of Catholic Women, Women's Alliance, Workers' Circles, Catholic University Youth, Catholic Youth Workers, and Brazilian Catholic Action.[148] But the most influential of these organizations was the Centro Dom Vital, established by Jackson de Figueiredo in 1922—the year that Bertha Lutz founded the FBPF. As the primary ideologue of right-wing Catholic thought, Figueiredo declared himself a reactionary. He believed that Catholic morality should underlie all human activity including national politics; he adamantly denounced liberalism, socialism, positivism, and evolutionism as both dangerous and false; and he preached that it was necessary to curb anarchy and revolution by preserving hierarchy and fostering a cult of order. His energy, passion, militancy, and polemic style infused the community of Catholic intellectuals with new life, and the Centro Dom Vital became an important meeting place. The center's conferences, debates, and courses helped solidify and popularize right-wing Catholic thought. In addition, Figueiredo actively supported the publication and distribution of Catholic literature by founding the journal *A Ordem* and by acquiring a publishing company, the Livraria Católica.[149]

Although Jackson de Figueiredo died an early death in 1928, his cause found renewed expression with the foundation of the Integralist Party (Ação Integralista Brasileira—AIB) in 1932. Ideologically, the AIB echoed Figueiredo's program in its commitment to defend the Catholic faith and to promote order and respect for authority. As a political party, it supported counterrevolution; its organization was profoundly antidemocratic, and its ethic was fascist. After the crushing defeat in 1935 of the National Liberation Alliance (Aliança Nacional Libertadora—ANL), a popular front coalition of left-wing and progressive organizations, the AIB became a mass movement that enjoyed a few years of considerable political strength.[150]

The AIB's militant antifeminism was made explicit in a book by Plínio Salgado, the party's leader. Salgado argued that since the solution of the woman problem had not been discovered by science, it was necessary to "return to the point of departure: religious morality."[151] He claimed that it was essential to give women a strict religious education because they were, by nature, impulsive and easily seduced by the first stimuli of novelty; thus they would be lost without a "single truth"—the "immutable principles" of Christianity—by which to guide their actions and orient their thoughts.[152] Salgado insisted that absolute adherence to Catholic dogma and morality was the sole path to women's elevation, liberation, and glory.[153] Feminism, or the establishment of equality between the sexes, represented not liberation but the violation of women's true nature, their degradation, and their enslavement.[154] Salgado appealed to modern women to accept the "realities of our time," which he defined to be the need for women to preserve their purity and piety; to embrace their "natural" role as wives, mothers, and educators of children; to strengthen the traditional Brazilian family; to maintain a strict separation of male and female spheres; and to avoid all competition with men.[155]

The organized feminist movement collapsed with the rise of a reactionary intellectual climate and the establishment of a dictatorship in 1937. Although feminists had played a crucial role in forcing a redefinition of acceptable social roles for women and securing new political rights, the limitations of the movement's achievements were reflected in the degree to which these new roles and rights were accommodated without fundamentally threatening Brazil's gender hierarchy. The successes of a few feminist leaders and professional women set important precedents but did not translate into female political power. The new model of the career woman was tolerated, but, given the limitations of Brazil's socioeconomic structure, few women could realistically hope to adopt it as their own. And the enshrining of traditional female stereotypes and roles—by feminists as well as antifeminists—helped preclude the possibility that the interests of women would be defined as antithetical to the interests of the male-dominated society at large.

Ironically, feminist successes most probably contributed to an undermining of urban middle- and upper-class women's discontent (which had so worried conservatives) and to an erosion of the constituency for feminist activism. Brazilians could now claim to be an "advanced" and "modern" nation, having accommodated demands for greater female social, economic, and political participation while attempting to endow women's familial roles with new dignity, respect, and prestige. Antonio Austregésilo Lima would probably have considered that his 1923 evaluation of Brazilian feminism remained valid for the next decade and a half:

> [W]e cannot deny that feminism in Brazil is making outstanding advances, in a peaceful, intelligent, and rapid manner. In Rio [de Janeiro] and in a few other Brazilian cities, women pursue [a great range of professions and occupations] with freedom and confidence.
>
> Our feminism . . . is not far from the most advanced in the Universe. Nevertheless, it is not ridiculous or sensational. . . . [The] peaceful, intelligent, and confident action [of Brazil's feminist leaders] has greatly contributed to the rapid evolution of feminism among us. Brazil is perhaps, of the countries in South America, the one that has made the greatest efforts to achieve the social emancipation of women. Women and girls, in the past decade, have achieved liberty and prerogatives that have surprised us all, without scandal, struggle, or radical changes in the family and good manners of Brazil's big cities.[156]

In short, Brazil's feminists contributed to the modernization of gender relations without fundamentally upsetting the organization of social and political inequality. Seeking to transform women into active "collaborators" with men, they avoided taking positions or adopting tactics that could be construed as "segregationist" or as fostering a "battle of the sexes." Accepting the values and norms of bourgeois capitalist society, they helped to integrate women more fully into it. Although individually and collectively urban middle- and upper-class women most certainly benefited, and although they introduced principles and set precedents that could be used later to pry open further the system for greater numbers of women, the immediate gains for the poor majority were negligible to nonexistent. Indeed, in their victories, feminists contributed to the strengthening and legitimization of the new bourgeois order.

CONCLUSION

From the point of view of U.S. suffragist leader Carrie Chapman Catt (who toured South America in 1922 in her role as acting president of the Pan American Association for the Advancement of Women), Brazil was a country of "curious contrasts." She was delighted to be the first woman ever received by the Brazilian Senate as a "distinguished foreigner" and impressed by the male senators who toasted to the success of female suffrage while they paid "fulsome compliments to United States women in general and suffragists in particular." She in turn lavished praise on Brazil's "advance column of women"—professionals and suffragists whom she described in glowing terms as "highly educated," "intelligent," "charming," "eloquent," "exceedingly able," "remarkable," "energetic," and "perennially optimistic." Catt clearly felt very much at ease among (and perhaps somewhat in awe of) Brazil's sophisticated and urbane feminist elite. But she noted that these women were isolated in a country where "very many women [were] held in almost harem restrictions." And she observed that throughout Latin America, deep ideological polarization and extreme class inequalities were not only hindering the organization of feminist movements but were dictating that feminist activists adopt an extremely conservative agenda.[1]

From the longer historical perspective of the late twentieth century, we can see the modernization of the gender system in early-twentieth-century Brazil as both part of larger international trends and particular to the specific social, economic, and political situation of that country. As in Europe and the United States, the bourgeois revolution in Brazil empowered urban middle- and upper-class women to contest male privilege. But heightened conflict between the sexes and measured victories for women were accompanied by increasing gender role rigidity. In each of these cases, progress in state building and rapid expansion of industrial capitalism were accompanied by attempts to streamline the family for more efficient reproduction. As the modernizing state usurped patriarchal authority within the family, it institutionalized the power of men over women in laws and social policies that brought gender inequality more in line with bourgeois notions of individual rights and modern scientific creeds. Legal reforms granted rights of citizenship to women while offering them "protection" that ensured continuing discrimination. Educational reforms expanded women's access to formal education while promoting their "proper" socialization into familial roles. The rationalization of the labor market required greater recruitment of educated women for tertiary sector jobs but rested on a sexual division of labor that mirrored and reinforced the sexual division of labor in the family. Public health initiatives valorized domestic hygiene and "scientific" child rearing but set escalating standards that bound "modern" women to subordinate caretaking roles and promoted highly gendered conceptions of mental health. In short, the explosive forces of early industrial-capitalist development were in part contained by assigning to the updated conjugal family (with women in a central—but still subordinate—position) a heightened role in defending social order and protecting public morality.[2]

Nonetheless, because the bourgeois revolution in Brazil began nearly a century after it had begun in Europe and the United States, in a dependent Third World country and in a very different cultural context, the struggle to manage the resistances of women and to transform the family into a more efficient locus of reproduction took on different forms. The Victorian ideal of the pure, asexual mother cloistered in the nurturing refuge of her home was anachronistic in the Jazz Age of the post–World War I era. And the bourgeois model of the competent housewife who was an efficient consumer and housekeeper, enlightened socializer of her children, and steady emotional support and charming social partner of her breadwinning husband could not realistically be applied across the enormous class boundaries and regional differences of Brazilian society.

The new gender system that emerged during the 1930s was profoundly shaped by Brazil's authoritarian traditions and hierarchical class structure, and it played a key part in maintaining those traditions in new forms. The corporatist model of an organic, cohesive, *saudavel* ("healthy," or medically sanitized and morally purified) *patria* ("fatherland") promoted modernization of gender roles but not democratization (or any "struggle" or "war") between the sexes. Women could—indeed, should—be mobilized to promote national "progress" by becoming more efficient producers and reproducers. But the mandate (accepted by Brazil's feminist leaders) to do so peacefully, without provoking "disorder," precluded radical change in the dominant social "order." Deeply rooted assumptions (shared by women and men) that gender distinctions were "natural" and necessary, requiring asymmetry of power and complementarity of roles, undermined the potentially radical impacts of women voting, obtaining higher education, and pursuing professional careers. New female roles could be accommodated within patriarchal traditions as long as they were rationalized as being an extension of women's innate abilities into the public sphere and thus would not emancipate women from mental, emotional, or economic dependence on (and therefore subordination to) men. In fact, these new roles, by creating an illusion of change, masked—and thereby helped to perpetuate—male dominance.

The effectiveness of corporatist ideology for modernizing gender inequality was buttressed by the structure of the Brazilian marketplace. On the one hand, Brazil's dependent economic growth allowed for a rapid expansion of the urban commercial economy along with the introduction of modern communications and foreign images of the "new woman." On the other hand, the narrowness of the market provided relatively few middle-class women with the material basis (economic independence and social status through employment) to promote or allow profound changes in life choices and consciousness. Wage labor was a means of emancipation more in theory than in practice. Given this reality, it is not surprising that Brazilian women—including the majority of self-proclaimed "feminists"—continued to accept at least some aspects of the sexual division of labor as "natural" and to seek dignity, self-realization, and empowerment primarily through their accomplishments as enlightened wives and mothers.

Finally, the enormous class divide as well as uneven regional economic development impeded cross-class and nationwide organizing among women, thereby undermining their power to contest male dominance effectively. The rapid growth of cities, which expanded opportunities and freedoms for urban middle-class women, did not bond Brazilian women together but set them apart and in competition across rural-urban and class divisions. While middle-class women gained individual rights, the privacy and rights of poor women were ignored—and often blatantly violated—by an authoritarian, increasingly interventionist state seeking to regulate their health, reproduction, living conditions, and social relations in the interests of economic development and social peace. Poor women could not have felt much of a bond of "sisterhood" with the growing corps of female charity and social workers whose efforts to remake them into respectable bourgeois housewives and mothers helped reinforce social hierarchy and the tutelary role of the state. Nor could the maids who worked for Brazil's "advance column of women" have shared their female employers' passion for securing "woman's rights" or viewed "emancipation" in the same way. At the other end of the social spectrum, the ability of women of the elite to (quietly) exploit the privileges of class to at least partially evade rigid gender roles also worked against the emergence of female solidarity and hindered organization for change. No issue united Brazilian women across the wide class divide (as did suffrage in the United States) or served as the basis for a mass movement against male privilege.

Brazil's deeply entrenched social hierarchy undermined gender equality in other, more subtle ways as well. As numerous scholars have pointed out, racial hierarchy was maintained after abolition in Brazil not through Jim Crow laws but thanks to the continued strength of a system of highly personalistic social relations in which the racial prejudices of the elite effectively undermined any challenges of (and reduced elite fear of) the free black population.[3] Similarly, this personalization of power allowed Brazil's male ruling class to grant greater legal equality to women (especially literate—or privileged—women) without fearing a serious challenge to male dominance. In such a hierarchical society, legal egalitarianism was ineffectual without transformations in social relations. Specifically, since female suffrage did nothing to reduce the paramount importance of "knowing one's place" for individual social "success," women continued to face insurmountable obstacles to challenging the deeply rooted sexist assumptions of their culture or to bringing about any true "revolution" in customs. Those few female radicals who refused to show the proper deference toward men faced an onslaught of hostility and rejection that often (and certainly in the cases of Patrícia Galvão and Maria Lacerda de Moura) severely jeopardized their physical and mental health. Most women who desired change trod delicately—not necessarily because they held conservative views, but because of the enormous power of ridicule within Brazil's personalistic and hierarchical culture to humiliate and to ostracize those who ignored the taboo against provoking conflict. Women's vulnerability to attacks of immorality and masculinization provided powerful protection (the threat of downward mobility along with social marginalization) for the principle and practice of male dominance.

The continuing strength of Brazil's patriarchal tradition was manifest in President Vargas's carefully cultivated and highly compelling image as the "father of the poor." He was an updated father—perpetually smiling rather than stern, accessible rather than distant, relaxed rather than formal, and disposed to cautious innovation rather than blindly wedded to tradition. But he was no less a virile father figure, whose legitimacy both rested on and reinforced assumptions about the "naturalness" of social hierarchy and thus the necessity of paternal (male and upper-class) authority. As a benevolent father—and very much in the spirit of an infallible ecclesiastical father—Vargas assumed the right and undertook the responsibility to "elevate" the downtrodden and "protect" the weak. But if the urban working class gained generous material benefits and women received "protection," as beneficiaries they were expected—indeed, required—to know their place and to stay in it. By making paternalism and authoritarian rule work for the benefit of the disenfranchised (at least temporarily), Vargas moralized and thus protected the principle of social hierarchy. In seeking to bond the nation together, Vargas cultivated a spirit of communion between himself (male ruler, head of the nation) and the "people" (socially inferior men as well as women and children, who formed the body of the nation) that obscured (although it never obliterated) conflicts between unequals and thereby reinforced vertical social identification over horizontal social solidarity. His skillful manipulation of the father image was key, for it shrouded the political process with a cloak of intimate familial sentiments—affection, trust, love, loyalty—that helped mask continuing exploitation and dependency. Thus even as the urban working class and women made advances, the principles of class privilege and male privilege were consolidated. If the fatherly Vargas sought to "elevate," "dignify," and "protect" the disenfranchised, he did not seek to empower them; on the contrary, he obstinately repressed their attempts to interpret their own reality and to act in their own behalf.

Since the late 1970s, Brazilian scholars and political activists seeking to democratize their country have identified male privilege and race privilege, as well as class privilege, as the powerful cultural and social underpinnings of political authoritarianism. And they have concluded that no real political democratization can occur without cultural and social democratization. Within this context, organized feminism in Brazil has evolved from a narrow bourgeois movement for equal rights to a far more theoretically sophisticated and politically potent movement against social hierarchy in general. But although Brazilian women's consciousness is again being transformed, and although feminists are renewing their attacks against male privilege in new more sophisticated ways, the increasingly unequal new international division of labor (and the limits it sets for political projects in the Third World) bodes ill for movements seeking social equality. Most likely, Brazilian feminists will succeed partially in forcing another, even more modern restructuring of patriarchy—the final results of which remain to be seen.[4]

NOTES

Abbreviations Used in the Notes

ACMSP   Arquivo da Cúria Metropolitana, São Paulo
AESP   São Paulo (State). Repartição de Estatística e Archivo. *Annuário estatístico de São Paulo*
AMJSP   Arquivo do Manicômio Judiciário do Estado de São Paulo
ATSP   Arquivo do Tribunal da Justiça, São Paulo
BMTIC   *Boletim do Ministério do Trabalho, Indústria, e Comércio*
FBPF   Federação Brasileira pelo Progresso Feminino
RF   *Revista Feminina*

Introduction

1. There had always been female rebels. In fact, Brazil's feminist movement has its roots in the nineteenth century. See Hahner, "Feminism, Women's Rights, and the Suffrage Movement," 65–111. But the nineteenth-century feminists were a very small number of isolated middle-class women who had little social impact. Chalhoub's interesting study of lower-class life, *Trabalho, lar e botequim*, shows that poor women were neither able nor willing to live up to the model of bourgeois womanhood. On the contrary, since they were self-supporting, they were relatively independent and powerful vis-à-vis men of their class. Yet these women's "deviant" behavior did not constitute an articulated critique of the dominant gender norms. See also Dias, *Quotidiano e poder*, and Esteves, *Mininas perdidas*.

2. Barbosa, "As classes conservadoras," 58–59.

3. The first eugenics society in Latin America was founded in 1918 in São Paulo, the Sociedade Eugénia de São Paulo, and counted among its membership 140 of the country's most prominent physicians as well as a few professionals from related fields (all of whom were men). In July 1929, the centennial of the founding of the National Academy of Medicine was celebrated with the First Brazilian Eugenics Congress, a week-long meeting of some 200 professionals including physicians, psychiatrists, medical hygienists, medical scientists, specialists in legal medicine, state sanitation officials, journalists, and federal deputies. Stepan, *"Hour of Eugenics,"* 46–54. Prominent among the many educators influenced by the eugen-

ics movement was pioneer reformer Fernando de Azevedo. See his *Da educação physica*, 88–107, and *Novos caminhos e novos fins*, 167–68.

4. Mainwaring, *Catholic Church*, 30–32; Iglésias, "Estudo sôbre o pensamento reacionário," 109–58; Miceli, *Intelectuais e classe dirigente*, 51–68; Salgado, *A mulher no século vinte*.

5. Mello, "Política da familia," 38–39.

6. Concerning the introduction of the model of the bourgeois family within elite society in mid- to late-nineteenth-century Brazil, see Costa, *Ordem médica e norma familiar*.

7. These connections were made explicitly at the time. Sueann Caulfield quotes the very revealing statement of Professor Rodrigues Doria (a leading authority in legal medicine): "Sex constitutes the most fundamental distinction between members of the human race." Caulfield, "Getting into Trouble," 148. The quote is from Doria's essay "O sexo e o crime," *Vida Policial* (8 August 1926).

8. On May Day 1938, President Vargas told the Brazilian public: "A country is not just a conglomeration of individuals within a stretch of land, but above all a unity of race, a unity of language, a unity of national spirit. To realize this supreme ideal, therefore, it is necessary that all march together, in a prodigious ascent, heroic and vibrant, with the feeling of collective collaboration and homogeneous effort for the prosperity and greatness of Brazil!" Vargas, *A Nova Política*, 5:205.

9. On the Estado Novo and corporatist ideology, see Carone, *O Estado Novo*; Malloy, *Authoritarianism and Corporatism*; Lenharo, *A sacralização da política*; Brasil, Congresso, *Cultura política e pensamento autoritário*.

10. This argument is developed in Besse, "Crimes of Passion."

11. In the conceptualization of my argument, I have been influenced by Joan Scott's article "Gender: A Useful Category of Historical Analysis." In it, she argues that "gender is a primary way of signifying relationships of power," or, "politics constructs gender and gender constructs politics" (1070). And she insists that studies of the construction of gender need to examine not only kinship but also the labor market, education, and the polity.

12. In Brazilian literature of the 1920s to 1930s, challenges to the sexual division of labor and to the stability of the nuclear family were described not just as unfortunate symptoms of larger disruptive changes but as potentially dangerous causes of the breakdown of social and political order. However, the history of women in Brazil only began to be written in the early 1970s. And only much more recently have historians begun to regard controversy over the (re)definition of gender roles as a politically significant issue of the period. One of the most recent—and best—studies that explores the political significance and meaning of gender conflict is Caulfield, "In Defense of Honor."

13. By the 1920s to 1930s, Brazilian society had diversified to a significant degree thanks to the expansion of industry, commerce, the bureaucracy, and professions. The upper classes consisted not only of the descendants of the nineteenth-century rural oligarchs but also nouveau riche industrialists. The middle classes, overwhelmingly concentrated in urban areas, included professionals, factory managers, technicians, office workers, civil servants, and small businessmen and merchants. They were distinguished by their literacy, their economic solvency, their familiarity with the rules of urban social etiquette, their ability to confront local political authorities more or less as social equals, and their ease in frequenting elite social spaces (such as fancy department stores and the opera). Still, the vast majority of the Brazilian population consisted of the lower classes, which were also increasingly diversified, including urban skilled and unskilled workers and poor rural laborers.

14. On the development of the urban labor market in Brazil, see Madeira and Singer, "Estrutura do emprego"; Hahner, "Women and Work"; Pena, *Mulheres e trabalhadores*; Moura, *Mulheres e menores no trabalho industrial*; Wolfe, *Working Women, Working Men*.

Chapter One

1. A useful definition of *patriarchalism* is "the principle that any group, familial or otherwise, will form a hierarchy from the lowest or youngest up to one senior figure under whose protection and dominance it stands and through whom advancement is obtained." Lockhart and Schwartz, *Early Latin America*, 7. Hence *patriarchalism* as I am using it has a specific historical meaning as a system of generational as well as gender relations, in which children and women are subordinated to the male head of family, who controls the wealth of the family, the sexuality of its women, and the labor power of all its members.

2. Gilberto Freyre's influential *Casa grande e senzala* (1933) generalized from a sociological study of elite families in the northeastern sugar-exporting region of Recife to establish a model of the large, extended patriarchal family for all of colonial Brazil. Since the 1950s, numerous authors have attacked this model as an ideological construction rather than an empirically accurate depiction of reality. They have demonstrated that very few families could realize this ideal and that even within the elite, alternative arrangements of family organization existed. See, for example, Candido, "Brazilian Family"; Corrêa, "Repensando a família patriarchal"; Almeida, Carneiro, and Paula, *Pensando a família no Brasil*. Nevertheless, even in regions such as São Paulo where small nuclear and female-headed families predominated, ties of blood, fictive kinship, friendship, and patronage, which existed outside the residential family unit, were essential in tying the society together. See Samara, *A família brasileira*; Kuznesof, *Household Economy and Urban Development*, 35–45.

3. The Englishwoman Maria Graham commented favorably on an unusual marriage in 1823 in which romance was said to have played a part. Nevertheless, if this marriage was indeed a "free match," it was between social equals and was considered advantageous by both families. Graham, *Journal of a Voyage to Brazil*, 305. An important study of changing marriage strategies within elite families in São Paulo is Nazzari, *Disappearance of the Dowry*. A useful study of a single elite family is Levi, *Prados of São Paulo*. For northeastern Brazil, Linda Lewin has demonstrated the importance of elite marriage strategies for consolidating political power in "Some Historical Implications of Kinship Organization," 273–81. See also her book *Politics and Parentela*, 144–60. For elite marriage patterns in late-nineteenth-century Rio de Janeiro, see Needell, *Tropical Belle Époque*, 117–24.

4. Hahner, *Emancipating the Female Sex*, 6.

5. Luccock, *Notes on Rio de Janeiro*, 111–15; Walsh, *Notices of Brazil*, 1:153–54; Fletcher and Kidder, *Brazil and the Brazilians*, 163–66, 175; Agassiz and Agassiz, *Journey in Brazil*, 270, 478–81; Expilly, *Mulheres e costumes*, 268–72.

6. Candido, "Brazilian Family," 295–96, 303; Russell-Wood, "Women and Society"; Russell-Wood, "Female and Family"; Levi, *Prados of São Paulo*, 22, 25, 45–47, 186; Lewin, *Politics and Parentela*, 190–94; Walsh, *Notices of Brazil*, 2:28, 263.

7. Historians have recently demonstrated the discrepancy between norms and practices and have concluded that illicit sexual relations were common even among elite women in colonial and nineteenth-century Brazil. See, for example, Kuznesof, "Sexual Politics,

Race, and Bastard-Bearing"; Lewin, "Natural and Spurious Children"; Silva, *Sistema do casamento.*

8. On the lives of poor women, free and slave, in nineteenth-century São Paulo and Rio de Janeiro, see Dias, *Quotidiano e poder*; Graham, *House and Street.*

9. On Brazilian politics during the Empire, see Carvalho, *A construção da ordem*; Faoro, *Os donos do poder*; Leal, *Coronelismo*; Queiroz, *O mandonismo local.* On political participation, see Love, "Political Participation." Love found that in 1886 less than 1 percent of the population actually cast votes in the parliamentary elections (7).

10. For the impacts of rising European demand and foreign investment on Brazilian development, see Graham, *Britain and the Onset of Modernization.* On the transition from slave to free labor in São Paulo, see Costa, *Da senzala à colônia.* On immigration, see Merrick and Graham, *Population and Economic Development*, 80–117. On economic development and early industrialization, see Leff, *Underdevelopment and Development*; Luz, *A luta pela industrialização*; Dean, *Industrialization of São Paulo*; Stein, *Brazilian Cotton Manufacture.* On urbanization, see Singer, *Desenvolvimento econômico e evolução urbana*; Morse, "Brazil's Urban Development"; and Costa, "Town and Country," in her *Brazilian Empire*, 172–201. On the rise of the middle classes, see Saes, *Classe média e sistema político.*

11. Costa, "The Fall of the Monarchy," in her *Brazilian Empire*, 202–33. Joseph Love found that 2.2 percent of all Brazilians cast votes in the first presidential election of 1894—many more than the 0.89 percent who had voted in 1886 but still a small percentage of all Brazilians. Love, "Political Participation," 7–9.

12. On the development of Rio de Janeiro, see Lobo, *História do Rio de Janeiro.*

13. On the elite's modernization projects, see Needell, *Tropical Belle Époque*, 19–51; Rocha, *A era das demolições*; Abreu, *Evolução urbana.*

14. European immigrants to São Paulo (state) represented 57 percent of the total European migration to Brazil between 1888 and 1928. Italians formed the largest single group, followed by Portuguese and Spaniards, as well as by lesser numbers of Syrians, Lebanese, Poles, eastern European Jews, Armenians, and Germans. Japanese immigrants began arriving in 1908. Not all of the immigrants stayed, however; during these same years, 960,000 people emigrated from the state through the port of Santos, and unknown numbers left overland. Holloway, *Immigrants on the Land*, 42–43, 179; Merrick and Graham, *Population and Economic Development*, 91–92.

15. Dean, *Industrialization of São Paulo*, 13, 83; Singer, *Desenvolvimento econômico e evolução urbana*, 19–58. For a general history of the growth of São Paulo, see Morse, *From Community to Metropolis.* See also Love, *São Paulo in the Brazilian Federation.*

16. Nazzari, *Disappearance of the Dowry*, pt. 3. According to Nazzari, elite families reallocated resources from dowries given to daughters to education given to sons, making sons the double winners in the changing family strategies. See also Lewin, *Politics and Parentela*, 195–98.

17. Lewin, "Some Historical Implications of Kinship Organization," 284; Lewin, *Politics and Parentela*, 187–88.

18. Graham, *Britain and the Onset of Modernization*, 116–20; Morse, *From Community to Metropolis*, 178–80, 190; Hahner, *Emancipating the Female Sex*, 8–9, 19, 77, 80.

19. An excellent summary of the efforts of nineteenth-century women's rights advocates in Brazil is chap. 2 of Hahner, *Emancipating the Female Sex.* See also her earlier articles: "Feminism, Women's Rights, and the Suffrage Movement," "Nineteenth-Century Feminist Press," and "Women and Work."

20. Leff, *Underdevelopment and Development*, 1:173; Dean, *Industrialization of São Paulo*, 10.

21. Americano, *São Paulo nesse tempo*, 18–19, 411; Ferreira, *Bairro da Sé*, 127; Gattai, *Anarquistas*, 40, 111–13; Oliveira, *Hontem e hoje*, 19; Cesario Julião, "Occupações de uma mocinha desoccupada: Chronica da vida elegante," *RF* 6:61 (June 1919). On the rise of consumer fetishism among the elite in late-nineteenth-century Rio de Janeiro, see Needell, *Tropical Belle Époque*, 156–77.

22. Americano, *São Paulo naquele tempo*, 63–64; Oliveira, *Hontem e hoje*, 19–21; Gattai, *Anarquistas*, 111–12.

23. Marinette, "A moda: A roupa branca e a moda," *RF* 5:45 (February 1918).

24. Oliveira, *Hontem e hoje*, 47–48, 100–101; Oliveira, *Passadismo e modernismo*, 40–43.

25. Americano, *São Paulo naquele tempo*, 111–19; Graham, *House and Street*, 42; Ewbank, *Life in Brazil*, 92–93.

26. Americano, *São Paulo naquele tempo*, 108; Americano, *São Paulo nesse tempo*, 58.

27. Lima, *A cura dos nervos*, 178. This book was a collection of some of the hundreds of short newspaper articles that the author wrote for popular audiences.

28. Azevedo, *Da educação physica*, 102; Vasconcellos, *Educação sexual da mulher*, 31.

29. On the professionalization of medicine in Brazil, see Luz, *Medicina e ordem política brasileira*; Costa, *Ordem médica e norma familiar*; Machado et al., *Danação da norma*; Stepan, *Beginnings of Brazilian Science*; Borges, *Family in Bahia*, chap. 3.

30. An outline of the type of training given to gynecologists may be found in Vasconcellos, *Educação sexual da mulher*, 58–67. The tone of this medical school thesis reflects the pride and pretentiousness of a young man highly impressed with the new scientific rigorousness and social importance of his profession.

31. Americano, *São Paulo naquele tempo*, 483; Americano, *São Paulo nesse tempo*, 319. Vasconcellos, *Educação sexual da mulher*, 64–65.

32. Americano, *São Paulo nesse tempo*, 319.

33. KYTTA, "Iniciação da maternidade," *Renascença* 1:3 (April 1923); Moura, "Eva."

34. Barreto, "Meninas feias e meninas bonitas," 141–42; "A mocidade artificial," *RF* 7:70 (March 1920); "O terror de envelhecer," *Estadinho* (São Paulo), 6 May 1920; Americano, *São Paulo nesse tempo*, 190, 314.

35. "A belleza dos dentes," *RF* 3:31 (December 1916); "A saude e os dentes: Conselhos indispensaveis," *RF* 5:44 (January 1918); "Arte da belleza: Os dentes," *RF* 8:84 (May 1921).

36. Lima, *A cura dos nervos*, 13–14; Lima, *A neurastenia sexual*, 18; Lima, *Pequenos males*, 78.

37. The state mental hospital in the São Paulo suburb of Juquerí accepted paying patients during this period and housed them in a separate pavilion. For a history of the Juquerí hospital, see Cunha, *O espelho do mundo*. See also Silva, *A assistência a psicopatas no Estado de São Paulo*. Many women of the middle and upper classes were also interned in the Instituto Paulista.

38. Americano, *São Paulo naquele tempo*, 342–44, 350, 356, 358–59; Americano, *São Paulo nesse tempo*, 83, 111, 211–13; Oliveira, *Passadismo e modernismo*, 81–85; Bosi, *Memória e sociedade*, 271; Azevedo, *A evolução do esporte*.

39. *AESP, 1915*, 374–75; *AESP, 1927*, 420.

40. Ferreira, *Bairro da Sé*, 124–25; Gattai, *Anarquistas*, 24–28; A., "Cinema," *Klaxon*, no. 8–9 (December 1922–January 1923): 30.

41. "Klaxon," *Klaxon*, no. 1 (15 May 1922): 2.

42. A., "Cinema," 30.

43. Anna Rita Malheiros, "Abril," *RF* 5:47 (April 1918). According to Adalzira Bittencourt, Anna Rita Malheiros was a pseudonym used by playwright Claudio de Souza, son of the director of the *Revista Feminina*, Virgilina de Souza Salles. See Bittencourt, *Dicionário bio-bibliográfico de mulheres*, 2:318.

44. Malheiros, "Abril"; "Os sátyros na penumbra," *RF* 10:110 (July 1923); "Julho," *RF* 12:134 (July 1925). Durval Marcondes, a respected *paulista* psychiatrist, agreed with the *Revista Feminina* that films could be dangerous because of their powers of suggestion. He reported the case of a woman who was suffering from strong unconscious desires to commit adultery and to see her husband dead. After attending a film in which the protagonist shot her husband and ran off with the man she loved, the patient, according to Marcondes, underwent a severe relapse. See Marcondes, "A influência do cinema," 37–38. On the rise of the Brazilian cinema industry and its representations of women, see Bicalho, "Art of Seduction."

45. Americano, *São Paulo nesse tempo*, 247; Gattai, *Anarquistas*, 224–25; "Na Radio Educadora Paulista," *A Cigarra* 15:320 (1–15 March 1928); Oliveira, *Passadismo e modernismo*, 82. For discussion of the cultural importance of the female singers who became radio stars during the 1940s to 1950s, see Lenharo, "Fascínio e solidão," and Avancini, "Na era de ouro das cantoras do rádio."

46. Brazil, Diretoria Geral de Estatística, *Recenseamento . . . 1872*, 21:1–2; Brazil, Diretoria Geral de Estatística, *Recenseamento . . . 1920*, vol. 4, pt. 4a, pp. xii–xiii, xvi, xxvi–xxvii. See also table 7.

47. *AESP, 1901*, 772; *AESP, 1910*, 2:192–93; *AESP, 1920*, 98–99; *AESP, 1927*, 180–81. From the early 1910s, São Paulo led all other states in Brazil (including Rio de Janeiro) in the number of periodicals published. Its largest newspapers also boasted the largest circulation in Brazil, thanks to a railroad network that could get daily papers to remote towns on the day of publication. See Love, *São Paulo in the Brazilian Federation*, 90–91.

48. "A *Revista Feminina* no Primeiro Congresso Brasileiro de Journalistas," *RF* 5:53 (October 1918).

49. They included Olavo Bilac, Coelho Netto, Magalhães de Azevedo, Felix Pacheco, Affonso Arinos, Claudio de Souza (writing both under his own name and under the pseudonym Anna Rita Malheiros), Amadeu Amaral, Cerqueira Mendes, Luis Guimarães Filho, Antonio Austregésilo Lima, Afrânio Peixoto, Monteiro Lobato, Guilherme de Almeida, René Thiollier, Cyro Costa, Julio Cesar da Silva, Júlia Lopes de Almeida, Francisca Júlia da Silva, B. Mendonça Lima, Cecilia Bandeira de Melo Rebêlo de Vasconcelos (pseud. Chrysanthème), Albina Pires de Campos, Dra. Alzira Reis, Presciliana Duarte de Almeida, Laurita de Lacerda, and Anna Cesar. See ibid.; "O nosso triumpho," *RF* 7:78 (November 1920).

50. "A nossa 'Revista,'" *RF* 4:43 (December 1917). Seven *mil-réis* was approximately equivalent to the cost of the fifty-mile train ride from São Paulo to Santos, or to one day's wages of a skilled worker, or to six kilos of good quality meat. Americano, *São Paulo nesse tempo*, 294; São Paulo (State), Secretaria da Agricultura, Comércio e Obras Públicas, *Boletim do Departamento Estadual do Trabalho* 15:56 (3d trimester of 1925): 318.

51. "Novo appello ás senhoras brasileiras," *RF* 5:51 (August 1918).

52. "A's senhoras brasileiras," *RF* 5:50 (July 1918). At the bottom of one page in issue 12:132 (May 1925), editors printed in bold type: "To spread the *Revista Feminina* is to perform an act of high patriotism."

53. "A's senhoras brasileiras."

54. The *Revista Feminina* published a regular column entitled "O que dizem de nós." See,

for example, this column in issues 3:31 (December 1916); 4:33 (February 1917); 4:34 (March 1917); 4:37 (July 1917); 5:48 (May 1918); and 9:92 (January 1922).

55. "O que dizem de nós," *RF* 4:41 (October 1917).

56. "A *Revista Feminina* no Primeiro Congresso Brasileiro de Journalistas."

57. When lawyer Orminda Bastos published an article about a federal loan to Amazonia, the editors noted: "The intransigent enemies of women, those who do not miss a chance to proclaim women's incapacity to deal with highly complex questions such as the government of nations and political economy, have in front of them, at every step, positive denials of their affirmations. The female mind is not, as these naive arguers maintain, typically unilateral. It can perfectly well encompass all social, moral, and human problems, including the most transcendental such as philosophy and strictly political or economic problems. It is solely a matter of adaptation and education." Orminda Bastos, "O governo federal e o emprestimo do Amazonas," *RF* 10:112 (September 1923).

58. An analysis of the magazine's "Catholic feminism" is included in Chapter 7 of this volume.

59. American companies, with the advice of international trade specialists, the encouragement of the U.S. Department of Commerce, and the help of international advertising agencies, began aggressive marketing and advertising campaigns in Latin America in the late 1910s. In order to compete, Brazilian companies were quick to copy the new advertising techniques. For a view of American companies' advertising and marketing strategies (in both domestic and foreign markets), see the trade journal *Printers' Ink*, established in New York in 1919. The earliest manuals for U.S. exporters to Latin America include Filsinger, *Exporting to Latin America*; Aughinbaugh, *Selling Latin America*; and Aughinbaugh, *Advertising for Trade in Latin America*.

60. The ten pages of advertisements at the beginning of each issue of the *Revista Feminina* not only displayed health and beauty aids, clothing, household appliances, and furniture but also insurance, automobiles, lottery tickets, and office supplies. In 1927, Remington Typewriter ran a full-page advertisement in *A Cigarra* entitled "An Impressive Event on a Daughter's Birthday." When asked what she wanted for her fifteenth birthday, the young woman in the advertisement replied not clothes, money, or jewels but a Remington portable typewriter! *A Cigarra* 14:293 (16–31 January 1927): 27.

61. The *Revista Feminina* did not seem to censor advertisements. Especially notable for the use of female sexuality to sell commodities were the prominent glossy advertisements for Lucy toothpaste and for the soft drink Guaraná Espumante that appeared regularly in *A Cigarra* during the early 1920s. Women's "indispositions"—or "female problems"—were also exploited by the patent medicine manufacturers, which became the heaviest American advertisers in Latin America during the late 1910s. See Filsinger, *Exporting to Latin America*, 264; Gattai, *Anarquistas*, 41–43; and Americano, *São Paulo nesse tempo*, 314. A typical advertisement was the one for Regulador Fontura in *A Cigarra* 14:259 (16–31 August 1925): 44. The advertisement claimed that the medicine was "very effective for morbid states and for functional disorders of the female organs," as well as essential for fighting "painful crises, nervous changes, and consequent physical decadence."

62. The success of the fad of printing snapshots was noted in Oliveira, *Passadismo e modernismo*, 82.

63. See, for example, "Qual é a moça mais bella de São Paulo?: Concurso de belleza d'*A Cigarra*," *A Cigarra* 9:180 (16–31 March 1922); "Qual é a moça mais culta de São Paulo? Outro concurso d'*A Cigarra*," *A Cigarra* 9:182 (16–30 April 1922); "Os concursos d'*A Ci-*

garra: Louras e morenas," *A Cigarra* 13:270 (1–15 February 1926): 30; "Concurso cine-matographico d'*A Cigarra*," *A Cigarra* 14:275 (16–31 April 1926): 19; "O melhor partido de casamento," *A Cigarra* 14:285 (16–30 September 1926).

64. "Qual é a mais bella mulher de Brasil?," *Revista da Semana*, nova série, 22:39 (24 September 1921); "Chronica: Olympiadas da formosura," *A Cigarra* 8:170 (16–31 October 1921); "Qual é a moça mais bella de São Paulo?"; "Chronica," *A Cigarra* 9:182 (16–30 April 1922); "Concurso de belleza," *A Cigarra* 10:196 (16–30 November 1922); "Concurso de belleza," *A Cigarra* 10:198 (16–31 December 1922); "Chronica," *A Cigarra* 10:204 (16–31 March 1923).

65. "Inquerito d'*A Vida Moderna*," *A Vida Moderna* 25:365 (28 August 1919); "As enquêtes d'*A Vida Moderna*," *A Vida Moderna* 24:527 (31 December 1927). Responses to the surveys are discussed at later points in the book.

66. "Consultorio feminina," *A Cigarra* 16:365 (16–31 January 1930).

67. Americano, *São Paulo naquele tempo*, 299–300, 303–11; Souza, *O espírito das roupas*.

68. Americano, *São Paulo nesse tempo*, 172–73, 184–97. See also the articles on fashion that appeared in every issue of the *Revista Feminina*.

69. Americano, *São Paulo naquele tempo*, 311; Americano, *São Paulo nesse tempo*, 102, 184, 188, 322; Oliveira, *Hontem e hoje*, 118–22.

70. See, for example, the covers of *O Cruzeiro* 3:9 (3 January 1931); *A Cigarra* 15:299 (16–30 April 1927); and *A Cigarra* 17:380 (1–15 September 1930).

71. "La beauté est um femme en marche," *A Cigarra* 14:285 (16–30 September 1926): 30.

72. Peregrino Junior, "A mulher, o 'sport,' e a moda," *O Cruzeiro* 1:43 (31 August 1929): 70.

73. Peregrino Junior, "A belleza 'standard' da mulher moderna," *O Cruzeiro* 3:53 (7 November 1931).

74. Oliveira, *Hontem e hoje*, 85–87, 140–41; Oliveira, *Passadismo e modernismo*, 42; Celso, *De relance*, 143–44; Barreto [Belmonte, pseud.], *Assim falou Juca Pato*, 15–17, 43–45; "A mulher angulosa nunca é bella," *RF* 10:109 (June 1923). Zélia Gattai, the daughter of modest Italian immigrants, remembered that the girls on her street enthusiastically followed local beauty contests and compared their measurements with those of the elected "beauty queens." Gattai, *Anarquistas*, 164.

75. Barreto [Belmonte, pseud.], *Assim falou Juca Pato*, 43–45.

76. Americano, *São Paulo nesse tempo*, 196.

77. Viviano, "Um Cigarro," *A Vida Moderna* 16:379 (25 March 1920).

78. "Chronica: Oh! A maravilha das tranças," *A Vida Moderna* 21:499 (25 July 1925).

79. "O senhor ou a senhora? Scenas da vida actual," *RF* 12:139 (December 1925).

80. [No title], *A Cigarra* 13:240 (1–15 November 1924); "Os caprichos da moda," *A Cigarra* 14:253 (16–31 May 1925); "Engano que se explica," *A Cigarra* 14:252 (1–15 May 1925); [no title], *A Cigarra* 13:243 (16–31 December 1924).

81. Numerous chronicles of Lola de Oliveira focused on the problem of generational conflict over the issue of modern fashions. See, for example, Oliveira, *Hontem e hoje*, 5–8; Oliveira, *Passadismo e modernismo*, 81–82; and Oliveira, *Gente de agora*, 5–7.

82. See, for example, Vasconcelos [Chrysanthème, pseud.], *Minha terra e sua gente*, 34–35.

83. See, for example, Martins, *A moda*, 6–13. The author dedicated her book, a scathing attack on modern fashions, to her children.

84. Anna Rita Malheiros, "Setembro," *RF* 5:52 (September 1918); Anna Rita Malheiros, "Fevereiro," *RF* 7:69 (February 1920).

85. Americano, *São Paulo nesse tempo*, 42; Oliveira, *Passadismo e modernismo*, 20; Oliveira, *Gente de agora*, 12–13; "Os sátyros na penumbra," *RF* 10:110 (July 1923).

86. "Hom'essa," *A Cigarra* 10:191 (1–15 September 1922).

87. Azevedo, "As regras do namôro no Brasil," 132, 141–42; Willems, "Structure of the Brazilian Family," 339–41; Americano, *São Paulo naquele tempo*, 311; Americano, *São Paulo nesse tempo*, 67; Oliveira, *Gente de agora*, 36–37.

88. Carvalho, "Avenida Paulista," *A Cigarra* 15:312 (1–15 November 1927).

89. "A moral do jazz," *O Cruzeiro* 2:54 (16 November 1929): 3; "A dansa de 1928," *Eu Sei Tudo*, anno 11, 10:130 (March 1928): 93.

90. "As dansas modernas ou a influencia dos antepassados," *Eu Sei Tudo*, anno 10, 11:119 (April 1927): 65; "A vida é um eterno recomeçar: Da barbaria á civilização, e da civilização á barbaria," *Eu Sei Tudo*, anno 10, 11:119 (April 1927): 84–85.

91. Americano, *São Paulo nesse tempo*, 108–10.

92. See the photograph of the event in *A Cigarra* 11:214 (16–31 August 1923).

93. Carlos Mello, "Idéas de importação," *RF* 4:37 (June 1917).

94. Ibid.

95. Amaral, *Tarsila*, 1:29.

Chapter Two

1. Clearly, the public controversy over marriage had deep historical roots in women's private discontentments and individual attempts to escape oppressive unions. María Beatriz Nizza da Silva found that although legal marital separation was unusual in colonial São Paulo, when it did occur, it was invariably the woman who took the initiative, and she most frequently alleged mistreatment. The author also argues that the number of marital separations granted in the late eighteenth to early nineteenth centuries increased not only because amicable separation had begun to be allowed but also because "women had begun to reject their previous passivity to mistreatment, a secluded life, and unconditional acceptance of the husband's supremacy" (336). See her "Divorce in Colonial Brazil," 313–40. For a similar argument for Mexico, see Arrom, *Women of Mexico City*.

2. These viewpoints, widely articulated in the post–World War I period, are well summarized in Leme, "Dos crimes contra a assistência familiar," 296, 299; Cesarino Júnior, "A família como objeto do direito social," 125–28; Hungria, *Comentários ao Código Penal*, 8:410–12 (these pages contain a reprint of a speech he published in 1940).

3. Marriage was defined as an indissoluble bond by church and state in Brazil until the legalization of divorce in 1977. The Catholic Church in colonial Brazil allowed the separation of estranged couples in extreme cases, but only with the provision that neither could remarry. Toward the end of the eighteenth century, separation by mutual consent began to be granted, but again, this did not free either partner to remarry. Silva, "Divorce in Colonial Brazil," 313, 333–34.

4. Although this is easily inferred from a great number of treatises on marriage, it comes closest to being explicitly stated at the beginning of the article "Como a esposa consegue atrair o amor do marido," *RF* 4:43 (December 1917).

5. On the values, expectations, and behavior of poor women and men, see Dias, *Quotidi-ano e poder*; Chalhoub, *Trabalho, lar e botequim*; Esteves, *Meninas perdidas*; Soihet, *Condição feminina e formas de violência*; and Kuznesof, "Sexual Politics, Race, and Bastard-Bearing." Sueann Caulfield provides ample evidence that during the 1920s to 1930s, Rio de Janeiro's poor and working-class population regarded stable consensual unions with great casualness, often accepting them as equivalent to formal marriages. In several cases she cites, parents accepted the informal conjugal arrangements of their daughters, only filing deflowering cases years later when the man abandoned the household and the responsibilities he had assumed (in the eyes of the community, at least) by taking their daughter's virginity and by "living maritally." See "In Defense of Honor," 320–29.

6. Mattos, "A questão do casamento," 50–51.

7. Cesar, *O problema feminino*, 266. On p. 5, the author states that the book was completed in 1922.

8. Francine Masiello, in her study of avant-garde Latin American women novelists of the 1920s, argues that they portrayed the family as an obstacle to women's well-being and helped subvert patriarchal discourse by writing fiction in which the heroines (who were usually childless and without male companions) escaped the family through orphanhood, fantasy, or bonding with other women. See her "Women, State, and Family in Latin American Literature of the 1920s," 36–44.

9. Bastos, *Justiça, alegria, felicidade*, 26, 45–46, 82, 116–17.

10. Vasconcelos, "Mussolini e a mulher," 36.

11. Iracema, "Carta da mulher," *O Cruzeiro* 1:18 (9 March 1929): 53; Iracema, "Porque o casamento emmudece o homem?," *RF* 8:91 (December 1921); Iracema, "A carta da mul-her," *O Cruzeiro* 1:32 (15 June 1929): 42.

12. Alma Martyr, "Ao '77 da Silva,'" *A Cigarra* 15:316 (1–15 January 1928).

13. Fada de bons conselhos, "A' Marqueza de Rabico," *A Cigarra* 15:327 (16–30 June 1928).

14. *A Vida Moderna* 16:338 (5 August 1920).

15. See Vasconcelos, *Gritos femininos*, 15–28; Vasconcelos, *O que os outros não veem*.

16. Martins, *Acção social brasileira*, 36; Martins, *Estudos sobre os problemas sociaes e o feminismo*, 29–31.

17. Vasconcelos, *Minha terra e sua gente*, 22, 24, 26, 29. See also Vasconcelos, *Matar! Romance sensacional e moderníssimo*.

18. Vasconcelos, *Gritos femininos*, 139–44, 190–92; Vasconcelos, "O amor no Brasil," *RF* 7:79 (December 1920); Vasconcelos, *O que os outros não veem*; Vasconcelos, *Minha terra e sua gente*, 63–70.

19. Vasconcelos, "A educação feminina de hoje," *RF* 7:68 (January 1920). On her support for women seeking divorces, see Vasconcelos, *Enervadas*, 106–7; Vasconcelos, "Mussolini e a mulher," 35.

20. Oliveira, *O divorcio*. The quotes are taken from pp. 7, 18. Other early female advocates of divorce included newspaper publisher Josefina de Azevedo, lawyer Mirtes de Campos, Paris-educated writer Inéz Sabino Pinho Maia, newspaper columnist Emília Moncorvo Bandeira de Melo (pseud. Carmen Dolores), and writer Júlia Lopes de Almeida. See Hah-ner, *Emancipating the Female Sex*, 118. By the 1920s, increasing numbers of women began to support divorce. See Coelho, *Evolução do feminismo*, 585–89; Oliveira, *Passadismo e moder-nismo*, 124; Moura, *Religião do amor*, 107–9; Moura, *Amai*, 224–25; Moura, "As conferen-cias de Maria Lacerda de Moura," 11. But despite significant support for divorce among

Brazil's female professional and intellectual community, its legalization never became a goal of the feminist movement. Strong opposition from the Catholic Church, as well as the ambivalence of many women themselves, led Brazilian feminists to avoid public discussion of the issue.

21. Bastos, *Justiça, alegria, felicidade*, 26, 45–46, 82, 116–17.

22. Ercília Nogueira Cobra's alienation from society was so extreme that all details of her personal life have disappeared from the historical record. Not even her relatives know for sure where she lived or how she earned a living. See Mott, "A igreja, a polícia, e a família a queriam pelas costas," 17. An excellent biography of Maria Lacerda de Moura is Leite, *Outra face do feminismo*. Maria Lacerda was influenced by the educational ideas of Spanish anarchist Francesco Ferrer and later by the writings of Russian feminist and socialist Alexandra Kolontai as well as free-love advocates Ellen Key and Han Ryner.

23. Moura, "As conferencias de Maria Lacerda de Moura," 11; Moura, *Amai*, 27, 66–69, 83–87, 98–100, 135, 154–59; Moura, *Religião do amor*, 93–95, 111–13, 131, 163–70; Moura, *Ferrer*, 87–88. Cobra, *Virgindade inútil*. Cobra's two books, *Virgindade anti-higiênica* (*Anti-hygienic Virginity*, 1924) and *Virgindade inútil* (*Useless Virginity*, 1927), were, upon publication, condemned by Church authorities and seized by the police. Although the São Paulo citywide catalog located at the University of São Paulo includes old cards from the municipal library for Cobra's books, they have disappeared from the collection. In 1979, used-book dealer Olynto Moura located a copy of *Virgindade inútil* in the library of one of his acquaintances, who kindly allowed me to make a photocopy. In 1980, Maria Lúcia Mott found a 1932 edition that included both of Cobra's works.

24. Galvão, *Parque industrial*. Finding no publisher for the book in 1932, Galvão's husband, Oswald de Andrade, footed the bill and published it privately. Galvão used a pseudonym, Mara Lobo, at the insistence of the Brazilian Communist Party. A rich collection of Galvão's writings, as well as testimonies by those who knew her and essays about her, is Campos, *Pagu*. A short biography of her in English is Besse, "Pagu."

25. Chalhoub, *Trabalho, lar e botequim*, 136–64.

26. Caulfield, "Getting into Trouble."

27. Celso, *De relance*, 64–72; Vasconcelos, *Gritos femininos*, 197–204; Vasconcelos, *Enervadas*; Vasconcelos, *Familias*; Vasconcelos, *O que os outros não veem*; Oliveira, *Gente de agora*, 5–7, 116–18, 127–28, 132–35; Oliveira, *Hontem e hoje*, 5–8, 59–65, 110–13, 138–39; Oliveira, *Passadismo e modernismo*, 81–82, 117–25. See also the series of cartoons by Belmonte (Benedicto Bastos Barreto) entitled "Hontem e hoje" published in *O Cruzeiro* from June through October 1930.

28. See, for example, Diamante Azul, "Verdades que impõem," *A Cigarra* 7:131 (1–15 March 1920).

29. Curt Degenthal, "Carta aberta á 'Thilde,'" *A Cigarra* 7:133 (1–15 March 1920); Antonio G. de Freitas, "Uma theoria do amor," *A Cigarra* 15:322 (1–15 April 1928).

30. Augusto Lima as quoted by Menotti del Picchia, "Caso ou não caso?," *RF* 7:68 (June 1920).

31. Britto, *Psychologia do adultério*, 22–23, 191.

32. Castro, *Os delictos contra a honra da mulher*, 21–22.

33. Cesar, *O problema feminino*, 208–14, 249–50, 269.

34. Raul Soares, "Palavras ao vento," *A Cigarra* 10:199 (1–15 January 1923); "Conselhos sociaes: O casamento," *Revista da Semana* 22:33 (13 August 1921) and 23:21 (20 May 1922); Castro, *Os delictos contra a honra da mulher*, 22; Renato Kehl, "Como escolher um

bom marido?," *Revista do Brasil*, anno 8, 23:92 (August 1923): 382–83; Antonio E. Gouveia, "O medico e a mulher: Dois grandes factores do progresso da patria," *RF* 10:107 (April 1923); Picchia, "Caso ou não caso?"

35. Celso, *De relance*, 75–78. Similar caricatures of the frivolousness of young women can be found in "Menina moderna," *A Cigarra* 7:134 (16–30 April 1920); Oliveira, *Gente de agora*, 24–25; Oliveira, *Passadismo e modernismo*, 23–26; Oliveira, *Hontem e hoje*, 32–33.

36. Azevedo, *A moda do desquite*, 87–104. João Aruda, in "Educação sexual e divorcio," *Arquivos Paulistas de Hygiene Mental* 3:5 (July 1930): 76, also claimed that one of his middle-class clients, desiring to be "chic," imitated the behavior of a certain man of the upper class by obtaining a *desquite* from his wife, who he admitted was a saint.

37. Gouveia, "O medico e a mulher"; Pereira, *A mulher no Brasil*, 151–54.

38. "Amor moderno," *Eu Sei Tudo* 133 (June 1928). Lola de Oliveira also underlined the supposed prevalence of this morality in many of her chronicles. See Oliveira, *Gente de agora*, 14–16, 67–69, and *Passadismo e modernismo*, 20, 28–29, 44–46.

39. *A Cigarra* 15:329 (16–31 July 1928).

40. *A Vida Moderna* 16:391 (23 September 1920), 16:389 (19 August 1920), 16:394 (3 November 1920).

41. Osiris, "Carta á Paquita," *A Cigarra* 7:132 (16–31 March 1920); Maldita, "Quando o amor morre," *A Cigarra* 11:208 (16–31 May 1923); Riscalla Asturian, "Amor," *A Cigarra* 10:206 (16–30 April 1923).

42. Cesar, *O problema feminino*, 248; KYTTA, "Iniciação da maternidade," *Renascença* 1:3 (April 1923).

43. "Antes que te cases," *RF* 9:103 (December 1922). The magazine *A Cigarra* printed an article that held up a presumably unusual model couple to be emulated as the "greatest exponents" of conjugal love. See "D. Maria Faria Dente: Um bello retrato," *A Cigarra* 6:127 (1–15 January 1920).

44. H., "Casar?," *A Vida Moderna* 20:473 (11 April 1924).

45. Rezende, "As mães solteiras," 211–16.

46. "Uma obra de assistencia a's celibatarias e velhas pobres," *RF* 12:136 (September 1925). Sophia Lyra in *Rosas de neve*, 121–23, described the life of her great-aunt Zefinha in similar terms. Having bravely refused to marry the son of her father's business partner in the 1880s, Zefinha lived out her adult life as an embittered and short-tempered spinster in the homes of various relatives, where she was charged with taking care of the children and keeping the books for the family business. See also Azevedo, "As regras do namôro no Brazil," 137–38.

47. Cobra, *Virgindade inútil*, 91–92.

48. Pereira, *A mulher no Brasil*, 88; Lima, *Perfil da mulher brasileira*, 101. The few articles that suggested the possibility of dignified alternatives to marriage clearly implied that these were second-best choices. See Lavinia, "O seu caminho," *RF* 9:102 (November 1922); "Reprise do amor," *RF* 5:54 (November 1918).

49. Rosa Barbara, "Caso ou não caso?," *RF* 7:74 (July 1920).

50. "Annullação de casamento," 402, 405–7; ACMSP, Processo de divorcio e nullidade de matrimonio, secção primeira F (1928), gaveta 54, estante 15, no. 694, p. 93.

51. ACMSP, Processo de divorcio e nullidade de matrimonio, secção primeira F (1928), 93–94.

52. "Annullação de casamento," 404–7.

53. Paulino José Soares de Souza Neto, as cited by Caulfield, "In Defense of Honor," 327–28. Souza Neto's article is "Repressão à fraude nas anulações de casamento," *Anais do Primeiro Congresso Nacional do Ministério Público*, vol. 9 (Rio de Janeiro: Imprensa Nacional, 1942), 123–32.

54. The examples that follow are taken from the records of marital separation of the São Paulo Arquivo do Tribunal. In numerous cases, it is difficult to judge whether a woman was truly forced to marry against her will or whether this was merely an argument marshaled in order to secure an annulment. I have therefore cited only cases in which the facts of the situation, the sequence of events, and agreement about details in the testimonies provide ample evidence that the claims made are indeed credible. Lawyers' arguments provide additional evidence that forced marriages had not ended. In one case, the lawyer claimed that the situation of his client represented "nothing extraordinary." (ATSP, "Acção ordinaria para annullação de casamento," no. 349 [1924], p. 38.) Another lawyer appealed to the judge to "embrace the new idea" that marriage had to be based on "reciprocal sincerity," and therefore to grant his client an annulment. (ATSP, "Acção ordinaria para annullação de casamento," no. 30 [1925], p. 30.) Because I was asked not to reveal the names of plaintiffs or defendants, the names used are false.

55. In 1919, official sources calculated that the cost of providing a family of five with basic, nutritionally adequate meals for one year was 1.6 *contos*. São Paulo (State), Secretaria da Agricultura, Comércio e Obras Públicas, *Boletim do Departamento Estadual do Trabalho* 9:34–35 (1st and 2d trimesters of 1920): 15.

56. ATSP, "Acção ordinaria para annullação de casamento," no. 52 (1925).

57. ATSP, "Acção ordinaria para annullação de casamento," no. 83 (1924).

58. ATSP, "Acção ordinaria para annullação de casamento," no. 331 (1924), no. 349 (1924), no. 362 (1925), no. 405 (1925).

59. "Sociedade harmonia," *RF* 7:76 (September 1920); Americano, *São Paulo nesse tempo*, 108–9.

60. "Sociedade harmonia." See also Americano, *São Paulo nesse tempo*, 108–9. Among Americano's list of young men and women who attended the Sociedade's dances, several Italian, German, and English names appear. Until 1918, certain immigrants were also barred from membership in the three most prestigious social clubs in São Paulo: the Jockey Clube, the Automóvel Clube, and Clube São Paulo. See Dean, *Industrialization of São Paulo*, 76–77.

61. Dean, *Industrialization of São Paulo*, 73–74, 76–77.

62. Oliveira, *Hontem e hoje*, 18–21; "O lar feliz," *RF* 6:67 (December 1919).

63. "As mulheres olham umas ás outras," *RF* 7:76 (September 1920).

64. Rosa Barbara, "Caso ou não caso?"

65. Cesar, *O problema feminino*, 197.

66. Americano, *São Paulo nesse tempo*, 121–22. Despite my searches in libraries and used-book stores, I was unable to locate a pre-1940 edition of *Boas maneiras*.

67. Linda Lewin argues that since Luso-Brazilian inheritance law did not exclude natural offspring (those born of merely illicit, but not prohibited, unions), the legal incentive to marry was reduced and the number of out-of-wedlock births was high for all social classes during the colonial period and the nineteenth century. Only after 1847 did the legal rules of heirship begin to discriminate against natural offspring, and Lewin suggests that it was only later (with increasing urbanization) that parents themselves began to discriminate against

natural offspring in their wills. See Lewin, "Natural and Spurious Children," 383–84, 394–95. For an analysis of census statistics, see Jardim, "La statistique par état matrimonial," 4:706. Muriel Nazzari argues that the disappearance of the dowry in nineteenth-century Brazil increased the chances for propertyless women to marry legally. This, combined with the growth of urban professions and employment, allowed a greater percentage of the population to marry legally. Nazzari, *Disappearance of the Dowry*, 142, 167.

68. Mortara, "A nupcialidade no Distrito Federal," 355.

69. Almeida Júnior, "Aspectos da nupcialidade paulista," 99. The same statistics for the years 1894–1927 appear in São Paulo (State), Serviço Sanitário, *Annuário Demográphico* 34:1 (1927): 27–28.

70. Mortara, "A nupcialidade no Distrito Federal," 333–34, 354–56.

71. Ibid., 350. See also table 2 in this volume.

72. Ibid., 350, 352.

73. Ibid., 350–51.

74. Almeida Júnior, "Aspectos da nupcialidade paulista," 105–6.

75. For a discussion of the prodivorce arguments of male professionals, see Chapter 3 in this volume.

76. Brazil, *Código Civil*, 2:65–67 (Article 207), and 2:82–90 (Articles 218–19). For a complete list of the grounds for annulment, see 2:65–97 (Chapter 4, Articles 207–24).

77. Brazil, *Código Civil*, 2:265–79 (Articles 315–18). Divorce was proposed and debated in the Congress in 1891 but rejected in favor of *desquite*. For a summary of the debate, see Bevilaqua's commentary on 2:268–71.

78. This practice was commented on by Americano, *São Paulo nesse tempo*, 272; Azevedo, *A moda do desquite*, 88.

79. Brazil, *Código Civil*, 2:280–81, 288 (Articles 320, 321, 326).

80. ATSP, "Acção ordinaria para annullação de casamento," no. 181 (1925). The name used here is false, since I was asked not to reveal the names of any of the plaintiffs or defendants.

81. Since researchers are not allowed free access to the records of marital separation in the São Paulo Arquivo do Tribunal, these figures were collected for me by an assistant of Judge Pedro Luiz Gagliardi in 1979. Unfortunately, I do not know how many requests for separation were rejected, how many were filed by women as opposed to men, or what the grounds were for these requests and for their acceptance or rejection. I am also lacking information about the numbers of separations granted per year prior to 1922. Judge Gagliardi advised me that the poor condition of the records from the years 1890 (when marriage became regulated by civil rather than ecclesiastical law) to the beginning of the 1920s made it impossible to gather statistics for this period.

82. Brazil, Comissão Censitária Nacional, *Recenseamento geral do Brasil . . . 1940*, série regional, pt. 17, São Paulo, tomo 1, p. 472. The 1920 census does not include any category for separated adults in statistics regarding civil status. The 1890 census recorded only sixteen men and twenty-four women as "*divorciados*," or 0.08 percent of the city's population of fifteen years or older. See Brazil, Diretoria Geral de Estatística, *Idades da população recenseado em 31 de dezembro de 1890*, 394–95; Brazil, Diretoria Geral de Estatística, *Sexo, raça e estado civil, nacionalidade, filiação culto e analphabetismo da população recenseada em 31 de dezembro de 1890*, 134–35.

83. A statistical summary and explanation of the classification of the Brazilian population

by civil status in the censuses of 1872, 1890, 1900, 1920, 1940, and 1950, as well as a discussion of the unreliability of these censuses, may be found in Jardim, "La statistique par état matrimonial," 4:705–14. See also Azevedo, "Family, Marriage, and Divorce," 305–6.

84. "Maternidade," *RF* 10:110 (July 1923).

Chapter Three

1. Hungria, *Comentários ao Código Penal*, 8:413. This quote is from a speech he published in 1940 in his *Questões jurídico-penais*.

2. Plinio Barreto, quoted by Kehl in *Certificado medico pré-nupcial*, 9.

3. Iracema, "Porque o casamento emmudece o homen?," *RF* 8:91 (December 1921). See also Rosa Barbara, "Caso ou não caso?," *RF* 7:74 (July 1920).

4. Iracema, "Porque o casamento emmudece o homen?" See also João do Norte, "As mulheres," *RF* 7:73 (June 1920).

5. Lima, *Conduta sexual*, 182–84.

6. Iracema, "Porque o casamento emmudece o homen?" See also Leme, "Dos crimes con tra a assistência familiar," 297.

7. Hermes, "El amor en el banquillo de los acusados," 466; Nelson Hungria, "Sentença, 7 de dezembro de 1931," in Lyra, *O amor e a responsabilidade*, 215–16.

8. Lyra, *Polícia e justiça para o amor!*, 13.

9. Ibid., 56, 58–59. For a more popular version of this new attitude, see the untitled article from *O Journal* (Rio de Janeiro), 14 May 1931, quoted in Lyra, *O amor e a responsabilidade*, 217–19.

10. "Maternidade," *RF* 10:110 (July 1923).

11. Izabel de León, "A educação da mulher—A esposa—A mãe," *RF* 10:108 (May 1923).

12. Brazil, *Código Civil*, 2:127 (Article 240), 2:113 (Article 233), and 2:131 (Article 242). The only power a wife enjoyed was the power to prevent her husband from alienating, mortgaging, lending, or donating their joint property without her consent. The husband also enjoyed this power over his wife. See 2:117 (Article 235) and 2:131 (Article 242).

13. Espinola, "O feminismo e a legislação civil," 7. This argument is developed throughout the text, 7–23. Clovis Bevilaqua likewise insisted on the necessity of submitting wives to the authority of their husbands in order to harmonize relations of conjugal life. Nevertheless, both he and Espinola constantly reemphasized that this in no way implied men's superiority or women's inferiority. It was explained as being solely the result of the diverse functions traditionally—and appropriately—assigned to husbands and to wives: whereas men were said to be endowed with the physical and intellectual energy necessary to represent the family in the public sphere, women were said to be endowed with the emotional qualities necessary to deal with matters pertaining to the interpersonal relations of domestic life. Brazil, *Código Civil*, 2:114–15, 133–36.

14. Lima, *Conduta sexual*, 187.

15. Brasilia Siqueira, "A influencia da literatura didactica sobre o destino dos povos," *RF* 7:73 (June 1920); Espinola, "O feminismo e a legislação civil," 8, 19.

16. León, "A educação da mulher—A esposa—A mãe"; "Maternidade," *RF* 10:110 (July 1923). See also the quote by J. J. Vieiro Filho in Lima, *Conduta sexual*, 185.

17. João A. Correa de Araujo, "O verdadeiro feminismo," *RF* 4:43 (December 1917); Orlando Machado, "A reivindicação feminina em New York," *Revista do Brasil*, anno 8, 23:89 (May 1923).

18. Espinola, "O feminismo e a legislação civil," 7–23; Albuquerque, *Moral sexual*, 145, 149; Gina de Lombroso, "A intelligencia da mulher," *Revista do Brasil*, anno 6, 18:72 (December 1921): 369–74.

19. *O lar feliz*, 7.

20. Aprígio Gonzaga, "A mulher na sociedade," *RF* 8:90 (November 1921).

21. Lemos, "O voto feminino," 248.

22. Bastos, *Justiça, alegria, felicidade*, 88; Coelho Netto, "Prefácio," in the unauthored book *O problema sexual*, 7; Vasconcelos, *Minha terra e sua gente*, 63–70; Vasconcelos, "O amor no Brasil," *RF* 7:79 (December 1920) (Chrysanthème develops this theme further in her many novels of social customs); "Conselhos sociaes: O casamento," *Revista da Semana* 22:33 (13 August 1921); Antonio Austregésilo Lima, "Poupae o vosso coração," *A Cigarra* 14:288 (1–15 November 1926); Lima, *O meu e o teu*, 55–58; Silva, *Arte de amar*, 3d ed., 14; Machado, *Um ensaio de moral sexual*, 117–18; "Como a esposa deve amar o marido," *RF* 4:37 (June 1917).

23. "Pre-texto," in Lyra, *Polícia e justiça para o amor*!; Humberto de Campos, "Eros vae morrer!," *O Cruzeiro* 2:78 (3 May 1930): 3; Renato Silva, "O funeral do romantismo," *O Cruzeiro* 2:94 (23 August 1930): 28; Riscalla Asturian, "Amor," *A Cigarra* 10:206 (16–30 April 1923); "Chronica," *A Cigarra* 15:313 (16–30 November 1927); Armando Bertoni, "A derrota do amor," *A Cigarra* 17:373 (16–31 May 1930).

24. Lima, *Educação da alma*, 68.

25. Peixoto, "Crimes passionaes," 67, 69; Peixoto, *Elementos de medicina legal*, 24.

26. R. Lyra, "Prefácio," 27; Lyra, "O amor no banco dos reus," 222–24.

27. "Como a esposa consegue atrair o amor do marido," *RF* 4:43 (December 1917); "Como a esposa deve amar o marido"; Silva, *Arte de amar*, 3d ed., 71.

28. Lima, *Meditações*, 27, 34–35, 37–41.

29. "Como a esposa deve amar o marido"; "Como a esposa consegue atrair o amor do marido"; Britto, *Psychologia do adultério*, 42, 47.

30. Bastos, *Justiça, alegria, felicidade*, 26.

31. Britto, *Psychologia do adultério*, 33, 53, 195–96; "Conselhos sociaes: O casamento."

32. Britto, *Psychologia do adultério*, 44–45.

33. "Como a esposa deve amar o marido."

34. Ibid.

35. Lima, *Educação da alma*, 235.

36. Lima, *A neurastenia sexual*, 145–46; Machado, *Um ensaio de moral sexual*, 86, 112, 116–18; *O problema sexual*, 120; Albuquerque, *Moral sexual*, 98–99.

37. Lima, *Conduta sexual*, 156–69. See also Marestan, *A educação sexual*, 352–53 (n. 23), and 356–58 (n. 28); Peixoto, *Eunice*, 262–63.

38. Lima, *Conduta sexual*, 159.

39. Ibid., 165.

40. Ibid., 159–60, 166–67, 173–74, 178. For a comparative perspective, see Grossman, "New Woman." She argues that the sex reform movement in Germany in the 1920s (as in Brazil) "recognized and encouraged female sexuality, but on male heterosexual terms—in defense of the family" (155). In both countries, reformers explicitly sought to redomesticate women and to solve the "crisis" of the family.

41. Moura, "As conferencias de Maria Lacerda de Moura," 11; Peixoto, *Sexologia forense*, 209. Interestingly, Sueann Caulfield found that during the 1920s to 1930s, the testimony in court cases of deflowering "contained a new language of sexual arousal." In many cases, the offended woman openly acknowledged that the defendant had greatly excited her physically before she "gave in." "In Defense of Honor," 352–54.

42. The following represents an undoubtedly incomplete list of books treating sexuality that were translated into Portuguese between 1928 and 1935. It does, however, include the works most commonly cited by Brazilian authors.

Augusto Forel, *A questão sexual*, 2d ed., rev. with a preface by Dr. Flaminio Favero (São Paulo, 1928).

Marie Carmichael Stopes, *Amor e casamento: Nova contribuição para a solução sexual*, trans. Godofredo Rangel (São Paulo, 1929); *Procreação racional* (São Paulo, 1929); *Radiante maternidade*, trans. Godofredo Rangel (São Paulo, [1929?]).

Havelock Ellis, *A educação sexual*, trans. and notes by Dr. Alvaro Eston (São Paulo, 1933); *O instinto sexual*, trans. and notes by Dr. Alvaro Eston (São Paulo, 1933); *O inversão sexual*, trans. and notes by Dr. Alvaro Eston (São Paulo, 1933); *O pudor, a periodicidade sexual e o auto-erotismo*, trans. and notes by Dr. Alvaro Eston (São Paulo, [193?]).

J. R. Bourdon, *A intimidade conjugal*, trans. Dr. Elias Davidovitch (São Paulo, [193?]); *A intimidade sexual: Guia moderno dos esposos*, trans. Dr. Odilon Galloti (Rio de Janeiro, 1935); *Impotencia sexual masculina*, trans. Dr. Odilon Galloti (São Paulo, 1935); *Perversões sexuais* (São Paulo, [193?]); *Tratamento prático da timidez*, trans. Luiz Martins (São Paulo, [193?]).

Theodoor Hendrik van de Velde, *Aversão conjugal*, trans. Manuel Bandeira (São Paulo, [193?]); *Capaz ou incapaz para o casamento* (São Paulo, [193?]); *A esposa perfeita: Efficiencia sexual pela cultura physica*, trans. Bruno Zander, with a preface by Arnaldo de Moraes (Rio de Janeiro, [193?]); *Fisiologia e tecnica das relações sexuais* (São Paulo, 1933); *O matrimonio perfeito*, with a preface by José de Albuquerque (São Paulo, [1933]).

Sigmund Freud, *Sexualidade*, trans. Osorio de Oliveira (São Paulo, [193?]).

Pierre Vachet, *A inquietação sexual* (São Paulo, 1929); *Conhecimento da vida sexual* (Rio de Janeiro, 1932).

Paolo Mantegazza, *Fisiologia da mulher* (Lisbon, 1924); *Fisiologia de amor* (Lisbon, 1932); *Higiene do amor* (Lisbon, [193?]).

Jean Marestan, *A educação sexual*, with a preface and notes by J. P. Porto-Carrero (Rio de Janeiro, 1930).

Gregorio Marañon, *Tres ensaios sobre a vida sexual* (São Paulo, 1933).

Julio R. Barcos, *Liberdade sexual das mulheres*, trans. and preface by Maria Lacerda de Moura (São Paulo, 1929).

Alexandra Kolontai, *A nova mulher e a moral sexual*, trans. and preface by Galeão Coutinho (São Paulo, [193?]).

Gilbert Van Tassel Hamilton and Kenneth MacGowan, *O que esta errado no casamento* (São Paulo, [193?]).

William Harrison, *Minha vida sexual* (Rio de Janeiro, [193?]).

43. J. P. Porto-Carrero, "Prefacio," in Marestan, *A educação sexual*, 6; Alvaro Eston, "Preambulo," in Ellis, *A educação sexual*, vi; José de Albuquerque, "Prefacio," in Velde, *O matrimonio perfeito*, xxxiii–xxxv; Flaminio Favero, "Prefacio," in Forel, *A questão sexual*, v.

44. Albuquerque, "Prefacio," in Velde, *O matrimonio perfeito*, xxxv.

45. Arnaldo de Moraes, "Prefacio," in Velde, *A esposa perfeita*, i–viii, 10–11, 278.

46. Albuquerque, *Moral sexual*, 99–100, 129–33; Lima, *Conduta sexual*, 186, 197–98;

Castro, *Os delictos contra a honra da mulher*, 51–54; Cesar, *O problema feminino*, 1, 268, 296–304, 314–35, 342–43, 356–60, 384–87; "Educação sexual e divorcio," 63–85. This last article republished the opinions of ten specialists in law and medicine who responded to an inquiry concerning sexual education and divorce organized by the *Diario da Noite* in May to June 1930. Of the eight who addressed the question of divorce, only Father Francisco de Assis Bastos categorically opposed it, upholding the official Church doctrine (78–79). Supporters included Franco da Rocha (64), Custodio de Carvalho (68), Flaminio Favero (69–70), Antonio Carlos Pacheco e Silva (73–74), João Arruda (74–77), Edgard Braga (81), and Fausto Guerner (85).

47. *O problema sexual*, 72–73; Pereira, *A mulher no Brasil*, 90, 163.

48. *O problema sexual*, 39, 74.

49. Nupciophilo, "Porque morrem mais solteiros do que casados? As vantagens do matrimonio," *A Cigarra* 15:336 (1–15 November 1928). The point of this article was didactic, not scholarly, and it contains no statistical evidence.

50. Lima, *Conduta sexual*, 196–97; Lima, *Perfil da mulher*, 100–101.

51. Pereira, *A mulher no Brasil*, 118, 123, 201–6. Renato Kehl agreed: "There is no happy life except in marriage." See his *Como escolher uma boa esposa*, 42.

52. Heitor Praguer Fróes, "Bases racionaes da felicidade conjugal," *RF* 11:118 (March 1924); "A educação da mulher: Esposa e mãe," *RF* 6:65 (October 1919); "Para as jovens solteiras," *RF* 12:129 (February 1925); "A mulher e o matrimonio," *RF* 10:108 (May 1923); Cesar, *O problema feminino*, 240; Britto, *Psychologia do adultério*, 191; Kehl, *Como escolher uma boa esposa*, 27, 55–61.

53. "A escolha de um noivo," *RF* 6:61 (June 1919); Britto, *Psychologia do adultério*, 200.

54. "A mulher e o matrimonio."

55. Fróes, "Bases racionaes da felicidade conjugal."

56. Kehl, *Como escolher uma boa esposa*, 18–19, 68–69, 75–91.

57. "A uma noiva," *RF* 12:139 (December 1925); Pericles Calvino Libero Mainardi, "Dia do lar," *Educação* (July–September 1930): 64–65; Fróes, "Bases racionaes da felicidade conjugal."

58. "Para as jovens solteiras"; Fróes, "Bases racionaes da felicidade conjugal."

59. Britto, *Psychologia do adultério*, 85–86.

60. Fróes, "Bases racionaes da felicidade conjugal"; Renato Kehl, "Como escolher um bom marido?," *Revista do Brasil*, anno 8, 23:92 (August 1923): 382; Kehl, *Como escolher uma boa esposa*, chap. 4; Marestan, *A educação sexual*, 368–70; Lima, *Conduta sexual*, 160–61; Vasconcellos, *Educação sexual da mulher*, 43, 45.

61. Arguments in favor of greater equality between spouses include Fróes, "Bases racionaes da felicidade conjugal"; "A educação da mulher: Esposa e mãe."

62. "A Cigarra commenta . . . : Vantagens e desvantagens," *A Cigarra* 19:422 (16–30 June 1923).

63. "Para as jovens solteiras"; Kehl, *Como escolher uma boa esposa*, 134–41.

64. "A escolha de um noivo."

65. Lima, *Perfil da mulher*, 61–71, 77–78, 81–120; Lima, *Conduta sexual*, 184.

66. Lima, *Livro de sentimentos*, 100.

67. Mello, "Política da familia," 38.

68. See Titulo IV, Article 121:1:h, Article 138, and Article 141 of the 1934 Constitution as reprinted in the *BMTIC* (September 1934).

69. *BMTIC* 6:64 (December 1939): 92–93.

70. "Decreto-Lei N. 3.200—De 19 de abril de 1941," *BMTIC* 7:81 (May 1941): 51–61. See also Cesarino Júnior, "A família como objeto do direito social." For further discussion of the incentives provided by this law for bearing children, see Chapter 4 in the present volume.

71. Azevedo, *Social Change in Brazil*, 17.

72. P. Desfosses, "A mulher de escol," *RF* 9:95 (April 1922); Mainardi, "Dia do lar," 66; "Conselhos sociaes: A mulher forte," *Revista da Semana* 22:35 (27 August 1921).

73. Lima, *Conduta sexual*, 187.

74. "O decálogo da esposa," *RF* 11:127 (December 1924); Peixoto, *Eunice*, 317–20.

75. Lemos, "O voto feminino," 248.

76. "A educação," *A Vida Moderna* 19:480 (23 August 1924); Cesar, *O problema feminino*, 236, 265 (the author states on p. 5 that the book was completed in 1922); "Como a esposa consegue attrahir o marido," *RF* 5:45 (February 1918); "A esposa deve conhecer bem seu marido," *RF* 4:36 (May 1917).

77. Desfosses, "A mulher de escol"; Marianno Macia, "A suavidade do lar," *RF* 9:103 (December 1922); "Qualidades moraes da esposa," *RF* 5:48 (May 1918); "Como a esposa consegue dar felicidade ao seu marido," *RF* 4:41 (October 1917); Odette Donais, "A felicidade no lar," *RF* 7:75 (August 1920); Rafael Mesa de la Pena, "Conselho de mãe," *RF* 12:132 (May 1925).

78. "O decálogo da esposa."

79. Mons. Solon Pereira, "O valor da mulher como esposa e como mãe," *RF* 10:106 (March 1923).

80. "Conselhos sociaes: A mulher forte."

81. "Divagações acerca da virtude," *RF* 11:126 (November 1924). See also Lima, *Perfil da mulher*, 87, 89; Lima, *Conduta sexual*, 187; Bastos, *Justiça, alegria, felicidade*, 117–18; *O problema sexual*, 83; "Em um doce colloquio," *RF* 11:121 (June 1924).

82. Lima, *Perfil da mulher*, 95.

83. Negreiros, "A acção da mulher no lar," 169; "Como a esposa consegue dar felicidade ao seu marido"; "Como a esposa consegue attrahir o marido"; "Qualidades moraes da esposa."

84. Silva, *Arte de amar*, 3d ed., 46; Peixoto, *Eunice*, 317–19; "Como a esposa consegue dar felicidade ao seu marido."

85. Desfosses, "A mulher de escol." See also "A felicidade no lar"; "Como a esposa consegue dar felicidade ao seu marido"; Pereira, "O valor da mulher como esposa e como mãe."

86. "As mulheres automnaes," *RF* 11:119 (April 1924).

87. Desfosses, "A mulher de escol"; Pereira, "O valor da mulher como esposa e como mãe"; Negreiros, "A acção da mulher no lar," 169.

88. "Qualidades moraes da esposa"; "Qualidades praticas e moraes da esposa," *RF* 5:47 (April 1918); "A educação da mulher—Esposa e mãe," *RF* 6:65 (October 1919); Silva, *Arte de amar*, 3d ed., 46.

89. León, "A educação da mulher—A esposa—A mãe."

90. Silva, *Arte de amar*, 3d ed., 75; Bastos, *Justiça, alegria, felicidade*, 126–27; Marilda Palinia, "Conselhos," *RF* 7:69 (February 1920); "Como fazer um bom matrimonio," *RF* 11:125 (October 1924).

91. Iracema, "Carta da mulher," *O Cruzeiro* 1:19 (16 March 1929): 46.

92. Marilda Palinia, "Conselhos"; Bastos, *Justiça, alegria, felicidade*, 133.

93. Claudio de Souza, "De Eva antiga á Eva moderna," *RF* 5:44 (January 1918).

94. "Qualidades praticas e moraes da esposa"; "Como a esposa consegue dar felicidade ao seu marido"; "O decálogo da esposa"; Negreiros, "A acção da mulher no lar," 169.

95. "Qualidades moraes da esposa."

96. "Como a esposa consegue dar felicidade ao seu marido."

97. "Qualidades praticas e moraes da esposa"; "Deveres de uma senhora," *RF* 4:34 (March 1917).

98. *O lar feliz*, 98.

99. "Qualidades praticas da esposa," *RF* 5:46 (March 1918).

100. "Deveres de uma senhora"; "Como a esposa consegue dar felicidade ao seu marido."

101. "Os segredos da felicidade," *RF* 12:132 (May 1925).

102. "Qualidades praticas e moraes da esposa"; "Qualidades praticas da esposa." In addition to the references already cited for this paragraph, see "O decálogo da esposa"; "Como a esposa consegue attrahir o marido"; Mainardi, "Dia do lar," 64; Madame X, "O lar," *A Vida Moderna* 17:401 (24 February 1921); Maria Rosa Ribeiro, "Prudencia, ordem, economia, e amor ao trabalho," in Brito, *Antologia feminina*, 92–93.

103. "Como a esposa consegue atrair o amor do marido"; "Como a esposa consegue attrahir o marido." See also Anna Rita Malheiros, "Março," *RF* 4:34 (March 1917); Iracema, "Porque o casamento emmudece o homem?"; "A elegancia na intimidade," *RF* 11:125 (October 1924); Angelo Mendes d'Almeida, "A educação da mulher," *A Vida Moderna* 15:351 (28 January 1919); Madame X, "A dona de casa," *A Vida Moderna* 16:396 (9 December 1920).

104. Cesar, *O problema feminino*, 257–58.

105. "As coquettes," *A Cigarra* 7:140 (16–31 July 1920). See also George, "Mlle. Coquetterie," *A Vida Moderna* 16:388 (5 August 1920).

106. Malheiros, "Março." See also Oliveira, *Gente de agora*, 102–6.

107. Maria Thereza, "Devemos amar mais os nossos filhos que os nossos esposos?," *RF* 6:61 (June 1919).

108. "Como a esposa consegue atrair o amor do marido."

109. Britto, *Psychologia do adultério*, 84, 86, 99–100.

110. Ibid., 114–15; *O problema sexual*, 58, 63; Silva, *Arte de amar*, 3d ed., 60; "Deveres de uma senhora"; Norte, "As mulheres."

111. Britto, *Psychologia do adultério*, 87, 160.

112. Silva, *Arte de amar*, 3d ed., 23–25.

113. "Como a esposa deve amar o marido"; Silva, *Arte de amar*, 3d ed., 63; Irene de Souza Pinto, "O primeiro amor," *RF* 9:94 (March 1922); Lima, *Educação da alma*, 238; Britto, *Psychologia do adultério*, 53; "Antes que te cases," *RF* 9:103 (December 1922); "Como a esposa deve amar o marido."

114. Silva, *Arte de amar*, 3d ed., 27, 73.

115. Ibid., 77. See also "Consultario feminino," *A Cigarra* 16:365 (16–31 January 1930).

116. Silva, *Arte de amar*, 2d ed., 288–98; Gonçalvo Maia, "*Arte de amar* de Julio Cesar da Silva," *A Cigarra* 8:172 (16–30 November 1921).

117. Marinette, "A intimidade do lar," *RF* 5:50 (July 1918); Desfosses, "A mulher de escol"; Marianno Macia, "A suavidade do lar," *RF* 9:103 (December 1922).

118. Lombroso, "A intelligencia da mulher," 371.

119. Desfosses, "A mulher de escol"; Araujo, "O verdadeiro feminismo"; Menezes Furtado, "O poder social da mulher Christã," *RF* 12:132 (May 1925).

120. Santiago Ramon y Cajal, "Como deve ser a esposa do sabio," *RF* 9:103 (December 1922).

121. Clotilde de Mattos, "As nossas leitoras," *RF* 5:46 (March 1918).

122. Lima, *Perfil da mulher*, 91, 106–8.

123. "Qualidades praticas da esposa"; Desfosses, "A mulher de escol"; Gonzaga, "A mulher na sociedade"; Pereira, "O valor da mulher como esposa e como mãe"; *O lar feliz*, 97, 140–42.

124. "Assumptos domesticos. A 'Liga Nacional das Donas de Casa' nos Estados Unidos: Conselhos á mulher brasileira," *RF* 10:110 (July 1923).

125. "Economia domestica: Conselhos de Mistress Julia Heath, presidente da 'Liga Nacional das Donas de Casa,' ás suas companheiras da associação," *RF* 10:108 (May 1923).

126. "Exposição de trabalhos," *RF* 4:40 (September 1917); "Nossa exposição de trabalhos," *RF* 4:36 (May 1917).

127. "Curso de trabalhos femininos," *RF* 4:36 (May 1917), 6:64 (September 1919), 6:67 (December 1919).

128. "Exposição de trabalhos," *RF* 4:33 (February 1917). Publicity for the exhibition became a regular feature of the magazine. The editors claimed that even women of well-known families sold handicrafts in the magazine's exhibition. Some of those named were Aurora de Carvalho, Vicentina Amaral, Flesbina Rudge, Livia Diniz, Zica Ribeiro, Nizia Amaral, Carolina Salles de Oliveira, and Dalila Barroso.

129. Lima, *Perfil da mulher*, 101–2.

130. Although husbands may have been in as much need of indoctrination as wives, their assigned roles—as considerate companions of their wives, responsible breadwinners, and upright citizens—were not nearly as problematic or as anxiety provoking. Given this, they would have had little interest in or reason for reading normative literature, and thus attempts to remold their behavior generally took on more coercive forms. See the following section of this chapter.

131. Mello, "Política da familia," 38–39.

132. For information on protective legislation, see Chapter 6 in this volume.

133. Brazil, *Código Civil*, 2:159.

134. In 1977 divorce was legalized in Brazil, but the new law allowed a person to divorce only once in his or her lifetime.

135. Leme, "Dos crimes contra a assistência familiar," 299. Judge Nelson Hungria concurred (in a speech published in 1940) that the "timid and easily evaded" civil sanctions had proved "innocuous" in protecting the family from "gradual annulment." This speech is republished in his *Comentários ao Código Penal*, 8:414–15.

136. Leme, "Dos crimes contra a assistência familiar," 292, 306–22.

137. Hungria, *Comentários ao Código Penal*, 8:342, 345–48, 352, 376.

138. Ibid., 8:346–48.

139. For a more lengthy discussion of this campaign, see Besse, "Crimes of Passion."

140. Celso, *De relance*, 31–32. Other female critics included Oliveira, *Passadismo e modernismo*, 124, and Moura, *Han Ryner e o amor plural*, 49. The *Revista Feminina* also mounted a strenuous campaign against wife killing, dedicating numerous editorials to the issue (some of which, however, were written by Claudio de Souza under the female pseudonym Anna Rita Malheiros). See Anna Rita Malheiros, "Junho," *RF* 9:97 (June 1922); "Os assassinos de mulheres," *RF* 7:71 (April 1920); and "O assassino de mulheres," *RF* 11:119 (April 1924). Although it was women who first decried the toleration of crimes of passion, it was

male professionals (mostly attorneys) who organized a campaign to change social and legal practices. And although women tended to be primarily concerned about the victimization of women, men tended to be more concerned about the negative impact of crimes of passion on the legitimacy of the institution of the family.

141. "Os crimes passionaes," *A Esquerda* (Rio de Janeiro), 28 April 1931, reprinted in Lyra, *O amor e a responsabilidade*, 86–88.

142. Hermes, "El amor en el banquillo de los acusados," 466.

143. Torres, "O jury e seu rigor contra os passionaes," 78; Hungria, *Questões jurídico-penais*, 113; Hungria, *Comentários ao Código Penal*, 5:129–39.

144. This terminology regarding their campaign was repeated ad infinitum. See, for example, Lyra, "O amor no banco dos reus," 221; Lyra, *Polícia e justiça para o amor!*, 43; Hermes, "El amor en el banquillo de los acusados," 466.

145. Besse, "Crimes of Passion," 661. As Mariza Corrêa has shown in her *Morte em família*, the practice of wife killing had changed little by the early 1970s, although legal defenses varied over time. Indeed, the practice continues to be an issue in Brazil in the 1990s (as it does elsewhere). But since the late 1970s, women active in the feminist movement have seized the initiative in Brazil in fighting this crime along with other forms of domestic violence.

146. Lima, *Perfil da mulher*, 102.

147. Donais, "A felicidade no lar."

148. Marinette, "A intimidade do lar"; Francisca Accidi Monteiro, "A frivolidade no lar," *RF* 9:101 (October 1922); Maria Thereza, "Devemos amar mais os nossos filhos que os nossos esposos?"; *O lar feliz*, 7; Mainardi, "Dia do lar," 64; Cesar, *O problema feminino*, 283.

149. See, for example, Gonzaga, "A mulher na sociedade"; Torres, "A mulher e o jury," 37–38.

150. Wolfe, *Working Women, Working Men*, 86; Pinheiro and Hall, *A classe operária*, 2:214–20.

151. Cava, "Igreja e estado"; Prandi, "Catolicismo e família." Prandi's essay analyzes the messages in the monthly journal *A Família Cristã*, the Catholic publication with the widest circulation in Brazil, from 1940 to 1970. See also Decca, *A vida fora das fábricas*, 90–91.

152. Silva, *Serviços sociais*, 186–87; Queiroz, "Assistencia social à infancia," 262. For more information about female charitable workers, see Chapter 6 in this volume.

153. Iamamoto and Carvalho, *Relações sociais e serviço social*, pt. 2, chaps. 1–2. The quote is taken from p. 175.

154. Ibid., chap. 3.

155. Cunha, *O espelho do mundo*; see esp. chap. 3. For a description of Brazil's oldest and most prestigious insane asylum at Juqueri during the 1920s and 1930s, see the work of one of its directors: Silva, *A assistência a psicopatas*. For numerous other case studies of women interned at the mental asylum in Juqueri, see Besse, "Freedom and Bondage," chap. 7.

156. Pinheiro and Hall, *A classe operário*, 2:213–20; Rago, *Do cabaré ao lar*, 175–99; Blay, *Eu não tenho onde morar*.

157. Joel Wolfe, in his *Working Women, Working Men* (57–58), quotes a 1931 letter to President Vargas from male unionists who dominated the union in the predominantly female sector of textile manufacturing (União dos Operários em Fábricas de Tecidos de São Paulo). They complained that the large number of women textile workers "serves to increase the number of unemployed men, creating . . . a ridiculous spectacle that is shameful and re-

volting: the woman at work in the factory and the husband at home taking care of domestic chores and bringing the children to the factory gate to be nursed."

158. Even Brazilian Communist Party (PCB) activist Laura Brandão, who played a major role in organizing female workers, was praised by her husband Octavio (founding member of the PCB) for working behind the scenes of the party to keep morale high and uphold socially acceptable sexual norms, for performing administrative tasks, and for raising their children. He thanked her publicly for being a loyal wife who "protected [his] life, health, and liberty." Brandão, *Combates e batalhas*, 303.

159. On the attitudes of male-directed labor unions toward women, see Pena, *Mulheres e trabalhadoras*, chap. 5; Beiguelman, *Os companheiros de São Paulo*; Rago, *Do cabaré ao lar*, 61–74.

160. An excellent study of the women's movements that emerged in Brazil during the 1970s and 1980s is Alvarez, *Engendering Democracy in Brazil*.

Chapter Four

1. The details of this case are taken from the newspaper article "Tribunal do juri: A impressionante cena da sangue da Rua Salete, examinada perante o juri," *Diario de São Paulo*, 3 May 1932, 5, and from AMJSP, "Laudo do exame medico-psicologico procedido na pessôa da acusada D. Antonia de Arujo" (entrance date, 25 December 1931).

2. AMJSP, "Laudo do exame da Antonia de Arujo," 2–3.

3. "Tribunal do juri: A impressionante cena da sangue da Rua Salete, examinada perante o juri," 5.

4. AMJSP, "Laudo do exame da Antonia de Arujo," 6–7.

5. Antonia may have suffered from manic depression, but the expression of her mental illness in the killing of her favorite son (rather than through some other channel) indicates that she experienced the frustrations of motherhood as especially traumatic. In addition, the compelling interest that this case had for many women of Antonia's class suggests that they could identify with her predicament even if they themselves would not have taken similar action.

6. Costa, *Ordem médica e norma familiar*, chap. 5. In the words of jurist Romão Côrtes de Lacerda: "[T]he idea of *pátrio poder*, since the Revolution of 1789, evolves toward that of *pátrio dever* [duty, rather than power, of the head of family toward offspring], losing, day by day, the Roman absolutism in favor of *liberty* and of *obligations* imposed on the father." See his commentary on crimes against the family in Hungria, *Comentários ao Código Penal*, 8:330.

7. See the articles in Priore, *História da criança*, especially Fernando Torres Londoño, "A origem do conceito *menor*," 129–45.

8. Mello, "Política da familia," 39.

9. Physician and leading eugenicist Renato Kehl rationalized assigning greater responsibility for child rearing to mothers on the basis of their supposedly greater biological contribution to reproduction, as well as the supposed nature of that contribution. In his words: "The influence of women in the future of the species is decisive. Its progressive improvement depends on female vigor and beauty. In human biology, women represent par excellence the conservative element of preservation, while men represent the active factor of evolution. They are intersecting forces for the indispensable equilibrium of the whole. Women

constitute, in other words, the reservoir of potential energy of the species, while men represent the active energy, in permanent state of propulsion. Since Adam and Eve (to trust in the divine origin of humanity) female influence over offspring is, let us say, 75 percent in relation to the 25 percent masculine influence." Kehl, *Perguntas a um eugenista*, 3.

10. Nagle, *Educação e sociedade*, 97–124. Nagle, using extensive quotes from the works of the leading Brazilian educators of the 1920s, demonstrates their tremendous enthusiasm for education and their boundless optimism in its transformative power. See also the citations in notes 49–51 in this chapter.

11. Leme, "Dos crimes contra a assistência familiar," 294.

12. Moncorvo Filho, *Histórico da protecção á infancia*, 134–44.

13. See Kehl, *Eugenía e medicina social*, 13–20. On the eugenics movements in Brazil, Mexico, and Argentina, see Stepan, *"Hour of Eugenics."*

14. Moncorvo Filho, *Histórico da protecção á infancia*, 283–89, 325.

15. Moncorvo Filho et al., *Hygiene infantil* (1907). This book consists of thirty short (one- to two-page) lectures given to poor women at the Dispensario Moncorvo between 1901 and 1907. Moncorvo Filho, *Histórico da protecção á infancia*, 156. These contests were apparently very popular and successful in setting modern standards. In 1927, a "Concurso de Eugenia" paid homage to the empress D. Leopoldina on the centenary of her death by selecting three children who came closest to the eugenic ideal. See Kehl, *A eugenía no Brasil*, 26–27. Later, the Johnson and Johnson Company exploited this idea, holding up an image of the perfect "Baby Johnson" to sell its products.

16. Moncorvo Filho, *Histórico da protecção á infancia*, 110–11.

17. Quoted in ibid., 132–33. See also Fernando Torres Londoño, "A origem do conceito *menor*," in Priore, *História da criança*, 129–45. Londoño examines the new interest among jurists from the end of the nineteenth century to the early twentieth century for children's welfare, especially the welfare of urban poor and abandoned children (who were regarded as potential—if not actual—criminals). In 1921, Lei 4.242 established the Serviço de Assistência e Protecção à Infancia Abandonada e aos Delinquentes (142).

18. Pena, *Mulheres e trabalhadoras*, 151–54; Werneck, "O trabalho das mulheres e dos menores," 134–49; "Decreto N. 21.417-A [and] Decreto N. 22.042," *BMTIC* 2:21 (May 1936): 37–49.

19. Sections of the 1934 Constitution concerning family and child welfare are printed in *BMTIC* 1:1 (September 1934).

20. "Decreto-Lei N. 3.200—De 19 de abril de 1941," *BMTIC* 7:81 (May 1941): 51–61. See also Mello, "Política da familia"; Cesarino Júnior, "A família como objeto do direito social."

21. Mello, "Trabalho de menores," 118–22.

22. For information on the labor movement's attitudes toward female and child labor, see Pena, *Mulheres e trabalhadoras*, chap. 5.

23. See the evaluation of a decade of work of the federação by its president: Alice Pinheiro Coimbra, "Federação Brasileira pelo Progresso Feminino," Arquivo da FBPF, folder "2º Congresso Feminista do Rio de Janeiro, 1931." See also the newspaper reports describing the first annual celebration of Mother's Day: "O dia das mães," *O Estado de São Paulo*, 7 May 1932, 1, and 10 May 1932, 5.

24. Bastos, *Justiça, alegria, felicidade*, 121.

25. Parédrinho, "Creimos uma escola onde a mulher apprenda a ser mulher," *RF* 12:135 (August 1925).

26. Maria Thereza, "Devemos amar mais os nossos filhos que os nossos esposos?," *RF* 6:61 (June 1919).

27. Ibid.

28. Santina Felizzola, "Femininidade e feminismo," *RF* 6:67 (December 1919).

29. P. Desfosses, "A mulher de escol," *RF* 9:95 (April 1922); Orlando Machado, "A reivindicação feminina em New York," *Revista do Brasil* anno 8, 23:89 (May 1923).

30. "Maternidade," *RF* 10:110 (July 1923).

31. Moncorvo Filho, *Hygiene infantil* (1917), 1:7–9, 36; Izabel de León, "A educação da mulher—A esposa—A mãe," *RF* 10:108 (May 1923); "A educação da mulher: Esposa e mãe," *RF* 6:65 (October 1919); Negreiros, "A acção da mulher no lar," 171; Lima, *Perfil da mulher*, 118; Lima, *Conduta sexual*, 85.

32. "Apprender a ser mãe," *RF* 5:47 (April 1918). See also Francisco Falcão, "A educação da mulher e as creanças," *Revista do Brasil*, anno 6, 17:68 (August 1921): 470–71.

33. Moncorvo Filho, *Histórico da protecção á infancia*, 127–28, 134–37, 318–19; Moncorvo Filho et al., *Hygiene infantil* (1907), 13, 45; Antonio E. Gouveia, "O medico e a mulher: Dois grandes factores do progresso da patria," *RF* 10:107 (April 1923); Kehl, *Eugenía e medicina social*, 68, 113.

34. Gouveia, "O medico e a mulher."

35. Lima, *Perfil da mulher*, 93.

36. This message was repeated ad infinitum not only to middle-class women but also to poor women who clearly did not possess the material resources to obey the "rules" even if they had wanted to. See the lectures given to poor women at the Dispensario Moncorvo and collected in the anthology by Moncorvo Filho et al., *Hygiene infantil* (1907). See also Kehl, *Pais, médicos, e mestres*, 12–13, 17.

37. See, for example, Moncorvo Filho et al., *Hygiene infantil* (1907); Moncorvo Filho, *Hygiene infantil* (1917); Silva, *A mulher e a criança*; Rocha Júnior, *Cartilha das mães*. Renato Ferraz Kehl, founder of the São Paulo Eugenic Society, also published dozens of books and countless articles during the 1920s and 1930s popularizing the principles of eugenic education.

38. *O lar feliz*, 24–25.

39. Vasconcellos, *Educação sexual da mulher*, 27; Madame Festoyer, "Da graça e da belleza infantil," *RF* 11:116 (January 1924).

40. Moncorvo Filho et al., *Hygiene infantil* (1907), 61–65, 78–79; Silva, *A mulher e a criança*; Rocha Júnior, *Cartilha das mães*; Vasconcellos, *Educação sexual da mulher*; Lima, *Conduta sexual*; Machado, *O physico feminino na adolescencia*; Moraes, *Ensaios de pathologia social*, 293–95, 306–7; Luiz Medeiros, "A educação sexual em face do problema venereo," *A Folha Medica* 3:7 (15 April 1922): 73–76, and 3:8 (30 April 1922): 85–86.

41. "Maternidade," *RF* 10:110 (July 1923); E. K., "O feminismo," *A Cigarra* 12:223 (1–15 January 1924); Odette Donah, "Um apello ás mães," *RF* 7:77 (October 1920); "A educação da mulher: Esposa e mãe."

42. Lima, *Perfil da mulher*, 119; Nogueira, "Dia do lar," 59.

43. Lima, *Perfil da mulher*, 94.

44. Chrysanthème, "A educação feminina de hoje," *RF* 7:68 (January 1920); Menotti del Picchia, "Caso ou não caso?," *RF* 7:68 (January 1920); "Os dois polos da educação," *Revista da Semana* 22:21 (20 May 1921).

45. Isa Eira, "A mãe como educadora," *RF* 7:79 (December 1920).

46. Lima, *Perfil da mulher*, 118.

47. Maria Clara de Alvear, "A funcção actual da mulher," *RF* 10:107 (April 1923).

48. Lemos, "O voto feminino," 249; Mainardi, "Dia do lar," 62. See also Parédrinho, "Creimos uma escola onde a mulher apprenda a ser mulher"; Moncorvo Filho et al., *Hygiene infantil* (1907), 80; Doria, *Educação moral*, 51; Leme, "Dos crimes contra a assistência familiar," 294.

49. Lima, *Perfil da mulher*, 116.

50. Nogueira, "Dia do lar," 57–59.

51. Negreiros, "A acção da mulher no lar," 171; Isa Eira, "A mãe como educadora"; Lima, *Perfil da mulher*, 89, 112.

52. Lima, *Perfil da mulher*, 110, 113; Magalhães, *A mulher*, 51–52.

53. Lima, *Perfil da mulher*, 106, 117; Vasconcellos, *Educação sexual da mulher*, 5; Magalhães, *A mulher*, 49, 51.

54. Lima, *Perfil da mulher*, 106.

55. Ibid., 118; Negreiros, "A acção da mulher no lar," 171; Isa Eira, "A mãe como educadora."

56. Magalhães, *A mulher*, 49.

57. Lima, *Perfil da mulher*, 109.

58. Ibid., 106.

59. León, "A educação da mulher—A esposa—A mãe"; "A educação da mulher: Esposa e mãe."

60. Lima, *Perfil da mulher*, 117–18.

61. Ibid., 111.

62. Lemos, "O voto feminino," 249; Nogueira, "Dia do lar," 60; "Paginas educativas," *RF* 11:126 (November 1924).

63. "O lar feliz," *RF* 6:67 (December 1919).

64. "A educação da mulher: Esposa e mãe."

65. Parédrinho, "Creimos uma escola onde a mulher apprenda a ser mulher."

66. Ibid.

67. "A educação da mulher: Esposa e mãe."

68. "Leituras," *RF* 4:34 (March 1917).

69. "A educação da mulher: Esposa e mãe."

70. Negreiros, "A acção da mulher no lar," 171–72.

71. "O lar feliz." See also "Entretenimento para moças," *RF* 8:91 (December 1921); B. Ayres, "Opiniões femininas sobre diversos themas: O matrimonio," *RF* 10:107 (April 1923).

72. "O lar feliz."

73. León, "A educação da mulher—A esposa—A mãe"; "A educação da mulher: Esposa e mãe"; Negreiros, "A acção da mulher no lar," 173.

74. "Maternidade," *RF* 10:110 (July 1923).

75. Machado, *O physico feminino na adolescencia*, 58.

76. Negreiros, "A acção da mulher no lar," 171.

77. Mortara, "Natalidade e fecundidade," 251; Leme, "Dos crimes contra a assistência familiar," 299; Negreiros, "A acção da mulher no lar," 171–72; Gouveia, "O medico e a mulher"; KYTTA, "Iniciação da maternidade," *Renascença* 1:3 (April 1923); Vasconcellos, *Educação sexual da mulher*, 50; Albuquerque, *Moral sexual*, 115; Lima, *Conduta sexual*, 191–93; Oliveira, *Hontem e hoje*, 90–93.

78. Moura, "Eva"; Albuquerque, *Moral sexual*, 115, 118; Lima, *Conduta sexual*, 194–96.

79. Moncorvo Filho, *Histórico da protecção á infancia*, 282; Fernando Magalhães, "A questão do aborto criminoso," *A Folha Medica* 1:7 (16 May 1920).

80. Lacroix, *Solução do problema sexual*, 165–66.

81. Vasconcellos, *Educação sexual da mulher*, 50–51; Machado, *Um ensaio de moral sexual*, 115–18; Albuquerque, *Moral sexual*, 114–15, 148.

82. Lima, *Perfil da mulher*, 92; Albuquerque, *Moral sexual*, 114–15.

83. I thank Emilia Viotti da Costa for bringing this expression to my attention.

84. Moura, *Amai*, 137, 139, 164–65; Moura, *A mulher é uma degenerada?*, 27, 29, 62–63.

85. Moura, *Amai*, 187; Moura, *Religião do amor*, 44–49, 104–7.

86. Moura, *Amai*, 183–85; Moura, *A mulher é uma degenerada?*, 28.

87. Moura, *A mulher é uma degenerada?*, 103.

88. Moura, *Amai*, 187, 236.

Chapter Five

1. Nagle, *Educação e sociedade*, 97–124. Nagle quotes extensively the leading Brazilian educators of the 1920s to demonstrate that they regarded education (broadly conceived) as the primary and essential instrument for resolving all national problems and for achieving "progress." See, for example, Doria, *Educação*, 11. In his words: "Education presents itself as the problem par excellence of civilized peoples: without it, men are no more than ravenous wolves. It is the dilemma of the world: education or misery, education or savagery, education or ruin. No father or country can escape it: either obtain education as a supreme duty or expect irremediable calamities."

2. This attitude was reflected in many of the chronicles of the period as well as in individual biographies. See Oliveira, *Passadismo e modernismo*, 86–88; Oliveira, *Hontem e hoje*, 39, 63–65; and Bosi, *Memória e sociedade*, 208–10, 238–39, 249.

3. The cost-of-living index rose from a base of 100 in 1914 to 267.4 in 1927 before it leveled off and declined. See Simonsen, *A evolução industrial*, 40.

4. Kehl, *Como escolher uma boa esposa*, 90.

5. The views of many of these women, as expressed in Brazil's feminist press of the late nineteenth century, are summarized in Hahner, *Emancipating the Female Sex*, 54–56. See also her earlier publication "Feminism, Women's Rights, and the Suffrage Movement," 77–84.

6. Mendes, *A preeminência social e moral da mulher*. The quotes are from p. 144.

7. Menses, *Estudos de sociologia*, 60, 78–81, 87.

8. Castro, *A mulher e a sociogenia*. The quote is from p. 320. For a more detailed discussion of late-nineteenth-century currents of thought regarding female education, see Saffioti, *A mulher na sociedade de classes*, 217–26; Hahner, *Emancipating the Female Sex*, 48–53.

9. Saffioti, *A mulher na sociedade de classes*, 204–8.

10. Hahner, "Women and Work," 94–95.

11. Saffioti, *A mulher na sociedade de classes*, 210, 214.

12. The Catholic Church dominated the teaching profession from the colonial period in Brazil, a domination that lasted well beyond the establishment of the principle of free, public, secular education by the 1891 Constitution. In addition, a few Protestant schools opened

during the late nineteenth century that were from the beginning coeducational and more innovative in their pedagogical techniques. The most notable was the American School (later renamed Mackenzie College), which opened in São Paulo in 1871, adding on a course of secondary studies in 1886 and a School of Commerce in 1902. See Saffioti, *A mulher na sociedade de classes*, 226–29; Azevedo, *Brazilian Culture*, 398–99, 420.

13. Saffioti, *A mulher na sociedade de classes*, 211, 213–16. Studies of nineteenth-century education include three works by Moacyr: *A instrução e o império*; *A instrução e as províncias*; *A instrução pública no Estado de São Paulo*. See also Rodrigues, *A instrução feminina em São Paulo*.

14. Ferreira, *A educação da mulher*, 44, 51. Similar attitudes were expressed by many prominent men and women who made statements in commemoration of the opening of classes for women at the School of Manual Arts and Trades. See Bellegarde, Ferreira, and Silva Junior, *Polyantheia commemorativa*.

15. Saffioti, *A mulher na sociedade de classes*, 205.

16. Faria, *Opusculo humanitario*, 119–20. This type of education continued to be the norm throughout the nineteenth century. See the letters of Ina von Binzer, a German schoolteacher who traveled to Brazil to work in 1881 and recorded her impressions of Brazilian customs and female education in a series of letters written to a friend. She not only worked as a tutor for children of wealthy families in Rio de Janeiro and São Paulo, but she also held a job in a private secondary school in Rio de Janeiro. Binzer, *Alegrias e tristezas*. See also Americano, *São Paulo naquele tempo*, 71–73, 439.

17. Azevedo, *Brazilian Culture*, 429.

18. Hahner, "Women and Work," 94–95.

19. In 1923, educational reformer Antonio Carneiro Leão criticized the "lamentable poverty" of female education in Brazil, characterizing it as superficial and useless (in the case of rich girls), "ultrarudimentary" (in the case of poor girls), and in all cases even more scarce and deficient than male education. Leão, *Os deveres das novas gerações*, 86–87.

20. Pereira, *A mulher no Brasil*, 240.

21. Peixoto, "A educação nacional." Peixoto later modified his position somewhat. In his *Eunice*, 205–31, 285 (first published in 1936), he reiterated his characterization of the differences between men and women but concluded that these were not sufficient to warrant providing a different education for boys and girls. The appropriateness of providing girls and boys with the same education remained a disputed issue. In 1942, Maria Kiehl, researcher for the Ministry of Labor, agreed with Peixoto's general characterization of female abilities and argued that female education *should* take into account these "natural" tendencies. Kiehl, "O trabalho da mulher fora do lar," 116–19.

22. Peixoto, "A educação nacional"; Peixoto, *Eunice*, 308–11, 314–16.

23. *A reconstrucção educational no Brasil*, 114; "Programma da Secção da Instrucção da Conferencia pelo Progresso Feminino," Arquivo da FBPF, vol. 23 (1922). While supporting coeducation at all levels, the FBPF also advocated better training of women of all social classes in domestic economy, hygiene, and child rearing.

24. Kiehl, "O trabalho da mulher fora do lar," 118–19. See also Branca de Canto e Mello, "Da instrucção da mulher," Arquivo da FBPF, vol. 23 (1922).

25. Clotilde de Mattos, "As nossas leitoras," *RF* 5:46 (March 1918); Angelo Menses d'Almeida, "A educação da mulher," *A Vida Moderna* 15:351 (28 January 1919).

26. See, for example, Aprígio Gonzaga, "A mulher na sociedade," *RF* 8:90 (November 1921); Lourdes Lambert, "Factos actuaes," *RF* 6:64 (September 1919); Francisco Falcão,

"A educação da mulher e das creanças," *Revista do Brasil*, anno 6, 17:68 (August 1921); Machado, *O progresso feminino*, 69–71; Pereira, *A mulher no Brasil*, 236–43, 255.

27. Mello, "Da instrucção da mulher"; Aprígio Gonzaga, "O papel da mulher," *RF* 8:89 (October 1921).

28. "Leituras," *RF* 4:34 (March 1917).

29. Advertisements for these collections were included in almost every issue of the magazine after May 1923. See, for example, "A influencia do livro na formação do caracter e na educação espiritual da raça," *RF* 10:108 (May 1923), and "A nossa contribuição em pról da cultura patria," *RF* 11:125 (October 1924). See *Revista do Brasil*, anno 5, 5:14 (May–August 1920): 76, for its positive review of the *Revista Feminina*'s collection of stories for children. And see "Romances para moças," *A Cigarra* 15:318 (1 February 1928), for its praise for two publishing companies—Livraria Castilho in Rio de Janeiro and Companhia Editôra Nacional in São Paulo—that "took upon themselves the highly noble task of editing romantic novels aimed principally at young women."

30. Lourenço Filho, "Um inquerito sobre o que os moços leem," 34–39. The books most frequently read by the young women surveyed were romantic novels written by Alencar, M. Delly, and Macedo. Girls from wealthy families, in addition to reading romantic novels, also had access to European classics and were sometimes encouraged to read voraciously. See Lyra, *Rosas de neve*, 108–9. Zélia Gattai, the daughter of "liberal" Italian immigrants, recounted that her mother loved to get together with her neighbors and have the older girls read serialized romantic novels out loud. Zélia too read the most popular romantic novels of the day (in editions borrowed from friends), along with classics by Zola and Victor Hugo and Dante's *Divine Comedy* (from her father's library). See Gattai, *Anarquistas*, 109, 263–65.

31. "Colégio Nossa Senhora de Sion," *RF* 8:81 (February 1921).

32. Borges, "Seminario de meninas orphãos e educandas."

33. For the view of a moderate, see Machado, *O progresso feminino*, 70–74. Machado, who worked as a schoolteacher at Mackenzie College in São Paulo and the normal school in Rio de Janeiro, considered herself a feminist and a Christian. Martins, *Estudos sobre os problemas sociaes*, 36. Azevedo, *Brazilian Culture*, 452–53. By Decree-Law 19.890, the Vargas government bowed to Church demands and effectively undermined the lay character of public education, as mandated by the 1891 Constitution. The experience of schoolteacher "Brites" (who was known for her anticlerical views) is interesting. In 1936, the school that she ran was placed on the "Index" by the Church, after which so many parents withdrew their children that she was forced to close the school. She also recounted that as a public school teacher, she never touched on the subject of religion. But she had to be very careful not to give the impression that she was standing in the way of the religious education of her students (which, she implied, was virtually mandatory in practice). See Bosi, *Memória e sociedade*, 263–64.

34. Oliveira, *Gente de agora*, 111.

35. Moura, *A mulher é uma degenerada?*, 205–44.

36. Gattai, *Anarquistas*, 267–69.

37. "A escola profissional feminina de São Paulo," *RF* 6:66 (November 1919). Schoolteacher and feminist activist Branca de Canto e Mello approved of the school's emphasis on exploiting the capacity of women in applied arts, since, according to her, men were by nature artists, whereas women were executors and craftspeople. See Mello, "Da instrucção da mulher."

38. "A escola profissional feminina de São Paulo." Even in coeducational primary schools,

the manual instruction given to girls and boys differed, with girls trained in needlework, dressmaking, and flower confection. See São Paulo, Secretaria dos Negócios da Educação e Saúde Publica, *Boletim da Diretoria do Ensino* 17 (1938): 23–24, and 18 (1938): 31–32.

39. I thank Barbara Weinstein for this information. Afrânio Peixoto lavished praise on another vocational school for poor girls, São Paulo's Escola Rivadavia Corrêa, a "beehive of useful and productive activity," where girls learned skills that would allow them to earn an honest living, "while not ignoring domestic skills . . . indispensable to the home." Peixoto, "A educação nacional." See also Nagle, *Educação e sociedade*, 228.

40. Schulz, "Trabalho de menores," 121–22.

41. Azevedo, *Novos caminhos e novos fins*, 167–68.

42. "Decreto-Lei N. 2.072—De 8 de Março de 1940," *BMTIC* 6:68 (April 1940): 60–61.

43. "A educação physica da mulher," *RF* 5:51 (August 1918); Azevedo, *Da educação physica*, 89, 101–2; Kehl, *Formulario da belleza*, 20. See also Peixoto, *Eunice*, 256–57. The First Brazilian Congress on Physical Education was held in December 1925. See Azevedo, *A evolução do esporte*, 95.

44. Rangel Sobrinho, *Educação physica feminina*, 25–26, 35, 167.

45. Rangel Sobrinho, *Educação physica feminina*, 82, 154; Lima, *Conduta sexual*, 136; Silva, "Esporte e sistema nervoso," 2–4.

46. Azevedo, *Da educação physica*, 3, 105. See also Rangel Sobrinho, *Educação physica feminina*, 17, and Vasconcellos, *Educação sexual da mulher*, 24–25.

47. Lima, *Conduta sexual*, 135, 137; Machado, *O physico feminino na adolescencia*, 49; "Educação sexual" (editorial), *A Folha Medica* 3:24 (15 December 1922): 279.

48. Lote Kretzchmar, "Cultura physica feminina," *Educação* (April–May 1932): 198. Kretzchmar argued that physical exercise was more important for women than for men because "in [a woman] the least defect represents an obstacle to her aspirations; she needs to do everything possible to obtain perfection." For similar views, see Kehl, *Formulario da belleza*, 18–20; Azevedo, *Da educação physica*, 92–93; and Vasconcellos, *Educação sexual da mulher*, 25.

49. "A mulher e a gymnastica," *RF* 6:67 (December 1919); "A cultura physica e a mulher," *Educação* (July–September 1929): 140–41; Kehl, *Formulario da belleza*, 18. Exhortations to women to practice sports abounded. See, for example, "A educação physica da mulher," *RF* 5:51 (August 1918); "A educação physica e seu papel na evolução da mulher normal: A mulher normal—Necessidades e vantagens de gymnastica racional no determinismo de sua perfeição esthetica," *RF* 10:108 (May 1923); "A educação physica da mulher," *RF* 10:111 (August 1923); Dr. Heitor Praguer Fróes, "A educação physica feminina e seu papel na evolução da mulher normal," *RF* 10:111 (August 1923).

50. The quote is from "A cultura physica e a mulher," 140. This article went on to say that in order to achieve "sure results," women should make up weekly lists, marking down their daily "gymnastic obligations" so as to "avoid confusion."

51. "Sports," *RF* 10:106 (March 1923); "A mulher e o esporte," *RF* 12:134 (July 1925); Azevedo, *Da educação physica*, 96.

52. "A belleza feminina e a cultura physica," *RF* 5:47 (April 1918).

53. Rangel Sobrinho, *Educação physica feminina*, 87, 109, 143–45, 152–53. In addition to his aesthetic concerns, Rangel Sobrinho insisted that since women's mission was "to procreate and not to fight," they should avoid sports that could result in blows "dangerous to the uterus." Vasconcellos, *Educação sexual da mulher*, 26, 29–30; Azevedo, *Da educação physica*,

96–98; Lima, *Conduta sexual*, 136; "Le tennis," *RF* 8:91 (December 1921); "Um grave problema," *RF* 8:87 (August 1921); "Sports," *RF* 10:106 (March 1923); "Os jogos olympicos femininos," *RF* 10:107 (April 1923); "A esgrima feminina," *RF* 10:109 (June 1923); "A mulher e os esportes: Conselhos e indicações," *RF* 10:110 (July 1923); "A educação physica da mulher," *RF* 10:111 (August 1923); "A mulher e os esportes," *RF* 10:118 (March 1924); "A mulher e o esporte," *RF* 12:134 (July 1925). Even the anarchist educator and radical feminist Maria Lacerda de Moura agreed that physical exercise should "develop women's physical energy without destroying the natural grace of their sex," and she therefore warned against excessive or violent exercise. See her *Lições de pedagogia*, 95–105.

54. Vasconcellos, *Educação sexual da mulher*, 8–12. Two decades later, Afrânio Peixoto reiterated these points. See his *Eunice*, 259–72.

55. *O problema sexual*, 23–24; Lima, *Pequenos males*, 163; Lima, *Conduta sexual*; Luiz Medeiros, "A educação sexual em face do problema venereo," *A Folha Medica* 3:7 (15 April 1922): 73–76, and 3:8 (30 April 1922): 85–86; "Educação sexual" (editorial), *A Folha Medica* 3:24 (15 December 1922): 278–79; Antonio E. Gouveia, "O medico e a mulher: Dois grandes factores do progresso da patria," *RF* 10:107 (April 1923); Heitor Praguer Fróes, "Bases racionaes da felicidade conjugal," *RF* 11:118 (March 1924); Machado, *Um ensaio de moral sexual*; Machado, *O physico feminino na adolescencia*; Albuquerque, *Moral sexual*, 22–24; Dra. Alzira Reis, "A educação sexual como media de protecção à infancia," and Dra. Francisca Praguer Fróes, "Hygiene e maternidade," in Arquivo da FBPF, folder "Segundo Congresso Internacional Feminista do Rio de Janeiro, Junho 1931"; Lyra, "Educação sexual e criminalidade," 43–44; Alvaro Eston, "Preambulo," in Ellis, *A educação sexual*, vi–x; Peixoto, *Sexologia forense*, 17; Peixoto, *Eunice*, 262–68; Silva, *Serviços sociais*, 51–52.

56. Kehl, *A cura da fealdade*, 215–17.

57. Padilha, "Educação sexual," 30–35. The 1931 convention organized by the FBPF also resolved that schools should provide sexual education to students beginning at the age of eleven. See Reis, "A educação sexual como media de protecção à infancia."

58. "Educação sexual e divorcio," 63–85. Those responding to the inquiry were Franco da Rocha, Durval Marcondes, Custodio de Carvalho, Osorio Cesar, Flaminio Favero, Antonio Carlos Pacheco e Silva, João Arruda, Edgard Braga, and Fausto Guerner.

59. Albuquerque, "Prefacio," in Velde, *O matrimonio perfeito*, xxxiii.

60. Lacroix, *Solução do problema sexual*, 219–23, 189–206. The book is dedicated to "Exo. e Revmo. Sr. Cardeal Arcebispo D. Sebastião Leme" and endorsed in the preface by Father João Baptista de Siqueira (doctor of law, philosophy, and theology, ecclesiastical censor, and canon of the Cabildo Metropolitano do Rio de Janeiro).

61. Ibid., 221.

62. Ibid., 196.

63. A notable exception was Maria Lacerda de Moura, an advocate of free love, who insisted that sexual education should be an antidote to the hypocrisy of conventional morality. Moura, *Religião do amor*, 173–76.

64. Doria, *Instrucção pelo estado*, 64.

Chapter Six

1. See Bertha Lutz, "Cartas de mulher," *Revista da Semana*, 28 December 1918; "O feminismo no Brasil," *RF* 5:53 (October 1918); Odette Donah, "Mulheres parasitas e o direito

de voto," *RF* 8:80 (January 1921); J. M. Gomes Ribeiro, "Ainda o voto feminino," *RF* 9:95 (April 1922); Lima, *Perfil da mulher*, 113; Leão, *Os deveres das novas gerações*, "Prefacio"; Celso, *De relance*, 28; Maria Eugenia Celso's and Goulart de Andrade's responses to a questionnaire in "As enquêtes d'*A Vida Moderna*," *A Vida Moderna* 24:529 (17 March 1928) and 24:531 (June 1928); and Moura, *Religião do amor*, 112. See also the references in the following three notes.

2. Clara Camara, "O lar futuro: O que devem fazer as nossas filhas," *RF* 6:58 (March 1919).

3. Vianna, "A evolução do trabalho da mulher," 104; B. F., "A evolução feminina," *RF* 6:64 (September 1919).

4. Branca de Canto e Mello, "Da instrucção da mulher," Arquivo da FBPF, vol. 23 (1922).

5. "Uma situação invejável," *A Classe Operário* 12 (18 July 1925): 1, as quoted in Pinheiro and Hall, *A classe operário*, 2:130–31.

6. Doliveira, *O trabalhador brasileiro*, 115–16.

7. See, for example, Castro, *Os delictos contra a honra da mulher*, 22–23; Machado, *Um ensaio de moral sexual*, 107–8; Castro, *A questão social*, 190, 202, 205; Salgado, *A mulher no século vinte*, 76–78.

8. Castro, *A questão social*, 189.

9. See, for example, ibid., 202, 205–6, 223; Rão, *Direitos da mulher casada*, 3–5.

10. Beginning in the 1930s, the miserable conditions of the urban poor began to be described in exhaustive detail by social workers commissioned by government agencies to conduct studies. Two of these studies are "Padrão de vida" and Vieira, "Monografia de uma familia."

11. Machado, *O progresso feminino*, 51; Pereira, *A mulher no Brasil*, 88–89; Edwiges de Sá Perreira, "Trabalho feminino," in Brito, *Antologia feminina*, 56; Peixoto, *Eunice*, 242–43; Castro, *A questão social*, 223.

12. "O feminismo no Brasil," *RF* 5:53 (October 1918); "Mais uma victoria do feminismo brasileiro," *RF* 9:96 (May 1922); "A mulher brasileira triumphante," *RF* 8:88 (September 1921).

13. Ribeiro, "Ainda o voto feminino."

14. Ibid.; Peixoto, "A educação nacional." A more unusual argument was that of Dr. Heitor Praguer Fróes, who applauded married women's pursuit of a profession on the grounds that it would allow couples to establish economic independence quickly. See Heitor Praguer Fróes, "A defficiencia de cultura intellectual: Principal factor da subordinação da mulher na sociedade," *RF* 10:105 (February 1923).

15. J. P. Fontenelle, "Visitadoras de hygiene," *A Folha Medica* 2:10 (16 May 1921): 93–94. Federal deputy Dr. Carlota Pereira de Queiroz argued for the growth of the social work profession on similar grounds: female social workers were needed to assist doctors and nurses in solving the problems of "deficient" (poor or morally corrupt) families and their children. Queiroz, "Assistencia social à infancia."

16. Doliveira, *O trabalhador brasileiro*, 116.

17. Reis, "Trabalho da mulher nas ferrovias."

18. Ibid., 8:90 (February 1942): 92.

19. "A fraca dona de casa," *RF* 5:45 (February 1918); Laura Vaz, "O trabalho," *RF* 8:80 (January 1921); Marilda Palinia, "O ideal feminino," *RF* 8:88 (September 1921); Nataly, "Historia de Honorina," *RF* 9:101 (October 1922); Mello, "Da instrucção da mulher"; Edwiges de Sá Perreira, "Trabalho feminino," 56; Goulart de Andrade's response to the ques-

tionnaire in "As enquêtes d'*A Vida Moderna*," *A Vida Moderna* 24:529 (17 March 1928); Kiehl, "O trabalho da mulher fora do lar," 85.

20. José de Castro Lagreca, "Mulheres lindas," *A Cigarra* 13:264 (1−15 November 1925).

21. Doliveira, *O trabalhador brasileiro*, 112−13.

22. Ibid., 123−36.

23. See, for example, Ribeiro, "Ainda o voto feminino"; Coelho, *Evolução do feminismo*, 20−23, 147, 157, 162−63, 242.

24. Anna Rita Malheiros, "Junho," *RF* 6:61 (June 1919).

25. "O feminismo no Brasil: Uma candidata a intendente municipal," *RF* 6:65 (October 1919).

26. Aprígio Gonzaga, "O papel da mulher," *RF* 8:89 (October 1921). This statement was quoted and endorsed by Mello, "Da instrucção da mulher."

27. Anna Rita Malheiros, "Outubro," *RF* 5:53 (October 1918). See also Anna Rita Malheiros, "Novembro," *RF* 5:54 (November 1918); "O feminismo em marcha: A *Revista Feminina* e o movimento feminista brasileiro," *RF* 6:62 (July 1919).

28. Vianna, "A evolução do trabalho da mulher," 103−5.

29. [Alice de Toledo Tibiriçá?], "O valor da educação profissional na evolução do Brasil," Arquivo da FBPF, folder no. 1, "Segundo Congresso Feminista de Rio de Janeiro, 1931."

30. See, for example, Vianna, "A evolução do trabalho da mulher," 104; Reis, "Trabalho da mulher nas ferrovias," 8:89 (January 1942): 74, and 8:90 (February 1942): 91; Americo Campos, "As damas da Cruz Vermelha," *A Folha Medica* 2:23 (16 December 1921): 238; Machado, *O progresso feminino*, 54−58; Lagreca, "Mulheres lindas."

31. Kiehl, "O trabalho da mulher fora do lar," 119−25. See also Cecília Meireles, "Trabalho feminino no Brasil," *O Observador Economico e Financeiro* 4:42 (July 1939): 100. Meireles lavished praise on Brazil's female wage workers, emphasizing the "extraordinary results" of women who worked in fields that required close attention to detail and nurturing care of others.

32. J. P. Porto-Carrero, "Annotações," in Marestan, *A educação sexual*, 361.

33. Arthur Osorio da Cunha Cabrera, "As actividades femininas no commércio," *Boletim da Associação dos Empregados no Commércio* 2:15 (September 1926): 167. For a lengthier discussion of the generally negative attitudes of the male-led labor movement toward female employment, as well as their efforts to reduce competition by keeping women's work complementary to men's work, see Pena, *Mulheres e trabalhadoras*, chap. 5.

34. Vianna, "A evolução do trabalho da mulher," 105.

35. "O feminismo no Brasil," *RF* 5:53 (October 1918); "Mais uma victoria do feminismo brasileiro."

36. Cristovão Camargo, "Uma confidencia triste," reprinted in the appendix of Magalhães, *A mulher.*

37. See, for example, Dr. MacDowell, "A mulher no pleno divino," *RF* 7:75 (August 1920); Orlando Machado, "A reivindicação feminina em New York," *Revista do Brasil*, anno 8, 23:89 (May 1923): 36−37; João A. Corrêa de Araujo, "O verdadeiro feminismo," *RF* 4:43 (December 1917); Coulet, *O problema da familia*, 9−12, 117−45.

38. Lemos, "O voto feminino," 249.

39. Pereira, *A mulher no Brasil*, 123−27.

40. See Oleno da Cunha Vieira's response to the questionnaire in "As enquêtes d'*A Vida Moderna*," *A Vida Moderna* 24:531 (June 1928).

41. See, for example, Doliveira, *O trabalhador brasileiro*, 115−16; Pereira, *A mulher no*

Brasil, 97–98; Lima, *Perfil da mulher*, 66–68; Albina A. Pires de Campos, "O despertar na ambulancia," *RF* 5 : 55 (December 1918).

42. Rão, *Direitos da mulher casada*, 9–11; Brazil, *Código Civil*, 2 : 113, 131, 141 (Articles 233 : 4, 242 : 7, 246). This provision remained in effect until 1943, after which women no longer needed permission from their husbands to work, but a woman could still at any time be prevented from continuing to work if, in the judgment of her husband, it was prejudicial to the interests of the family or to the woman herself.

43. Xavier Carvalho de Mendonça, as quoted in "Mulher comerciante? Isto dava até desquite," *Jornal da Tarde* (São Paulo), 2 July 1975.

44. A transcription of Decree-Law 21.417-A may be found in *BMTIC* 2 : 21 (May 1936): 37–42.

45. Vianna, "A evolução do trabalho da mulher," 107, 110. See also Tappen, *Status of Women in Brazil*, 2, 9.

46. Lopes, "O trabalho feminino no Brasil," 99, 110. Even today in Brazil, the gap between the law and practice continues to be wide; it is not uncommon for pregnant women to be fired or demoted by employers seeking to avoid the costs of maternity leaves.

47. The discussion of women's labor force participation that follows is largely based on the Brazilian national censuses of 1872, 1920, and 1940. I have not used the 1890 or the 1900 censuses because their statistics on occupations are highly unreliable. No national census was carried out in 1910. Despite the numerous problems with these censuses—the lack of standardization, errors, and significant undercounting of women in the labor force, especially those who worked part-time, irregularly, and in family businesses (including agriculture)—they are nevertheless the only comprehensive source available for studying the occupational structure in Brazil. Unfortunately, they do not permit analysis of short-term effects of such events as World War I or the depression on patterns of female employment. For a more detailed evaluation of Brazilian censuses and female workforce participation from 1920 to 1970, see Madeira and Singer, *Estrutura do emprego e trabalho feminino*. For a discussion of female employment from the mid-nineteenth century to the early twentieth century, see Hahner, "Women and Work."

48. Studies of female industrial workers include Blay, *Trabalho domesticado*; Rodrigues, *A mulher operária*; Moura, *Mulheres e menores no trabalho industrial*; and Pena, *Mulheres e trabalhodoras*. More general studies on the history of Brazilian industrialization are Stein, *Brazilian Cotton Manufacture*; Dean, *Industrialization of São Paulo*; Luz, *A luta pela industrialização*.

49. Moura, "Além da indústria têxtil," 86–96.

50. Brazil, Diretoria Geral de Estatística, *Recenseamento . . . 1920*, vol. 4, pt. 5, tomo 1, pp. 27, 173.

51. [Alice de Toledo Tibiriçá?], "O valor da educação profissional na evolução do Brasil." See also Meireles, "Trabalho feminino no Brasil," 99. Meireles explained that although schoolteaching paid very little, it had numerous advantages for women, including the nature of the work: "so much in harmony with women's vocation."

52. The growth and professionalization of nursing (which had previously been considered a very low status, menial occupation) was marked by the establishment of the Associação Nacional de Enfermeiras Diplomadas Brasileiras (Brazilian Association of Registered Nurses). See Lutz, *O trabalho feminino*, 113–17. One of the leading advocates of the nursing profession was Rachel Haddock Lobo. The daughter of a well-to-do family whose sons both became doctors, she traveled to France, where she finished her nursing degree in 1924. She

later received more training in the United States before assuming the directorship of the Anna Nery Nursing School. See "Morreu Rachel Haddock Lobo: Symbolo perfeito das virtudes da mulher brasileira," *Boletim da Sociedade de Assistência aos Lázaros e Defesa Contra a Lepra* 5:55 (October 1933): 25.

53. The quote is from Queiroz, "Assistencia social à infancia," 272. For a history of the social work profession in Brazil, see Iamamoto and Carvalho, *Relações sociais e serviço social.*

54. Vidal, *Precursoras brasileiras*, 237.

55. Leite, *Subsídios para a história*, 261. Saraiva herself discontinued practicing law after a short time. See Bittencourt, *A mulher paulista*, 69.

56. Brazil, Diretoria Geral de Estatística, *Recenseamento . . . 1920*, vol. 4, pt. 5, tomo 1, pp. 27, 173.

57. According to the 1940 census, the total number of women in Brazil who held degrees in medicine was 543, compared with the 1,225 women who held degrees in dentistry and the 1,841 women who held degrees in pharmacology. Not all of these degree holders, of course, practiced their profession. Brazil, Comissão Censitária Nacional, *Recenseamento geral do Brasil . . . 1940*, série nacional, tomo 2, pp. 32–33.

58. "O feminismo no Brasil," *RF* 5:53 (October 1918).

59. Adilia de Albuquerque Morais, "Bertha Lutz," *Boletim da FBPF* 1:2 (November 1934): 1.

60. Tappen, *Status of Women in Brazil*, 1, 3.

61. Cannon, *Women in Brazil Today*, 7–8; Hahner, *Emancipating the Female Sex*, 177–78.

62. Mariana Coelho, in her book *Evolução do feminismo*, 499–517, devoted fifteen pages to listing women in the arts and letters and little more than three pages to mentioning prominent female professionals in other fields. Antonio Austregésilo Lima also found prominent women writers, poets, and artists to be far more numerous and far more worthy of lengthy praise than other professional women (with the single notable exception of Bertha Lutz). See Lima, *Perfil da mulher*, 37–48. See also Bittencourt, *Dicionário bio-bibliográfico de mulheres.*

63. Lima, *Perfil da mulher*, 37–42, 44–45; "A mulher na arte," *RF* 11:117 (February 1924).

64. Bittencourt, *Dicionário bio-biográfico de mulheres*, 2:318. This was an interesting reversal of tradition, whereby women had commonly adopted male pseudonyms to get published and to be taken seriously.

65. "A mulher brasileira triumphante," *RF* 8:88 (September 1921). Women were not, however, admitted to the academy as members until years later. See Coelho, *Evolução do feminismo*, 518–20.

66. For an account of her life and her work, see Amaral, *Tarsila.*

67. Brazil, Diretoria Geral de Estatística, *Recenseamento . . . 1920*, vol. 5, pt. 2, p. xiv.

68. Ibid., xvi–xvii.

69. For a personal account of the appalling conditions in such shops, see Bosi, *Memória e sociedade*, 57–60 and passim.

70. Domestic workers—nearly all of whom were women—did not even enjoy the right to earn the legally established minimum salary. Rebouças, "O problema do salário minimo," 89–90.

71. On the meager wages paid to these women see Doliveira, *O trabalhador brasileiro*, 118, 124, 130, 135, 137–39.

72. Ibid., 138–39.

73. Ibid., 118.

74. For personal comments on the difficulty of surviving economically as a schoolteacher, see Bosi, *Memória e sociedade*, 223, 257, 263, 283–84, 290. The very low salaries of female white-collar workers and schoolteachers is also discussed in Tappen, *Status of Women in Brazil*, 10.

75. See Article 1 of Decree-Law N. 21.417-A, reprinted in *BMTIC* 2:21 (May 1936): 37, and Article 121.1.a of the 1934 Constitution, reprinted in *BMTIC* 1:1 (September 1934).

76. "Padrão de vida," 87.

77. Tappen, *Status of Women in Brazil*, 9.

78. See, for example, Cott, *Bonds of Womanhood*; Berg, *Remembered Gate*.

79. Although a few Brazilian women participated in the nineteenth-century abolitionist movement, there was (to borrow Nancy Hewitt's terminology) no strong tradition of "ultraist" (radical, feminist) female social reformism in Brazil (Hewitt, *Women's Activism and Social Change*). Maria Lacerda de Moura, for example, who entered social activism in the 1910s through participation in campaigns for literacy, educational reform, and female suffrage, quickly joined other female radicals in violently rejecting suffragism and charity as classist, bourgeois instruments of domination. Brazil's female radicals tended to work as isolated individuals within overwhelmingly male-dominated political parties and unions. Only during, and especially after, World War II did neighborhood organizations of poor women arise to fight for amnesty and for quality-of-life issues including child welfare and price controls. See Saffioti, *A mulher na sociedade de classes*, 290–96.

80. Leão, *Os deveres das novas gerações*, 83–89, 168–73.

81. Pereira, *A mulher no Brasil*, 99–102.

82. Lima, *Perfil da mulher*, 109–11. These views were echoed by many other male professionals and intellectuals. See, for example, Coelho Netto, "O feminismo brasileiro," *RF* 7:68 (January 1920); Silva, *A mulher paulista*, 13, 15; Claudio de Souza, as quoted in "Uma associação feminina de Petrópolis," *RF* 9:96 (May 1922); Andrade Bezerra, "O feminismo e a questão social," *RF* 6:66 (November 1919).

83. Maria Jacobina de Sá Rabello, "A mulher," *RF* 10:105 (February 1923).

84. Vianna, "A evolução do trabalho da mulher," 106.

85. *AESP, 1901*, 788; *AESP, 1910*, 2:258; *AESP, 1915*, 336–40, 370; *AESP, 1920*, 226–30, 280–82; *AESP, 1921*, 384–90, 444–46; *AESP, 1922 a 1926*, 242–44, 312; *AESP, 1927*, 356–60, 405. A few Brazilian women dedicated themselves to charitable work during the late nineteenth century; however, their organizations were very small and socially inconspicuous. See Hahner, "Feminism, Women's Rights, and the Suffrage Movement," 74. The rapid emergence of female charity organizations was frequently noted in the writings of the early twentieth century. See Bezerra, "O feminismo e a questão social"; Lima, *Perfil da mulher*, 46; Americano, *São Paulo naquele tempo*, 160; Americano, *São Paulo nesse tempo*, 153, 271, 318.

86. Martins, *Acção social brasileira*, 35–36.

87. For short biographical sketches of *paulista* women active in charitable organizations, see Bittencourt, *A mulher paulista*, 143–67. See also "Uma das maiores organisações cristãs em nosso paiz: A Liga das Senhoras Católicas," *RF* 10:112 (September 1923); "Fevereiro," *RF* 10:105 (February 1923); "Patriotismo feminino: A mulher portuguesa," *RF* 4:37 (June 1917); "Vida feminina: Alliança Feminina," *RF* 6:59 (April 1919); "O feminismo brasileiro em fóco," *RF* 6:66 (November 1919); "Uma conferencia de D. Palmyra Wanderly," *RF* 8:85 (June 1921); Bittencourt, *Dicionário bio-bibliográfico de mulheres*, 1:153–60; and Mello, "Trabalho de menores," 118–21. For information about the activities of female char-

ity organizations in São Paulo during the 1932 military uprising, see Rodrigues, *A mulher paulista*, and Ribeiro, "A mulher paulista em 1932," 247–62. Although a few women attempted to organize a temperance movement similar to the one in the United States, the idea had relatively little appeal in Brazil.

88. Mello, "Trabalho de menores," 120–21.

89. Bittencourt, *A mulher paulista*, 187–88.

90. Martins, *Acção social brasileira*, 9–13, 30, 107–8, 112–13. A short biographical sketch of Martins and a list of her copious publications may be found in Bittencourt, *Dicionário bio-bibliográfico de mulheres*, 2:244–48.

91. Martins, *Acção social brasileira*, 31–33.

92. Ibid., 9.

93. Ibid., 8, 18–20, 22, 26–29, 36–37, 39–40, 50–57.

94. Ibid., 38, 110–11.

95. "Uma associação feminina de Petrópolis," *RF* 9:96 (May 1922).

96. "Flôr de caridade," *A Cigarra* 15:307 (16–31 August 1927); "Flôr de caridade," *A Cigarra* 15:308 (1–15 September, 1927); "O dia da rasa," *A Cigarra* 15:310 (1–15 October 1927); "Flôr de caridade," *A Cigarra* 16:332 (1–15 September 1928). According to Jorge Americano, selling flowers for charity became a veritable social institution in downtown São Paulo. See Americano, *São Paulo nesse tempo*, 153.

97. While these benefits were dismissed by some critics as self-serving and frivolous events, others offered apologies for their ostentation. See Celso, *De relance*, 211–19; Oliveira, *Hontem e hoje*, 25–28, 34–36; Oliveira, *Gente de agora*, 86–89; "Festa de caridade," *RF* 4:32 (January 1917).

98. Mariana Coelho, "A principal emancipação feminina," *Renascença* 1:5 (July 1923).

99. Ibid.

100. Marilda Palinia, "O idéal feminino," *RF* 8:88 (September 1921).

101. Lima, *Perfil da mulher*, 42–44, 130–42; Adilia de Albuquerque Morais, "Bertha Lutz," *Boletim da FBPF* 1:2 (November 1934): 1; "O facto do mez: A representante da mulher na camara federal," *Boletim da FBPF* 2:7 (July 1936): 2.

102. Valdir Sanches, "Lola Delgado, uma pionera dos anos 20," *Jornal da Tarde* (São Paulo), 2 July 1975.

103. Amaral, *Tarsila*, 1:14, 27, 39, 41, 47, 51.

104. Cited in ibid., 1:39.

105. Moura, *A mulher é uma degenerada?*, 141.

106. Ibid., 62, 105–6.

107. Quote from ibid., 138.

108. An excellent biography of Maria Lacerda de Moura is Leite, *Outra face do feminismo*.

109. Moura, *Religião do amor*, 88.

110. Moura, *Amai*, 190.

111. Bosi, *Memória e sociedade*, 273, 283–84, 289–90.

112. Ibid., 293.

113. Quoted by Cunha, *O espelho do mundo*, 151.

114. Arquivo do Hospital do Juquerí, case 52 (1927).

115. Bosi, *Memória e sociedade*, 270.

116. See the response of Anna Amelia de Queiroz Mendonça to the questionnaire in "As enquêtes d'*A Vida Moderna*," *A Vida Moderna* 24:530 (16–30 April 1928). Mendonça, it would seem, strove to conquer her own "terrestrial happiness" outside as well as inside the

"secluded charm of her home." In addition to marrying and raising three children, she published numerous books, wrote regularly for the press, gave frequent public lectures, and was an active member of many professional, feminist, and charity organizations. See Bittencourt, *Dicionário bio-bibliográfico de mulheres*, 2:263–64.

117. Bittencourt, *Dicionário bio-bibliográfico de mulheres*, 3:434–35.

118. Bosi, *Memória e sociedade*, 226, 231, 239–40, 273.

119. Paquita, "Violencia e severidade," in the column "Collaboração das leitoras," *A Cigarra* 8:165 (1–15 August 1921).

120. "O lar feliz," *RF* 6:67 (December 1919).

121. Kiehl, "O trabalho da mulher fora do lar," 93–95.

122. Bosi, *Memória e sociedade*, 300–327 and passim. For further evidence that working-class women took pride not only in the money they contributed to the family but also in the skills they acquired as factory workers, see Theresa R. Veccia, "Women, Work, and Family Life: São Paulo Textile Workers, 1900–1950" (paper delivered at the Eighth Berkshire Conference on the History of Women, Douglass College, Rutgers University, 9 June 1990), 27–28.

Chapter Seven

1. The quote is from "O nosso centenario," *RF* 9:100 (September 1922).

2. It has not become any easier with the perspective of historical distance to define this stage of Brazilian feminism. Indeed, the ambiguity of determining where feminism stopped and antifeminism (or "antifeminist feminism") began suggests that they existed on a continuum, rather than in strict opposition to each other. It is clear (to borrow Karen Offen's conceptualization) that the "individualist feminist tradition" (which emphasized equal rights and personal autonomy) had less appeal within the Brazilian cultural context than did "relational feminism," which "emphasized women's rights *as women* (defined principally by their childbearing and/or nurturing capacities) in relation to men." Offen, "Defining Feminism," 136. But the FBPF made powerful use of both equal rights arguments and arguments that emphasized women's special contributions as women. Outside the FBPF, "relational feminism" prevailed; but it would be odd to lump together Brazil's "anarchist and libertarian feminists" (as they were called) with those who labeled themselves "Catholic feminists." The latter, although they sought to improve women's disadvantaged status, did so without offering any serious critique of male dominance. This chapter, which explores the full continuum between Brazilian feminism and antifeminism of the period, seeks to demonstrate both how the specific circumstances of Brazilian society and culture influenced the practice of feminism and how feminist practice contributed to the restructuring of the gender order in Brazil.

3. See the newspaper reports describing the first annual celebration of Mother's Day: "O dia das mães," *O Estado de São Paulo*, 7 May 1932, 1, and 10 May 1932, 5.

4. Alice Pinheiro Coimbra, "Federação Brasileira pelo Progresso Feminino," speech delivered 17 October 1932, Arquivo da FBPF, folder no. 1, "Segundo Congresso Feminista do Rio de Janeiro, 1931."

5. June Hahner, in her article "Feminism, Women's Rights, and the Suffrage Movement," traces the roots of Brazilian feminism. She uncovered the history of a few nineteenth-century women who protested the subordination of women in the family, championed im-

proved female education, and demanded access to paid employment. However, because they worked in isolation from one another, they were generally ignored and dismissed. Unlike European and North American women, Brazilian women neither led nor participated in large numbers in nineteenth-century progressive reform movements. When they did participate, such as in the abolitionist movement, their participation did not serve as a basis from which to organize autonomously as women.

6. Martin, *Who's Who*, 226; Adilia de Albuquerque Morais, "Bertha Lutz," *Boletim da FBPF* 1:2 (November 1934): 1.

7. Bertha Lutz, "Cartas de mullher," *Revista da Semana*, 28 December 1918.

8. See Lutz's appeal to the Ministry of Education reprinted in "Gymnasios para senhoras," *RF* 8:87 (August 1921).

9. Bertha Lutz, "O feminismo no Brasil," *RF* 6:63 (August 1919). This article is a reprint of a speech.

10. Bertha Lutz, "A mulher brasileira e o voto," *RF* 7:78 (November 1920). This article is an interview reprinted from the newspaper *A Noite*.

11. Martin, *Who's Who*, 226.

12. See Lutz's own account of the conference in Lima, *Perfil da mulher*, 136.

13. Catt, a brilliant organizer and leading suffragist in the United States, was active in the international suffrage movement. In 1922, she was president of both the International Woman Suffrage Alliance and the newly formed Pan American Association for the Advancement of Women.

14. A brief history and description of the FBPF may be found in "Victory in Brazil: A Short Report on Fifteen Years Work," *Boletim da FBPF* 1:4 (February 1935): 2–3. It is interesting that this article was published in English, indicating the strong international links that the FBPF leadership cultivated.

15. Ibid. See also Nazario, *Voto feminino e feminismo*, 61.

16. Coelho, *Evolução do feminismo*, 248.

17. Ibid., 248–51; Nazario, *Voto feminino e feminismo*, 60; Lima, *Perfil da mulher*, 145–46.

18. See the following communications presented to the convention: "O trabalho feminino nas fabricas"; "These apresentada pela União dos Empregados do Commércio do Rio de Janeiro"; "Algumas considerações sobre o 'trabalho': Notas colhidas no Bureau de Empregados da Associação Christã Feminina"; Branca de Canto e Mello, "Da instrucção da mulher," Arquivo da FBPF, vol. 23 (1922).

19. "Protecção da mulher na industria, commércio, e agricultura, e no serviço do estado," Arquivo da FBPF, vol. 23 (1922).

20. Ibid.; Lutz, *O trabalho feminino*, 70.

21. "Programma da Secção da Instrucção da Conferencia Pelo Progresso Feminino," Arquivo da FBPF, vol. 23 (1922).

22. Coelho, *Evolução do feminismo*, 249–50; Nazario, *Voto feminino e feminismo*, 60.

23. Nazario, *Voto feminino e feminismo*, 61–66.

24. Their primary manifesto was the "Declaração dos direitos da mulher," *Educação* (May 1928): 212.

25. See, for example, their lengthy attack on Congressman Basilio Magalhães's amendment to the female suffrage bill that would have required married women to obtain permission from their husbands in order to vote. Coelho, *Evolução do feminismo*, 240–46. See also their letter of congratulations to Washington Luis upon his inauguration as president reprinted in the same work, 261–63.

26. Coelho, *Evolução do feminismo*, 238. Nazario, *Voto feminino e feminismo*, 21–28. Nazario described her attempt to register to vote, reprinted the letter she received from Judge Affonso José de Carvalho justifying the denial of her request, and attacked the judge's argument.

27. Morais, "Bertha Lutz," 1.

28. "Victory in Brazil: A Short Report on Fifteen Years Work," 2.

29. Nazario, *Voto feminino e feminismo*; Coelho, *Evolução do feminismo*.

30. Lutz, *O trabalho feminino*, 70–72, 117–20, 135; Arquivo da FBPF, folder no. 1, "Segundo Congresso Feminista do Rio de Janeiro, 1931."

31. Suffrage was, however, still restricted to literates who had reached their twenty-first birthday.

32. Lutz, *Treze principios básicos*.

33. Lutz, *O trabalho feminino*, 72.

34. "Medidas entradas na Constituição pelo esforço de Bertha Lutz," *Boletim da FBPF* 1:1 (October 1934): 8. See also the Brazilian Constitution of 1934, Articles 106, 108, 113, 121, 138, 141, 168, 170. In fact, although the FBPF campaigned for new guiding principles for labor legislation, it was Brazil's socialist parties and workers' movements that had led this campaign since the 1890s.

35. Bertha Lutz, "Idealistas e garimpeiros," *Boletim da FBPF* 2:2 (February 1936): 7.

36. Bertha Lutz, "É prohibido pagar," *Boletim da FBPF* 2:3 (March 1936): 9.

37. "Novo plano de acção," *Boletim da FBPF* 1:9–10 (August–September 1935): 46–47.

38. The resolutions of the 1934 convention held in Bahia may be found in the *Boletim da FBPF* 1:1 (October 1934): 4–7. Resolutions of the 1936 convention held in Rio de Janeiro may be found in the *Boletim da FBPF* 2:11 (November 1936): 1–4, and in 2:12 (December 1936): 1–3.

39. Lutz, "É prohibido pagar," 9.

40. The FBPF's proposal for a "Statute on Women" may be found in the *Boletim da FBPF* 2:11 (November 1936): 3–4, and 2:12 (December 1936): 1–3.

41. *Boletim da FBPF* 2:11 (November 1936): 4. See item I:4 of the "Estatuto Económico." This demand was also made in a radio broadcast aired in Rio de Janeiro. For a transcript of the broadcast, see "Trabalho feminino," *Boletim da FBPF* 2:5 (May 1935): 4.

42. "O trabalho nocturno das mulheres," *Boletim da FBPF* 1:3 (December 1934): 2–3. Although this point was not made directly in the proposal for the Statute on Women, item I:5 of the "Estatuto Económico" specified that adult female labor should be subject to different regulations than was child labor.

43. *Boletim da FBPF* 2:11 (November 1936): 3. See item C, no. 5.

44. Lutz, "É prohibido pagar," 9.

45. *Boletim da FBPF* 2:11 (November 1936): 4. See items IV:21–23 of the "Estatuto Económico."

46. The proposed reforms in the Civil and Penal Codes may be found in the *Boletim da FBPF* 1:1 (October 1934): 4–5, and 2:12 (December 1936): 2–3.

47. *Boletim da FBPF* 1:1 (October 1934): 5.

48. Ibid., 6–7.

49. Lutz, *O trabalho feminino*, 103–4.

50. Ibid., 95.

51. Ibid., 111.

52. Ibid., 111–13, 120–25.

53. Article 103 of the 1934 Constitution specified that every ministry of the government should be assisted by "technical councils" of experts that would give advice in the elaboration of public policies. Although ministers were not bound by the advice given, they were prohibited from acting against the unanimous opinion of a council. The FBPF proposal may be found in Lutz, *O trabalho feminino*, 101–3. See also the resolutions of the FBPF's 1934 and 1936 conventions concerning women's participation in technical councils in *Boletim da FBPF* 1:1 (October 1934): 7, item III:II:8, and 2:11 (November 1936): 2, items I:3:c–e.

54. *Boletim da FBPF* 2:11 (November 1934): 4. See items III:12–13 of the "Estatuto Económico."

55. Lutz, *O trabalho feminino*, 87–89; Coelho, *Evolução do feminismo*, 258.

56. *Boletim da FBPF* 1:1 (October 1934): 5–6; 2:11 (November 1936): 2–3; and 1:4 (February 1935): 3. See also issue 2:1 (January 1936): 2 for the statutes of the League of Independent Women Voters.

57. *Boletim da FBPF* 2:11 (November 1936): 1–2; Lutz, *O trabalho feminino*, 151–54. Lutz modeled her proposed bureau on the U.S. Women's Bureau.

58. Lutz had been elected as an alternative in her 1934 campaign for a congressional seat, and she entered two years later when the death of a congressman created a vacancy.

59. Cannon, *Women in Brazil Today*, 8; Hahner, *Emancipating the Female Sex*, 177–78.

60. Hahner, *Emancipating the Female Sex*, 164–68.

61. Bertha Lutz, "A palavra da mulher no legislativo brasileiro: Discurso da Deputada Bertha Lutz na sua posse na Camara dos Deputados," *Boletim da FBPF* 2:7 (July 1936): 4.

62. Lutz, "Idealistas e garimpeiros," 7.

63. Carlota Pereira de Queiroz, quoted in Saffioti, *A mulher na sociedade de classes*, 285.

64. Coelho, *Evolução do feminismo*, 40–46.

65. Ibid., 55–62, 66.

66. The attention Coelho paid to private relationships between the sexes was focused not on the family per se but on the possibilities for and conditions of love between men and women. Ibid., chap. 7.

67. Luiza Roberti Soares, "Feminismo," *A Cigarra* 18:403 (1–15 September 1931): 36.

68. Arquivo da FBPF, folder no. 1, "Segundo Congresso Feminista do Rio de Janeiro, 1931."

69. Coimbra, "Federação Brasileira pelo Progresso Feminino."

70. My interpretation of Brazilian feminism differs from the interpretation of other scholars who claim that Latin American feminists sensed no conflicts between motherhood and professionalism or feminism. (See, for example, K. Lynn Stoner's history of Cuban feminism, *From House to the Streets*, 194.) As I have shown, Brazilian feminists celebrated motherhood, exploited this role as the basis of their moral authority, and used it to justify expanded rights and freedoms for women. Nevertheless, it is surely no coincidence that throughout Latin America, feminist activists (who tended also to be professionals) remained unmarried and childless in far greater numbers than did other women of their class. This was true even though, as members of the middle and upper classes, they had servants who freed them from domestic chores. And it was true in Cuba as well as in Brazil (see Stoner, 80). For further evidence that Brazilian feminists perceived marriage and motherhood as conflicting with professionalism (and, by extension, feminist activism), see the quotes cited in Chapter 6, notes 107, 117–19. Whereas the leaders of the organized feminist movement were generally guarded in discussing the conflicts between women's domestic and professional roles, Brazil's "anarchist and libertarian feminists" (as they were called by their foes)

were far more open. See the discussions of Maria Lacerda de Moura and Patrícia Galvão that follow. One might conclude from the popularity of Maria Lacerda de Moura's books—many of which sold out numerous editions—that her vehement attacks on marriage resonated with a large group of readers who were less willing than she to express their views publicly.

71. An excellent biography of Maria Lacerda de Moura is Leite, *Outra face do feminismo*.

72. Quoted by Leite, "Quem foi Maria Lacerda de Moura?," 14.

73. Moura, *A mulher é uma degenerada?*, 12.

74. Ibid., 263.

75. Reference to Ellen Key can be found in Moura, *Religião do amor*, 128. References to all three of these writers can be found in Moura, *Han Ryner e o amor plural*, 123–24, 151–52. For the author's own arguments, see Moura, *Religião do amor*, 44–45, 83–85, 93–95, 105–7, 111–12, 128–32, 185–86; Moura, *Amai*, 66–69.

76. In the dedication to her 1932 edition of *A mulher é uma degenerada?*, Maria Lacerda de Moura addressed her husband as follows: "Today, we are merely two great and true friends . . . merely two loyal siblings" (9). In the same year, she dedicated her new book, *Amai*, to "my dear friend A. Neblind—liberated man [and] social deserter" with the hope that it would serve to increase understanding between the sexes (9).

77. Moura, *Amai*, 11–13.

78. Ibid., 48–49.

79. Moura, *Ferrer*, 87–88.

80. A movement launched by Oswald de Andrade in 1928, Antropofagia adamantly rejected stale nineteenth-century European formulas and sought inspiration in Brazil's "primitive," indigenous past. Oswald's May 1928 "Manifesto" advocated a ritual, symbolic "devouring" of European values in order to wipe out patriarchal and capitalist society with its rigid social and psychological boundaries. See Oswald de Andrade, "Manifesto antropofago," *Revista de Antropofagia* 1 : 1 (May 1928).

81. Campos, *Pagu*, 321–23. Mystery still shrouds many of the intimate details of Patrícia Galvão's life, but the persistent efforts of Augusto de Campos, who spent years searching for lost pieces of information and assembling her widely scattered writings, resulted in this invaluable anthology.

82. Ibid., 320, 323–24. See also Oswald de Andrade's "Romance da época anarquista ou livro das horas de Pagu que são minhas," reprinted on 63–77. According to Pagu's sister, Sidéria, their parents were delighted with Pagu's marriage to Waldemar and sensed no abnormality. When they discovered that the marriage was a pretext for Pagu and Oswald to run off together, they were mortified. They cut their vacation short, refused to see anyone but relatives, and forbade Sidéria to enter into contact with Pagu, whose "pernicious influence" they feared might corrupt her. The ban wore off after a certain time. See pp. 276–77.

83. Quoted in Antonio Riserio, "Pagu: Vida-obra, obravida, vida," in ibid., 325.

84. Campos, *Pagu*, 261–62, 324–25.

85. Galvão's columns, from Oswald de Andrade's short-lived journal *O Homen do Povo*, are reprinted in ibid., 81–87. See also Galvão, *Parque industrial*, 87–89. It is interesting that when Patrícia Galvão was finally rescued from oblivion in 1982, it was in an anthology that, apart from her own writings, contains all male voices (with the single exception of her sister Sidéria's testimony). Perhaps it is fitting—given that she lived in the very male world of the artistic avant-garde and the political Left—that this impressive anthology was compiled by an avant-garde male writer of the next generation, Augusto de Campos, and that it contains

only the voices of her male admirers, past and present. But it stands as a dramatic testimony of Patrícia's alienation from female culture and the difficulty (or disinterest) she had in finding female allies.

86. In 1950, she wrote an extraordinary reflection on her involvement in the party. See Patrícia Galvão, "Verdade e liberdade," reprinted in Campos, *Pagu*, 188–89.

87. Brandão, *Combates e batalhas*, 303. Another party activist attacked Pagu directly as a "pernicious" influence, who, he claimed, like other middle-class intellectuals, approached her political activism as "supremely entertaining and exciting." Basbaum, *Uma vida em seis tempos*, 119.

88. Feminine movements on the political Left during this period grew up around class issues such as the cost of living and only secondarily addressed issues of women's rights. They also tended to be very ephemeral, as was the União Feminina, which existed only between 1934 and 1935, when it was banned along with the leftist Alliança Nacional Libertadora. See Saffioti, *A mulher na sociedade de classes*, 290. Brazil did not have a tradition of organized anarchist feminism, as did Argentina. See Molyneux, "No God, No Boss, No Husband."

89. Anna Rita Malheiros, "Outubro," *RF* 8:89 (October 1921). As noted earlier, Anna Rita Malheiros was the pseudonym used by Claudio de Souza, son of the founder of the *Revista Feminina*, Virgilina de Souza Salles. Presumably, the magazine's editorial policy reflected a coincidence of views between Claudio and Virgilina and, as I argue below, probably expressed fairly accurately the views of the magazine's tens of thousands of middle-class urban housewife readers.

90. "O nosso centenario."

91. Ibid.

92. Anna Rita Malheiros, "Outubro," *RF* 8:89 (October 1921). The same theme is developed in "O voto feminino," *RF* 9:98 (July 1922); Anna Rita Malheiros, "Novembro," *RF* 8:90 (November 1921).

93. A Direcção, "A's mulheres brasileiras! O feminismo no seu maior triumpho!," *RF* 5:55 (December 1918); Anna Rita Malheiros, "Outubro," *RF* 6:65 (October 1919).

94. "Idéa perseguida—idéa triumphante: A mulher moderna—suas reivindicações—suas responsabilidades," *RF* 10:111 (August 1923).

95. A Direcção, "A's mulheres brasileiras! O feminismo no seu maior triumpho!"

96. Anna Rita Malheiros, "Outubro," *RF* 8:89 (October 1921).

97. "Idéa perseguida—idéa triumphante: A mulher moderna—suas reivindicações—suas responsabilidades."

98. Ibid.; Anna Rita Malheiros, "Fevereiro," *RF* 9:93 (February 1922).

99. A Direcção, "A's mulheres brasileiras! O feminismo no seu maior truimpho!"

100. "Chronica," *RF* 10:106 (March 1923).

101. Maria Clara Alvear, "Feminismo brasileiro," *RF* 10:109 (June 1923); Anna Rita Malheiros, "Novembro," *RF* 8:90 (November 1921).

102. Anna Rita Malheiros, "Novembro," *RF* 8:90 (November 1921).

103. "Um factor de dissolvimento social: O divorcio," *RF* 10:111 (August 1923).

104. "Chronica," *RF* 10:106 (March 1923).

105. Anna Rita Malheiros, "Outubro," *RF* 4:41 (October 1917); "O feminismo no Brasil," *RF* 6:56 (January 1919).

106. "Junho," *RF* 8:85 (June 1921).

107. Ibid.

108. "O bom feminismo," *RF* 10:111 (August 1923); Anna Rita Malheiros, "Agosto," *RF*

8:87 (August 1921); Anna Rita Malheiros, "Outubro," *RF* 6:65 (October 1919); A Direcção, "O feminismo e sua imprensa," *RF* 5:54 (November 1918); "A mulher brasileira e o direito feminino de voto em nosso paiz," *RF* 10:110 (July 1923).

109. Anna Rita Malheiros, "Agosto," *RF* 8:87 (August 1921).

110. Anna Rita Malheiros, "Outubro," *RF* 5:53 (October 1918); "O feminismo em marcha: A *Revista Feminina* e o movimento feminista brasileiro," *RF* 6:62 (July 1919); Anna Rita Malheiros, "Novembro," *RF* 5:54 (November 1918); "O feminismo no Brasil," *RF* 5:53 (October 1918); "Mais uma victoria do feminismo brasileiro," *RF* 9:96 (May 1922).

111. Delminda Silveira, "A mulher brasileira é ou não é cidadão brasileiro," *RF* 8:91 (December 1921).

112. Villela, "A mulher e o homen," *RF* 10:104 (January 1923).

113. Machado, *O progresso feminino*, 63–64. See also Delminda Silveira, "A mulher brasileira"; Costa, *A mulher*, 30–32, 39–40, 48–49, 57.

114. Costa, *A mulher*, 14.

115. Apelecina, "Washington Luis e o voto feminino," *A Vida Moderna* 24:257 (31 December 1927).

116. Machado, *O progresso feminino*, 54–59.

117. Alzira Reis, "Uma escriptora mineira," *RF* 5:51 (August 1918). Editors of the *Revista Feminina* published Reis's letters, but they felt uncomfortable about her combative tone and noted that they could not agree with all of her ideas.

118. Joanita de Souza, "Pro-feminismo," *RF* 10:107 (April 1923).

119. Male politicians well known for their support of female suffrage included Justo Chermont, who introduced a suffrage bill into the Senate in 1919; Juvenal Lamertine, who, as a congressman, introduced a suffrage bill into the Chamber of Deputies in 1920 and, as governor of the state of Rio Grande do Norte, secured an amendment to the state voting law that permitted women to vote; Senators Lopes Gonçalves, Moniz Sodré, and Lauro Muller; Congressman Maurício de Lacerda; and Ruy Barbosa.

120. See, for example, Herotides da Silva Lima, "O voto feminino," *Revista dos Tribunais* (São Paulo) 18:72 (November 1929): 18–26; Magalhães, *A mulher*; Pereira, *A mulher no Brasil*; Silva, *A mulher paulista*.

121. See the responses by Rubens de Amaral, Oswaldo Chateaubriand, Braz de Souza Arruda, and Goulart de Andrade to the questionnaire in "As enquêtes d'*A Vida Moderna*," *A Vida Moderna* 24:528 (31 January 1928); 24:529 (17 March 1928); 24:530 (16–30 April 1928). See also J. M. Gomes Ribeiro, "Ainda o voto feminino," *RF* 9:95 (April 1922). He declared feminism, socialism, and pacifism to be the "three great hopes" of the times. Congressman Maurício de Lacerda not only supported female suffrage but also sponsored progressive legislation to guarantee working women minimum employment security.

122. Most of the authors cited in this paragraph proclaimed their support for women's political equality, but none wished to see women emancipated from their traditional domestic roles. It is interesting to note that Basilio de Magalhães introduced an amendment to the female suffrage bill in 1924 that required married women to obtain the consent of their husbands in order to vote. See Coelho, *Evolução do feminismo*, 239.

123. "As enquêtes d' *A Vida Moderna*," *A Vida Moderna* 24:527 (31 December 1927). Nearly the same opinion was expressed by Belmiro Braga, whose response was also printed in this issue.

124. "As enquêtes d' *A Vida Moderna*," *A Vida Moderna* 24:531 (June 1928).

125. "As enquêtes d' *A Vida Moderna*," *A Vida Moderna* 24:530 (16–30 April 1928). See

also the article he published in *O Journal do Brasil* that is reprinted in Lima, *Perfil da mulher*, 126–28.

126. "As enquêtes d' *A Vida Moderna*," *A Vida Moderna* 24:528 (31 January 1928) and 24:530 (16–30 April 1928).

127. "As enquêtes d' *A Vida Moderna*," *A Vida Moderna* 24:528 (31 January 1928).

128. "As enquêtes d' *A Vida Moderna*," *A Vida Moderna* 24:529 (17 March 1928).

129. Lima, *Perfil da mulher*, 8, 61.

130. Ibid., 7.

131. Ibid., 65, 77–78, 96.

132. Ibid., 7, 10, 65–66, 71, 87–89, 100–103.

133. Ibid., 65–66.

134. Ibid., 38–48, 147.

135. Moura, *Amai*, 37–38.

136. See, for example, Julio Dantas, "Para Miss Kate ler," *A Cigarra* 6:127 (1–15 January 1920); João de S. Paulo, "O feminismo em 1990," *A Cigarra* 9:175 (1–15 January 1922); Lellis Vieira, "Chronicas da época," *A Vida Moderna* 24:528 (31 January 1928); Mello Nogueira, "A emancipação feminina," *A Vida Moderna* 19:463 (16 November 1923).

137. Pedro Tacques, "Feminismo," reprinted in Nazario, *Voto feminino e feminismo*, 87. The article appeared first in the *Folha da Noite*.

138. Ibid.

139. "Effeminisação dos direitos politicos," reprinted in Nazario, *Voto feminino e feminismo*, 80–82. This article was also reprinted from the *Folha da Noite*.

140. See articles by Azevedo Amaral and Mário de Alencar reprinted in Lima, *Perfil da mulher*, 123–26.

141. Tristão da Cunha, "A' beira do styx," *Revista do Brasil*, anno 9, 26:103 (July 1924): 199.

142. Paulo de Tharso, "Labios . . . de fogo," *RF* 4:41 (October 1917). Similar statements were made by Coulet, *O problema da familia*, 133–34, 137–38, 142.

143. Dr. MacDowell, "A mulher no pleno divino," *RF* 7:75 (August 1920).

144. Orlando Machado, "A reivindicação feminina em New York," *Revista do Brasil*, anno 8, 23:89 (May 1923): 36.

145. MacDowell, "A mulher no pleno divino."

146. João A. Corrêa de Araujo, "O verdadeiro feminismo," *RF* 4:43 (December 1917); Coulet, *O problema da familia*, 9–12, 117–45; Machado, "A reivindicação feminina em New York," 36–37; Lemos, "O voto feminino," 248–50.

147. Pedro Tacques, "Feminismo," reprinted in Nazario, *Voto feminino e feminismo*, 87–88; Araujo, "O verdadeiro feminismo"; "Effeminisação dos direitos politicos," reprinted in Nazario, *Voto feminino e feminismo*, 80–82. See also Laurindo de Brito's response to the questionnaire in "As enquêtes d' *A Vida Moderna*," *A Vida Moderna* 24:529 (17 March 1928).

148. Mainwaring, *Catholic Church*, 30–32.

149. Iglésias, "Estudo sôbre o pensamento reacionário," 109–58.

150. See, for example, Trindade, *Integralismo*.

151. Salgado, *A mulher no século vinte*, 23.

152. Ibid., 53, 59–60.

153. Ibid., 45–46.

154. Ibid., 108–9.

155. Ibid., 97–103, 114–17.
156. Lima, *Perfil da mulher*, 146–47.

Conclusion

1. Catt, "Busy Women in Brazil," 9–10; Catt, "Summing Up South America," 7–8, 26.

2. Among the many works of interest are Boris and Bardaglio, "Transformation of Patriarchy"; Smith-Rosenberg, *Disorderly Conduct*; Ryan, *Womanhood in America*; Donzelot, *Policing of Families*; Walkowitz, *Prostitution and Victorian Society*; Walkowitz, *City of Dreadful Delight*; Bridenthal, Grossmann, and Kaplan, *When Biology Became Destiny*; Kessler-Harris, *Out to Work*; Tilly and Scott, *Women, Work, and the Family*; and Friedlander, *Women in Culture and Politics*.

3. See, for example, Skidmore, *Black into White*, and Andrews, *Blacks and Whites in São Paulo*.

4. For scholarly analyses of the social and cultural roots of political authoritarianism, see, for example, Lenharo, *A sacralização da política*; Chauí and Franco, *Ideologia e mobilização popular*; Chauí, *Conformismo e resistência*; Weffort, "Why Democracy?"; and DaMatta, *Carnivals, Rogues, and Heroes*. For a history and analysis of the Workers' Party (the Brazilian political party that has developed the most serious critique of authoritarianism), see Keck, *The Workers' Party and Democratization*. For an analysis of the rise of feminism in Brazil since the late 1970s, see Alvarez, *Engendering Democracy in Brazil*.

BIBLIOGRAPHY

Archives

Arquivo da Cúria Metropolitana, São Paulo
Arquivo da Federação Brasileira pelo Progresso Feminino, Arquivo Particular 46, Arquivo
   Nacional, Rio de Janeiro
Arquivo do Hospital do Juquerí, Juquerí, São Paulo
Arquivo do Manicômio Judiciário do Estado de São Paulo, Juquerí, São Paulo
Arquivo do Tribunal da Justiça, São Paulo

Magazines and Periodicals

Dates are given for periodicals of limited duration and for the period in which they were
   consulted.
Archivos Paulistas de Hygiene Mental, São Paulo, 1930
Boletim da Associação dos Empregados no Commércio, Rio de Janeiro, 1925–27
Boletim da Federação Brasileira pelo Progresso Feminino, Rio de Janeiro, 1934–37
Boletim da Sociedade de Assistência aos Lázaros e Defesa contra a Lepra, São Paulo, 1929–33
Boletim do Ministério do Trabalho, Indústria, e Comércio, Rio de Janeiro, 1934–42
A Cigarra, São Paulo, 1920–32
O Cruzeiro, Rio de Janeiro, 1929–32
Diario de São Paulo, São Paulo
Educação, Orgão da Diretoria Geral da Instrução Pública e da Sociedade de Educação de
   São Paulo, São Paulo, 1927–32
O Estado de São Paulo, São Paulo
Eu Sei Tudo, Rio de Janeiro, 1927–28
A Folha Medica, Rio de Janeiro, 1920–22
Klaxon: Mensario de Arte Moderna, São Paulo, 1922–23; reprint ed., São Paulo: Revista
   dos Tribunais, 1976
A Ordem, Orgão do Centro Dom Vital, Rio de Janeiro, 1931–32
Renascença, São Paulo, 1923
Revista da Semana, Rio de Janeiro, 1921–27
Revista de Antropofagia, São Paulo, 1928–29; reprint ed., São Paulo: Abril, 1975

Revista do Brasil, São Paulo, 1918–24
Revista de Direito Penal, Rio de Janeiro, 1933–34
Revista Feminina, São Paulo, 1916–25
A Vida Moderna, São Paulo, 1918–28

Government Publications

Brazil. *Código Civil dos Estados Unidos do Brasil.* 6 vols. Comments by Clovis Bevilaqua.
    Rio de Janeiro: Francisco Alves, 1916–17.
————. *Código Penal: Comentários.* 2 vols. Comments by Ribeiro Pontes. Curitiba: Guaíra,
    1942.
————. *Constituições do Brasil.* 4th ed., rev. Edited by Fernando H. Mendes de Almeida.
    São Paulo: Saraiva, 1963.
————. Comissão Censitária Nacional. *Recenseamento geral do Brasil, 10. de setembro de
    1940.* 3 vols. Rio de Janeiro: IBGE, 1943–50.
————. Congresso. *Cultura política e pensamento autoritário.* Introduction by Ricardo
    Vélez Rodriguez. Brasilia: Câmara do Deputados, Centro de Documentação e Infor-
    mação, Coordinação de Publicações, 1983.
————. Diretoria Geral de Estatística. *Recenseamento da população do Império do Brazil a
    que se procedeu no dia 10. de agosto de 1872.* 22 vols. Rio de Janeiro: Leuzinger, 1873–76.
————. Diretoria Geral de Estatística. *Recenseamento do Brazil realizado em 1 de setembro
    de 1920.* 5 vols. Rio de Janeiro: Typ. da Estatística, 1922–30.
————. Diretoria Geral de Estatística. *Sexo, raça e estado civil, nacionalidade, filiação culto
    e analphabetismo da população recenseado em 31 de dezembro de 1890.* Rio de Janeiro:
    Oficina da Estatística, 1898.
————. Diretoria Geral de Estatística. *Synopse do recenseamento realizado em 1 de setembro
    de 1920. População do Brazil. Resumo do censo demographico por estados, capitaes e munici-
    pios. Confronto do numero de habitantes em 1920 com as populações recenseadas anterior-
    mente.* Rio de Janeiro: Typ. da Estatística, 1922.
São Paulo (State). Departamento de Estatística. *Boletim do Departamento Estadual de Es-
    tatística* 5 (May 1939).
————. Diretoria Geral do Ensino. Secção de Estatística e Arquivo. *Estatística escolar de
    1930.*
————. Repartição de Estatística e Arquivo. *Annuário estatístico de São Paulo.* 1901–27.
————. Secretaria da Agricultura, Comércio e Obras Públicas. *Boletim do Departamento
    Estadual do Trabalho* 9:34–35 (1st and 2d trimesters of 1920); 14:52 (3d trimester of
    1924); 15:56 (3d trimester of 1925).
————. Secretaria dos Negócios da Educação e Saúde Publica. *Boletim da Diretoria do En-
    sino* 17 (1938): 23–24, and 18 (1938): 31–32.
————. Serviço Sanitário. *Annuário Demográphico* 34:1 (1927).

Other Published Materials and Theses

Abreu, Mauricio de A. *Evolução urbana do Rio de Janeiro.* Rio de Janeiro: Instituto de
    Planejamento, Jorge Zahar, 1988.

Agassiz, Louis, and Elizabeth Agassiz. *A Journey in Brazil*. Boston: Ticknor & Fields, 1868.

Albuquerque, José de. *Moral sexual*. Rio de Janeiro: N.p., 1930.

Almeida, Angela Mendes de; Maria José Carneiro; and Silvana Gonçalves de Paula, eds. *Pensando a família no Brasil: Da colônia à modernidade*. Rio de Janeiro: Espaço e Tempo/ UFRRJ, 1987.

Almeida, Candido Mendes de. *As mulheres criminosas no centro mais populoso do Brasil: Distrito Federal, Estados do Rio de Janeiro, São Paulo, Minas Gerais, e Espirito Santo*. Rio de Janeiro: Imprensa Nacional, 1928.

Almeida, Júlia Lopes de. *Livro das donas e donzellas*. Desenhos de Jeanne Mahieu. Rio de Janeiro: Francisco Alves, 1906.

———. *Livro das noivas*. 2d ed. Rio de Janeiro: Francisco Alves, 1905.

Almeida Júnior, A. "Aspectos da nupcialidade paulista." *Revista do Arquivo Municipal* (São Paulo) 6:66 (April–May 1940): 97–106.

Alvarez, Sonia E. *Engendering Democracy in Brazil: Women's Movements in Transition Politics*. Princeton: Princeton University Press, 1990.

Alves, Branca Moreira. *Ideologia e feminismo: A luta da mulher pelo voto no Brasil*. Petrópolis: Vozes, 1980.

Amaral, Aracy A. *Tarsila: Sua obra e seu tempo*. 2 vols. São Paulo: Perspectiva, 1975.

Americano, Jorge. *São Paulo naquele tempo, 1895–1915*. São Paulo: Saraiva, 1957.

———. *São Paulo nesse tempo, 1915–1935*. São Paulo: Melhoramentos, 1962.

Andrade, Oswald de. "Manifesto da poesia pau-brasil." *Correio da Manhã* (São Paulo), 18 March 1924.

Andrews, George Reid. *Blacks and Whites in São Paulo, Brazil, 1888–1988*. Madison: University of Wisconsin Press, 1991.

"Annullação de casamento. Coacção. Conceito desse vicio de vontade. Sua prova." *Revista dos Tribunais* (São Paulo) 18:72 (November 1929): 402–7.

Arrom, Silvia M. *The Women of Mexico City, 1790–1857*. Stanford: Stanford University Press, 1985.

Aughinbaugh, William E. *Advertising for Trade in Latin America*. New York: Century Co., 1922.

———. *Selling Latin America: A Problem in International Salesmanship*. Boston: Small, Maynard & Co., 1915.

Avancini, Marta. "Na era de ouro das cantoras do rádio." *Luso-Brazilian Review* 30:1 (Summer 1993): 85–93.

Azevedo, Aluísio. *Livro de uma sogra*. 12th ed. Introduction by Homero Silveira. São Paulo: Martins, 1973.

Azevedo, Fernando de. *Brazilian Culture: An Introduction to the Study of Culture in Brazil*. Translated by William Rex Crawford. New York: Macmillan, 1950.

———. *Da educação physica: O que ella é, o que tem sido, o que devia ser*. São Paulo: Weiszflog Irmãos, 1920.

———. *A educação publica em São Paulo: Problemas e discussões (Inquerito para O Estado de São Paulo em 1926)*. São Paulo: Companhia Editôra Nacional, 1937.

———. *A evolução do esporte no Brasil*. São Paulo: Melhoramentos, 1930.

———. "Meninas feias e meninas bonitas." In *Annaes de Eugenía*, edited by the Sociedade Eugenica de São Paulo, 146–53. São Paulo: Revista do Brasil, 1919.

———. *Novos caminhos e novos fins: A nova política de educação no Brasil*. Vol. 7 of *Obras completas*. 1937. 3d ed., São Paulo: Edicões Melhoramentos, [1958].

Azevedo, Noe'. *A moda do desquite: O velho instituto do casamento defendido pelo advogado Noe' Azevedo*. São Paulo: Revista dos Tribunais, 1927.

Azevedo, Thales de. "Family, Marriage, and Divorce in Brazil." In *Contemporary Cultures and Societies of Latin America: A Reader in the Social Anthropology of Middle and South America and the Caribbean*, edited by Richard N. Adams and Dwight B. Heath, 288–310. New York: Random House, 1965.

———. "As regras do namôro no Brazil: Um padrão tradicional." *América Latina* (Rio de Janeiro) 13:2–3 (April–October 1970): 128–52.

———. *Social Change in Brazil*. Gainesville: University of Florida Press, 1963.

Azzi, Riolando. *A vida religiosa feminina no Brasil*. Rio de Janeiro: Ceris, 1969.

Barbosa, Ruy. "As classes conservadoras." In *Obras completas de Ruy Barbosa*, vol. 46, tomo 1, 5–60. Rio de Janeiro: Ministerio do Educação e Cultura, 1956.

———. "A questão social e politica no Brasil." In *Obras completas de Ruy Barbosa*, vol. 46, tomo 1, 63–130. Rio de Janeiro: Ministerio do Educação e Cultura, 1956.

Barcos, Julio R. *Liberdade sexual das mulheres*. Translated and preface by Maria Lacerda de Moura. São Paulo: Editôra Paulista, [1929].

Barreto, Benedicto Bastos [Belmonte, pseud.]. *Assim falou Juca Pato: Aspectos divertidos de uma confusão dramatica*. São Paulo: Companhia Editôra Nacional, 1933.

Barreto, Luiz Perreira. "Meninas feias e meninas bonitas." In *Annaes de Eugenía*, edited by the Sociedade Eugenica de São Paulo, 137–45. São Paulo: Revista do Brasil, 1919.

Barros, Maria Paes de. *No tempo de dantes*. Preface by Monteiro Lobato. São Paulo: Brasiliense, 1946.

Basbaum, Leôncio. *Uma vida em seis tempos (memórias)*. 2d ed. São Paulo: Alfa Omega, 1978.

Bastos, Elisabeth. *Justiça, alegria, felicidade: Os novos rumos do feminismo brasileiro*. Rio de Janeiro: Jacintho, 1935.

Bastos, Orminda. "Emancipação civil e politica da mulher." *Boletim do Instituto da Ordem dos Advogados Brasileiros* (Rio de Janeiro) 5 (April 1929): 282–84.

Beiguelman, Paula. *Os companheiros de São Paulo*. São Paulo: Símbolo, 1977.

Bellegarde, Guilherme; Félix Ferreira; and José Maria da Silva Junior, eds. *Polyantheia commemorativa da inauguração das aulas para o sexo feminino do Imperial Lycéo de Artes e Officios*. Rio de Janeiro: Lombaerts, 1881.

Berg, Barbara J. *The Remembered Gate: Origins of American Feminism: The Woman and the City, 1800–1860*. New York: Oxford University Press, 1978.

Besse, Susan K. "Crimes of Passion: The Campaign against Wife-Killing in Brazil, 1910–1940." *Journal of Social History* 22:4 (Summer 1989): 653–66.

———. "Freedom and Bondage: The Impact of Capitalism on Women in São Paulo, Brazil, 1917–1937." Ph.D. diss., Yale University, 1983.

———. "Pagu: Patrícia Galvão—Rebel." In *The Human Tradition in Latin America: The Twentieth Century*, edited by William H. Beezley and Judith Ewell, 103–17. Wilmington, Del.: Scholarly Resources, 1987.

Bicalho, Maria Fernanda Baptista. "The Art of Seduction: Representation of Women in Brazilian Silent Cinema." *Luso-Brazilian Review* 30:1 (Summer 1993): 21–33.

Binzer, Ina von. *Alegrias e tristezas de uma educadora alemã no Brasil*. Translated by Alice Rossi and Luisita da Gama Cerqueira. São Paulo: Anhembí, 1956.

Bittencourt, Adalzira. *Dicionário bio-bibliográfico de mulheres ilustres, notáveis, e intelectuais do Brasil*. 3 vols. Rio de Janeiro: Pongetti, 1969–72.

————. *Mulheres e livros*. Catálogo da Bibliotéca Pública Feminina Brasileira. Rio de Janeiro: N.p., 1948.

————. *A mulher paulista na história*. Rio de Janeiro: Livros de Portugal, 1954.

Blachman, Morris J. "Eve in an Adamocracy: The Politics of Women in Brazil." Ph.D. diss., New York University, 1976.

Blay, Eva Alterman. *Eu não tenho onde morar: Vilas operárias*. São Paulo: Nobel, 1985.

————. *Trabalho domesticado: A mulher na indústria paulista*. São Paulo: Ática, 1978.

Borges, Dain. *The Family in Bahia, Brazil, 1870–1945*. Stanford: Stanford University Press, 1992.

Borges, Wanda Rosa. "Seminario de meninas orphãos e educandas de Nossa Senhora da Gloria: Primeiros ensaios para a profissionalização feminina em São Paulo, 1825–1935." Ph.D. diss., Faculdade de Filosofia, Ciências e Letras de Rio Claro (São Paulo), 1973.

Boris, Eileen, and Peter Bardaglio. "The Transformation of Patriarchy: The Historic Role of the State." In *Families, Politics, and Public Policy: A Feminist Dialogue on Women and the State*, edited by Irene Diamond, 70–90. New York: Longman, 1983.

Bosi, Ecléa. *Memória e sociedade: Lembranças de velhos*. São Paulo: T. A. Queiroz, 1979.

Bourdon, J. R. *A intimidade sexual: Guia moderno dos esposos*. Translated by Odilon Galloti. Rio de Janeiro: Civilização Brasileira, 1935.

Brandão, Octavio. *Combates e batalhas: Memórias*. Preface by Paulo Sérgio Pinheiro. São Paulo: Alfa Omega, 1978.

Brant, Alice Dayrell. *The Diary of Helena Morley*. Translated by Elizabeth Bishop. New York: Ecco Press, 1957.

Bridenthal, Renate; Atina Grossmann; and Marion Kaplan, eds. *When Biology Became Destiny: Women in Weimar and Nazi Germany*. New York: Monthly Review Press, 1984.

Brito, Candida de, ed. *Antologia feminina: Escriptoras e poetisas contemporaneas*. 2d ed. Rio de Janeiro: Editôra da "A Dona de Casa," 1929.

Britto, José Gabriel de Lemos. *Psychologia do adultério*. Rio de Janeiro: Castilho, 1921.

Camargo, Candido Procópio Ferreira de. "Catholicismo e família no Brasil contemporáneo." *Estudos CEBRAP* 12 (April–June 1975): 151–60.

Campos, Augusto de, ed. "Patrícia Galvão." *Atraves* 2 (1978): 2–62.

————, ed. *Pagu: Patrícia Galvão: Vida-obra*. São Paulo: Brasiliense, 1982.

Candido, Antônio. "The Brazilian Family." In *Brazil: Portrait of Half a Continent*, edited by T. Lynn Smith and Alexander Marchant, 291–311. New York: Dryden Press, 1951.

Cannon, Mary M. *Women in Brazil Today*. Washington, D.C.: U.S. Department of Labor, [1943].

A Capital Paulista: Commemorando o centenario da independencia. São Paulo: Editôra Independencia, 1920.

Cardone, Marly A. "A mulher nas constituições brasileiras." *Revista dos Tribunais* 360 (October 1965): 48.

Carneiro, Justino. "A legítima defesa da honra nos crimes de adultério." *Revista de Jurisprudencia Brasileira* (Rio de Janeiro) 5 (September 1929): 13–18.

Carone, Edgard. *O Estado Novo, 1937–1945*. São Paulo: Difel, 1977.

Carvalho, José Murilo de. *A construção da ordem: A elite política imperial*. Rio de Janeiro: Campus, 1980.

Castro, Augusto Olympio Viveiros de. *A questão social*. Rio de Janeiro: Livraria Editôra Conselheiro Candido de Oliveira, [1920].

Castro, Francisco José Viveiros de. *Os delictos contra a honra da mulher*. 2d ed. Rio de Janeiro: Freitas Bastos, 1932.

Castro, Tito Lívio de. *A mulher e a sociogenia*. Posthumous work published under the direction of Manoel da Costa Paes. Rio de Janeiro: Francisco Alves, [1894].

Catt, Carrie Chapman. "Busy Women in Brazil." *The Woman Citizen*, 24 March 1923, 9–10.

———. "Summing Up South America." *The Woman Citizen*, 2 June 1923, 7–8, 26.

Caulfield, Sueann. "Getting into Trouble: Dishonest Women, Modern Girls, and Women-Men in the Conceptual Language of *Vida Policial*, 1925–1927." *Signs* 19:1 (Autumn 1993): 146–76.

———. "In Defense of Honor: The Contested Meaning of Sexual Morality in Law and Courtship, Rio de Janeiro, 1920–1940." Ph.D. diss., New York University, 1994.

Cava, Ralph Della. "Igreja e estado no Brasil do século vinte." *Estudos CEBRAP* 12 (April–June 1975).

Celso, Maria Eugenia. *De relance: Chronicas de B. F.* São Paulo: Monteiro Lobato, 1923.

Cesar, Augusto. *O problema feminino e o divorcio: Aspétos da sociedade em crise*. Rio de Janeiro: Freitas Bastos, 1937.

Cesarino Júnior, A. F. "A família como objeto do direito social." *Boletim do Ministério do Trabalho, Indústria, e Comércio* 9:99 (November 1942): 109–33.

Chalhoub, Sidney. *Trabalho, lar e botequim: O cotidiano dos trabalhadores no Rio de Janeiro da Belle Époque*. São Paulo: Brasiliense, 1986.

Chauí, Marilena. *Conformismo e resistência: Aspectos da cultura popular no Brasil*. São Paulo: Brasiliense, 1985.

Chauí, Marilena, and Maria Sylvia Carvalho Franco. *Ideologia e mobilização popular*. Rio de Janeiro: Paz e Terra, CEDEC, 1978.

Cobra, Ercília Nogueira. *Virgindade inútil: Novella de uma revoltada*. N.p.: By the author, 1927.

Coelho, Mariana. *Evolução do feminismo: Subsídios para a sua história*. Rio de Janeiro: Imprensa Moderna, 1933.

Corrêa, Luiz Moraes. "Amor e crime." *Revista de Direito Penal* 4 (1934): 179–87.

Corrêa, Mariza. *Os crimes da paixão*. São Paulo: Brasiliense, 1981.

———. *Morte em família: Representações jurídicas de papéis sexuais*. Rio de Janeiro: Graal, 1983.

———. "Repensando a família patriarchal brasileira." In *Colcha de retalhos: Estudos sobre a família no Brasil*, edited by Maria Suely Kofes de Almeida et al., 13–38. São Paulo: Brasiliense, 1982.

Costa, Emília de Sousa. *A mulher*. Rio de Janeiro: Alvaro Pinto, 1923.

Costa, Emília Viotti da. *The Brazilian Empire: Myths and Histories*. Chicago: University of Chicago Press, 1985.

———. *Da senzala à colônia*. São Paulo: Difusão Européia do Livro, 1966.

Costa, Jurandir Freire. *Ordem médica e norma familiar*. 2d ed. Rio de Janeiro: Graal, 1983.

Cott, Nancy F. *The Bonds of Womanhood: "Women's Sphere" in New England, 1780–1835*. New Haven: Yale University Press, 1977.

Coulet, (Padre), S.J. *O problema da familia na sociedade contemporanea*. Preface by P. Leonel Franca, S.J. Rio de Janeiro: Livraria Catholica, 1933.

Cunha, Maria Clementina Pereira. *O espelho do mundo: Juquery, a história de um asilo*. Rio de Janeiro: Paz e Terra, 1986.

DaMatta, Roberto. *Carnivals, Rogues, and Heroes: An Interpretation of the Brazilian Dilemma*. Translated by John Drury. Notre Dame: University of Notre Dame Press, 1991.

Dantas, Arruda. *Dona Olivia: Olivia Guedes Penteado*. São Paulo: Impressora Pannartz, 1975.

Dean, Warren. *The Industrialization of São Paulo, 1890–1945*. Austin: University of Texas Press, 1969.

Decca, Maria Auxiliadora Guzzo. *A vida fora das fábricas: Cotidiano operário em São Paulo, 1920–1934*. Rio de Janeiro: Paz e Terra, 1987.

Dias, Maria Odila Leite da Silva. *Quotidiano e poder em São Paulo no século XIX: Ana Gertrudes de Jesus*. São Paulo: Brasiliense, 1984.

Doliveira, Clodoveu. *O trabalhador brasileiro: Esbôço anthropo-sociologo seguido de inqueritos sobre salarios e sobre o trabalho feminino no Brasil*. Rio de Janeiro: A. Balança, 1933.

Donzelot, Jacques. *The Policing of Families*. Foreword by Gilles Deleuze. Translated by Robert Hurley. New York: Pantheon, 1979.

Doria, Antonio de Sampaio. *Educação*. São Paulo: Companhia Editôra Nacional, 1933.

———. *Educação moral*. São Paulo: Melhoramentos, [1928].

———. *Instrucção pelo estado: Coaduna-se a instrucção primaria obrigatoria com os principios que regem a acção social do estado?* São Paulo: Monteiro Lobato, 1922.

———. *A questão social*. São Paulo: Monteiro Lobato, 1922.

Drummond, Magalhaes. "É possivel o flagrante de adultério commissivel por marido?" *Revista de Direito Penal* 1 (1933): 342–46.

"Educação sexual e divorcio." *Archivos Paulistas de Hygiene Mental* 3:5 (July 1930): 63–85.

Ellis, Havelock. *A educação sexual*. Translation and notes by Dr. Alvaro Eston. São Paulo: Companhia Editôra Nacional, 1933.

———. *O instinto sexual*. Translation and notes by Dr. Alvaro Eston. São Paulo: Companhia Editôra Nacional, 1933.

Ensaios Paulistas. 2 vols. Contribuição do "O Estado de São Paulo" as comemorações do IV centenário da cidade. São Paulo: Anhembí, 1958.

Espinola, Eduardo. "O feminismo e a legislação civil: A psychologia feminina comparada com a psychologia masculina." *Pandectas Brasileiras: Registro de Doutrina, Jurisprudencia dos Tribunaes e Legislação* (São Paulo) 9 (1st semester of 1931): 7–23

Esteves, Martha de Abreu. *Meninas perdidas: Os populares e o cotidiano do amor no Rio de Janeiro da Belle Époque*. Rio de Janeiro: Paz e Terra, 1989.

Ewbank, Thomas. *Life in Brazil; or, a Journal of a Visit to the Land of Cocoa and Palm*. New York: Harper & Brothers, 1856.

Expilly, Charles. *Mulheres e costumes do Brasil*. 2d ed. Translation, preface, and notes by Gastão Penalva. São Paulo: Companhia Editôra Nacional, 1977.

Faoro, Raymundo. *Os donos do poder: Formação do patronato político brasileiro*. 2 vols. 2d ed. Pôrto Alegre: Globo, 1975.

Faria, Nisia Floresta Brasileira Augusta. *Opusculo humanitario*. Rio de Janeiro: M. A. Silva Lima, 1853.

Fausto, Boris. *Crime e cotidiano: A criminalidade em São Paulo (1880–1924)*. São Paulo: Brasiliense, 1984.

Ferreira, Barros. *O nobre e antigo bairro da Sé*. São Paulo: Secretaria de Educação e Cultura da Prefeitura do Municipio de São Paulo, Departamento da Cultura, 1971.

Ferreira, Félix. *A educação da mulher: Notas collegidas de varios autores*. Preface by Guilherme Bellegarde. Rio de Janeiro: Hildebrandt, 1881.

Filsinger, Ernst B. *Exporting to Latin America: A Handbook for Merchants, Manufacturers, and Exporters.* Foreword by Leo S. Rowe. New York: D. Appleton & Co., 1916.

Fletcher, James C., and Daniel P. Kidder. *Brazil and the Brazilians.* 6th ed. Boston: Little, Brown & Co., 1866.

Forel, Augusto. *A questão sexual.* 2d ed. Preface by Flaminio Favero. São Paulo: Companhia Editôra Nacional, 1928.

Foucault, Michel. *Madness and Civilization: A History of Insanity in the Age of Reason.* Translated by Richard Howard. New York: Pantheon Books, 1965.

Franca, P. Leonel, S.J. *O divorcio.* Rio de Janeiro: F. Briguiet, 1931.

———. "Divorcio e suicidio." *A Ordem* (Rio de Janeiro) 12:16 (June 1931): 327–39.

Freitas, Affonso Antonio de. *A imprensa periodica de São Paulo desde os seus primordios em 1823 até 1914.* São Paulo: Typ. do "Diario Official," 1915.

Freixo, José Teixeira Portugal. *Matercracia, ou tratado scientifico do amor de mãe.* São Paulo: Oficinas d' "O Estado de São Paulo," 1914–15.

Freyre, Gilberto. *Casa grande e senzala.* Rio de Janeiro: Maia & Schmidt, 1933.

Friedlander, Judith; Blanche Wiesen Cook; Alice Kessler-Harris; and Carroll Smith-Rosenberg, eds. *Women in Culture and Politics: A Century of Change.* Bloomington: Indiana University Press, 1986.

Fundação Carlos Chagas. *Mulher brasileira: Bibliografia anotada.* São Paulo: Brasiliense, 1979.

Galvão, Patrícia [Mara Lobo, pseud.]. *Parque industrial: Romance proletário.* São Paulo: By the author, 1933; reprint, São Paulo: Editôra Alternativa, 1981.

Gattai, Zélia. *Anarquistas, graças a Deus.* Rio de Janeiro: Record, 1979.

Graham, Maria Dundas [Lady Maria Calcott]. *Journal of a Voyage to Brazil and Residence There during Part of the Years 1821, 1822, 1823.* Reprint, New York: Praeger, 1969.

Graham, Richard. *Britain and the Onset of Modernization in Brazil, 1850–1914.* Cambridge: Cambridge University Press, 1968.

Graham, Sandra Lauderdale. *House and Street: The Domestic World of Servants and Masters in Nineteenth-Century Rio de Janeiro.* Cambridge: Cambridge University Press, 1988.

Grossmann, Atina. "The New Woman and the Rationalization of Sexuality in Weimar Germany." In *Powers of Desire: The Politics of Sexuality,* edited by Ann Snitow, Christine Stansell, and Sharon Thompson, 153–71. New York: Monthly Review Press, 1983.

Hahner, June E. *Emancipating the Female Sex: The Struggle for Women's Rights in Brazil, 1850–1940.* Durham, N.C.: Duke University Press, 1990.

———. "Feminism, Women's Rights, and the Suffrage Movement in Brazil, 1850–1932." *Latin American Research Review* 15:1 (1980): 65–111.

———. "The Nineteenth-Century Feminist Press and Women's Rights in Brazil." In *Latin American Women: Historical Perspectives,* edited by Asunción Lavrin, 254–85. Westport, Conn.: Greenwood Press, 1978.

———. "Women and Work in Brazil, 1850–1920: A Preliminary Investigation." In *Essays Concerning the Socio-economic History of Brazil and Portuguese India,* edited by Dauril Alden and Warren Dean, 87–117. Gainesville: University Presses of Florida, 1977.

———, ed. *A mulher no Brasil.* Translated by Eduardo F. Alves. Rio de Janeiro: Civilização Brasileira, 1978.

Hermes, Fonseca. "El amor en el banquillo de los acusados: El crime pasional desde el punto de vista psicologico y social." *Revista de Direito Penal* 3 (1933): 443–66.

Hewitt, Nancy A. *Women's Activism and Social Change: Rochester, New York, 1822–1872.* Ithaca, N.Y.: Cornell University Press, 1984.

Holloway, Thomas H. *Immigrants on the Land: Coffee and Society in São Paulo, 1886–1934.* Chapel Hill: University of North Carolina Press, 1980.

Hungria, Nelson. *Comentários ao Código Penal (Decreto-Lei n.o 2.848, de 7 de dezembro de 1940).* 8 vols. 3d ed. Rio de Janeiro: Revista Forense, 1956.

———. *Questões jurídico-penais.* Rio de Janeiro: Livraria Jacintho Editôra, 1940.

Iamamoto, Marilda Villela, and Raul de Carvalho. *Relações sociais e serviço social no Brasil: Esboço de uma interpretação histórico-metodológica.* 5th ed. São Paulo: Cortez, 1986.

Iglésias, Francisco. "Estudo sôbre o pensamento reacionário: Jackson de Figueiredo." In *História e ideologia,* 109–58. São Paulo: Perspectiva, 1971.

Irmandade da Santa Casa da Misercordia de São Paulo. *Relatorio.* São Paulo: Casa Espinola, 1921.

Jardim, Germano. "La statistique par état matrimonial dans les recensements brésiliens." In *Proceedings of the World Population Conference.* 6 vols., 4:705–14. New York: United Nations, 1954.

Jiménez de Asúa, Luis. *Ao serviço da nova geração.* Translated by J. Catoira and A. Blay. Preface by Galeão Coutinho. São Paulo: Edições e Publicações Brasil, 1933.

Keck, Margaret E. *The Workers' Party and Democratization in Brazil.* New Haven: Yale University Press, 1992.

Kehl, Renato Ferraz. *Certificado medico pré-nupcial: Regulamentação eugenica do casamento.* Rio de Janeiro: Sodré & Companhia, 1930.

———. *Como escolher uma boa esposa.* Rio de Janeiro: Pimenta de Mello, 1925.

———. *A cura da fealdade: Eugenia e medicina social.* São Paulo: Monteiro Lobato, 1923.

———. *Eugenia e medicina social: Problemas da vida.* 2d ed. São Paulo: Francisco Alves, 1923.

———. *A eugenia no Brasil: Esboço historico e bibliographico.* Rio de Janeiro: Sodré & Companhia, 1929.

———. *Formulario da belleza: Formulas escolidas.* Rio de Janeiro: Francisco Alves, 1927.

———. *Livro do chefe de familia.* Rio de Janeiro: Canton & Berger, 1930.

———. *Pais, médicos, e mestres: Problemas de educação e hereditariedade.* Rio de Janeiro: Francisco Alves, 1939.

———. *Perguntas a um eugenista.* Rio de Janeiro: Canton & Beger, 1927.

———. *Porque sou eugenista: Vinte anos de Campanha Eugenica, 1917–1937.* Rio de Janeiro: Francisco Alves, n.d.

Kessler-Harris, Alice. *Out to Work: A History of Wage-Earning Women in the United States.* New York: Oxford University Press, 1982.

Kiehl, Maria. "O trabalho da mulher fora do lar." *Boletim do Ministério do Trabalho, Indústria, e Comércio* 8:96 (August 1942): 83–95; 9:97 (September 1942): 97–129.

Kolontai, Alexandra. *A nova mulher e a moral sexual.* Translated and preface by Galeão Coutinho. São Paulo: Guaira, [193?].

Kuznesof, Elizabeth Anne. *Household Economy and Urban Development: São Paulo, 1765–1836.* Boulder, Colo.: Westview Press, 1986.

———. "Sexual Politics, Race, and Bastard-Bearing in Nineteenth-Century Brazil: A Question of Culture or Power?" *Journal of Family History* 16:3 (1991): 241–60.

Lacroix, P. Pascoal. *Solução do problema sexual.* Petrópolis: Vozes, 1935.

Langenbuch, Juergen Richard. *A estruturação da grande São Paulo: Estudo de geografia urbana*. Rio de Janeiro: Instituto Brasileira de Geografia, Departamento de Documentação e Divulgação Geográfica e Cartográfica, 1971.

O lar feliz: Manual de economia domestica, de jardinagem, de avicultura, etc. para uso das jovens mães e de todos quantos amam seu lar. São Paulo: Livraria Agricola da "Chacaras e Quintares," 1916.

Leal, Victor Nunes. *Coronelismo, enxada e voto. O município e o regime representativo no Brasil: Da colônia à Primeira República*. Rio de Janeiro: Revista Forense, 1949.

Leão, Antonio Carneiro. *Os deveres das novas gerações brasileiras*. Rio de Janeiro: Sociedade Editôra de Propaganda dos Paizes Americanos, 1923.

———. *São Paulo em 1920*. Rio de Janeiro: Annuario Americano, 1920.

Leff, Nathaniel. *Underdevelopment and Development in Brazil*. 2 vols. London: George Allen & Unwin, 1982.

Leite, Aureliano. *Subsídios para a história da civilização paulista*. São Paulo: Saraiva, 1954.

Leite, Míriam Lifchitz Moreira. *Outra face do feminismo: Maria Lacerda de Moura*. São Paulo: Ática, 1984.

———. "Quem foi Maria Lacerda de Moura?" *Educação e Sociedade* 1:2 (January 1979): 5–24.

Leme, Cândido de Morais. "Dos crimes contra a assistência familiar." In *Anais do 1.o Congresso Nacional do Ministério Público*. Vol. 4 of *Comentários ao Código Penal*. Parte Especial. Rio de Janeiro: Imprensa Nacional, 1943.

Lemos, Floriano de. "O voto feminino." *Educação* (October–November 1932): 248–50.

Lenharo, Alcir. "Fascínio e solidão: As cantoras do rádio nas ondas sonoras do seu tempo." *Luso-Brazilian Review* 30:1 (Summer 1993): 75–84.

———. *A sacralização da política*. Campinas: Papirus, 1986.

Levi, Darrell E. *The Prados of São Paulo, Brazil: An Elite Family and Social Change, 1840–1930*. Athens: University of Georgia Press, 1987.

Lewin, Linda. "Natural and Spurious Children in Brazilian Inheritance Law from Colony to Empire: A Methodological Essay." *The Americas* 48:3 (January 1992): 351–96.

———. *Politics and Parentela in Paraíba: A Case Study of Family-Based Oligarchy in Brazil*. Princeton: Princeton University Press, 1987.

———. "Some Historical Implications of Kinship Organization for Family-Based Politics in the Brazilian Northeast." *Comparative Studies in Society and History* 21:2 (April 1979): 262–92.

Lima, Antonio Austregésilo. *Conduta sexual*. Rio de Janeiro: Guanabara, 1934.

———. *A cura dos nervos: Conselhos medicos*. Rio de Janeiro: Jacintho Ribeiro dos Santos, 1918.

———. *Educação da alma: Preceitos de hygiene moral*. 2d ed. Rio de Janeiro: Francisco Alves, 1932.

———. *Livro dos sentimentos: Maximas e comentarios*. Rio de Janeiro: Leite Ribeiro, 1923.

———. *Meditações*. Rio de Janeiro: Francisco Alves, 1923.

———. *O meu e o teu: Forças psicologicas*. Rio de Janeiro: Flores & Mano, 1932.

———. *A neurastenia sexual e seu tratamento*. 2d ed., enl. Rio de Janeiro: Francisco Alves, 1928.

———. *Pequenos males*. Rio de Janeiro: Jacintho Ribeiro dos Santos, 1919.

————. *Perfil da mulher brasileira: Esbôço acêrca do feminismo no Brasil.* Rio de Janeiro: Francisco Alves, 1923.

————. *Preceitos e conceitos.* Rio de Janeiro: Leite Ribeiro & Maurillo, 1921.

Lima, Herotides da Silva. "O voto feminino." *Revista dos Tribunais* (São Paulo) 18:72 (November 1929): 18–26.

Lima Sobrinho, Barbosa. "O sensacionalismo: Influencia do noticiario jornalistico sobre a criminalidade." *Revista de Direito Penal* 5 (1934): 167–75.

Lobo, Eulália Maria Lahmeyer. *História do Rio de Janeiro: Do capital comercial ao capital industrial e financeiro.* 2 vols. Rio de Janeiro: Instituto Brasileiro de Mercado de Capitais, 1978.

Lockhart, James, and Stuart B. Schwartz. *Early Latin America: A History of Colonial Spanish America and Brazil.* Cambridge: Cambridge University Press, 1983.

Lopes, Helvecio Xavier. "Auxilio à gestante solteira." *Boletim do Ministério do Trabalho, Indústria, e Comércio* 4:39 (November 1937): 224–28.

————. "O trabalho feminino no Brasil." *Boletim do Ministério do Trabalho, Indústria, e Comércio* 3:32 (April 1937): 99–111.

Lourenço Filho, M. Bergstrom. "Um inquerito sobre o que os moços leem." *Educação* (October 1927): 33–39.

Love, Joseph L. "Political Participation in Brazil, 1881–1969." *Luso-Brazilian Review* 7:2 (1970): 3–24.

————. *São Paulo in the Brazilian Federation, 1889–1937.* Stanford: Stanford University Press, 1980.

Luccock, John. *Notes on Rio de Janeiro and the Southern Parts of Brazil; Taken during a Residence of Ten Years . . . 1808–1818.* London: Samuel Leigh, 1820.

Lutz, Bertha. *A nacionalidade da mulher casada.* Rio de Janeiro: Irmãos Pongetti, 1933.

————. *O trabalho feminino: A mulher na ordem económica e social.* Rio de Janeiro: Imprensa Nacional, 1937.

————. *Treze princípios básicos: Sugestões ao Ante-projecto da Constituição.* Rio de Janeiro: Editôra da Federação Brasileira pelo Progresso Feminino, 1933.

Luz, Madel. *Medicina e ordem política brasileira: Políticas e instituições de saúde, 1850–1930.* Rio de Janeiro: Graal, 1982.

Luz, Nícia Vilela. *A luta pela industrialização no Brasil.* São Paulo: Difusão Européia do Livro, 1961.

Lyra, Roberto. *O amor e a responsabilidade criminal.* Preface by Afrânio Peixoto. São Paulo: Saraiva, 1932.

————. "O amor no banco dos reus." *Revista de Direito Penal* 1 (1933): 219–25.

————. "Educação sexual e criminalidade." Palavras proferidas no Centro de Educação Sexual a 20 de julho de 1933. *Revista de Direito Penal* 2 (1933): 43–44.

————. *Polícia e justiça para o amor! (Criminalidade artística e passional).* Rio de Janeiro: A Noite, [1937?].

————. "Préfacio." In *O delicto passional na civilização contemporania*, by Enrico Ferri, translated by Roberto Lyra. São Paulo: Saraiva, 1934.

Lyra, Sophia A. *Rosas de neve: Como eram as mulheres no começo do século.* Rio de Janeiro: Cátedra, 1974.

Machado, Else Mazza Nascimento. *O physico feminino na adolescencia: Para mães e professoras.* Rio de Janeiro: Mendonça, Machado & Companhia, 1925.

————. *O progresso feminino e sua base.* São Paulo: Imprensa Methodista, 1922.

Machado, Pedro de Alcantara Marcondes. *Um ensaio de moral sexual.* Thesis, Faculdade de Medicina e Cirurgia de São Paulo. São Paulo: Secção de obras d'"O Estado de São Paulo," 1925.

Machado, Roberto; Angela Loureiro; Rogerio Luz; and Katia Muricy. *Danação da norma: Medicina social e constituição da psiquiatria no Brasil.* Rio de Janeiro: Graal, 1978.

Madeira, Felícia R., and Paul I. Singer. *Estrutura do emprego e trabalho feminino no Brasil: 1920–1970.* Cadernos CEBRAP 13. São Paulo: CEBRAP, 1973.

Magalhães, Basilio de. *A mulher: Os seus direitos politicos e o papel que lhe incumbe na actual evolução do Brasil.* Conferencia realizada a 15 de novembro de 1927 no salão nobre da Liga de Defesa Nacional, a convite da Federação Brasileira pelo Progresso Feminino. Rio de Janeiro: Leite Ribeiro, 1928.

Maia, Jorge de Andrade. *Catálogo-dicionario das theses inauguraes defendidas perante a Faculdade de Medecina da Universidade de São Paulo, 1919–1935.* São Paulo: N.p., 1935.

————. *Indice catálogo médico paulista, 1860–1936.* São Paulo: Revista dos Tribunais, 1938.

————. *Indice geral da Revista de Medicina, 1916–1931.* São Paulo: N.p., 1931.

Mainardi, Pericles Calvino Libero. "Dia do lar." *Educação* (July–September 1930): 61–66.

Mainwaring, Scott. *The Catholic Church and Politics in Brazil, 1916–1985.* Stanford: Stanford University Press, 1986.

Malloy, James M., ed. *Authoritarianism and Corporatism in Latin America.* Pittsburgh: University of Pittsburgh Press, 1977.

Marcondes, Durval. "A influência do cinema na agravação das neuroses." *Revista da Associação Paulista da Medicina* 3:1 (July 1933): 37–39.

Marestan, Jean. *A educação sexual.* Preface and notes by J. P. Porto-Carrero. Rio de Janeiro: Freitas Bastos, 1930.

Martin, Percy Alvin, ed. *Who's Who in Latin America.* Stanford: Stanford University Press, 1935.

Martins, Amélia de Rezende. *Acção social brasileira, 1925–1929.* Rio de Janeiro: Papelaria Brasil, n.d.

————. *Estudos sobre os problemas sociaes e o feminismo.* São Paulo: Escolas Prof. Salesianas do Lyceu C. de Jesus, 1925.

————. *A moda.* Niteroi: Salesiana, [1921?].

Masiello, Francine. "Women, State, and Family in Latin American Literature of the 1920s." In *Women, Culture, and Politics in Latin America,* edited by the Seminar on Feminism and Culture in Latin America, 27–47. Berkeley and Los Angeles: University of California Press, 1990.

Mattos, José Veríssimo de. "A questão do casamento: O propósito do *Livro de uma sogra* do Sr. Aluísio Azevedo." In *Estudos de literatura brasileira,* 49–60. 1a. série. São Paulo: Universidade de São Paulo, 1976.

Meireles, Cecília. "Trabalho feminino no Brasil." *O Observador Econômico e Financeiro* 4:42 (July 1939): 93–107.

Mello, Affonso Bandeira de. "Trabalho de menores." *Boletim do Ministério do Trabalho, Indústria, e Comércio* 3:25 (September 1936): 118–22.

Mello, Baptista de. "Política da familia." *Arquivo Judiciário (Supplemento)* 56:3 (5 November 1940): 37–40.

Mendes, Raimundo Teixeira. *A preeminência social e moral da mulher (segundo os ensinos da verdadeira sciência pozitiva)*. Rio de Janeiro: Igreja Pozitivista do Brasil, 1908.

Menses, Tobias Barreto. *Estudos de sociologia*. Rio de Janeiro: Instituto Nacional de Livro, 1962.

Merrick, T. W., and D. Graham. *Population and Economic Development in Brazil, 1808 to the Present*. Baltimore: Johns Hopkins University Press, 1979.

Miceli, Sergio. *Intelectuais e classe dirigente no Brasil, 1920–1945*. São Paulo: Difel, 1979.

Moacyr, Primitivo. *A instrução e a república*. 4 vols. Rio de Janeiro: Imprensa Nacional, 1941–42.

———. *A instrução e as províncias: Subsídios para a história da educação no Brasil, 1834–1889*. 3 vols. São Paulo: Companhia Editôra Nacional, 1939–40.

———. *A instrução e o império: Subsídios para a história da educação no Brasil*. 3 vols. São Paulo: Companhia Editôra Nacional, 1936–38.

———. *A instrução pública no Estado de São Paulo*. 2 vols. São Paulo: Companhia Editôra Nacional, 1942.

Molyneux, Maxine. "No God, No Boss, No Husband: Anarchist Feminism in Nineteenth-Century Argentina." *Latin American Perspectives* 13:1 (Winter 1986): 119–45.

Moncorvo Filho, Arthur. *Histórico da protecção á infancia no Brasil*. Rio de Janeiro: Emprenza Graphica Editôra, 1926.

———. *Hygiene infantil: Prelecções do "Curso Popular" realizado em 1915 no Instituto de Protecção e Assistencia á Infancia do Rio de Janeiro*. 2 vols. Rio de Janeiro: Imprensa Nacional, 1917.

Moncorvo Filho, Arthur, et al. *Hygiene infantil: A's mães pobres: Conferencias realizadas no Dispensario Moncorvo, 1901–1907*. Rio de Janeiro: Imprensa Nacional, 1907.

Moraes, Evaristo de. *Un caso de homocidio por paixão amorosa: Estudo de psychologia criminal seguido da sentença absolutoria*. Rio de Janeiro: Martins de Arujo, 1914.

———. *Criminalidade passional: O homocidio e o homocidio-suicidio por amor em face da psychologia criminal e da penalistica*. São Paulo: Saraiva, 1933.

———. *Ensaios de pathologia social: Vagabundagem, alcoolismo, prostituição, lenocinio*. Rio de Janeiro: Leite Ribeiro & Maurillo, 1921.

Morse, Richard M. "Brazil's Urban Development: Colony and Empire." In *From Colony to Nation: Essays on the Independence of Brazil*, edited by A. J. R. Russell-Wood, 155–81. Baltimore: Johns Hopkins University Press, 1975.

———. *From Community to Metropolis: A Biography of São Paulo, Brazil*. 2d ed. New York: Octagon Books, 1974.

Mortara, Giorgio. "The Brazilian Birth Rate: Its Economic and Social Factors." In *Culture and Human Fertility*, edited by Frank Lorimer, 405–501. New York: UNESCO, 1954.

———. "A fecundidade feminina na Capital Federal e na Capital de São Paulo." In *Estudos sobre a natalidade em algumas grandes cidades do Brasil*, 54–65. Rio de Janeiro: IBGE, 1952.

———. "Natalidade e fecundidade no Brasil." *Boletim do Ministério do Trabalho, Indústria, e Comércio* 6:69 (May 1940): 251–59.

———. "A nupcialidade no Distrito Federal." *Revista Brasileira de Estatística* 9:33 (January–March 1948): 343–56.

Mott, Maria Lúcia de Barros. "A igreja, a polícia, e a família a queriam pelas costas: O crime de Ercília Cobra? Defender o prazer sexual da mulher." *Comtudo* (Ribeirão Preto, São Paulo) 13 (1–15 October 1980): 17.

Moura, Esmeralda Blanco B de. "Além da indústria têxtil: O trabalho feminino em ativida-des 'masculinas.'" *Revista Brasileira de História* 9:18 (August–September 1989): 86–96.

————. *Mulheres e menores no trabalho industrial: Os fatores sexo e idade na dinâmica do capi-tal.* Petrópolis: Vozes, 1982.

Moura, Maria Lacerda de. *Amai e . . . não vos multipliqueis.* Rio de Janeiro: Civilização Bra-sileira, 1932.

————. "As conferencias de Maria Lacerda de Moura na Argentina e no Uruguay." *Diario de São Paulo*, 2 July 1929, p. 11.

————. *Em torno da educação.* São Paulo: Teixeira, 1918.

————. "Eva." *Renascença* 1:3 (April 1923).

————. *Ferrer, o clero romano e a educação laica.* São Paulo: Editôra Paulista, 1934.

————. *Han Ryner e o amor plural.* Rev. ed. São Paulo: Unitas, 1933.

————. "O individualismo neo-estoico de Han Ryner: Estudo." *Feira Literaria* (São Paulo) 11 (November 1929): 59–104.

————. *Lições de pedagogia.* São Paulo: Typ. Paulista, 1925.

————. *A mulher é uma degenerada?* 3d ed. Rio de Janeiro: Civilização Brasileira, 1932.

————. *Religião do amor e da belleza.* 2d ed. São Paulo: Editôra "O Pensamento," 1929.

————. *O silêncio.* Palestra realizada no Departamento Cultural da Fraternidade Rosa Cruz do Brasil no dia 19 de julho de 1944. Rio de Janeiro: N.p., 1948.

Nagle, Jorge. *Educação e sociedade na Primeira Republica.* São Paulo: EPU, Editôra da Uni-versidade de São Paulo, 1974.

Nazario, Diva Nolf. *Voto feminino e feminismo.* São Paulo: Monteiro Lobato, 1923.

Nazzari, Muriel. *Disappearance of the Dowry: Women, Families, and Social Change in São Paulo, Brazil, 1600–1900.* Stanford: Stanford University Press, 1991.

Needell, Jeffrey D. *A Tropical Belle Époque: Elite Culture and Society in Turn-of-the-Cen-tury Rio de Janeiro.* Cambridge: Cambridge University Press, 1987.

Negreiros, Odila Ferraz de. "A acção da mulher no lar." *Educação* (November–December 1928): 169–73.

Nogueira, Iracema S. "Dia do lar." *Educação* (July–September 1930): 57–60.

Offen, Karen. "Defining Feminism: A Comparative Historical Approach." *Signs* 14:1 (Au-tumn 1988): 119–57.

Oliveira, Andradina. *O divorcio.* Pôrto Alegre: Universal, 1912.

Oliveira, José Feliciano de. *O ensino em São Paulo: Algumas reminiscencias.* São Paulo: Si-queira, 1932.

Oliveira, Lola de. *Gente de agora.* 2d ed. São Paulo: Typ. Paulista, 1927.

————. *Hontem e hoje.* São Paulo: Typ. Paulista, 1928.

————. *Passadismo e modernismo.* 2d ed. São Paulo: Est. Graphico "Rossolillo," 1932.

Padilha, Celina. "Educação sexual." *Educação* (January 1928): 30–35.

"Padrão de vida (Relatorio do inquerito que a Escola Livre de Sociologia e Politica realizou sobre 221 familias operarias na cidade de São Paulo)." *Boletim do Ministério do Trabalho, Indústria, e Comércio* 1:10 (June 1935): 77–97.

Pedreira, Mario Bulhões. "O amor no banco dos reus." *Revista de Direito Penal* 1 (1933): 445–65.

Peixoto, Afrânio. "Crimes passionaes." *Arquivo Judiciário (Supplemento)* 20 (October–December 1931).

————. "A educação nacional: Aspectos femininos." *Revista Feminina* 7:79 (December 1920).

————. *Elementos de medicina legal.* Rio de Janeiro: Francisco Alves, 1910.

————. *Eunice; ou, A educação da mulher.* Rev. ed. Rio de Janeiro: W. M. Jackson, 1947.

————. *Marta e María: Documentos de acção pública.* Rio de Janeiro: N.p., 1930.

————. *Sexologia forense.* 2d ed., enl. Rio de Janeiro: Guanabara, 1934.

Pena, Maria Valéria Junho. *Mulheres e trabalhadoras: Presença feminina na constituição do sistema fabril.* Rio de Janeiro: Paz e Terra, 1981.

Pereira, Manuel Francisco Pinto. *A mulher no Brasil.* São Paulo: Teixeira, 1916.

Perreira, Lucia Miguel. "Chronica feminina: O perigo do feminismo." *A Ordem* (Rio de Janeiro) 12:34 (December 1932): 449–50.

Pimentel, Silvia. *Evolução dos direitos da mulher: Norma, fato, valor.* São Paulo: Revista dos Tribunais, 1978.

Pinheiro, Paulo Sérgio, and Michael M. Hall, eds. *A classe operário no Brasil: Documentos, 1889 a 1930.* 2 vols. São Paulo: Alfa Omega, 1979–81.

Prandi, José Reginaldo. *Catolicismo e família: Transformação de uma ideologia.* Cadernos CEBRAP 21. São Paulo: CEBRAP, 1975.

Priore, Mary del, ed. *História da criança no Brasil.* São Paulo: Contexto, 1991.

O problema sexual. Prefaces by Ruy Barbosa and Coelho Netto. Rio de Janeiro: N.p., 1913.

Queiroz, Carlota Pereira de. "Assistencia social à infancia." *Boletim do Ministério do Trabalho, Indústria, e Comércio* 3:28 (December 1936): 260–83.

Queiroz, Maria Isaura Pereira de. *O mandonismo local na vida política brasileira.* São Paulo: Instituto de Estudos Brasileiros, USP, 1969.

Rachum, Ilan. "Feminism, Woman Suffrage, and National Politics in Brazil: 1922–1937." *Luso-Brazilian Review* 14 (Summer 1977): 118–34.

Rago, Margareth. *Do cabaré ao lar: A utopia da cidade disciplinar: Brasil, 1890–1930.* Rio de Janeiro: Paz e Terra, 1985.

Rangel Sobrinho, Orlando. *Educação physica feminina.* Rio de Janeiro: Typ. do Patronato, 1930.

Rão, Vicente. *Da capacidade civil da mulher casada.* São Paulo: Saraiva, 1922.

————. *Direitos da mulher casada sobre o producto de seu trabalho.* Dissertação para concurso a cadeira de direito civil da Faculdade de Direito de São Paulo. São Paulo: N.p., [1937?].

Rebouças, Alberto. "O problema do salário minimo." *Boletim do Ministério do Trabalho, Indústria, e Comércio* 5:52 (December 1938): 85–97.

A reconstrucção educational no Brasil: Ao povo e ao governo. Manifesto dos pioneiros da educação nova. Introduction by Fernando de Azevedo. São Paulo: Companhia Editôra Nacional, 1932.

Reis, Arthur Henock dos. "Trabalho da mulher nas ferrovias." *Boletim do Ministério do Trabalho, Indústria, e Comércio* 8:89 (January 1942): 61–82; 8:90 (February 1942): 81–93.

Rezende, Astolpho. "As mães solteiras. Sua protecção e dignidade. Pesquiza da paternidade. Penalidade pecuniaria na fecundação extra-legal." *Revista de Jurisprudencia Brasileira* (Rio de Janeiro) 4 (June 1929): 207–18.

Ribeiro, Carolina. "A mulher paulista em 1932." *Revista do Instituto Histórico e Geográfico de São Paulo* 59 (1961): 247–62.

Ribeiro, Sergio Nogueira. *Crimes passionais e outras temas.* Rio de Janeiro: Itambé, 1975.

Rocha, Oswaldo Porto. *A era das demolições: Cidade do Rio de Janeiro, 1870–1920.* Rio de Janeiro: Secretaria Municipal de Cultura, 1986.

Rocha Júnior, Martinho da. *Cartilha das mães.* Rio de Janeiro: N.p., 1930.

Rodrigues, Jessita Martins. *A mulher operária: Um estudo sobre tecelãs.* São Paulo: Hucitec, 1979.

Rodrigues, João Batista Cascudo. *A mulher brasileira: Direitos políticos e cívis.* Forteleza: Imprensa Universitária do Ceará, 1962.

———. *A mulher paulista no movimento pró-constituinte.* São Paulo: Revista dos Tribunais, 1933.

Rodrigues, Jorge Martins. *São Paulo de ontem e de hoje.* 2d ed. São Paulo: Imprensa Oficial do Estado, 1940.

Rodrigues, Leda Maria Pereira. *A instrução feminina em São Paulo: Subsídios para sua história até a proclamação da república.* São Paulo: Faculdade de Filosofia "Sedes Sapientiae," 1962.

Russell-Wood, A. J. R. "Female and Family in the Economy and Society of Colonial Brazil." In *Latin American Women: Historical Perspectives,* edited by Asunción Lavrin, 60–100. Westport, Conn.: Greenwood Press, 1978.

———. "Women and Society in Colonial Brazil." *Journal of Latin American Studies* 9:1 (May 1977): 1–34.

Ryan, Mary P. *Womanhood in America: From Colonial Times to the Present.* 3d ed. New York: F. Watts, 1983.

Saes, Décio. *Classe média e sistema político no Brasil.* São Paulo: T. A. Queiroz, 1984.

Saffioti, Heleieth Iara Bongiovani. *A mulher na sociedade de classes: Mito e realidade.* São Paulo: Quatro Artes, 1969.

Salgado, Plínio. *A mulher no século vinte.* 3d ed. São Paulo: Guanumby, 1949.

Samara, Eni de Mesquita. *A família brasileira.* São Paulo: Brasiliense, 1983.

Schulz, Maria Rita Lira. "Trabalho de menores." *Boletim do Ministério do Trabalho, Indústria, e Comércio* 7:75 (November 1940): 115–25.

Scott, Joan. "Gender: A Useful Category of Historical Analysis." *American Historical Review* 91:5 (December 1986): 1053–75.

Silva, Antonio Carlos Pacheco e. *A assistência a psicopatas no Estado de São Paulo: Breve resunha dos trabalhos realizados durante o periodo de 1923 a 1937.* São Paulo: Oficinal Gráficas da Assistência a Psicopatas de Juquerí, 1945.

———. "Esporte e sistema nervoso." *Archivos Paulistas de Hygiene Mental* 2–3:3–4 (January 1930).

———. *A mulher paulista no atual momento brasileiro.* Conferencia realizada no salão do Club Comercial sob o patrocínio da Associação Cívica Feminina, em 29 de abril de 1933. São Paulo: Oficinas Gráficas do Hospital de Juquerí, 1933.

———. *Serviços sociais.* São Paulo: N.p., 1937.

Silva, Julio Cesar da. *Arte de amar.* 2d ed., enl. São Paulo: Monteiro Lobato, 1924.

———. *Arte de amar.* 3d ed., enl. São Paulo: Companhia Editôra Nacional, 1928.

Silva, María Beatriz Nizza da. "Divorce in Colonial Brazil: The Case of São Paulo." In *Sexuality and Marriage in Colonial Latin America,* edited by Asunción Lavrin, 313–40. Lincoln: University of Nebraska Press, 1989.

———. *Sistema do casamento no Brasil colonial.* São Paulo: T. A. Queiroz, 1984.

Silva, Peregrino da. *A mulher e a criança.* 3d ed. São Paulo: N.p., 1931.

Simonsen, Roberto C. *A evolução industrial do Brasil.* São Paulo: Revista dos Tribunais, 1939.

Singer, Paul I. *Desenvolvimento econômico e evolução urbana: Análise da evolução econômica de São Paulo, Blumenau, Pôrto Alegre, Belo Horizonte e Recife.* São Paulo: Companhia Editôra Nacional, 1968.

————. *Fôrça de trabalho e emprêgo no Brasil, 1920–1969.* São Paulo: CEBRAP, 1971.

Skidmore, Thomas E. *Black into White: Race and Nationality in Brazilian Thought.* New York: Oxford University Press, 1974.

Smith-Rosenberg, Carroll. *Disorderly Conduct: Visions of Gender in Victorian America.* New York: Knopf, 1985.

Sociedade Eugenica de São Paulo. *Annaes de eugenía.* São Paulo: Revista do Brasil, 1919.

Soihet, Rachel. "Bertha Lutz e a ascensão social da mulher, 1919–1937." Master's thesis, Universidade Federal Fluminense, Rio de Janeiro, 1974.

————. *Condição feminina e formas de violência: Mulheres pobres e ordem urbana, 1890–1920.* Rio de Janeiro: Forense Universitária, 1989.

Souza, Gilda de Mello e. *O espírito das roupas: A moda no século dezenove.* São Paulo: Companhia das Letras, 1987.

Stein, Stanley J. *The Brazilian Cotton Manufacture: Textile Enterprise in an Underdeveloped Area, 1850–1950.* Cambridge: Harvard University Press, 1957.

Stepan, Nancy Leys. *Beginnings of Brazilian Science: Oswaldo Cruz, Medical Research, and Policy, 1890–1920.* New York: Science History Publications, 1976.

————. *"The Hour of Eugenics": Race, Gender, and Nation in Latin America.* Ithaca, N.Y.: Cornell University Press, 1991.

Stoner, K. Lynn. *From the House to the Streets: The Cuban Women's Movement for Legal Reform, 1898–1940.* Durham, N.C.: Duke University Press, 1991.

Tappen, Kathleen B. *The Status of Women in Brazil.* Washington, D.C.: U.S. Office of Inter-American Affairs, 1944.

Tilly, Louise A., and Joan W. Scott. *Women, Work, and the Family.* New York: Holt, Rinehart and Winston, 1978.

Torres, Magarinos. "O jury e seu rigor contra os passionaes ou o amor no banco dos reos." *Revista de Direito Penal* 1 (1933): 65–79.

————. "A mulher e o jury." *Revista de Direito Penal* 3 (1933): 33–42.

Trindade, Hélgio. *Integralismo: O fascismo brasileiro na década de 30.* São Paulo: Difusão Européia do Livro, 1974.

Vargas, Getúlio. *A Nova Política do Brasil.* 11 vols. Rio de Janeiro: José Olympio, 1938–43.

Vasconcellos, Francisco Figueira de Mello e. *Educação sexual da mulher.* Thesis, Faculdade de Medicina do Rio de Janeiro. Rio de Janeiro: N.p., 1915.

Vasconcelos, Cecilia Bandeira de Melo Rebêlo de [Chrysanthème, pseud.]. *Enervadas: Novella.* Rio de Janeiro: Leite Ribeiro, 1922.

————. *Familias: Romance.* Rio de Janeiro: Renascença, 1933.

————. *Gritos femininos.* São Paulo: Monteiro Lobato, 1922.

————. *Matar! Romance sensacional e moderníssimo.* Rio de Janeiro: N.p., 1927.

————. *Minha terra e sua gente.* Rio de Janeiro: João do Rio, 1929.

————. "Mussolini e a mulher." In *Antologia feminina: Escriptoras e poetisas contemporaneas*, 2d ed., edited by Candida de Brito, 32–36. Rio de Janeiro: Editôra da "A Dona de Casa," 1929.

————. *O que os outros não veem: Romance moderno de psycho-analyse feminina.* Rio de Janeiro: Francisco Alves, 1929.

Velde, Theodoor Hendrik van de. *A esposa perfeita: Efficiencia sexual pela cultura physica.*

Translated by Bruno Zander. Preface by Dr. Arnaldo de Moraes. Rio de Janeiro: Marisa, [193?].

———. *O matrimonio perfeito: Estudo de sua fisiologia e sua técnica.* Translated by Dr. Pedro Gouvêa Filho. Preface by José de Albuquerque. Rio de Janeiro: Civilização Brasileira, 1933.

Vianna, Maria Sophia Bulcão. "A evolução do trabalho da mulher." *Boletim do Ministério do Trabalho, Indústria, e Comércio* 4:37 (September 1937): 99–110.

Vidal, Olímio Barros. *Precursoras brasileiras.* Rio de Janeiro: A Noite, [1945?].

Vieira, Margarida Maria Motta. "Monografia de uma familia." *Boletim do Ministério do Trabalho, Indústria, e Comércio* 6:65 (January 1940): 379–89; 6:66 (February 1940): 369–79.

Walkowitz, Judith R. *City of Dreadful Delight: Narratives of Sexual Danger in Late-Victorian London.* Foreword by Catharine R. Stimpson. Chicago: University of Chicago Press, 1992.

———. *Prostitution and Victorian Society: Women, Class, and the State.* Cambridge: Cambridge University Press, 1980.

Walsh, Robert. *Notices of Brazil in 1828 and 1829.* 2 vols. London: Frederick Westley and A. H. Davis, 1830.

Weffort, Francisco. "Why Democracy?" In *Democratizing Brazil: Problems of Transition and Consolidation,* edited by Alfred Stepan, 327–50. New York: Oxford University Press, 1989.

Werneck, Heloisa Cabral da Rocha. "O trabalho das mulheres e dos menores." *Boletim do Ministério do Trabalho, Indústria, e Comércio* 3:27 (November 1936): 134–50.

Willems, Emílio. "The Structure of the Brazilian Family." *Social Forces* 31:4 (May 1953): 339–45.

Wolfe, Joel. *Working Women, Working Men: São Paulo and the Rise of Brazil's Industrial Working Class, 1900–1955.* Durham, N.C.: Duke University Press, 1993.

INDEX

38–40; Church influence in, 83–84; necessity of female education in, 110–11; effect of female employment on, 132; feminist influence in, 165, 192, 197–98; diversification of, 206 (n. 13)

Sodré, Moniz, 248 (n. 119)

Solteironas. See Women: unmarried

Souza, Claudio de, 24, 149, 210 (n. 49); on role of women, 74; pseudonyms of, 210 (n. 43), 247 (n. 89); on crimes of passion, 225 (n. 140)

Souza, Joanita de, 189–90

Special Commission on the Status of Women (1937), 156

Sports: popularity of, 21–22; for women, 124–26, 234 (nn. 49, 50, 53). *See also* Physical education

State, Brazilian: regulation of gender roles, 5; socialization in, 6; protection of family, 6, 70–71, 80; intervention in gender roles, 6–7; control over social life, 59; family as microcosm of, 62; social action programs of, 85–86; child-rearing policies of, 92, 94–96, 228 (n. 17); women as socializing force in, 102–3, 111, 185–86, 192, 195, 200; role of education in, 110, 232 (n. 1); regulation of female employment, 140–41; regulation of poor women, 201. *See also* Brazil, government and politics

Statute on Women (FBPF proposal), 171–72, 244 (nn. 40, 42); Special Congressional Commission on, 174

Stereotypes, female: of fragility, 8, 20; effect of cinema on, 23; in education, 123; in workforce, 132, 133, 134, 135, 136, 138, 140, 149; in charitable work, 151; use by FBPF, 176, 177; in *Revista Feminina*, 186–87; of submissiveness, 188, 189. *See also* Character traits, female

Stoner, K. Lynn, 245 (n. 70)

Stopes, Marie Carmichael, 65

Suffrage:

—in nineteenth century, 14; debated in Constituent Congress (1891), 18; in 1894 presidential election, 208 (n. 11)

—female, 1, 98; implementation of, 9, 148, 170, 171; role of FBPF in, 164; challenge to patriarchy, 165; Lutz on, 167; voter registration for, 169, 173, 244 (n. 26); in Constitution of 1934, 170; FBPF's campaign for, 182; *Revista Feminina* on, 186; male support of, 190, 248 (nn. 119, 121); proposed restrictions on, 243 (n. 25), 248 (n. 122)

—literacy requirement for, 165, 244 (n. 31)

Suffragists, depiction in print media, 194

Tango, 33, 45

Teachers' League, 168

Teatro Lírico (Rio de Janeiro), 21

Telephone, effect on courtship, 33

Temperance movement, 241 (n. 87)

Textile industry, women in, 110, 146, 226 (n. 257)

Thiollier, René, 210 (n. 49)

Thirteen Principles (Lutz), 170

U.S. National Organization of Housewives, 78

União de Funcionárias Pública (Association of Women Civil Service Workers), 169

União dos Operários em Fábricas de Tecidos de São Paulo, 226 (n. 157)

União Profissional Feminina (Professional Women's Association), 169

União Universitária Feminina (Association of University Women), 169

Unisexuality, in fashion, 29, 32

University of São Paulo, Faculty of Philosophy, Sciences, and Letters, 115, 116

Upper class: urban, 2, 9, 18; effect of social and economic change on, 2, 17–18; legitimation of male domination, 9; marriage in, 12, 16, 38, 39; seclusion of women in, 13, 17, 19, 199; modernization projects of, 15, 208 (n. 13); marriage strategies of, 51–53, 207 (n. 3); bourgeois morality of, 88; fertility rates in, 106, 108; moral authority of, 154; composition of, 206 (n. 13). *See also* Families, upper-class

Urban-industrial economy, Brazilian. *See* Economy, Brazil: urban-industrial

Urbanization, Brazilian, 15–16; effect on national culture, 36; effect on child rearing, 101; effect on birth rates, 105–6; effect on women, 151, 174, 201; effect on legitimacy rates, 217 (n. 67). *See also* Modernization

—widowed: social status of, 49; in workforce, 132, 133

—working-class: political campaigns against, 8; suffrage for, 9; social freedom for, 71; and labor unions, 87, 97, 226 (n. 157), 227 (n. 159); vocational education for, 121–23; as factory workers, 162, 242 (n. 122); FBPF programs for, 175

Workers, women, 4; political campaigns against, 8; threat to family, 8, 130, 132, 133, 136–37; suffrage for, 9; middle-class, 10; sexual abuse of, 44–45; wages of, 110, 149–50, 238 (n. 51), 239 (nn. 70–71); praise for, 135, 237 (n. 31); maternity leave for, 141, 170, 238 (n. 46); in industry, 146–47, 238 (n. 48); in factories, 162, 242 (n. 122); in censuses, 238 (n. 47). *See also* Employ-

ment, female; Labor force: women in; Professionals, women; Service sector: women in; White-collar jobs; names of specific occupations

Workforce. *See* Labor force

Working class, 3; nuptiality rates of, 4; state control of, 5–6, 201, 202–3; effect of Estado Novo on, 9, 202–3; model of family for, 10; model villages for, 59, 86, 87; industrial bourgeoisie's support of, 86–87; composition of, 206 (n. 13)

Writers, women, 25, 40–44, 148–49, 169, 214 (n. 8); contributing to *Revista Feminina*, 24, 210 (n. 49); use of pseudonyms, 239 (n. 64). *See also* names of specific writers

YWCA, 152; Bureau of Employees, 168